T0373893

The Logics of Gender Justice

When and why do governments promote women's rights? Through comparative analysis of state action in 70 countries from 1975 to 2005, this book shows how different women's rights issues involve different histories, trigger different conflicts, and activate different sets of protagonists. Change on violence against women and workplace equality involves a logic of status politics: feminist movements leverage international norms to contest women's subordination. Family law, abortion, and contraception, which challenge the historical claim of religious groups to regulate kinship and reproduction, conform to a logic of doctrinal politics, which turns on relations between religious groups and the state. Publicly-paid parental leave and child care follow a logic of class politics, in which the strength of Left parties and overall economic conditions are more salient. The book reveals the multiple and complex pathways to gender justice, illuminating the opportunities and obstacles to social change for policymakers, advocates, and others seeking to advance women's rights.

MALA HTUN is Professor of Political Science at the University of New Mexico. She is the author of *Inclusion Without Representation in Latin America* and *Sex and the State*. She has been named an Andrew Carnegie Fellow, held the Council on Foreign Relations International Affairs Fellowship in Japan, and was a fellow at the Kellogg Institute of the University of Notre Dame and the Radcliffe Institute of Harvard. She has received grants from the National Science Foundation, the National Institutes of Health, and the Norwegian Research Council.

S. LAUREL WELDON is Distinguished Professor of Political Science and Director of the Purdue Policy Research Institute at Purdue University. Weldon has authored more than twenty articles and book chapters and two books, including *When Protest Makes Policy: How Social Movements Represent Disadvantaged Groups* (2011), which won the Victoria Schuck Award. She is co-editor of the *Oxford Handbook on Politics and Gender* (2013) and of the journal *Politics, Groups and Identities*. She has served on the editorial board of the American Political Science Review, Politics & Gender, Women, Politics and Policy and European Journal of Politics and Gender.

Cambridge Studies in Gender and Politics

Cambridge Studies in Gender and Politics addresses theoretical, empirical, and normative issues at the intersection of politics and gender. Books in this series adopt incisive and comprehensive approaches to key research themes concerning the construction and impact of sex and gender, as well as their political and social consequences.

General Editors

Karen Beckwith, Case Western Reserve University (Lead)
Lisa Baldez, Dartmouth College
Christina Wolbrecht, University of Notre Dame

Editorial Advisory Board

Nancy Burns, University of Michigan
Matthew Evangelista, Cornell University
Nancy Hirschmann, University of Pennsylvania
Sarah Song, University of California at Berkeley
Ann Towns, University of Gothenburg
Aili Mari Tripp, University of Wisconsin at Madison
Georgina Waylen, University of Manchester

Books in This Series

J. Kevin Corder and Christina Wolbrecht, *Counting Women's Ballots*
Mala Htun, *Inclusion without Representation in Latin America*
Aili Mari Tripp, *Women and Power in Postconflict Africa*
Kristin N. Wylie, *Party Institutionalization and Women's Representation in Democratic Brazil*

The Logics of Gender Justice

State Action on Women's Rights around the World

MALA HTUN

University of New Mexico

S. LAUREL WELDON

Purdue University

CAMBRIDGE
UNIVERSITY PRESS

CAMBRIDGE
UNIVERSITY PRESS

University Printing House, Cambridge CB2 8BS, United Kingdom

One Liberty Plaza, 20th Floor, New York, NY 10006, USA

477 Williamstown Road, Port Melbourne, VIC 3207, Australia

314–321, 3rd Floor, Plot 3, Splendor Forum, Jasola District Centre, New Delhi – 110025, India

79 Anson Road, #06–04/06, Singapore 079906

Cambridge University Press is part of the University of Cambridge.

It furthers the University's mission by disseminating knowledge in the pursuit of education, learning, and research at the highest international levels of excellence.

www.cambridge.org
Information on this title: www.cambridge.org/9781108417563
DOI: 10.1017/9781108277891

First published 2018
Reprinted 2019

Printed in the United Kingdom by TJ International Ltd. Padstow Cornwall

A catalogue record for this publication is available from the British Library.

Library of Congress Cataloging-in-Publication Data
NAMES: Htun, Mala, 1969- author. | Weldon, S. Laurel, author.
TITLE: The logics of gender justice : state action on women's rights around the world / Mala Htun, University of New Mexico, S. Laurel Weldon, Purdue University.
DESCRIPTION: Cambridge, United Kingdom ; New York, NY : Cambridge University Press, 2018. | Includes bibliographical references and index.
IDENTIFIERS: LCCN 2017054699| ISBN 9781108417563 (hardback : alk. paper) | ISBN 9781108405461 (pbk. : alk. paper)
SUBJECTS: LCSH: Women's rights. | Women–Government policy. | Women–Legal status, laws, etc.
CLASSIFICATION: LCC HQ1236 .H799 2018 | DDC 305.42–DC23 LC record available at https://lccn.loc.gov/2017054699

ISBN 978-1-108-41756-3 Hardback
ISBN 978-1-108-40546-1 Paperback

To our families, and to the memories of our grandmothers

Contents

List of Figures		*page* ix
List of Tables		xi
Preface and Acknowledgments		xiii
1	Introduction: States and Gender Justice	1
2	Feminist Mobilization and Status Politics: Combatting Violence against Women	28
3	Governing Women's Legal Status at Work	84
4	Doctrinal Politics: Religious Power, the State, and Family Law	120
5	Class Politics: Family Leave and Childcare Policy	158
6	Reproductive Rights: Class, Status, and Doctrinal Politics	201
7	The Multiple Logics of Gender Justice	229
	Conclusion	245
Appendix A	*Data and Methods*	257
Appendix B	*Family Law in the World's Legal Traditions*	273
References		303
Index		339

Figures

2.1 Violence against Women Index, 1975   *page* 35
2.2 Violence against Women Index, 1985   35
2.3 Violence against Women Index, 1995   36
2.4 Violence against Women Index, 2005   36
2.5 Violence against Women Index and women's share of
     parliamentary seats   50
2.6 Coefficient plot of Models 2 and 8 of Table 2.9   76
3.1 Legal equality in the workplace, 1975   97
3.2 Legal equality in the workplace, 1985   97
3.3 Legal equality in the workplace, 1995   98
3.4 Legal equality in the workplace, 2005   98
3.5 Coefficient plot of Model 7 of Table 3.4   113
4.1 Map of Family Law Index, 1975   131
4.2 Map of Family Law Index, 1985   131
4.3 Map of Family Law Index, 1995   132
4.4 Map of Family Law Index, 2005   132
4.5 Family Law Index in Muslim-majority and non-Muslim-
     majority countries   145
4.6 Family Law Index and Religious Legislation Index, pooled
     1995 and 2005   150
4.7 Family Law Index coefficient plot of models 1, 2, and 3 of
     Table 4.2   150
4.8 Family Law Index and religiosity scale, pooled 1995
     and 2005   151

4.9 Adjusted predictions of religious legislation at varying levels
    of religiosity scale   153
5.1 Overall leave generosity by region, 1975–2005   180
6.1 Mean value of Abortion Law Index, by region, 1975–2005   214

Tables

1.1	Typology of policies to promote women's rights	*page* 9
1.2	Most salient actors and institutions for each policy type	17
2.1	Violence against Women Index, Anglo countries, 1975–2005	39
2.2	Violence against Women Index in Europe, 1975–2005	40
2.3	Violence against Women Index in Latin America, 1975–2005	41
2.4	Violence against Women Index in Eastern Europe, 1975–2005	43
2.5	Violence against Women Index in Africa, 1975–2005	44
2.6	Violence against Women Index in the Middle East and North Africa, 1975–2005	45
2.7	Violence against Women Index in Asia, 1975–2005	48
2.8	Percentage of parliamentary seats held by women and biggest changes in violence against women policy, 1995–2005	51
2.9	Coefficients, Violence against Women Index, linear regression with panel corrected standard errors, 1975–2005	72
2.10	Coefficients, Violence against Women Index, linear regression, 1985 and 2005	74
3.1	Overview of policy relating to women's legal status at work	86
3.2	Means by year, indices of legal equality at work	94
3.3	National laws relating to women's legal status at work. Number of countries with the legal provision in question, of a total of seventy	95
3.4	Coefficients, Overall Legal Equality at Work Index, GLS random effects models, 1975–2005	111
4.1	Family Law Index	129

4.2   Coefficients, Family Law Index, GLS random effects models,
        1975–2005   146
5.1   Coefficients, overall family leave generosity, random effects
        linear models, 1975–2005   183
5.2   Government action on childcare (seventy countries)   187
5.3   Coefficients, national childcare policy, random effects
        logistic regression models, 1975–2005   192
5.A.1   National childcare policy, by region   198
5.A.2   Coefficients, random effects logit, national childcare
        policies, high- and low-fertility countries, 1975–2005   200
6.1   Abortion Law Index   211
6.2   State Funding Index   212
6.3   Mean value of Abortion Law Index, by year   213
6.4   State funding for reproductive rights, by year   213
6.5   Abortion legality and reproductive rights indices, various
        regression techniques, 1975–2005   223
7.1   Typology of policies to promote gender justice and equality   230
7.2   Most salient actors and institutions for each policy type   231
7.3   Multiple areas of women's rights, linear regression with
        panel-corrected standard error, seventy countries,
        1985–2005   233
A.1   Family Law Index   262
A.2   Guide to family law coding in countries with multiple
        legal systems   263
A.3   Summary of three workplace equality indices   265
A.4   Abortion Law Index   266
A.5   Independent variables   268
B.1   Main features of classical Muslim family law   281
B.2   Main features of civil law   298
B.3   Socialist family law   300

Preface and Acknowledgments

When and why do governments promote women's rights? When we began to talk about this question in 2005, each of us brought to the table different theoretical perspectives and regional expertise. Laurel, whose work had focused mainly on policies regarding violence against women in the established democracies, emphasized the role of feminist movements, and saw religion mainly as a footnote. Laurel's scholarship showed how the autonomous mobilization of feminist activists outside of political parties and state agencies created the conditions for women to articulate, develop, and promote violence against women as a priority policy issue. Autonomous women's movements constituted a more effective channel for policy influence on violence than mixed-gender organizations – many of which had historically marginalized women's concerns – or women in elected office or other governmental positions.

As a result of her work on gender quotas, Mala shared Laurel's skepticism about whether getting women into power would produce policy changes on women's rights. Mala's earlier study of family law and reproductive rights in Latin America focused instead on religious claims to govern kinship, as well as the broader context of state–society relations in transitional polities. The links between Church and state and the power of religious organizations shaped the context in which feminist movements, modernizing lawyers, and liberal politicians advanced demands for policy change. Yet religious groups did not object to change on all issues; ecclesiastical leaders supported some advances in women's rights. To understand the chances for change, we needed to disaggregate gender issues.

Both of us had an intuition that policies promoting greater class equality among women, such as publicly paid parental leave and subsidized child care, followed a different logic altogether. The prospect of expanding the state's responsibility for care work seemed to animate different political conflicts, invoke different political philosophies and policy legacies, and call to arms different sets of actors than combatting violence against women, liberalizing family law, or expanding reproductive freedom. But neither one of us had explored these issues systematically in a global context.

We had extensive experience studying gender and feminist theory, state theory, and critical social theory more generally under the influence and teaching of Iris Marion Young, Jane Mansbridge, Kimberlé Crenshaw, Uma Narayan, Susan Moller Okin, Seyla Benhabib, Lisa Brush, and Nancy Fraser. Due to this background, we were aware of the variety of feminist approaches to state and society, the complexity of gender, the differences among women, and the importance of adopting a critical approach to the deep structure of society.

Serendipity, and the network centrality of Pippa Norris, helped to spark our collaboration. In the spring of 2005, Laurel ran into Pippa at the annual meeting of the Midwest Political Science Association in Chicago, and asked her for advice about expanding the study in her 2002 book on social movements, institutions, and policies on violence against women to a wider group of countries, as well as taking on some other issue-areas beyond violence to explore the impact of social movements on gender politics. Pippa suggested talking to Mala, whom she knew was similarly interested in applying the approach of her 2003 book to a broader group of countries and women's rights issues. We had already been acquainted, thanks to the 1998 Frontiers in Women and Politics workshop at Harvard's Kennedy School, so it was not difficult to connect.

Over the late spring and summer of 2005, we worked over phone and email to develop a theoretical approach that took account of what we knew about our own issues and regions, as well as our best hunches about other world regions and issue-areas. We also worked out a methodology to test our approach by building a dataset of laws and policies from around seventy countries across four decades. Our plan was to create an index for each issue-area, enabling us to compare state action on women's rights across issues, across countries, and over time. We submitted a collaborative research proposal to the Political Science Division at the National Science Foundation (NSF) and were fortunate to receive funding and then an additional supplemental award.

Sitting down to do the research that would explore the validity of our approach in a global study of seventy countries over thirty years was daunting at times. The sheer complexity and scale of this project sometimes scared the heck out of us. Were we crazy to take on a project of this scale? Perhaps we were! Could we say anything meaningful about such a set of phenomena, issues, and contexts?

More than a dozen years later, we think the answer is yes. We have renewed appreciation for the slow political science required to take on big questions. Making sense out of large, complex phenomena involves thousands of hours of reading, talking, considering the views of others, and arguing. Some of our biggest insights arose during periods of occupation or distraction with other tasks, such as caring for children or serving as Vice-Provost of Purdue.

We have received help from generous colleagues who are country and region experts, and we have had the good fortune to try these ideas out in presentations on nearly every continent and with practitioners and theoretical folks alike. We have had flashes of understanding gleaned both from field visits and from looking at scatterplots. We have written and rewritten these chapters and argued about nuance and terminology. What we offer here, though flawed, is our best effort at distilling what we learned from these investigations.

This book also reflects personal as well as professional struggles and triumphs. We jointly produced four babies during the course of this project: Laurel's second child and all three of Mala's. Once, while we were both in Washington, DC for APSA, we jumped in a cab with a new baby and a graduate student to go to the World Bank to discuss how our research might inform data they were collecting on women's rights. Mala participated in the meeting from a blanket on the floor, sometimes breastfeeding, sometimes playing with the baby (who was very quiet!).

We had many discussions while feeding babies, and many phone calls and meetings were rescheduled or adjusted for sick kids or other family issues. Whether missing them or taking them with us on trips to Tokyo, Kuala Lumpur, Buenos Aires, Beijing, Delhi, Jerusalem, or Oslo, our children are part of the fabric of this book. We both took on administrative, research, and teaching roles during this project that both informed our work and made it more challenging. There were certainly times when the finished product and final goal – the book – seemed like a distant possibility – and maybe an impossibility – but it always seemed important.

Many people, agencies, and institutions have contributed to this project over the past dozen years. We have benefited from the diligent work of research assistants hailing from nearly every region of the world, including Maura Bahu, Amanda Burke, Eric Cleven, Paul Danyi, Holly Gastineau Grimes, Vagisha Gunesekera, José Kaire, Meng Lu, Cheryl O'Brien, Crystal Shelton, and Sara Wiest from Purdue; Eddie Gonzales, Nami Ishihara, Lauren Paremoer, and Natasha van der Zwan from the New School; and Anna Calasanti, David Nunnally, Melina Juárez, and Kimberly Proctor at the University of New Mexico. Chris Erwin and Vanessa Cornwall provided a ton of help at the end. Olga Avdeyeva, who was a newly minted Ph.D. at the time (but now has tenure!), assisted with the research on Russia and Eastern Europe and has offered considerable help at several stages.

We are grateful for support from Brian Humes and the National Science Foundation, Shahra Razavi at UN Women, and Aline Coudouel and Tazeen Hasan at the World Bank. Laurel received support from the O'Brien Fellowship Program at the Center for Human Rights and Legal Pluralism as well as the Research Group on Constitutional Studies at McGill University, and Mala's work on this project was supported by the Council on Foreign Relations International Affairs Fellowship in Japan, sponsored by Hitachi Ltd., and got a boost at the end from the Andrew Carnegie Fellowship and the Norwegian Research Council (project 250753). Though this material is based upon work supported by the National Science Foundation under Grant No. SES-0550284, any opinions, findings, and conclusions or recommendations expressed in this material are those of the authors and do not necessarily reflect the views of the National Science Foundation.

Many colleagues provided comments and suggestions, including Lisa Baldez, Jane Mansbridge, Christina Wolbrecht, Karen Beckwith, Amy Mazur, Mieke Verloo, Amy Elman, Aaron Hoffman, Leigh Raymond, Pat Boling, Rosalee Clawson, Louise Chappell, Georgina Waylen, Mary John, Jacob Levy, Catherine Lu, Joni Lovenduski, Jay McCann, Ann Clark, Olga Avdeyeva, Jorge Domínguez, Ann Shola Orloff, Kimberly Morgan, Jeffrey Isaac, Elisabeth Friedman, Sara Niedzwiecki, Kendra Koivu, Jami Nelson Nuñez, Richard Wood, Bill Stanley, Mark Peceny, Tamara Kay, Vicky Murillo, Kathy Thelen, Dawn Teele, John Carey, Francesca Jensenius, Jennifer Hochschild, Frances Rosenbluth, Jacqui True, Tamir Moustafa, Cyndi Daniels, Jonathon Fox, Bob Kulzick, Tong Fi, Scott Mainwaring, Bill Shaffer, Bert Rockman, Mark Jones, Irwin Weiser, Kira Sanbonmatsu, Aili Tripp, Claire Annesley, Susan Franceshet, Pratap Banu Mehta, Bina Agarwal, Tom Clark, Suzanne Mettler, Vivien Schmidt, Ruth Halperin-Kaddari, Galia Golen, Aryeh Neier, and several anonymous reviewers. Anne Marie Goetz provided invaluable assistance in connecting with interviewees in Delhi. Several people provided data which we may not have used in the final version; however, we are grateful for those people's willingness to share, including Nita Rudra, who gave us her data on Potential Labor Power (PLP), and Michael Ross, who provided his data on oil rents. Special thanks goes to our many interviewees, including activists, policy makers, scholars, and others, whom we cannot thank by name, for sharing their thoughts and devoting their time to helping us understand their contexts and experiences.

We presented parts of this project at various workshops, public lectures, and colloquia, including at Cornell, Notre Dame, McGill, Carleton, Emory, Harvard, University of Illinois, University of Indiana, Yale, New School for Social Research, Columbia, Johns Hopkins, Purdue, Christian Michelsens Institute, Bergen Resource Center for International Development, Social Science Research Council, Albuquerque Council on Foreign Relations, Universiti Kebangsaan Malaysia, University of Chicago, University of Minnesota, Case Western Reserve University, University of New Mexico, National University of Singapore, Center for Women Development Studies (Delhi), Vancouver Rape Relief (Canada), Simon Fraser University, UC-Irvine, the United Nations Research Institute for Social Development (UNRISD), United Nations Office of the High Commissioner for Human Rights, Department for International Development (DFID-UK), United Nations Development Program (UNDP), UN Women, American Academy of Arts and Sciences, and on panels at the annual meetings of the American Political Science Association, Midwest Political Science Association, Latin American Studies Association, Social Science History Association, European Conference on Politics and Gender, European Consortium for Political Research, and the Law and Society Association. Participants in these spaces shared experiences and perspectives that helped to provoke and refine our thinking.

Earlier versions of some chapters were presented in *Perspectives on Politics*, *American Political Science Review*, *Politics & Gender*, a working paper for the World Bank's World Development Report, a working paper for UN Women's Progress of the World's Women, *Indiana Journal of Global Legal Studies*, and the coedited volume by Kimberly Morgan and Ann Shola Orloff entitled *Many Hands of the State* (Cambridge University Press, 2016).

We present our book with a great sense of accomplishment, for having completed the task we set ourselves so long ago to the best of our abilities. We think we have offered some insights that can be helpful to activists, policy makers, and scholars who wrestle with change in different contexts in far-flung parts of the globe. We want to celebrate and express our gratitude to colleagues, mentors, students, sisters, and brothers in the struggle for gender justice, as well as the global and local communities that made this book possible. We know this book would not have been written without the support of our husbands, Aaron Hoffman and Doug Turner, and our children, Zed and Audrey Hoffman-Weldon and Zander, Livia, and Elinor Turner. We hope our research helps them see the way to new, more gender-equal worlds.

I

Introduction

States and Gender Justice

The state's approach to women's rights has changed dramatically over the past century. In an earlier era, many states legally classified women as the property of their male relatives, endorsed gender discrimination, ignored violence against women, and treated care work as solely a private responsibility, outside the sphere of official state action. As part of a broader transformation in gender roles, relations, and identities, many states began to uphold principles of equality and autonomy for women and men. Today, it is becoming increasingly common for women to enjoy equal legal status with men in many areas, for laws to prohibit sex discrimination and violence, and for governments to support working families through parental leave and childcare provisions.

Still, government action on women's rights varies across countries. In Norway and Sweden, parents of young children are entitled to thirteen months of paid parental leave, two months of which is typically taken by men. In the United States, federal law does not guarantee any *paid* leave, mandating only that firms of a certain size allow workers to take twelve weeks of *unpaid* leave. In Egypt and Jordan, family laws stipulate that men are in charge of the household and other family members must follow their will, while in Cuba, the family code implores men to do their share of the housework. In Catholic Ireland, abortion is a crime, while in Italy, seat of the Vatican, access to abortion is legally guaranteed and provided at state expense.

Women's rights vary not only *across* countries but also *within* them, depending on the issue. In the United States, the federal government fails to mandate public funding for maternity or parental leave, but it was relatively early to adopt policies combating violence against women and to liberalize abortion laws. Governments in Argentina and Costa Rica were early adopters of gender quota laws establishing minimum levels for women's participation as candidates in legislative elections, as well as comprehensive legislation on violence against women, but have failed to reform restrictive abortion laws or to promote more gender-neutral legislation on parental leave.

The mobilization of transnational and domestic feminist movements, the emergence of international norms on women's rights, and the proliferation of governmental women's agencies have been more successful at inducing policy changes on some women's rights than on others. Over the past few decades, scores of countries have adopted new policies to combat violence against women, introduced candidate quotas and reserved parliamentary seats to promote women's inclusion in political decision-making, and reformed constitutions to incorporate principles of equality. Meanwhile, a significant number of countries continue to deny women equal rights to seek a divorce and make decisions about the welfare of their minor children. In some countries, women may not inherit, own property, or work on the same terms as men. Dozens of countries keep laws on the books that prevent women from exercising certain professions, and a handful have entrenched greater inequality in the law and have rolled back previous progress. These examples suggest that a state can be both progressive and regressive: It can extend greater rights and freedoms to women and men with one hand, while it takes them away with the other (see, e.g., Morgan & Orloff, 2016; O'Connor, Orloff, & Shaver, 1999).

In this book, we delineate and attempt to make sense of these patterns. Each women's rights issue is a critical area for achieving gender justice, and yet the bewildering array of government actions can prompt skepticism about the existence of a common thread linking concepts of women's rights, sex equality, or gender justice.[1] We offer an approach that takes account of the multiplicity of gender while illuminating the connections among gender issues. We argue that gender equality is not one issue but many linked issues (Htun, 2003; Mazur, 2002; Sanbonmatsu, 2002; Sen, 2001). We identify several distinct dimensions of gender, and show

---

[1] When we speak of gender justice, we refer to equality and autonomy for people constructed by gender institutions, including people of all sexes, genders, sexual identities, and gender identities. Women's rights, a subcategory of gender justice, concerns questions of equality and autonomy for women and men. We explore these differences in more detail below.

how they propel different types of political dynamics in each area of women's rights. Scholars and policy makers need to disaggregate women's rights – and measures that promote gender justice in general – in order better to understand the possibilities of change and the logics of continuity.

All policies promoting gender justice seek changes to the social and political institutions that construct – often in binary ways – the categories of sex and gender, imbue them with social meaning, and embed them in our material surroundings (buildings, clothes, wages). Gender justice policies challenge prevailing patterns of cultural value and require changes to societal norms at the macro level as well as at the micro level of social practices, in the interstices of daily life.

The common project of institutional challenge does not mean, however, that all policies confront the same institutions, or that they engage them in the same ways. In this book, we show that different types of women's rights challenge different aspects of social and political relations, in different ways, and to different degrees. Not all historical legacies, institutions, background conditions, or social and political actors are equally relevant for all areas of women's rights. Identifying which ones matter for which issues, and in which ways, allows us to identify and explain patterns of continuity and change.

Some policies that promote gender equality, such as measures to combat violence against women, seek primarily to transform the power and the meaning of particular bodies. Other gender equality initiatives, such as family law and the liberalization of restrictions on abortion, touch directly upon the claim of religious and cultural communities to govern the terms of kinship and reproduction. Still other gender equality policies, such as publicly paid parental leave and public provision of childcare, alter the cultural meanings, social organization, and material consequences of care work and domestic labor. In this book, we characterize these projects as *status politics*, *doctrinal politics*, and *class politics*, respectively. Though status politics, doctrinal politics, and class politics commonly seek a transformation of gender institutions to advance equality and autonomy, they trigger different dimensions of those institutions, as we explain below.

Existing literature has not given much emphasis to variation across women's rights. Many studies of gender and public policy tend to focus on a single issue or set of issues, such as parental or family leave (see, e.g., Gornick & Meyers, 2003, 2008; Henderson & White, 2004; Kittilson, 2008; Ruhm, 1996); reproductive rights (Ferree, 2002; Githens & Stetson, 2013; Lovenduski & Outshoorn, 1986; Norgren, 2001); family law

(Charrad, 2001; Glendon, 1989; Sezgin, 2013); violence against women
(Heise & Germain, 1994; Katzenstein, 1989; True, 2012; Weldon,
2002a); childcare (Bratton & Ray, 2002; Morgan, 2006); gender quotas
(Dahlerup, 2006; Jones, 2009; Krook, 2009); and so forth. Fewer studies
explore variation across multiple policy areas (for exceptions see Blofield
& Haas, 2005; Gelb & Palley, 1982; Htun, 2003; Kang, 2015; Mazur,
2002; Tripp, Casimiro, Kwesiga, & Mungwa, 2009; Weldon, 2011).
Other studies claim, at least implicitly, that matters of women's rights
are a more unified set of issues, by arguing that advances in equality
policy form part of a general trend toward secularization and economic
modernization (Inglehart & Norris, 2003), or by claiming that women's
presence in government advances all areas of women's rights to the
same degree.

We propose a typology of equality-promoting policies and develop
a framework to analyze patterns of variation, continuity, and change
for each type of women's rights issue. The typology implies that models
accounting for crossnational variation in policy patterns should vary
across issue-types. In the rest of the book, we explore the utility of this
framework using qualitative analysis and comparisons, as well as
regression analysis of a database covering seventy countries over four
decades. Our dataset on these women's rights issues is based on fieldwork
(including visits to countries in Asia, Africa, North America, and Europe);
analysis of primary sources such as legal codes and constitutions, policy
statements, and official reports; and secondary sources.

The book shows that the logic of gender justice on one issue is not the
same as the logic on another issue. The complexity of gender, combined
with the diversity of the world's political and socioeconomic contexts,
accounts for these different political dynamics. We begin this chapter,
therefore, by disaggregating the concept itself. What is gender? What
do we mean by gender equality? By women's rights? How can policies
promote women's rights? Our hypotheses about change flow directly
from this picture of gender as a configuration of institutions.

DIMENSIONS OF GENDER

Gender is not just an attribute of individual identity or a type of
performance but a collection of institutions: a set of rules, norms,
and practices, widely held and somewhat predictable – though not
uncontested – that constructs what it means to be or to belong to a
particular sex group (cf. Fraser, 2007; Htun, 2005; Ridgeway, 2001,

p. 637; Young, 2002).[2] Different gender systems construct sex categories in different ways. Historically, people in the West believed in the model of a single sex (Laqueur, 1990). In the West and many other places today, sex is constructed in the familiar binary of man/woman, masculine/feminine, but other systems create more than two sex categories and uphold multiple gender identities. Though many people assume that biology clearly defines two distinct sex groups (women and men), scholarship has shown that biology may define as many as five sex groups, or none at all (Connell, 1987; Devor, 1989; Fausto-Sterling, 1993, Hawkesworth, 2013).

Gender is the mechanism through which "woman" and "man" and "masculine" and "feminine" come to be known as legitimate conceptual categories (Butler, 2004). Institutions of gender organize social behavior, furnishing incentives for some actions (girls playing with dolls; men proposing marriage to women) and sanctions for others (bullying and harassment of boys who want to wear dresses or who speak in high voices). Conceptualizing gender as an institutional phenomenon helps account for its structural and historical character: It cannot be reduced to the actions and preferences of individuals, and derives much of its weight from its endurance over time.

The social construction of gender in most contemporary societies positions sex groups against one another and also divides them against themselves. Gender, for example, situates men and women in unequal relations of power, often intersecting (or combining) with other institutions to uphold patterns of status hierarchy and economic inequality. As Young puts it, "What we call categories of gender, race, ethnicity, etc. are [less individual identities than] a set of structures that position persons ... in relations of labor and production, power and subordination, desire and sexuality, prestige and status" (2002, pp. 417, 420). Social groups do not exist by virtue of a shared identity or attributes alone, but rather because they are similarly positioned by institutions.

Gender is composed of distinct institutions that Young calls the "basic axes of gender structures" (2002, p. 422), which one might think of as dimensions of gender. They include the status hierarchy, the sexual

---

[2] Ridgeway refers to gender as an "institutionalized system of social practices for constituting males and females as different in socially significant ways and organizing inequality in terms of those differences" (Ridgeway, 2001, p. 637). To be sure, there are a wide variety of legitimate scholarly conceptions of gender, which we do not review here for reasons of space. For an overview and further discussion, see Hawkesworth (2013).

division of labor, and normative heterosexuality. The *status hierarchy* refers to those institutionalized patterns of cultural value that privilege men and the masculine and devalue women and the feminine (Fraser, 2003, 2007). By virtue of their low status, women are the feminine and are marginalized, rendered "other," lesser beings less worthy of rights and dignity. Patriarchal norms treat women as the sexual property of men; as objects rather than subjects; as goods to be exchanged, ignored, or belittled; or as disposable beings who may be abused or even killed – in short, as less than full persons (Brush, 2003; Williams, 1988; Young, 1990, 2005). Promoting women's rights involves the transformation of these patterns that designate some groups as normative and constitute others as inferior, different, or unworthy. The status hierarchy devaluing women and the feminine in favor of normative models of masculinity is an obstacle to the achievement of dignity and equality (Fraser, 2001, 2007; Young, 2000, 2002).

The *sexual division of labor* refers to the tendency, across most societies, for women to shoulder a disproportionate burden of repro-ductive and care work. This work tends to be unpaid or underpaid, less valued, and concealed in the domestic or private sphere. By contrast, most societies allocate public, paid, and valued work to men. This division of labor has tended to put women at a disadvantage in relation to men by reinforcing economic inequalities including occupational sex segregation, gender wage gaps, and the scarcity of women in upper management (Estevez-Abe, 2006; Fuchs, 1990; Iversen & Rosenbluth, 2010). Promoting parity in opportunities and chances for economic independence requires changing the way we organize work (both paid and unpaid) and allocate resources (Fraser, 1997; Okin, 1989; Orloff, 1993; Young, 2000).

Normative heterosexuality locates heterosexual coupling as the legit-imate site of rights, reproduction, and romance. It assumes a natural sexual and social pairing of male and female bodies as the basis for the family and community (Butler, 1990; Rich, 1980). The regime of norma-tive heterosexuality renders "unintelligible" – and often wrong, sinful, and abhorrent – those people, relationships, and modes of behavior that deviate from gender dimorphism and heterosexuality, including same-sex relationships, same-sex parenting, and transgender expressions, among other phenomena (Butler, 2004).

We understand gender equality as an ideal condition or social reality that gives groups constituted by gender institutions similar opportunities to participate in politics, the economy, and social activities; that values their roles and status, and enables them to flourish; in which no gender group suffers from disadvantage or discrimination; and in which all are considered free and autonomous beings with dignity and rights. This conception of equality pertains to men and women. It also pertains to groups constituted in other ways, including by sexuality and gender identity. Gender justice, or equality and autonomy for people of all sex groups and gender identities, thus includes the emerging developments in LGBTQ law and policy that combat normative heterosexuality, such as legitimizing gay marriage and adoption, decriminalizing homosexuality, and so on.[3] It involves the widening set of laws and policies protecting transgender people from violence and forced gender identity. Gender justice also encompasses the radical notion that "women are human," and are entitled to the full range of rights and responsibilities, and the fullest degree of autonomy, consistent with the status of personhood.

No single book could explore all these questions of gender justice, and we do not try. We focus on women's rights as a subcategory of gender justice and sex equality. Women's rights are legitimate claims for greater parity in the well-being, life chances, and opportunities of women and men.[4] Advancing women's rights involves changes in many spheres of life, such as politics, the family, the market, and civil society, and requires reimagining our communities and nations as more inclusive and egalitarian. We think many of our arguments about women's rights will prove useful for those focused on LGBTQ rights or other issues of gender, and we explore these applications in our conclusion. But we do not claim to exhaust the study of gender justice in this book.

---

[3] In this book, we often use the terms gender justice and gender equality as synonyms. Some people may prefer the concept of gender justice, since the equality concept often triggers confusion over whether it implies equality of treatment (formal equality) or equality of outcome (substantive equality). As we discuss in Chapter 4, formal and substantive equality have different implications for women's rights and neither, on its own, is adequate to overcome historical disadvantages.

[4] Throughout this text, we occasionally use the terms "women's rights," "gender equality policies," "sex equality policies," and "gender issues" as synonyms. Our usage is occasionally ambiguous since, as we make clear in the present discussion, the terms are not equivalent. Women's rights and sex equality issues are a subset of a larger group of "gender equality issues" and "gender issues."

DISAGGREGATING POLICIES THAT PROMOTE
GENDER EQUALITY

Scholars of public policy have long argued that different types of issues involve different sorts of politics.[5] For example, in his seminal 1964 work, Ted Lowi differentiated between distributive, redistributive, and regulatory policies and showed that each involved different modes and loci of decision making (Lowi, 1964). Peter Hall distinguished between policy changes affecting the instruments of policy, the settings on those instruments, and the underlying paradigm setting the parameters of policy (Hall, 1993). Depending on the level of policy, different causal factors are at work.

Gender and politics researchers have refined this idea by introducing distinctions between women's rights policies. For example, Gelb and Palley distinguished between "role equity" and "role change" policies in their study of feminist achievements in the United States during the 1970s (Gelb & Palley, 1982). They showed that "role equity" policies (such as fair credit laws and Title IX) granting women equal access to privileges formerly held by men and minorities were easier to accomplish than policies promoting change in the social meaning of women's roles (see also Skrentny, 2002). Advocating these policies, which meant greater sexual freedom and independence, generated controversy and proved costly to politicians (Sanbonmatsu, 2002).

Gelb and Palley's typology is helpful because it focuses on the varying degrees to which policies challenge established patterns. Since they provoke more radical changes, "role change" policies have been more controversial and provoked greater opposition than "role equity" policies. Yet policies that provoke opposition in some contexts encounter less in others. Unpaid leave to care for family members was finally adopted in the United States in 1993 after two presidential vetoes and considerable controversy (Bernstein, 2001). Yet the same policy had been in place in Norway since the end of the nineteenth century and its expansion was hardly controversial. The difference owed not to the nature of the policy but to the varying contexts of class politics in the two countries (Mazur, 2002; Stetson, 1998; Weldon, 2011). As this suggests, prevailing institutions, and not just the inherent features of a policy, determine the political dynamics at work.

---

[5] The writing and analysis in this part builds on Htun & Weldon (2010) and Htun and Weldon's contribution to Morgan & Orloff, 2016.

In her study of family law and abortion in Latin America, Htun suggests a different way to disaggregate gender policy dynamics (Htun, 2003). Did policy change challenge the core tenets of the dominant religion (in this case, Roman Catholicism)? Or were ecclesiastical leaders agnostic about reform? Her analysis suggests that policy controversies derive from a clash of normative traditions – authoritative scripts furnishing standards of morality and the good life – and their implications for the respective roles of men, women, the state, and religion. Family law and abortion reforms have been far more controversial in contexts where they present challenges to established religious doctrine.

Building on these accounts, we focus on the degree to which gender equality policies challenge prevailing patterns of social organization. Though women's rights commonly question sexuality, work, and family life, as well as the authority of religious institutions and the reach of markets, they do so in different ways. Our typology classifies policies along two dimensions: (1) whether it touches upon state–market relations and questions of socioeconomic redistribution, or whether it promotes the social and legal position of women, or some subsector of women, as a status group (*the class–status dimension*) and (2) whether or not the policy challenges the religious doctrine, cultural traditions, or sacred discourse of a major social group (*the doctrinal–nondoctrinal dimension*) (see Table 1.1).

TABLE 1.1 *Typology of policies to promote women's rights*

		Do the policies challenge the doctrine of religious organizations or the codified tradition or sacred discourse of major cultural groups?	
		No: Nondoctrinal	Yes: Doctrinal
Does the policy advance women's rights primarily as a status group or as a gender-class group?	Status	Violence against women Gender parity/quotas Constitutional equality Legal equality in the workplace	Family law Abortion legality Reproductive freedom
	Class	Maternity/parental/daddy leave Public funding for childcare	Public funding for abortion and contraceptives

Source: Htun & Weldon, 2010 (modified from its original version).

Status versus Class Policies

Under the influence of intersectional approaches to social research, scholars of women's rights have come to consider "women" as a collection of categories, not a single category. Women are internally divided along the lines of class, race, ethnicity, sexual orientation, and the like. Multiple social positions intersect to shape women's opportunities, their chances for well-being, and the respect they receive from others (Crenshaw, 1993; Hancock, 2007).[6] In any particular circumstance, the effects of these distinct positions may be difficult to disentangle. Is my employer's reluctance to promote me due to the fact that I am Muslim, or because I am physically impaired, or a woman? From the perspective of lived experience, these positions are not detachable either: The experience of being female or male, for example, cannot be cleanly distinguished from the experience of being black or white (Jordan-Zachery, 2007; Moi, 2001; Spelman, 1998; Young, 2002).

From an analytical angle, however, we can identify the degree to which women suffer some injustices primarily because they are women and not as a function of their other positions, such as poor, immigrant, or dark-skinned.[7] "Institutionalized patterns of cultural value" (Fraser, 2000) that privilege masculinity and devalue behaviors and characteristics associated with femininity inflict harm on women as a status group. These patterns cast men as normative and women as subordinate, "other," and lacking in value, denying women the recognition and dignity they merit as human beings (Young, 2002). As Fraser argues:

---

[6] This recognition of intersectionality implies that women do not inherently share common interests or perspectives. The forging of a common front among women is the result of politics, not the premise of politics (Htun & Ossa, 2013; Weldon, 2006, 2011). Feminist work on intersectionality has become a voluminous, multidisciplinary, and global literature in recent years: See work by Kimberlé Crenshaw, Patricia Hill Collins, Nira Yuval-Davis, Ange-Marie Hancock, Leslie McCall, Julia Zachery-Jordan, and Iris Marion Young, among others. For a nice discussion see Chepp and Collins (2013). See Hancock (2016) for a comprehensive history of the roots of intersectionality approaches.

[7] Many scholarly works, for example, attempt to disentangle the effects of gender, race, and education on pay scales and occupational segregation. In addition, although particular types of injustice may take different forms for different subgroups of women (such as poverty or violence), women are uniquely vulnerable to some of these. Women are raped because they are women, but this does not mean that women in every country are equally vulnerable to custodial rape by police or gang rape in fraternities. Women who are fired or not promoted because they are pregnant are fired or not promoted because they are women, regardless of their occupation or income.

Women suffer gender-specific forms of status subordination, including sexual assault, sexual harassment, and domestic violence; trivializing, objectifying, and demeaning stereotypical depictions in the media; disparagement in everyday life; exclusion or marginalization in public spheres and deliberative bodies; and denial of the full rights and equal protections of citizenship (2007, p. 26).

Though status injustices are inflicted on women as women, they do not necessarily affect all women in the same way or to the same extent. Nor do all women subjectively experience them in similar fashion.[8]

We refer to remedies for status-based injustices as "status policies." They attack those practices and values that constitute women as a lesser group vulnerable to violence, marginalization, exclusion, and other injustices that prevent them from participating as peers in political and social life. Such policies include, among others: (1) reforms to family law, which historically cast women as inferior to men and gave them few or no rights over marital property or minor children, nor the ability to work; (2) measures to combat violence against women, rooted in patriarchal attitudes and misrecognition; (3) laws mandating equal treatment and non-discrimination in the workplace; (4) liberalization of laws on abortion, contraception, and others related to women's reproductive capacities and decisions over their bodies; and (5) gender quotas, which promote women's presence in positions of decision-making and leadership, thereby changing gendered social meanings.[9]

Gender systems inflict other harms on women that are more directly related to their connection to reproductive labor or care work. By reproductive labor, we refer not to gestational carriers and egg donation but to the entire range of work needed to reproduce and maintain human life – childcare; food production; cleaning; care for the sick and elderly; keeping track of schedules, transportation, household expenses, and the like. The sexual division of labor assigns women primary responsibility for reproductive labor, which has economic value (albeit value that, when informal

---

[8] In some cases, women may be excluded from the category of women. For example, First Nations women got the right to vote some four decades after nonindigenous Canadian women: They were not considered women at all.

[9] Status policies are not a category that can be conceptually opposed to material considerations (Young, 1994). The experience of police brutality, rape, and sexual harassment is not fundamentally a question of changing identities so much as of securing bodily integrity and freedom from violence for some groups (Young, 2002). Presence in government involves concrete access to power and authority. As a result, "status" issues – including the meaning of bodies, and body politics – cannot be reduced to "cultural politics" or the politics of recognition, or otherwise mapped onto an ideal–material binary.

or unpaid, does not directly figure into calculations of gross domestic product).[10] Reproductive labor helps workers arrive, well slept and well fed, to their jobs, and maintains the labor supply over generations. When performed in the home without pay, women's reproductive labor saves the state and private companies the expense of childcare, elder care, food, cooking, sanitation, care of the sick and injured, the delivery of water, and other activities essential for human survival.

As this discussion suggests, gender equality touches upon more than the position of women relative to men. It also raises the question of inequalities among women. In societies structured by class and race, some women and men enjoy opportunities denied to others.[11] Since people can purchase reproductive labor, women of different class positions have different experiences vis-à-vis care work. Better-off women can buy at least some reproductive labor on the market by hiring domestic workers as nannies, cooks, and cleaners, or by exiting the labor market to spend time on these same duties. Poor and working-class women are less able to hire others to do care work, and may be too dependent on extrahousehold income to be able to leave the labor market. As a result, poor women are far more dependent on the state and kinship networks for help in alleviating their care work duties (Razavi & Staab, 2012).

Some gender equality policies intend to promote more equal access to resources among women of different social classes. We call these "class-based policies," and they include paid maternity or parental leave and government-funded childcare. State funding for abortion and for contraceptives is also a class policy. Though the legality of abortion and contraceptives is a status issue affecting all women, funding for these practices is not. Middle-class women, but not poor ones, can pay market rates for contraceptive services. The ability of poor and working-class

---

[10] We do not mean to suggest that this particular form of the sexual division of labor is universal. Indeed, human biology has combined with a wide variety of forms of social organization, including varying ways of organizing gender. In contemporary states, however, dominant norms mostly reinforce the sexual division of labor as described here, though of course there is variation across tradition and context in the degree and form of this division.

[11] Class differences pervade global society: The labor of migrant women in care chains bolsters the status and autonomy of women in advanced economies. Transnational policies to promote greater equality seem infeasible in a world of multiple sovereign states, though some experts have recommended independent ethical action on the part of employers (such as paying for an immigrant domestic worker's trips home to visit her family; Ehrenreich & Hochschild, 2003).

women to exercise reproductive rights often hinges on public funding, which increases the availability of reproductive services.

Whereas gender status policies pose a challenge to institutionalized patterns of cultural value privileging masculinity and denigrating femininity, class-based policies touch upon the historic division of responsibility between state, market, and family for social provision and reproduction (cf. Orloff, 1993). How much autonomy does this division provide to women, whether they are seeking to establish an independent household of their own or trying to make ends meet in a dual earner or single-breadwinner family (Lewis, 1992; Orloff, 1993)? Does the social policy regime assume that care work will be performed entirely in the family, by women, for no wages? Is reproductive labor – including maids, nannies, day care, modern appliances, home health aides, and the like – provided primarily through private transactions in the market? Or does the state socialize reproductive labor by providing childcare and communal kitchens and paying for housework, as Russian Communist and feminist theorist Alexandra Kollontai envisioned? Different societies have forged the balance between the respective roles of state, market, and family in different ways. Changes to this balance – for example, by state mandates of parental leave or childcare centers – often expand the boundaries of the welfare state, threaten to upset historic relations between state and market, and pose challenges to existing economic interests.

Advocates of class policies are concerned about the justice of existing economic arrangements and are committed to using state power to modify them. For these reasons, we hypothesize that the power of Left parties and other dimensions of class politics will be the main drivers of change on these types of policies. Historic patterns of social provision and the degree and kind of market regulation are critical for understanding resistance and innovation in this area.[12]

Status policies, by contrast, are less likely to challenge established patterns of state–market relations. Rather, changing the social, legal, and political status of a group often requires legal reforms, innovations to civil and criminal justice procedures, changes to electoral rules, public awareness campaigns, and greater monitoring and accountability of state officials (such as police and judges). At stake is the degree to which the polity recognizes the worth of certain groups, affords them autonomy (or conversely, the degree of regulation and invasion of privacy that is

---

[12] Blofield and Haas (2005) work with a similar distinction, which they refer to as "distributive" versus "regulatory."

acceptable), and considers their security a priority. Since status policies affect women as women, and require challenging the elevated status of some men and specific forms of masculinity, we expect that they will be driven primarily by feminist movements.

The demarcation of some policies as "class-based" should not be taken as an indication that they are any less important for gender equality than status policies. All the policies considered here are gender equality policies. Some touch more squarely on class, the politics of redistribution, and state–market relations than others, however. In addition, classed and gendered policies are also implicated in race. For example, some countries historically restricted access to contraceptives for women who were considered to approximate a eugenic ideal, while sterilizing those who were not. Gender equality should mean greater rights and autonomy for *all* women, not just for rich, Northern, white, or heterosexual women.

Doctrinal versus Nondoctrinal Policies

One of the more controversial turns of modern life has been the state's claim to regulate kinship relations and sexuality (Htun, 2003, p. 1). Before the modern state came into being, other organizations – including churches, clans, tribes, and traditional authorities – were largely responsible for upholding the rules and managing the processes related to the reproduction of life, which we today refer to as "family law." In Europe and Latin America, for example, the Roman Catholic Church maintained registries of births and deaths, ran hospitals and cemeteries, presided over marriages and separations, and castigated people for interfering in pregnancies. In sub-Saharan Africa, clans and tribes controlled marriage, family relations, and the use and inheritance of land. In much of the Middle East, religious courts administered rules related to family, marriage, and inheritance (Charrad, 2001; Glendon, 1987, 1989; Tripp et al., 2009).

As states grew, rulers faced crucial decisions over whether to impose central authority over family law, or whether to recognize subnational and religious control. Rulers' choices of how much religious and tribal authority to usurp have forged a patchwork of legal authority, seen in the coexistence of multiple legal systems, in much of Asia, Africa, and the Middle East (Charrad, 2001; Kang, 2015; Sezgin, 2013). In Nigeria and Kenya, civil law upheld by the state coexists alongside customary and religious laws. In India and Egypt, state courts apply ecclesiastical laws to members of different religious groups, many of which were codified from above by the state. Israel kept intact the Ottoman *millet* system of separate religious courts. People are ruled by a different set of legal norms depending on their identity, where they live, and the resources to which they have access. In these situations, women's rights are often restricted by the principle of cultural autonomy over family law (Cohen, 2012).

In the West too, the church's power over much of social life persisted well into the nineteenth and twentieth centuries. Even when the state succeeded in extending its authority, it often imported ecclesiastical principles into its own philosophy of governance. Catholic doctrine on the indissolubility of marriage, for example, influenced civil and constitutional law until 1977 in Brazil, 1983 in Argentina, and 2004 in Chile (Htun, 2003). Elsewhere, the church was incorporated into the structure of the state (as in the United Kingdom, Norway, and Sweden). In other places, the separation between church and state has been more marked, as in Turkey, the United States, and France (though each of these countries institutionalizes secularism in a different way).

The liberalization of many laws on gender and the advancement of women's rights thus tracks the course of relations between the state on the one hand and religious and cultural groups on the other. In twentieth-century North Africa, for example, changes in family law depended on whether or not the state needed the help of clan groups to consolidate its power. When the state was strong, it marginalized clan groups by usurping their power over family law and introducing secular codes. When the state was weak, it allowed the clans to preside over kinship and reproduction (Charrad, 2001). In Uganda, politicians who wanted to preserve clan power helped defeat a clause in the 1998 Land Act that would have given women coownership rights to land with their spouses (Tripp et al., 2009, pp. 133–4). In Latin America, the legalization of divorce depended on the eruption of conflict between Roman Catholic bishops and the state over education, human rights, and authoritarian rule (Htun, 2003).

Not all women's rights provoke such conflicts between the state and other organizations over their respective jurisdictional authority. Some women's rights are more distant from religious doctrine and codified tradition. They concern zones of life rarely touched upon by scripture (such as government versus private provision of childcare) or more modern dilemmas that traditional religions and customs failed to anticipate (such as equality in the workplace).

We call the first set of issues "doctrinal" and the second "nondoctrinal." Doctrinal issues touch upon the core tenets of religious doctrine and codified cultural traditions, particularly concerning the regulation of reproduction, inheritance, and other intimate matters. They include family law, the legality of abortion, reproductive freedom, and funding for abortion and contraceptives. Nondoctrinal issues include violence against women, gender quotas, equality at work, parental leave, child care, and constitutional provisions for sex equality.[13]

Our classification of some issues as "doctrinal" and others as "non-doctrinal," some as "class" and others as "status," is not a scheme that applies in a fixed way for all issues, all countries, and all times. Political struggles involve attempts by actors to reframe issues. What is more, issues that play out as "nondoctrinal" in some contexts – through a dynamic that fails to invoke or involve religion – may be more doctrinal in others. For example, though religious authorities did not oppose measures to combat violence against women in North America, Latin America, and Europe, advocates of some types of violence against women policies in some Middle Eastern and North African countries have encountered religiously based opposition. In Sudan, for example, rules condemning marital rape have provoked objections framed by religious discourse emphasizing a woman's marital duties and a husband's prerogatives (Tønnessen, 2014).[14]

DIFFERENT ISSUES, DIFFERENT POLITICAL DYNAMICS

Each women's rights issue takes on a different aspect of the constellation of institutions that together comprise gender. Each issue therefore involves different actors, activates different cleavages, and motivates different types of political conflicts. Whereas "status" issues involve challenges mainly to institutionalized patterns of cultural value that subordinate women, "doctrinal" issues touch primarily upon state–church relations, and "class" issues animate the politics of redistribution and division of responsibility between state and market for social provision. We therefore expect that different actors and political conditions will

---

[13] We do not define an issue as doctrinal according to whether it does *in fact* provoke religious opposition. It is defined as doctrinal if the policy contradicts the explicit doctrine, codified tradition, or sacred discourse of the dominant religion or cultural group. For more clarification, see Htun & Weldon (2010).

[14] In addition, religious power was historically important in the development of welfare policies (which we classify here as class-based and nondoctrinal issues) in several European countries (Morgan, 2006).

TABLE 1.2 *Most salient actors and institutions for each policy type*

	"Nondoctrinal" policies	"Doctrinal" policies
Gender status policies	Feminist movements (+) International agreements (+) I	Religion (–) Feminist movements (+) II
Class policies	Left parties (+) Socioeconomic conditions (+) III	Religion (–) Left parties (+) IV

be differentially relevant for patterns of variation, continuity, and change on each women's rights issue.

The empirical chapters of this book develop testable hypotheses about the factors associated with more and less egalitarian policies. Table 1.2 provides a guide to the actors and factors that are most relevant for each issue, discussed in greater detail in the chapters to come. The table depicts the different clusters of variables we expect to be significantly associated with more and less progressive laws in each quadrant of our typology. Now, we describe the distinctive political logics characterizing policy reform and policy status for each quadrant.

Status politics. For quadrant I (gender status/nondoctrinal policies), we focus on autonomous feminist movements. Like other scholars, we expect feminist movements to be important players in driving processes of change for all women's rights. Their importance, however, will be greater for issues concerning women's status *as women*. Feminist movements are the main forces driving discursive and normative change in relation to the categories of masculine and feminine. It is feminist movements that identify and frame women's issues as such, and put them on the policy agenda as such. Feminist mobilization articulated the need for change on status issues; conceptualized women's rights as human rights; found allies, forged coalitions, and created networks; and lobbied politicians and state officials. Working within and across national borders, feminist movements built global norms on women's rights and organized to apply and translate these norms in local contexts (Benhabib, 2009; Merry, 2006).

For example, the rise of women's autonomous organizing – outside of political parties and the state – created the conditions for violence against women to be seen as a problem and its eradication championed as a political cause. Women organizing as women – a distinct social group – helped generate a collective perspective, an oppositional consciousness, and a set of priorities that reflected their distinctive experiences and concerns, including the problem of violence (Keck & Sikkink, 1998; Mansbridge, 1995; Mansbridge & Morris, 2001; Sternbach, Navarro-Aranguren, Chuchryk, & Alvarez, 1992; Weldon, 2002a, 2002b, 2006, 2011). It is far more difficult for a group to generate such a perspective in a mixed setting with other priorities (Weldon, 2011). Political parties, unions, civic organizations, or state agencies have seen women's concerns as tangential to established priorities or as secondary, less important issues. As a result, even organizations seeking economic justice, racial equality, and other objectives have previously neglected women's issues, including violence (Strolovitch, 2007). But when women organized as women, they did not need to defend the broader significance of violence in order to make it a priority (Weldon, 2002a). Instead, women recognized a striking similarity in "problems, social attitudes, and feminist strategies" vis-à-vis violence across contexts, "even while the manifestations of violence varied as they intersected with the particularities of culture, race, class, and other factors" (Bunch, 2012, p. 31).

Religious politics. For quadrant II (doctrinal status issues), we expect that the political role of religion will be important. When religious organizations are strong, people are devout, and attitudes toward gender and the family are conservative, we would expect many women's rights policies to be restrictive. Religious groups can credibly pressure state officials to do their bidding, and politicians will be reluctant to incur ecclesiastical wrath by supporting liberalizing reforms. In less devout societies, by contrast, state officials will have less to lose by promulgating secular and feminist policy changes.

Institutionalized relations between the state on the one hand and religious, cultural, and tribal organizations on the other will also influence the possibility of change on doctrinal policy issues. When church and state are close, political legitimacy, national identity, and public values are frequently linked to, and derived from, ecclesiastical principles. In such a context, groups that challenge particular religious principles related to women's rights are often perceived to challenge the entire configuration of church–state relations. Advances in women's rights come to involve far more than the status of women. They imply shifts in the bargains tying religious groups to state authorities and to dominant conceptions of the nation. Change on women's rights becomes a referendum on the role of religion in the polity and on the public and legitimizing character of religious doctrines. Defenders of patriarchal policies support religion's public status, while supporters of egalitarian reforms challenge the relationship between church and state. These practical political linkages between women's rights and the institutionalization of religious power raise the stakes and intensify the obstacles to reform.

In Malaysia, for example, colonial policies and Islamicization measures of the 1980s bound Malay identity and political legitimacy to religious family laws that subordinated women (Hussin, 2007; Nasr, 2001). In the twenty-first century, the influence of religious–secular conflict and the defense of national identity has thwarted progress on women's rights. State officials and the media branded Muslim feminists who proposed family law reforms – which feminists framed and justified in religious terms! – as "traitors" and accused them of insulting Islam (Anwar & Rumminger, 2007; Hamayotsu, 2003; Mohamad, 2010; Neo, 2003). At the same time, the state's control of religious interpretation has promoted the erroneous view that Muslim law is fixed, uniform, and divine in origin, and that only the *ulama* – or Muslim clergy – has the authority to speak on religious matters. The state's view has shaped public opinion, leading to pervasive misunderstandings of the nature of Islamic law and legal theory.

Class politics. Quadrant III consists of class issues that are nondoctrinal, including maternity and parental leave and public funding for childcare services.[15] Feminist movements may play a role here, especially with respect to childcare (because childcare outside of the home represents more of a challenge to traditional gender roles), but the key actors that catalyze policies in this category are Left parties. We expect to find that the varying strength of Left parties and other actors involved in class politics (such as unions) will be correlated with differences in the extent and nature of policy provision. Left parties and labor mobilization played a pivotal role in the expansion of the universalistic welfare state (Esping-Andersen, 1990; Huber & Stephens, 2001; Korpi, 2006; Korpi, 1983). When pushed by feminist mobilization, the spread of new ideas about women's roles, and women's growing participation in the paid labor force, Left party power fostered the development and expansion of social policies such as parental leave and day care.

---

[15] Some readers might wonder why issues concerning women's roles as mothers are classified as "nondoctrinal," since the world's religions have had a lot to say about motherhood and families. Though many religious doctrines define family roles and emphasize the family's importance in society, they have not rejected state support for working parents and their children. In fact, many religious organizations and leaders have endorsed the expansion of family policies. Pope Francis, for example, supports maternity leave, declaring that women "must be protected and helped in this dual task: the right to work and the right to motherhood" (Bruenig, 2015).

For example, forty-four years of Social Democratic rule in Sweden helped promote the adoption of the world's first parental leave policy in 1974. The gender-neutral policy, which granted six months of paid leave following birth, affirmed women's dual roles as mothers and workers, the importance of fathers, the state's responsibility to promote work–life balance, and the idea that care for children was a political and not merely a private matter (Chronholm, 2009; Haas, 1992).[16]

In Norway, Social Democratic rule created the conditions for enactment of the Day Care Act of 1975, which guaranteed that public childcare would be available for all working parents who needed it (Leira, 1992, 2002). Then, in 1993, Norway adopted the world's first law establishing a nontransferable parental leave entitlement (widely called "daddy leave"). Social Democrats led the special commission created by the government in 1986 to examine men's gender roles, masculinity, and fatherhood. In order to promote gender equality as well as improve the father–child bond, the committee recommended reserving a special period for fathers in the parental leave scheme (Leira, 2002, p. 95). "Daddy leave" policies were later adopted in Sweden (in 1995), Denmark (though later repealed), Finland, Iceland, and Germany (in 2007). Over time, the policies led to pervasive changes in gender roles in parenting (Skorge, 2016).

Both Sweden and Norway have a long tradition, dating from the end of the nineteenth century, of state provision of maternity leave. These patterns of past social provision influence the extent to which more recent policies, such as gender-neutral parental leave and "daddy leave," generate controversy. The United States, by contrast, did not even go through the phase of public support of paid maternity leave, which, along with gender-neutral paid leave, continues to be politically divisive. US federal policy has been limited only to mandating *unpaid* leave since the Family and Medical Leave Act of 1993. Policy legacies established by decades of Left power shape the possibilities in the present.

For the category of class politics, economic development will affect crossnational policy differences. Larger tax bases make allocation decisions less existential for many actors, which reduces the degree of conflict

---

[16] It is important to note that many policy makers at the time believed that women would be the vast majority of workers who took advantage of parental leave. These expectations were correct. Men did not participate in parental leave in a significant way until "daddy leave" (nontransferable parental leave) was introduced under a Liberal government (though the policy was later expanded under a Social Democrat government).

in this policy area. States with larger informal sectors and weaker institutions, by contrast, will find implementation of paid parental leave and subsidized childcare regimes more difficult. As middle-income countries have grown economically, family policies have expanded (Blofield & Martínez Franzoni, 2014a).

Religion and class. When doctrinal issues also involve a class dimension (quadrant IV), we expect Left parties and the politics of redistribution to be important alongside religious factors and feminist movements. Consider public funding for abortion and contraception. On the one hand, we would expect that the politics surrounding the *de jure* (as opposed to the *de facto*) situation of abortion and contraception – including the conditions under which abortion is permitted by law, which types of contraceptives are legally available, and for whom this is the case – will, like family law, be shaped by religious politics. Across dozens of countries, for example, Christian churches and civic organizations have mobilized their followers and lobbied politicians so that laws conform to ecclesiastical doctrine on the sanctity of life, and on the nature and purposes of marital sex. Whether or not governments have liberalized access to abortion has depended, in part, on their willingness to incur the political costs of confronting religious organizations (Htun, 2003, 2009).

On the other hand, the politics surrounding the *de facto* situation of abortion and contraception involve an additional dimension. Whether women exercise reproductive autonomy *in practice* – which is a separate and distinct issue from the *legality* of reproductive rights – often depends on public funding. Do government funds subsidize these services so they are accessible to, and safe for, all women? Do clinics and hospitals provide contraceptives and perform legal abortions free of charge? Whereas decisions about the legality of reproductive rights are influenced by religious politics, decisions about access involving state spending are more shaped by the politics of socioeconomic redistribution. The trajectory of the welfare state and the strength of actors – such as Left-leaning parties and labor unions – who advocate a greater governmental role in guaranteeing social rights will influence policy patterns on this issue.

In summary, change in quadrant I follows a logic of *status politics*, change in quadrant II is primarily driven by *doctrinal politics*, change in quadrant III conforms to a *class politics* logic, and quadrant IV is driven by a combination of all three sets of actors and contexts. Since countries vary in terms of the clusters of actors, cleavages, and conflicts that influence policy dynamics on each issue, policy outcomes exhibit distinct

patterns. For example, different configurations of religion–state relations
will produce, and be reflected in, the situation of family law in a particular
country. Variation in the mobilization of autonomous women's movements is important for explaining the degree and scope of legislative
activity on status issues such as violence against women. The varying
strength of Left parties and welfare state trajectories shape differences in
parental leave lengths and reimbursement rates.

   In the empirical chapters of this book, we use this framework to
more fully develop our approach to each issue and clarify the specific
theoretical expectations implied in relation to that issue. In each chapter, we examine the relative role of each of these sets of factors in
accounting for crossnational variation in women's rights. We examine
one or more policy issue from each cell of our two-by-two table to
illustrate cross-issue variation and to demonstrate the utility of our
theoretical approach. The chapters focus on violence against women
(a nondoctrinal status issue), workplace equality (a nondoctrinal status
issue), family law (a doctrinal status issue), parental leave and childcare
(nondoctrinal class issues), and reproductive rights (which include both
doctrinal status and doctrinal class issues, as we compare the legality
of abortion as well as funding for abortion and contraceptives). The
final chapter aims to add force to our argument about the diversity of
explanatory logics across issues, as well as the utility of the categories
we offer, by comparing the analysis of all issue areas using the same
statistical model. In our conclusion, we consider extensions to other
gender-related policy areas.

RESEARCH DESIGN

To assess the utility of our approach to variation, change, and continuity
in women's rights, we created an original dataset of laws and policies on
women's rights in seventy countries. The dataset includes seven distinct
policy domains (violence against women, family law, equality at work,
family leave, childcare, abortion legality, and reproductive rights funding)
in order to cover the multiple ways that states promote (or undermine)
gender justice. We gathered data for four points in time (1975, 1985,
1995, and 2005), and developed indices for each of our analyses of
women's rights. They are measures of the degree to which the government
promotes equality and autonomy in each area. The empirical chapters
of the book, as well as Appendix A, describe in detail the components of
each index.

A team of more than a dozen researchers working from 2006 to 2011 gathered the data for this study. The team reviewed primary source documents on national laws and policies (such as national labor codes, legislative language and preambles, and Supreme Court decisions) and secondary literature such as legal doctrine, law review articles, newspaper articles, and studies and databases maintained by women's rights organizations and intergovernmental organizations (such as the International Labour Organization's database of labor laws by country, NATLEX, and the maternity protection database). We also relied on the reports produced by intergovernmental organizations such as the United Nations (UN) and the World Bank, as well as transnational activist groups (such as Musawah and Women for Women's Human Rights) and NGOs (such as the Center for Reproductive Law and Policy). Government reports to the Convention on the Elimination of All Forms of Discrimination against Women (CEDAW) and shadow reports compiled by activist groups provided another source of information. Finally, we consulted country-specific scholarship (for more details see Appendix A).

Based on these data sources, our team members completed country sheets (small monographs on each country), answering a standard set of questions about all countries in each year. Then, a trained team of coders coded the information in these sheets using a shared set of code rules. Two or three researchers coded each variable in each country and there was a high degree of agreement. We thoroughly reviewed the coding. In addition, parts of the database, particularly pertaining to family law, were checked against the World Bank's Women, Business, and the Law database (2011), confirming its validity. It took approximately five years to gather the most basic data for seventy countries, and then more time to code, check, and analyze these data across the seven policy domains (some of which cover dozens of items) for use in our indices, which is why the most recent year covered is 2005. In addition, we created an original dataset on the strength and autonomy of women's movements in the seventy countries, using a similar approach (more on this in Chapter 2 and Appendix A).

The dataset contains measurements at the national level. In most cases, national governments establish the laws and policies on women's rights in the areas we study. In some federal countries, these responsibilities fall to state governments, and in some plural legal systems, women's rights may be determined by particular religions or by the state courts that apply interpretations of those religions. We take note of these exceptions and explain our coding decisions in the empirical chapters. Even in these cases, national governments sometimes play a role in establishing model policies, funding state-level initiatives, and otherwise shaping women's rights.

The seventy countries that comprise our dataset were selected to ensure variation in our independent variables. Our dataset includes countries with a full separation of religion and state and others where they are significantly intertwined, as well as those with high and low religiosity, high and low levels of feminist mobilization, many and few women in parliament, and varying levels of democracy, among other factors, as well as both parties and nonparties to the Convention on the Elimination of All Forms of Discrimination Against Women (CEDAW). These countries, drawn from every region of the world, encompass some 85 percent of the global population.[17]

Our indices measure laws and policy that have been formally adopted, including laws, constitutions, Supreme Court decisions, national programs and initiatives (that may not be legislation or court decisions), and other official policy documents. We measure variation in the things governments are doing and promising, not how well they do them or the degree to which they follow through on promises, and definitely not changes in attitudes or behavior in response to policy. We do not examine whether laws are enforced, whether policies are adequately funded, and whether citizens comply with the law. While these considerations are important and will determine the degree to which policy changes induce transformations in women's rights on the ground, they are beyond the scope of the present study. When we say we focus on policy adoption, we mean variation in government action.

In most of the countries of the study, there is a gap between the law on the books and the law in action. The countries in our study vary in the extent of their lawfulness (see, e.g., Kaufman, Kraay, & Mastuzzi, 2011). Regardless of the degree of the gap (an account of which is beyond the scope of this study), the law on the books remains important for scholarly

---

[17] The countries included in this study include: Algeria, Argentina, Australia, Austria, Bangladesh, Belgium, Botswana, Brazil, Bulgaria, Canada, Chile, China, Colombia, Costa Rica, Croatia, Cuba, Czech Republic, Denmark, Egypt, Estonia, Finland, France, Germany, Greece, Hungary, Iceland, India, Indonesia, Iran, Iraq, Ireland, Israel, Italy, Ivory Coast, Japan, Jordan, Kazakhstan, Kenya, Lithuania, Malaysia, Mexico, Morocco, Netherlands, New Zealand, Nigeria, Norway, Pakistan, Peru, Poland, Portugal, Romania, Russia, Saudi Arabia, Slovak Republic, Slovenia, South Africa, South Korea, Spain, Sweden, Switzerland, Taiwan, Tanzania, Thailand, Turkey, Ukraine, United Kingdom, United States, Uruguay, Venezuela, and Vietnam.

analysis and for human lives on the ground. Scholars cannot measure, explain, or compare the divergence of the law from social practice without having a sense of what the law is. And the law, even when violated, constitutes a central reference point for political struggles, as it represents the outcome of collective decision making on moral and ethical matters and has great symbolic power (Glendon, 1987; Habermas, 1996).

The statistical analyses presented in this book explore the relationship between various areas of government action (our dependent variables) and various explanatory factors (the independent variables) for all seventy countries. The dataset pools single-year cross-sections of all countries in 1975, 1985, 1995, and 2005. In some cases we examine "snapshots" of particular years, but in most we use regression analysis techniques that take into account both the cross-sectional and over-time nature of the dataset. This type of data is sometimes called "panel data" because it is analogous to studying the same people in different waves of a survey, or panels, over time. This larger, over-time dataset provides more explanatory leverage than standard cross-sectional studies, as we are able to incorporate repeated measurements of the same countries at different times.

The best statistical models in the world will not offer insight into political phenomena if they are incomplete, or missing critical aspects of context and action. Qualitative work and deep knowledge of the subject of study is the best way to ensure that one is capturing, as much as possible, the most important elements in the explanatory account one is offering. Such qualitative work is also useful on its own, of course, but here we use it in combination with our statistical analysis to offer a more robust picture of the comparative politics of women's rights.

Fortunately, we were able to ground our theories and hypotheses in our own longstanding expertise in particular regions and countries (primarily in North America, Europe, and Latin America), which was supplemented and enriched by the fieldwork undertaken as part of this project. The fieldwork on which this book is based included document study and interviewing in Argentina, China, India, Israel, Japan, Malaysia, and Nigeria, combined with prior interview materials and field research in the United States, Canada, Norway, and the various Latin American countries studied by Htun over the course of her career (including Bolivia, Brazil, Chile, Colombia, Mexico, and Peru). We selected these cases not as "critical cases" or as theory-testing exercises but rather for what they offered us in terms of deepening, honing, and refining our theoretical expectations about state action on women's rights. Our fieldwork offered us a sense of the reactions of feminist activists, scholars, and politicians on the ground in some of the countries we study – reactions that helped us to elaborate and clarify our approach. This rich contextual material is reflected in the examples and specific comparisons we offer in each chapter.

Over the past decade or so, the international development community has made great strides in the collection, analysis, and dissemination of data on women's legal rights and public policies related to gender equality. These projects, such as the World Bank's Women, Business, and the Law (WBL) reports and the OECD's Social Institutions and Gender Index (SIGI), cover many of the same areas analyzed in this book, and in at least one case (WBL) are more up to date. The World Bank project includes indicators on property and inheritance rights, decision-making authority in the family, maternity and parental benefits, reproductive rights, provisions on violence, quota laws, and equal rights at work. The OECD project covers many of these same legal areas, though its measurement of "social institutions" also includes data on social practices, such as missing women, child marriage, incidence of and attitudes toward violence, unmet demand for contraceptives, and numbers of women in parliament.

Our project differs from these other efforts in a few important respects. Since the logic and politics of different women's rights differ, we should disaggregate issues in order to make explanations and policy recommendations. Our dataset is organized to permit such disaggregation, but not all international organizations involved in the study of gender and advocacy of equality engage in a similar practice of analytical disaggregation.[18] What is more, their measures often combine measures of policy with measurements of behavioral outcomes, which may make sense for other purposes, but not for our policy-focused project.

Our measures do not combine policy and outcomes, and they do not combine different policy issues into a single index to measure women's rights or gender equality on a single dimension. We do not presume there

---

[18] OECD's SIGI, for example, combines issues of violence against women and reproductive autonomy into a single subindex of "restricted physical integrity" (OECD, 2015, p. 8). And their report regularly aggregates their subindices into an aggregate "social institutions and gender index" to classify and rank countries (Ibid, pp. 9–11, 24–5). The World Bank project identifies seven clusters of indicators, including "accessing institutions," "using property," "going to court," "providing incentives," "building credit," "getting a job," and "protecting women." Though all deal with the conditions of women's economic agency, some of the clusters combine issues that we argue should be separated analytically. "Accessing institutions," for example, contains measures of family law and measures of quotas for women in politics, two issues that we claim conform to different policy logics.

is a uniform explanatory model that produces more gender equality in the same way across all issues. Instead, we explore, and seek to explain, differences *across* women's rights (as well as across countries and over time). This disaggregated approach is beneficial. If there are differences across issues, it allows us to identify, chart, and account for them. If there are similarities across issues, we can identify those as well. By not presuming homogeneity across gender issues from the start, our approach is open to patterns *both* of diversity *and* of similarity.

CONCLUSION

Our analysis is premised on the idea that gender equality is a complex concept spanning different dimensions. Advancing women's status and promoting equality involves massive social changes and challenges entrenched patterns of state–society relations. Whether or not a policy touches upon women's status with respect to men, their gendered class positions and redistributive politics, or the authority of the state against religious and cultural groups, sets in motion distinct political dynamics.

Not every policy will pose the same challenge in every national context. Paid maternity leave is more of a challenge in the United States than it is in Norway or even Egypt. Affirmative action policies are more of a challenge in Sweden than they are in Canada, where such action is specifically permitted by the constitution (Constitution Act of 1982, section 15(2)). Policies challenging religious authority are more controversial in Iran than in the United Kingdom, where state authority upholds religion but where a secular culture and ideology prevails. The key thing to note, however, is that the contexts that make *some* women's rights initiatives controversial will not necessarily make *all* women's rights issues controversial to the same degree or in the same way. We theorize the impact of these contextual factors on each gender equality issue in the chapters that follow.

The analyses presented in the chapters that follow reveal support for our arguments. We show that women's rights cannot be considered part of a single basket, and we begin to explain why and how the dynamics of reform and resistance vary across issues. Each women's right challenges fundamental, though distinct, values and institutions set by the status order; class inequalities; and the power of religious and cultural doctrine.

2

Feminist Mobilization and Status Politics

Combatting Violence against Women

Violence against women is a global problem.[1] Research from North America, Europe, Africa, Latin America, the Middle East, and Asia has documented astonishingly high rates of sexual assault, stalking, trafficking, violence in intimate relationships, and other violations of women's bodies and psyches, acts which collectively constitute the phenomenon of violence against women.[2] No region of the world is immune to violence against women. Differing definitions and methodologies mean data about prevalence is not strictly comparable across countries, but there is sufficient evidence to show that these problems are serious in all of our study countries and regions. In Europe, violence against women is far more dangerous to the female population than cancer or terrorism (Elman, 2007, p. 85). As many as 45 percent of European women have been victims of physical or sexual violence (Martinez & Schrottle, 2006; see also Europe, 2006). Rates are similarly high in North America, Australia, and New Zealand,[3]

---

[1] An earlier version of this chapter was published as Mala Htun and S. Laurel Weldon, "Civic origins of progressive policy change: combating violence against women in global perspective." *American Political Science Review*, 106(3) (August 2012), 548–69.

[2] Article 1 of the UN Declaration of Elimination of Violence against Women defines violence against women as "any act of gender-based violence that results in, or is likely to result in, physical, sexual or psychological harm or suffering to women, including threats of such acts, coercion or arbitrary deprivation of liberty, whether occurring in public or in private-life."

[3] In Canada, about half of all women have experienced physical or sexual violence in their lifetime; in the United States, a national survey found that a quarter of all women have experienced such violence (Johnson & Sacco, 1995; Tjaden & Thoennes, 1998). In Australia, one national study (1996) found that 3 percent of women had been assaulted

and studies in Asia, Latin America, and Africa show that violence against women is ubiquitous.[4]

Assaults on women violate human rights, undermine democratic transitions, harm children, and are tremendously costly.[5] Today, violence against women is widely seen as a question of fundamental human rights. Many national governments and international organizations have adopted a wide variety of measures to address violence against women, including legal reform, public education campaigns, and support for shelters and rape crisis centers, among others. In spite of this growing and deepening consensus about violence, there are puzzling differences in national policy. Why do some governments have more comprehensive policy regimes than others? Why are some governments quick to adopt policies to address violence while others are slow?

In this chapter, we present a global comparative analysis of the development of policies on violence against women from 1975 to 2005. We show that the autonomous mobilization of feminists in domestic and transnational contexts – not Left parties, women in parliament, or national wealth – is the critical factor accounting for policy change. Autonomous social movements develop oppositional consciousness, imagine new forms of social organization, and mobilize broad societal action to generate understanding and support (Mansbridge & Morris, 2001). In these ways, they champion progressive social policies that explicitly challenge the established social order by reshaping relations among groups. Further, our analysis reveals that the impact of global norms on domestic policy

---

in the past year while 8 percent had been assaulted in their current relationship. In New Zealand, a national study found that 35 percent of women had been assaulted in an intimate relationship.

[4] For example, a national study of Bangladeshi villages found that nearly half (47 percent) of all women reported being subject to male violence in an intimate relationship. In Korea, an older (1989) national study found that somewhere from 12 to 38 percent of adult women were physically assaulted by an intimate in the last year. Surveys of women in five Latin American countries found that more than half had suffered violence (Heise & Germain 1994). In Africa, rates of women ever assaulted by an intimate male partner range from 13 percent in South Africa to 30 percent in Nigeria (Heise, Ellsberg, & Gottemoeller, 1999). In Morocco, an emergency room in Casablanca reports that 30–40 percent of women admitted each month are suffering injuries from domestic violence (UNFP 2007).

[5] For excellent overviews of prevalence rates for different types of violence by country, see Heise, Ellsberg, and Gottemoeller (1999) and Heise and Germain (1994). For European research see Martinez & Schrottle (2006). See also Aromaa & Heiskanen, eds. (2008). For a discussion of different kinds of data in the United States see Greenfeld (1997). For summaries of police statistics, survey, and other data for thirty-six established democracies see Weldon (2002a), Appendix A. For data on effects of violence against women, see also Chalk & King, 1998; Heise & Germain, 1994; Martinez & Schrottle, 2006. For figures on cost see World Health Organization (2010).

making is to some degree conditional on the presence of feminist movements in local contexts, pointing to the importance of ongoing activism and a vibrant civil society. Autonomous feminist movements play important roles for other types of gender issues as well, as we show later in the book, but often in addition to or alongside other factors.

Public policy scholars have long identified the importance of social movements in softening up the political environment, changing the national mood, and putting new issues on the agenda (e.g., Baumgartner & Mahoney, 2005; Kingdon, 1984; McAdam & Su, 2002; Weldon, 2002a; 2011). Democratic theorists argue that social movements are critical for advancing inclusion and democracy (Costain, 2005; Dryzek, 1990; Dryzek, Downes, Hunold, Sclosberg, & Hernes, 2003; Young, 1990, 2000). Yet our standard cross-national datasets for the study of social policy include few indicators of this type of political phenomenon. Much of the large-n literature is state-centric, focusing on the structure of state institutions, such as veto-points, or on formal political actors, such as political parties and women in parliament (e.g., Brady, 2003; Däubler, 2008; Esping-Andersen, 1990; Huber & Stephens, 2001; Kittilson, 2008; Kittilson & Schwindt-Bayer, 2012; Rudra, 2002; Schwindt-Bayer & Mishler, 2005; Swank, 2001).[6] Other cross-national studies focus on economic factors, such as globalization, women's labor force participation, or national wealth (e.g., Brady, Beckfield, & Seeleib-Kaiser, 2005; Huber & Stephens, 2001; Rudra, 2002). Existing measures of civil society-related phenomena are underdeveloped compared to those pertaining to economic or formal political variables.[7]

More qualitative, historical studies of social policy take greater account of civil society, exploring women's activism, labor movements, and the ways that civil society and the state intertwine (e.g., Banaszak, Beckwith, & Rucht, 2003; Mazur, 2002; 2005; Piven & Cloward, 1993; Skocpol, 1992, 2003) but their nuanced theoretical arguments tend to get lost in larger-scale, cross-national, and cross-regional studies. As a result, large-n analyses of social policy tend to neglect the broader context of normative political contestation outside the state (Amenta, Bonastia, &

---

[6] The power resources school sees class struggle as being determined by political battles, but even when scholars say they aim to measure labor mobilization, they tend to do so by focusing on political parties rather than civil society itself (See, e.g., Esping-Andersen, 1990; Huber & Stephens, 2001; Korpi, 2006).

[7] This may be remedied to some degree by the Varieties of Democracy project indicators on civil society. However, even for those indicators, only one measure focuses on women's organizations, and none distinguish feminist from women's organizing more generally.

Caren, 2001; Amenta, Caren, Chiarello, & Su, 2010). This chapter blends qualitative and historical insights with a cross-national perspective to show that autonomous mobilization of feminists in civil society triggered global transformations in government action on violence against women.

DEFINING GOVERNMENT RESPONSIVENESS TO VIOLENCE AGAINST WOMEN

Most of the world's governments now take some kind of action to address the problem of violence against women, though the remedies vary. Which policies are most likely to address violence effectively? To answer this question, we need to understand the causes of violence and the most common barriers to an effective government response. A growing body of research, mainly in the disciplines of public health, criminology, anthropology, and psychology, shows that the causes of violence against women in general (and rape and domestic violence in particular) are complex and operate at multiple levels (e.g., Chalk & King, 1998; Crowell & Burgess, 1996; Heise et al., 1999; Heise & Germain, 1994; World Health Organization, 2010). Individual and societal attitudes about gender are an important cause of violence (Crowell & Burgess, 1996; Davies, 1994; Graham-Kevan & Archer, 2003; Johnson, 1995). Cross-cultural studies have found that cultural norms endorsing male dominance; female economic dependency; patterns of conflict resolution emphasizing violence, toughness, and honor; and male authority in the family predict high societal levels of domestic violence and rape (Heise & Germain, 1994; Levinson, 1989; Sanday, 1981). Social and legal norms make women vulnerable to violence and others more likely to abuse them with the expectation of impunity (Carillo, Connor, Fried, Sandler, & Waldorf, 2003; World Health Organization, 2010). At the level of individual relationships, the causes of intimate violence and rape include sexist attitudes or "gender schemas," though poor relationship skills and vulnerability (e.g., economic, social, and legal dependence) on the part of the victim also contribute (Brush, 2011; Crowell & Burgess, 1996; Raphael, 1996; World Health Organization, 2010). As this suggests, violence against women is not primarily the result of "single factor" causes or solely attributable to individual-level risk factors such as alcohol use or mental illness (Crowell & Burgess, 1996; Heise et al., 1999; Heise & Germain, 1994; World Health Organization, 2010).

There is an emerging international consensus about the causes of violence and about which policy actions would be most likely to prevent violence and provide appropriate services to victims. In adopting the Vienna Declaration at the World Conference on Human Rights in 1993, governments agreed that "violence against women is a manifestation of historically unequal power relations between men and women . . . it is one of the crucial social mechanisms by which women are forced into a subordinate position." The Beijing Declaration and Platform for Action (United Nations, 1995), agreed to by 189 governments and supported by NGOs from 180 countries in 1995, outlines a series of measures to address violence against women in a wide variety of policy areas.

The research on responses to violence against women also supports this multipronged approach. It suggests that responding to violence against women requires action on the many dimensions and types of abuse that occur in contemporary societies. Legal reforms need to specify that violence against women is a crime, even where one might think that general laws against assault and murder should apply to women (Carillo et al., 2003; Chalk & King, 1998; Crowell & Burgess, 1996; Davies, 1994; Martinez & Schrottle, 2006). Counseling, shelters, and other housing and legal assistance help women leave abusive relationships (Carillo et al., 2003; Chalk & King, 1998; Martinez & Schrottle, 2006). Training and dedicated units for police, social workers, judges, and other professionals improve victims' experiences with these agencies (Carillo et al., 2003; Chalk & King, 1998; Martinez & Schrottle, 2006). Specific efforts to address the concerns of particularly vulnerable populations of women, such as immigrant or racialized minority women, are also important (Carillo et al., 2003; Crenshaw, 1993; Richie & Kanuha, 2000). In addition to responding to victims, governments can seek to reduce violence through preventative measures such as public education and "social marketing" (Carillo et al., 2003; Chalk & King, 1998). Finally, governments should adopt explicit efforts to coordinate antiviolence measures so that agencies are working together to combat violence instead of at cross-purposes (Chalk & King, 1998; Weldon, 2002b).

We examined each of these dimensions of government response to violence against women for all countries in our study to build an index to facilitate comparison. The index assigns higher values to those policy regimes that address more types of violence and whose actions span these categories of services, legal reform, policy coordination, and prevention of violence. This measure adapts the approach employed by Weldon (Weldon, 2002b, 2006), in order to take into account the varied types of violence that are salient in different contexts. Assessing this range of policies produces a score out of a total of ten points:

(1) Three points for *services to victims* (1 for each of the following):
 – Government funds domestic violence shelters
 – Government funds rape crisis centers
 – Government provides crisis services for other forms of violence (stalking, female genital mutilation, honor killings, and so forth);
(2) Three points for *legal reform* (1 for each of the following):
 – Government has adopted specialized legislation pertaining to domestic violence
 – Government has adopted specialized legislation pertaining to sexual assault and rape
 – Government has adopted specialized legalization pertaining to other forms of violence (such as trafficking, sexual harassment, female genital mutilation, and so forth);
(3) One point for policies or programs targeted to *vulnerable populations* of women (one point for any of the following programs or policies):
 – Government provides specialized services to women of marginalized groups (defined by ethnicity, race, and so forth). Examples include bilingual hotlines, specialized crisis centers, and specially trained police officers
 – Government recognizes violence against women as a basis for refugee status
 – Government protects immigrant women in abusive relations from deportation;
(4) One point for *training professionals* who respond to victims:
 – Government provides training for police, social workers, nurses, and so forth;[8]
(5) One point for *prevention* programs:
 – Government funds public education programs or takes other preventative measures;

---

[8] There is not space here to engage the criticism of so-called "professionalization" of services for violence against women. Some critics have argued that services such as counseling and social work pathologize women victims and do not advance social change (Elman, 2001; Goodey, 2004; Incite Women of Color against Violence, 2007). On the other hand, some scholars have argued that professionalization has furthered feminist principles (Johnson & Zaynullina, 2010), and that actual "professionalization" itself is less extensive than these critics would suggest. For example, shelter workers are not paid high wages, provided benefits, or treated with the respect generally accorded "professionals," nor are shelters otherwise integrated into state bureaucracies in the ways critics suggest, since even with state funding they are often staffed largely by volunteers and low-paid but committed activists (Weldon, 2011).

(6) One point for *administrative* reforms:
  – Government has an organization or agency to provide research, policy analysis, and coordinate different levels of government response on violence against women.

Our index sums these elements, so that more points imply more types of government response. The most responsive governments score a 10 and those that do nothing score a zero. Like the index developed by Weldon in earlier work (2006b, 2002a), this measure of policy *scope* encompasses a variety of different types of policies as a way of getting at the many different dimensions of the problem. Responsiveness means addressing as many of these dimensions as possible, both responding to women and preventing future violence.[9]

GLOBAL OVERVIEW OF GOVERNMENT ACTION ON VIOLENCE AGAINST WOMEN

No region of the world is immune to violence against women. Differing definitions and methodologies mean data about prevalence is not strictly comparable across countries, but there is sufficient evidence to show that these problems are serious in all of our study countries and regions. What does vary across countries and regions is the scope of government response to this problem. Maps shown in Figures 2.1 through 2.4 depict the ways in which global responses to violence against women changed over decades from 1975 to 2005. These maps show that at the beginning of the period there was not much cross-national variation in government response: Most countries did little or nothing to address violence. By 2005, however, great variation in government response had emerged, both across and within regions.

---

[9] Since this is a measure of scope, the measure's strength consists in the fact that it considers a variety of policies. Analysis of each individual item will not tell us about the scope of the policy. Experts have emphasized, for example, that responding to violence requires legal reform, provision of shelter, and measures such as raising awareness. Moreover, since this index is based on conceptual, not practical, relatedness, standard measures used to assess indices (such as Cronbach's alpha) are inappropriate for this type of index construction (Weldon, 2011). For those who are nevertheless interested, Cronbach's alpha is .88. Analysis of the individual items in the index might be interesting for answering other types of questions (for example, what factors determine whether a response is more focused on legal reform or changing awareness?) but is beyond the scope of this chapter.

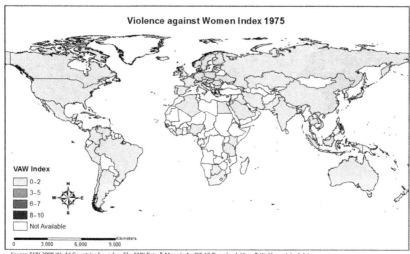

FIGURE 2.1 Violence against Women Index, 1975

FIGURE 2.2 Violence against Women Index, 1985

FIGURE 2.3 Violence against Women Index, 1995

FIGURE 2.4 Violence against Women Index, 2005

The four figures show that both rich and poor countries have seen a trend toward greater responsiveness to violence against women over time. This chapter argues that the trend reflects not a smooth process of convergence toward equality and recognition of women's rights (perhaps as a result of modernization, industrialization, or the spread of Western enlightenment ideals), but rather a process of political struggle and contestation. Official responses to violence against women are complex and shaped by both national and international factors, including global and regional activism, institutions, and norms. These dynamics vary considerably by country and region.

International Women's Rights Meetings and Conventions

International agreement that violence against women is a fundamental question of human rights emerged in the mid-1990s, but neither intergovernmental conferences nor international activist meetings focused on violence against women before the late 1960s or early 1970s.[10] Of course, there were discussions of sexual violence in the international women's movement even in the early 1900s, since rape in war and peacetime was presented by feminist activists in their discussions at the time as one of the reasons women should organize internationally (Rupp, 1999, p. 378). Although women have experienced and criticized rape, wife abuse, and other forms of violence against women throughout the ages, it was not until the late 1960s and early 1970s that activists began to use the term "violence against women" (Brownmiller, 1975; Weldon, 2002b, 2006a).

When the UN organized the first intergovernmental meeting on women during International Women's Year (1975), violence against women was not a major agenda item. The same was true at the next world meeting in 1980 in Copenhagen. Even when the major women's rights Convention, the Convention on the Elimination of Discrimination against Women, was adopted by the General Assembly of the UN in 1979, violence against women was not a major category. As a result, the process the UN developed for monitoring the implementation of the Convention on the Elimination of All Forms of Discrimination against Women (CEDAW), which involves periodic reports by state parties to an expert panel with critical discussion, did not initially include a requirement to discuss

[10] This section draws on Weldon (2006a).

government action on violence against women. Indeed, even though CEDAW entered into force in 1981, reporting on violence against women was not a major part of the process of monitoring CEDAW implementation until the late 1980s.

The Third and Fourth UN Conferences on Women, major intergovernmental meetings in Nairobi (1985) and Beijing (1995) with concomitant NGO sessions, were major turning points at which violence against women assumed greater prominence as a global human rights issue. These developments are reflected (to varying degrees) in the national and regional stories we tell in the following sections. Governments' and activists' participation in international meetings provides the backdrop for the development of many national policies (for more on CEDAW and the CEDAW Process, see Baldez, 2014).

North America, Europe, Australia, and New Zealand

In Canada, Australia, and the United States, feminist movements made violence against women a priority item starting in the late 1960s and early 1970s. In addition, in response to feminists, governments began to press for international agreements, and introduced many resolutions on violence against women at meetings of the United Nations Commission on the Status of Women. Government action on violence began to gather steam in the late 1970s and early 1980s, but the biggest transformation in policies on violence in these countries occurred between 1985 and 1995. For example, in 1979 and 1983 the Canadian government revised the country's criminal code to address sexual assault, and in the mid- to late 1980s the government began to fund major initiatives on both domestic violence against women and family violence more generally. These included the Secretary of State's Women's Program, the Family Violence Initiative (1988), and Project Haven, which provided funding for shelters. In the United States, legal and administrative reforms were introduced in the 1970s and 1980s, and the Violence against Women Act was passed in 1994. In both countries, feminist activists mobilized and skillfully deployed institutional resources in domestic politics to compel governments to take action on women's rights. By the early 1990s, government policy had incorporated the language of radical feminists, using the terms violence against women and even the "War against Women"(the latter in the Canadian context) (Gotell, 1998; Weldon, 2002a, 2011). As this discussion suggests, government action in Canada, the United States, and Australia was already advanced by 1995, when the international community established global norms on violence

TABLE 2.1 *Violence against Women Index, Anglo countries, 1975–2005*

Country	1975	1985	1995	2005
Canada	0	5	10	10
Australia	2	3	9	10
United States	1	4	8	10
New Zealand	0	3	5	8
United Kingdom	0	3	4	7

against women. Table 2.1 shows that some of these countries had achieved very high scores (8, 9, 10) on our index measuring government action on violence against women by that year.

Many European states took action on violence against women later (see Table 2.2, which shows that in 1995, scores on the index of government responsiveness to violence against women were lower in Europe than in the Anglo countries – no country in Europe scored an 8, 9, or 10 in 1995 – even lower than in Latin America), and their efforts were far more likely to be shaped by international organizations and transnational activist networks. In Finland, at the beginning of the 1990s, domestic violence could be dealt with only under the 1889 Criminal Law. International factors were responsible for growing awareness of the importance of tackling domestic violence there (Kantola, 2006). Montoya (2010) notes that the first wave of policy reform in the European Union (EU) (involving changes in Denmark, France, Sweden, and the United Kingdom) occurred "in the early 1990s, concurrently with the rise in international activism on behalf of violence against women, as seen at the Vienna and Beijing conferences" (p. 297).

The second wave of reform occurred in the late 1990s and 2000s, after the EU started promoting policy on violence against women. Although a few European governments took some early action (for example, this was the case in both the United Kingdom and Sweden), even in these countries the major developments occurred after 1995. Sweden's 1998 Violence against Women Act represented a major shift in government action (Ekberg, 2004; Elman, 2003; but see Elman, 2007 on the Child Contact Act of 1995). Before the 1990s, the Swedish government had been somewhat slower to adopt measures to redress violence than other established democracies had been (Elman, 1996; Weldon, 2002a). Indeed, as Elman (2003) notes, orders of protection were endorsed by the Riksdag (Swedish parliament) only in 1988, "over a decade after their original use in the United States and Britain" (p. 108).

TABLE 2.2 *Violence against Women Index in Europe, 1975–2005*

Country	1975	1985	1995	2005
Austria	0	2	4	9
Belgium	1	2	3	8
Denmark	0	0	1	9
Finland	0	1	4	7
France	0	3	5	8
Germany	0	2	7	8
Greece	0	0	1	6
Iceland	0	1	3	7
Ireland	0	1	5	10
Italy	0	0	0	4
Netherlands	0	1	3	7
Norway	0	2	7	10
Portugal	0	0	3	9
Spain	0	1	4	5
Sweden	1	4	6	8
Switzerland	0	0	3	9
United Kingdom	0	3	4	7

Latin America

Latin America's regional organizing and national action on violence occurred somewhat earlier than in Europe. Latin American regional activism preceded the global meetings of the mid-1990s that proved so influential elsewhere. Feminists held five regional feminist meetings (*Encuentros feministas*) between 1982 and 1990 and, at the fifth, formed the Latin American and Caribbean Feminist Network against Domestic and Sexual Violence (Friedman, 2009). In 1986, the OAS women's commission announced that violence against women was a special area of concern. July 1990 saw the Inter-American Consultation on Women and Violence, which opened with a proposal for the Inter-American Convention on Violence, which ultimately became the Inter-American Convention on the Prevention, Punishment and Eradication of Violence against Women (Convention of Belém do Pará) adopted in 1994. The language used in this Convention served as a basis for the language of the 1993 Vienna Declaration. The Convention of Belém do Pará was intended to be hard law, not just a declaration (Friedman, 2009; Merry, 2006; Weldon, 2006). There is a provision for monitoring compliance through the appointment of a rapporteur. In addition, the declaration endorsed by heads of state at the first Summit of the Americas, held in

TABLE 2.3 *Violence against Women Index in Latin America, 1975–2005*

Country	1975	1985	1995	2005
Argentina	0	0	7	8
Brazil	0	2	7	8
Chile	0	0	6	7
Dominican Republic	1	1	2	8
Peru	0	0	6	7
Costa Rica	2	2	7	8
Mexico	1	1	5	6
Venezuela	0	4	4	6
Colombia	0	1	5	6
Uruguay	0	0	4	5
Cuba	1	1	1	2

Miami in 1994, called on governments to "undertake appropriate measures to address and reduce violence against women."

In the 1990s, twelve Latin American countries adopted legislation on domestic violence and rape. Many took additional measures, such as establishing women's police stations, training judges and law enforcement officials, offering more services to survivors, and launching public awareness campaigns (Htun, 1998). Brazil, for example, was the first country in the world to create special police stations, staffed by women officers and counselors, to receive victims of violence (Nelson, 1996). Table 2.3 shows that by 1995, many countries had taken multiple forms of action to combat violence. Indeed, Latin American governments were slightly more likely to have adopted policies on violence against women than European ones (compare Tables 2.2 and 2.3). Scholars emphasize the roles of domestic feminist mobilization and the effectiveness and design of women's policy machineries in pushing for these actions (Franceschet, 2010; Haas, 2006; Weldon, 2002a). The impact of UN instruments such as the Vienna Declaration or CEDAW is less prominent, especially in these earlier reforms, than in Europe, especially Eastern Europe.

In the 2000s, though often after the period of our study, many Latin American governments adopted a fresh round of legislation to combat violence against women, as well additional public policies to document, combat, and prevent the practice. This "second generation" legislation adopted a feminist framing of the problem of violence and explicitly recognized the wide variety of forms of violence and locations where violence occurs (in the home, street, workplace, public institutions). The 2007 Mexican Law Guaranteeing Women Access to a Life Free from

Violence is exemplary in this regard, and evidence suggests that adoption of the law is related, at a national level, to some reduction in the frequency of physical intimate partner violence as well as a rise in the likelihood that women will report such violence to the authorities (Htun & Jensenius, 2016b). Yet impunity remains a severe problem in the region, for crimes of violence against women as well as other types of crimes (Htun, O'Brien, & Weldon, 2014).

Eastern Europe

Compared to other regions, action on violence in Eastern Europe occurred later and was weaker, but not nonexistent. Domestic feminist movements, transnational feminist networks, the pressures of EU accession, and international organizations were triggers for policy reforms on violence against women. Funding from the United Nations Fund for Women (UNIFEM, now called UN Women) and from organizations in the United States, especially the Open Society Institute (based in Budapest and New York City), offered critical support for movements against domestic violence in Poland, the Czech Republic, and Hungary.

International networking on domestic violence among women's groups was not palpably evident until the beginning of the twenty-first century when NGOs to help victims of rape and domestic violence started to emerge in Post-communist Europe and Eurasia. The NGOs appeared partly in response to domestic needs and partly because Western feminist concepts were now seen as applicable, and Western governments' and international governmental organizations' (IGOs') funding were unarguably appealing (Fabian, 2010, p. 7).

In Ukraine as well, international conferences and funding were key initiators of mobilization and policy reform. "First, attendance at international conferences and exposure to foreign funding initiated local interest in the issue of domestic violence. Next, Western grants allowed local advocates to experiment with new techniques and models" (Hrycak, 2010, p. 67). The government endorsed the Beijing Platform for action, and the United Nations Development Programme (UNDP) supported the creation of a women's policy agency to monitor compliance with CEDAW. The agency helped to raise awareness and support networks of activists working to eliminate violence against women. In 1997, the United States government began to make fighting trafficking a priority, and funding from U.S. organizations facilitated some organizing against violence. These activities, particularly the activities of the women's agency, helped lead to adoption of the 2001 Law on the Prevention of Domestic Violence.

TABLE 2.4 *Violence against Women Index in Eastern Europe, 1975–2005*

Country	1975	1985	1995	2005
Bulgaria	0	0	0	0
Croatia	0	0	0	5
Czech Republic	0	0	0	3
Estonia	0	0	0	1
Hungary	0	0	1	2
Kazakhstan	0	0	0	2
Lithuania	0	0	0	2
Poland	0	0	0	5
Romania	0	0	0	3
Russia	0	0	0	3
Slovak Republic	0	0	0	2
Slovenia	0	0	3	5
Turkey	0	0	1	6
Ukraine	0	0	0	1

In Kazakhstan, women's groups used CEDAW and other human rights instruments to pressure the government. Funding from the Open Society Institute helped local organizations raise awareness and pressure for legal reform on violence (Snajdr, 2010). Scholarship on Poland and Slovenia suggests that legal reforms to redress violence were adopted as a way to comply with EU gender equality directives and conform to European norms (Chivens, 2010; Robnik, 2010). In other countries as well, the process of EU accession has been a critical source of external pressure, sparking policy reforms in the later waves of change across Europe (Avdeyeva, 2007, 2010; Montoya, 2010). As this suggests, transnational feminist activists helped to stimulate policy change indirectly by pressuring governments for an opening and by providing resources to domestic and transnational activists. In some cases, they even created or strengthened domestic mobilization where that mobilization was absent or weak (Brunell & Johnson, 2010; Fabian, 2010; Hrycak, 2010).

Africa

In Africa, women's mobilizing around violence accelerated after the Nairobi conference. In the 1990s, feminist mobilization helped push through a new generation of legislation that marked a break from past reforms, including many measures on violence against women (Tripp, Casimiro, Kwesiga, & Mungwa, 2009). The support of legislative commissions, parliamentarians, media, foreign donors, and other civil society organizations has also been

TABLE 2.5 *Violence against Women Index in Africa, 1975–2005*

Country	1975	1985	1995	2005
Botswana	1	1	1	5
Tanzania	0	0	1	4
Nigeria	0	0	0	3
Kenya	0	0	0	5
Ivory Coast	0	0	2	5
South Africa	0	0	1	8

important in Tanzania, for example, pressure from the feminist move ment led to new legislation including the Sexual Offenses Act, and in Mozambique, women's groups worked with the Legal Reform Commission (created in 1997) to combat domestic violence (Tripp, Casimiro, Kwesiga, & Mungwa, 2009, p. 127). Women's rights activists in South Africa pushed for action on violence against women starting in the early 1990s. Laws establishing minimum sentences for rape and tightening bail requirements for those accused of rape were enacted in 1997, and guidelines for the handling of sexual offenses were passed the following year. Also in 1998, both men and women legislators helped pass the Domestic Violence Act (Casimiro, Kwesiga, & Mungwa, 2009).

In some countries, however, women's activism has been unable to secure government compliance with international agreements. In Nigeria, many bills to combat violence against women have been introduced, mainly at the behest of women's movement activists and their allies in the legislature, and many of these measures make reference to CEDAW. Yet the only measures to combat violence adopted by the legislature reject a women's rights framing. For example, a law on child marriage was framed as a question of children's rights, while a law on human trafficking was framed as a national security and border control issue. The women's movement in Nigeria has tended to be weak, and there are few women in the legislature. Public opinion tends to accept violence against women as inevitable (Kimani, 2016).

Middle East and North Africa

In the Middle East and North Africa (MENA) region, most policy changes on violence occurred between 1995 and 2005 – the period after the Beijing Conference – though there is significant variation within the region in terms of the scope and timing of responsiveness. The two

TABLE 2.6 *Violence against Women Index in the Middle East and North Africa, 1975–2005*

Country	1975	1985	1995	2005
Algeria	0	0	0	4
Iraq	0	0	0	0
Morocco	0	0	0	4
Jordan	0	0	0	0
Saudi Arabia	0	0	0	0
Egypt	0	0	0	2
Iran	0	0	0	2
Turkey	0	0	1	6
Israel	0	0	2	6

governments in the region that were most responsive to violence against women (Turkey and Israel) had taken some action before 1995, while the Iraqi government had undertaken no legal measures at all to address violence against women by 2005. What explains the overall tendency to respond after 1995, as well as this difference in response?

At first blush, it may seem that democratization or authoritarian back-lash conditions policy adoption on violence against women across the region. Israel is the only established, stable democracy in the region (so classified in spite of the situation regarding Palestinian human rights), and policy change in Turkey may also be due to a greater degree of democracy. Women's rights campaigns in Iran were shut down by authoritarian repression (Moghadam & Gheytanchi, 2010). But democratization, authoritarian backlash, and women's movements combine in more complex ways than this story would suggest. Sometimes, authoritarian governments seek to enhance their human rights record by undertaking what may seem like easy or symbolic measures on women's rights.

Feminist organizing plays an important role in drawing attention to violence against women in the MENA region as elsewhere. Women's movements have been active across the MENA region, and constitute a significant presence not only in Israel, but also in Algeria, Iran, Morocco, and Turkey (Moghadam & Gheytanchi, 2010). It is no coincidence that these are the countries that were more likely to address violence against women than the region as a whole (see Table 2.6).

In one of the most well-known campaigns, in Morocco, women launched a successful campaign (the 1 Million Signatures Campaign), mostly focused on family law (Charrad, 2001), that prompted movements in other countries (such as Iran) to emulate them (Moghadam & Gheytanchi, 2010). In the context of the broader political opening in Morocco, women's movement activists (including those working on violence against women) were able to advance their calls for women's rights in several areas (Moghadam & Gheytanchi, 2010). Moroccan women's groups used the CEDAW process to pressure the government to adopt changes in relation to women's rights. In 2002, the government announced a National Action Plan to address gender-based violence. This plan was developed and implemented through consultation and coordination with women's groups (among other NGOs and experts) (Carrillo, Connor, Fried, Sandler, & Waldorf, 2003). Government-sponsored shelters were established, a special police investigatory unit was set up, and changes to the criminal code strengthened protections for battered women. In addition, the government adopted a measure against trafficking in 2003.[11] These changes stemmed from international pressure combined with a supportive domestic elite and women's NGOs (Carrillo et al., 2003; Moghadam & Gheytanchi, 2010).

In Jordan, feminist activism combined with international pressures to move a government – even one trending toward authoritarianism – to begin addressing violence against women (albeit later than Morocco). The 1996 rape and police mistreatment of a British–Iraqi woman thrust violence against women to the forefront of the international community's view of the country.[12] Over the next two years, at the prompting of a member of Prince Hassan's staff, the police created a unit to attend to family violence.[13] In 1998, a series of investigative newspaper reports brought violence against women to public attention again but little government action followed (Forester, 2016).

A change in regime in the subsequent year (1999) put a halt to what had been greater democratization with the dissolution of Parliament.

---

[11] Critics note that the adoption of this strategy has not changed the fact that a large swath of Moroccan society still sees domestic violence as acceptable and that the police are mostly unresponsive to complaints. The government has not undertaken to ensure that social workers, police, and other professionals who respond to calls for help are trained to provide assistance.

[12] This section on Jordan draws on work by Summer Forester. See, in particular, Forester (2016).

[13] This initiative is not reflected in the coding for police training in the Regional Table presented in Figure 2.6 because in 1998 this unit was formed to focus on children and families, not primarily women. It does appear to have also handled rape and sexual violence against girls, and also against mothers, but it is not clear that police training was intended to (or even actually did) focus on issues unique to violence against women (in fact, some examples given suggest insensitivity to issues confronting women victims of violence). We did run our main regression analysis with a dataset that included "1" for Jordan in 2005 (in our current coding, this is "0"), and it made negligible difference to the main findings (not shown).

Nearly simultaneously, the monarchy undertook a review of international human rights treaties. Though this produced no direct action on violence against women, it did prompt the establishment of a women's rights body that was helpful to later efforts on violence against women (Forester, 2016). The monarchy initiated some proposals for policies addressing violence against women, but they were unsuccessful. In 2003, the lower house of Parliament voted against a measure aimed at establishing a women's shelter, reportedly because it was seen as encouraging immorality (Forester, 2016). Feminists protested, but the groups were too weak and fragmented to sustain coordinated action or follow-up. Parliament once again rejected proposals aimed at addressing violence against women when they were introduced a few years later.

As a result, in spite of these protests, and in spite of a close relationship between the activists and the monarchy, the first government-sponsored shelter did not open until 2007. Also in 2007, CEDAW took effect in Jordan. That year, women's groups were able to submit a shadow report to CEDAW outlining both progress and concerns about women's rights in the country, including concerns about violence against women. It was in the following year (2008) that the Family Protection Act was passed to address violence against women in Jordan (Forester, 2016).

In both these cases – one of democratic opening and one of increasing repression – feminist activists demanded action on violence against women, but the weak women's movement in Jordan meant that action there was delayed and partial. In both cases, as well, the international community was a key audience for whom reforms were intended to signal the monarch's commitment to human rights.

International pressures can operate on a global as well as a regional scale (Moghadam & Gheytanchi, 2010; Forester, 2016): For example, Turkey's progress has been attributed largely to the scrutiny applied to its efforts to join the European Union (Htun, Weldon, & O'Brien, 2010), and Morocco's reforms may also be due to the combination of the vibrant civil society groups taking advantage of the democratic opening and global pressures also proving favorable (Moghadam & Gheytanchi, 2010). Overall, however, it seems that in both favorable and unfavorable global contexts, in democracies and nondemocracies, it is feminist movements that spark the process of government response to violence. Women's activism and global pressures appear to have combined to prompt policy action where it occurred; where women's movements were weak and fragmented, government action was less likely and more delayed.

TABLE 2.7 *Violence against Women Index in Asia, 1975–2005*

East Asia	1975	1985	1995	2005
Taiwan	0	0	1	8
Vietnam	0	1	1	2
China	0	0	2	2
Thailand	1	1	1	7
Malaysia	0	0	2	6
South Korea	0	0	1	8
Indonesia	0	0	0	7
Japan	0	0	0	7
South Asia				
Pakistan	0	1	1	3
Bangladesh	0	0	3	5
India	0	1	5	6

Asia

Feminist movements in India mobilized against violence in the late 1970s and early 1980s, pushing for legal reforms to address rape, dowry deaths, widow abuse, and other salient forms of violence. Although these movements were effective at getting violence on the national agenda at a fairly early stage, the movement was most successful in procuring legal and policy change only after the mid-1980s, when a new bill addressing sexual assault was passed (1983) and measures to address domestic and dowry violence were adopted (such as the 1986 amendments to criminal procedure or the Dowry Prohibition Amendment Bill passed in 1984). Indian feminists have also appealed to CEDAW. In 2005, the Protection of Women from Domestic Violence Act was passed. This legislation was first drafted by the Lawyers Collective in 1994 (Sharma, 2012).

By contrast, there was little discussion of violence against women in China until domestic violence was included as a cause for divorce in the 2001 marriage law reform, which added some causes for divorce to modify what had previously been a no-fault only law.[14] In China, the feminist movement has long been weak and unable to operate outside government control. Today, in spite of expanding numbers of women's organizations (and civil society organizations in general), and in spite of

[14] Mala Htun, interview with officials at the Shanghai Women's Federation, Shanghai, June 2007.

the expansion and increased activity of China's official women's policy machinery (the AWCF), the women's movement still is not very strong, and autonomous organizing of any kind is very difficult.[15] As Human Rights Watch (2014) noted: "Although the government acknowledges that domestic violence, employment discrimination, and gender bias are widespread, it limits the activities of independent women's rights groups working on these issues by making it difficult for them to register, monitoring their activities, interrogating their staff, and prohibiting some activities." For example, five women's rights activists who had been planning a protest to draw attention to sexual harassment on public transport were jailed by the government and then released only after human rights groups launched an international campaign calling for their release, a campaign joined by the European Union and the United States (The Guardian, 2015).

This climate of repressiveness in general, and toward women's movements in particular, makes it difficult for activists to push for government action on violence against women. Under these circumstances, it is not surprising that the Chinese government has been one of the slowest in the world to respond to such violence. Although the government adopted laws to address domestic violence in 2001, 2005, and 2011, critics contend that these laws are still too general and many problems remain. A new law to fix these problems is promised, and the ACWF, the government's agency on women, worked with UNPF on a pilot project to address violence against women in two regions. This range of government action, however, seems belated and anemic compared to what has been seen in China's democratic counterparts.

It is important to note that the lack of response is not due to a lack of need. Violence against women is a serious problem in China. It is estimated that more than a third of families suffer from domestic violence, and more than 90 percent of victims in these cases are women. Spousal abuse typically goes unreported, especially in rural areas. An ACWF study found that only 7 percent of rural women who suffered domestic

---

[15] Civil society in China expanded in the 1990s in general, and the 1995 Fourth World Conference on Women and the parallel NGO conference in Beijing brought many more feminist activists to China. However, this expansion in women's organizing coincided with new government controls on NGOs. After the tragic events of Tiananmen Square in 1989, many types of organizations were prohibited, especially those perceived as a threat to state authority, including student unions and independent trade unions. In addition, all new organizations are required to register with the Ministry of Civil Affairs (Howell, 2003). Further controls were introduced in 1998.

violence sought help from police (State, 2012). By 2005, the government had still not adopted comprehensive legislation on violence against women.

Summary of Global Overview

These regional surveys show that action on violence against women did not emerge first in the richest regions of the world, nor in the richest countries in the richest regions. It did not spread from the West to the Global South. Latin American and North American activists were demanding government action long before European governments began to address violence, and long before the Vienna Declaration or the Beijing Conference (though these meetings no doubt helped domestic movements). Nor does it seem that Catholicism or Islam precludes government action, as the experiences of Ireland and Turkey make clear.

Finally, having many women in parliament does not lead to early, innovative action on violence. As Figure 2.5 shows, the Index of Government Responsiveness to Violence against Women rose much more sharply

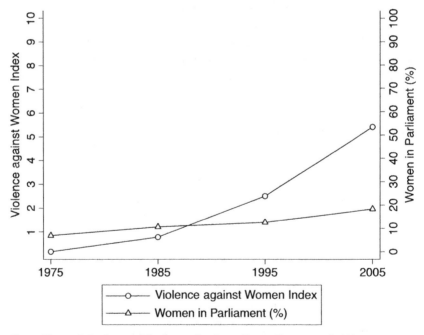

Notes: Women in Parliament (%) refers to the share of Lower House seats held by women.

FIGURE 2.5 Violence against Women Index and women's share of parliamentary seats

TABLE 2.8 *Percentage of parliamentary seats held by women and biggest changes in violence against women policy, 1995–2005*[16]

	% Women 1975	% Women 1985	% Women 1995	% Women 2005	Change '95–'05 (in % pts)	VAW index change '95–'05
Japan	1.4	1.6	2.7	7	4.3	8
Denmark	15.1	26.3	33.5	38	4.5	7
Indonesia	7.2	9.1	12.2	11.3	–.9	7
South Africa	.5	1	33	32.8	–.2	7
South Korea	4	2	1	13.4	12.4	7
Dom Republic	14.3	5.8	11.7	17.3	5.6	6
Portugal	8	7.2	13	19.1	6.1	6
Switzerland	5.5	11	17.5	25	7.5	6
Thailand			4.2	8.6	4.4	6

for all countries over our study period than did the share of parliamentary seats held by women. Many of the most responsive countries tend to have fewer women in government (France, United States, Australia, Canada). Moreover, some of the largest improvements in our Index of Government Responsiveness to Violence against Women happened when there were decreases in the number or proportion of women, as in South Africa or Indonesia, or when very small (less than 10 percent, even) proportions of women were in government, as in Japan and Thailand (see Table 2.8). Without a strong, autonomous feminist movement to push for change, even wealthy, democratic countries appear unlikely to take comprehensive action on violence against women. How do we account for these complex, and somewhat puzzling, global patterns?

MOVEMENTS, GLOBAL NORMS, AND PROGRESSIVE POLICY CHANGE: THEORY AND HYPOTHESES

In this section we apply the theoretical approach to government action on women's rights that we developed in the Introduction to the issue of violence against women, a status policy. Recall that status policies seek to address injustices that stem from the devaluation, denigration, and humiliation of people because of their identification as members of a

[16] Government action in Taiwan showed one of the biggest changes, but is omitted here because of a lack of data about women in parliament.

particular group. Further recall that this is a type of gender equality issue for which autonomous social movements are particularly decisive. In the case of violence against women, autonomous feminist movements are the primary drivers of change because they articulate social group perspectives, disseminate new ideas and frames to the broader public, and demand institutional changes that recognize these meanings. In this section we explain how movements work within and across national borders and how they demand the creation of new institutions to encode their ideas and to advance feminist interests. We argue that the impact of movements includes but goes well beyond agenda setting.

Feminist Movements

Most people today think that violence against women ought to be a crime and see it as a violation of human rights. This was not always the case. As late as 1999, the Eurobarometer survey found that as many as one in three Europeans thought violence against women should probably **not** be considered a crime (Eurobarometer Survey 2010). And although it may seem obvious now that rape, trafficking, domestic violence, honor crimes, female genital mutilation, and other forms of abuse are violations of women's human rights, it is important to recognize that such violence has not always been seen as central to human rights activism or even to women's rights. The Universal Declaration of Human Rights fails to mention violence against women, though it does touch upon other gender issues such as family law. As noted earlier in this chapter, even when the United Nations Convention on the Elimination of All Forms of Discrimination against Women (CEDAW) was presented to the intergovernmental meeting at Copenhagen in 1980, there was no mention of violence against women as a priority for action except for specific, minor provisions dealing with traffic in women, prostitution, and "crimes of honor." Violence against women was not recognized as a priority in its own right and the links between various forms of violence against women and male domination were not acknowledged. "Family violence," FGM, and other violations of women's human rights were treated as distinct issues (Weldon 2006).

Violence against women is rarely raised as an issue, much less as a priority, without pressure from feminists (Weldon 2002a). This is true even in progressive social justice organizations and human rights groups (Friedman 1995). Indeed, in her study of interest groups in the United States, Dara Strolovitch (2007) finds that organizations that are not focused explicitly and primarily on women (including economic justice organizations and organizations focusing on particular ethnic or racial groups) fail to address violence against women, even though women are clearly part of the group they are representing. This is because they fail to see it as important for the group more broadly. Similarly, many human rights groups did not recognize rape and intimate violence as violations of human rights until they were pressed to do so by feminist activists in the 1990s.

Indeed, some women themselves did not (and some still do not) see forced penetration as rape, as indicated by the title of the classic feminist text *I Never Called It Rape* (Warshaw 1994). Of course, women knew they had been assaulted, but they considered it a fact of life, unalterable like earthquakes, or something that happened only to them. These attitudes persist to some degree today even in places like the United States. For example, a large number of college students in the United States do not recognize themselves as victims of rape in spite of the fact that the behavior they report meets the legal definitions of the crime (Fisher, Cullen, & Turner, 2000). Today, in places with less active feminist movements (such as Kuwait), as many women as men support "rape myths," that is, commonly believed falsehoods about sexual assault (Nayak, Byrne, Martin, & Abraham, 2003). In spite of women's universal exposure to the threat of violence, and although political leadership on this issue is predominantly female, one cannot assume that women are aware of, active on, and prioritize this issue just because they are women. Women outside of women-focused organizations rarely articulated and championed issues of rape prevention and intimate violence in formal, public settings such as legislatures until the feminist movement pushed the issue into mainstream public discourse.

Women organizing to advance women's status defined the concept of violence against women, raised awareness, and put the issue on national and global policy agendas. Feminist movements – as opposed to movements of women organized for other purposes – were the critical actors. Looking at thirty-six stable democracies from 1974 to 1994, Weldon (2002b) found that in each of these instances it was "strong, autonomous women's movements" that first articulated the issue of violence against women and were the key catalysts for government action. Government action on violence is usually adopted in response to domestic or transnational activists demanding action from the outside. Individual women, sometimes female legislators, have become spokespersons on the issue, but they have generally owed their awareness and motivation to their participation in or connection to women's autonomous organizing (Weldon, 2002a).

There are three reasons for this. First, women organizing as women generate social knowledge about women's position as a group in society. When social groups self-organize, they develop oppositional consciousness as well as a set of priorities that reflect their distinctive experiences and concerns as a group. (Mansbridge, 1995; Mansbridge & Morris, 2001; Young, 2000). This social perspective cannot be developed in more generally focused organizations or in settings where group concerns must be subordinated to other sorts of imperatives (Weldon, 2011). When women come together to discuss their priorities as women, the problem of violence comes to the fore (Joachim, 1999; Keck & Sikkink, 1998; Sternbach et al., 1992; Weldon, 2006, 2011, 2002a). This is why the issue of violence against women was first articulated by and diffused from women's autonomous organizing.

Second, the issue of violence against women is one that challenges, rather than reinforces or works within, established gender roles in most places (Weldon, 2002a). In contrast with more "maternalist" issues such as maternity leave or childcare, for which women can advocate without deviating too far from traditional gender scripts, addressing violence against women requires challenging male privilege in sexual matters and social norms of male domination more generally (Gelb & Palley, 1996; Htun & Weldon, 2010; Weldon, 2011). In criticizing such violence, women refuse to be silent victims.

Women are more likely to speak up in spaces that are secure from bureaucratic reprisals from superiors and social censure. For example, activists attempting to raise the issue of violence in Sweden were characterized as shrill and divisive, and prominent feminist bureaucrats lost their jobs when they were unwilling to attribute male violence against women to individual pathologies such as alcoholism (Brush, 2003; Elman, 1996; MacKinnon, 1989). It is difficult for legislative insiders (such as members of parliament and bureaucrats) to take on social change issues without the political support of broader mobilization.

This observation leads to the third reason for the importance of autonomous self-organization, which concerns the way social privilege shapes organizational agenda setting. Agenda setting means identifying and ordering priorities. When women's movements are organized within broader political institutions such as political parties, or are entirely contained in the state, they must argue for the relevance of their concerns to these established, often already defined priorities. In these contexts, women's concerns are often seen as tangential to established priorities or as secondary, less important issues. Organizational imperatives seem to sideline "women's" issues such as violence against women or equal pay because such issues are perceived as being of importance "only" to women. This perception results in the subordination of women's issues to other, seemingly more important, established or universal goals such as "environmental protection," "better wages and working conditions," or "free elections." "Women's issues" fall through the cracks of organizational entities aimed at purposes other than sex equality, because they are not the explicit mission of any of these agencies (Bachrach & Baratz, 1962). Women need not struggle to get sex equality and women's empowerment recognized as priorities in autonomous feminist organizations. They need not highlight the connection to more general issues or stress their importance to men and children, which means these issues can be articulated as being important in their own right (Elman, 1996).

Autonomy as defined here implies independence not only from the state, but also from all institutions with a more general focus. An autonomous feminist movement is a form of women's mobilization that is devoted to promoting women's status and well-being independently of political parties and other associations that do not have the status of women as their main concern.[17] For example, if the only women's organizations are women's wings or caucuses within the existing political parties, the women's movement is not autonomous. "Autonomous organizations ... are characterized by *independent* actions, where women organize on the basis of self-activity, set their own goals, and decide their own forms of organization and struggle" (Molyneux, 1998, p. 70; Strolovitch, 2007; Weldon, 2002a). Autonomous feminist organizations are not subsidiaries, auxiliaries, or wings of larger, mixed-sex organizations.

In addition to the importance of autonomy, movements must also be strong. Existing research suggests that a high level of mobilization is required for a movement to be influential (Bashevkin, 1998; Molyneux, 1998). Strong women's movements can command public support and attention, while weaker movements have trouble convincing the media and others that their positions and opinions are important for public discussion. Note that strong movements do not always influence policy outcomes (Amenta et al., 2010) and that strength (a potential capacity for high levels of political mobilization and support) is analytically distinct from policy influence, even if in practice strong movements often do influence policy (a point to which we return later).

---

[17] This sense of "autonomy" incorporates both independent and associational forms of women's movements as described by Weldon (2006, 2002a, 2011).

How exactly do these autonomous, strong movements exert their effects? Like other social movements, autonomous feminist organizations influence policy through a variety of mechanisms. It is well established that social movements shape public and government agendas and create the political will to address particular issues. They also demand institutional reforms that have broad consequences (Rochon & Mazmanian, 1993). They engage in lobbying (Gelb & Palley, 1996), change cultures so that people see issues differently (Rochon, 1998), bring lawsuits and submit briefs to international meetings. They protest and create public disruptions (McAdam & Su, 2002), though in the case of women's feminist movements, some of the most important actions have been "unobtrusive" disruptions poorly captured by the 1960s stereotype of protests, such as sit-ins and street protests (Weldon, 2004). In addition, they organize networking and other activities that bring autonomous activists into contact with government officials, businesswomen and the like (Katzenstein, 1998). More distinctively for feminist movements, and perhaps new social movements in general, they adopt particular ways of living, sometimes called "everyday politics," that model new forms of social organization, such as nonsexist language, equal sharing of parenting, and organizing cooperative farms, bookstores, grocery stores, and shelters (Katzenstein, 1995; 1998; Mansbridge 1995). They produce women's newspapers and magazines and organize cultural events (Weldon, 2004). They organize conferences and symposia, such as the "color of violence" conferences organized by and for women of color in the United States that sought to understand and highlight the specific forms and dimensions of violence against women of color (Incite Women of Color against Violence, 2007). These movement activities shape public opinion and disseminate new ideas (Amenta et al., 2010; Kingdon, 1984). This broader process conditions the sometimes seemingly more influential or direct activities of lobbyists and other more state-oriented actors (Costain, 1998). These arguments and observations, then, lead us to hypothesize that:

H1: We expect that strong, autonomous feminist movements will be significant influences on policies on violence against women at all points in time.

Cross-national, quantitative studies rarely examine the activity of women's movements, much less the autonomous or feminist nature of such activity (partly because it is so hard to measure). When they do, the usual measures are numbers of groups based on national directories or registrants at international conferences.[18] Organizational counts do not capture the degree of movement autonomy from political parties and the state. Yet the literature identifies autonomy as the critical factor in a movement's ability to promote the adoption of feminist policy, detailing the ways in which these movements precede and spark government action (Alvarez, 1990; Gelb & Palley, 1996; Molyneux, 1998; Randall & Waylen, 1998). Nonautonomous movements champion some women's rights changes but not in relation to violence against women (Elman 1996; Weldon, 2002a, 2002b). Social movements are defined as sustained, organized, voluntary challenges to an established authority,[19] while women's movements are defined as social movements in which a preponderance of participants and leaders are women (Beckwith, 2000; McBride & Mazur, 2010).

Most cross-national studies of women's movements use data on formally existing organizations. For the analysis in this chapter and the rest of the book, we used an original dataset on the strength and autonomy of the feminist movement. Feminist movements are distinguished by their stated efforts to improve the status of women (or some subgroup of women), promote sex equality, or end patriarchy. Feminists identify the status quo as being disadvantageous to women.[20] Determining autonomy requires us to ask about movement activities: Do they originate outside of nonfeminist political parties and bureaucracies (autonomous)? Or do all the ideas and initiatives come from the women's wing of the social democratic party or state women's commission (not autonomous)? Are there any activists located outside government (autonomous)? Are all activists members of the government commission on women, or of the ruling party, or the family of the ruling party (not autonomous)? Data on

---

[18] For example, Kenworthy and Malami (1999) examine the strength of the women's movements in terms of number of organizations, as does Weldon (2004, 2006).

[19] This definition is adapted from Tarrow's canonical 1998 work. "Authority" here does not refer exclusively to state authority. It can also mean religious or other social authorities. Social movements may be inside or outside the state, inside or outside other institutional settings (see also Meyer, 2005). What matters for defining social movements as well as for civil society more generally is not where these activities are located, but rather what they are doing: whether the activity is voluntary, whether it represents a challenge to authority, whether it is sustained (Armstrong & Bernstein, 2008). The characteristics of the activity (for example, autonomy from male-dominated institutions, as we discuss later) may determine its effectiveness, but not whether or not it is a social movement.

[20] Note that an analytic definition of feminism should be descriptively accurate, and may not necessarily capture our normative ideal of feminism (for example, some feminist movements or activists have been racist, but our ideal of feminism would include antiracism) (Katzenstein, 1998; Young, 2002). Such movements may or may not refer to themselves as feminist, especially since the context may not be an English-language one.

activities and organizations (including magazines, writer's collectives, and so forth) are taken from a wide variety of primary and secondary sources, including journal articles and books, activist websites, media reports, and encyclopedias of women's organizations (Barrett 1993). Movements judged to be autonomous are coded "1." Movements judged to be not autonomous are coded "0."[21]

In this study, strength is assessed through an integrated examination of organizations, protests, and public opinion. A large number of organizations, or a few well-supported and highly visible organizations, generally indicate the strength of women's movements.[22] Strength can also be indicated by massive protests and by a strong media presence. Reports of protests and media presence can be determined by electronic searches of print and other media using LexisNexis and other similar databases and sources. Measures of popular support for women's movements are available in survey data for many cases, such as the World Values Survey. Narrative accounts of women's movements often explicitly assess the strength of women's movements over time and/or relative to other countries. We gave most weight to region- and country-specific expertise. Movements that were moderately strong were scored "1," and movements that were very strong were scored "2." This was especially useful for capturing instances where that strength dramatically increased or decreased.

These data were collected following a similar process as the violence against women index (dependent variable), with a team of researchers gathering qualitative and quantitative data about women's movement activities and organizations over the period from 1975 to 2005 from primary and secondary sources. A datasheet summarizing the contents of these materials was prepared for each country, including a narrative of the women's movement over four decades. These datasheets were then coded and discussed at periodic meetings to ensure the clarity and replicability of the code rules.[23]

---

[21] This approach to autonomy is taken from Weldon (2002a).

[22] Care must be taken, however, in contexts where the state has tight control over civil society in general or women's organizations in particular. A large number of state-controlled associations (state-funded does not necessarily mean state-controlled) may merely reflect the state's strength in marketing political issues to women.

[23] For a summary of codes for strength and autonomy of feminist movements, as well as other details of coding rules and definitions, please see supplementary materials to Htun and Weldon 2012 (cf. Beckwith, 2000; Stetson & Mazur, 2010). These materials are also available on S. Laurel Weldon's personal website.

Women's Policy Machineries or State Feminism

About half the national governments considered here have created one or more government institutions (that is, an office, department, commission, or ministry) whose main purpose is to promote the status of women. There is great variety in institutional form: some are women's desks stationed in lowly subdepartments while others include a complex array of agencies, including both advisory bodies and agencies focused directly on service provision. Some policy machineries, such as that in Australia, have at times included mechanisms through which women's movement activists can be included in national policy-making processes (Stetson & Mazur, 1995; McBride & Mazur, 2010; True & Mintrom, 2001; Weldon, 2002a).

Scholars have found that women's policy machineries promoted policies on violence against women in both established and emerging democracies (e.g., Avdeyeva, 2007; Franceschet, 2010; Haas, 2010; Johnson, 2007; Nelson, 1996; Weldon, 2002a). These agencies tend to add to, rather than replace, the work of autonomous women's movements. Indeed, in many places, women's policy machineries are formed in response to women's movement demands, though they are also adopted as a way to comply with international agreements such as CEDAW. This institutional momentum furthers feminist policy making.

Policy agencies can help feminist movements put the issue of violence against women on the public agenda by providing research and other institutional supports that assist movements in their efforts to influence government. Even weaker movements can profit from these resources. Agencies are more likely to be effective if they are cross-sectoral, high-level agencies with significant resources. However, even these well-designed and resourced policy agencies are neither necessary nor sufficient for reform on their own. Any impact on policy depends on reforms creating real institutions that are more than mere publicity, not just a desk in a back office (Mazur, 2002; McBride & Mazur, 2010; Stetson & Mazur, 1995; True & Mintrom, 2001; Weldon, 2002a).

H2: The presence of an effective women's policy machinery will make the adoption of more comprehensive policies on violence against women more likely.

We employ True & Mintrom's (2001) measure of women's policy machinery effectiveness, supplemented by additional data sources for missing countries and years (e.g., United Nations, 1993; Avdeyeva 2009).

Transnational Feminism

Feminist activism has shaped policies on violence not only through domestically focused activism but also through transnational advocacy. Through such advocacy, activists have pushed for the inclusion of violence against women in international agreements on human rights. Autonomous feminist organizing across borders began independently of government processes (indeed, initially it was sharply critical of the UN process) in the mid-1970s and gathered strength in the late 1980s after a common agenda was forged at Nairobi (Keck & Sikkink, 1998; Sternbach et al., 1992; Weldon, 2006). Commencement of the "social cycle" of UN conferences in the 1990s, in combination with the end of the Cold War, dramatically increased the political opportunities for transnational organizing (Friedman, 2003; Joachim, 1999). Transnational advocacy networks working to promote women's rights disseminated ideas about violence against women and pressed for government action. These networks helped to spark and support local women's organizing, indirectly affecting policy processes on violence against women (Avdeyeva, 2009; Finnemore & Sikkink, 1998; Moghadam, 2005). As a result of this activism, declarations, treaties, and agreements proliferated over the four decades of our study, especially after 1995.

Though many national women's groups attend international conferences, there is a weak correlation between strong, autonomous women's movements and numbers of transnational women's rights organizations (measured as the number of women's organizations attending UN conferences, .27, p = .02). Since data on the number of transnational women's rights organizations is spotty and somewhat unreliable for early years, analysis of this data could be misleading. Moreover, such organizational counts, we have argued, are poor measures for getting at the impact of mobilization.[24] For these reasons, we have not included the numbers of transnational women's organizations in the models in this chapter.[25]

---

[24] As noted, the best data for this type of analysis is the record of those organizations participating in the NGO forums and registered at the various UN conferences for women. Yet these records are missing data for some key country cases (such as Canada and Australia) and for some years. It is also unknown if all attendees were registered correctly by country.

[25] The density of NGO connections to intergovernmental meetings is uncorrelated or weakly correlated with policy adoption. In 1995, the number of organizations attending the Beijing meeting (and registering with the IWTC) was uncorrelated with government responsiveness to violence against women and for 2005, and the number of organizations

There is no doubt that transnational feminism is important for domestic policy making on violence against women, but we expect most of the impact of transnational feminist networks (TFNs) to be observable through the norms they help to create. We turn to these phenomena in the subsequent sections.

International Norms and Global Civil Society

A growing body of scholarly literature focuses on the consolidation of international law and norms on human rights. Scholars have also examined how international norms affect women's rights in particular, and some of this work focuses specifically on violence against women.[26] International norms, or standards of appropriate behavior shared by a critical mass of states, affect domestic policymaking along a variety of causal pathways (Merry, 2006; Finnemore & Sikkink, 1998; Amirthalingam, 2005; Fabian, 2010; Tripp, Casimiro, Kwesiga, & Mungwa, 2009). These pathways include creating standards in global civil society, creating shared expectations in regional communities of nations, and mobilizing domestic civil society (Khagram et al., 2002; Simmons, 2009). The dynamics of each of these pathways, all of which focus on civil society at some level, are slightly different and warrant separate theoretical discussion. In this section we discuss three different mechanisms by which the norms of an international society might affect national policy making: (1) influence of global treaties and documents on women's rights, such as CEDAW; (2) influence of regional agreements on violence against women (particularly after certain tipping points); and (3) regional demonstration effects or pressures for conformity, captured as diffusion within regions. Through these mechanisms, we also capture the effect of transnational feminist activism. As we will see, feminists created even greater institutional pressure by pushing for international institutional measures (such as CEDAW and regional agreements) as well.

registered with the UN was weakly correlated (r = .30, significant only at .05 level). Strong, autonomous feminist movements have a stronger correlation (.45, p = 0.000) across all decades.

[26] On human rights in general see Checkel (1997); Khagram, Riker, & Sikkink (2002); Simmons (2009); Williams (2004); on women's rights in particular see Chan-Tiberghien (2004); Cook (1994); Kittilson, Sandholz, & Gray (2006); on violence against women, see Avdeyeva (2007); Friedman (2009); Joachim (1999, 2003); Merry (2006); Htun & Weldon (2012a).

Global Norms

The first major document recognizing violence against women as a violation of women's human rights was the United Nations Declaration on the
Elimination of Violence against Women, a product of the World Conference on Human Rights, held in Vienna in 1993 (Clark, Caetano, &
Schafer, 1998; Friedman, 2009; Simmons, 2009). The global women's
movement worked to transform the Vienna conference from a general
conference on human rights to a conference on women's rights. In the late
1960s and the 1970s, when many activists in Latin America and North
America were agitating for governmental action on violence, many people
in the human rights community did not recognize rape and domestic
violence as core issues of human rights. Although Human Rights Watch
had published several early and important articles on specific forms of
violence against women (sterilization, police abuse, rape, and domestic
violence), the broader concept of violence against women did not have
much currency in the 1970s. At that time, many people in the human
rights community believed that abuses of women's human rights resulted
from private action and were therefore inappropriate for a human rights
organization, which should be dealing with violations by the state (Brown
Thompson, 2002; Elman, 2007; Weldon, 2006).[27]

Nevertheless, activism on women's rights and violence against women
in the human rights community and beyond began to take effect in the
run-up to Vienna. Under Aryeh Neier's leadership, Human Rights Watch
launched its Women's Rights Project, headed by Dorothy Thomas, in
1989 (Neier, 2005, 2012). Amnesty International also established a
women's rights project around the same time (Neier, 2012, p. 228;
Thomas, 2012, p. 325). The Vienna Declaration was adopted by consensus of 171 states, though some characterized it as a mere exhortation with
no "teeth" (Freidman, 1995, pp. 25N6). In spite of these criticisms of the
formal results of the Vienna Conference, it is still seen by many as the
point at which the broader human rights system began to incorporate
violence against women as a core concern of women's human rights.

The global movement gathered steam and successfully pushed for
stronger language and clearer recognition of the issue at the 1995 Fourth

---

[27] In fact, when Human Rights Watch created its women's rights program in 1989, the Ford
Foundation signaled its opposition to the expansion of the human rights agenda by
reducing its funding for the organization. Only after a personnel change in the mid-
1990s did Ford stop opposing the notion that women's rights are a core component of
human rights (Neier, 2012, pp. 228–9).

World Conference on Women in Beijing. More than 180 governments affirmed the 1995 Beijing Declaration, which named violence against women a critical area of concern. The Beijing and Vienna meetings signaled the development of new international norms. They have been widely cited by activists and governments proposing legislation or other action to redress violence (Joachim, 1999; Meyer, 1999). These influences, however, were mainly felt after the Beijing meeting, when violence was incorporated more fully into the CEDAW process. As noted earlier, the original (1979) text of CEDAW did not explicitly mention violence against women.

Scholars of international norms do not expect norms to produce uniform effects across governments. Some ratify treaties and comply with agreements, others do not. International treaties such as CEDAW are unlikely to have many visible effects in those countries that already comply with the directives (Brown Thompson, 2002; Fabian, 2010; Weldon, 2006). But countries that already adopt policies that conform to treaty requirements are most likely to ratify the treaties. On the other hand, countries that seek wider international legitimacy, but that expect difficulties in complying with aspects of these international treaties, will ratify with reservations. In this latter case, the aim is to communicate a commitment to women's rights to a wide (global) audience. Yet the mere fact of signing these treaties raises expectations and mobilizes citizens. Governments are held to account in public forums such as the CEDAW Committee for failing adequately to honor their commitments. Removing reservations to a treaty such as CEDAW reflects a degree of acceptance of a norm of recognizing the legitimacy of women's rights. State socialization to global norms on women's rights should lead to more progressive policies on violence against women.

H3: We expect that those states that withdraw reservations to CEDAW will be most likely to adopt policies on violence against women, especially after the CEDAW process began to include violence against women as an issue (after 1989). We expect the withdrawal of reservations to be a stronger predictor of changing policy than mere ratification.

Following standard practice in the literature (Simmons, 2009), we took data on ratification and reservations from the UN Treaty database. CEDAW Ratify is coded 1 if the country ratified the Convention; Withdraw Reservations is coded 1 if the country withdrew a reservation to CEDAW in the preceding decade.

Regional Norms

The Vienna and Beijing meetings were part of (and likely accelerated) a proliferation of regional and other international agreements on violence against women. But, as noted, many countries and regions had active discussions of violence against women well before Vienna and Beijing. In the Americas, regional activists and organizations were developing strong regional treaties to address violence against women long before these issues were accepted more generally as core areas of human rights (e.g., Friedman, 2009; Sternbach et al., 1992). In fact, the Vienna Declaration may have taken language that had been proposed for the Organization of American States (OAS) declaration but that had not been formally announced (Meyer, 1999; Weldon, 2006). The OAS began formulating the convention before the Vienna meeting and adopted the Inter-American Convention on Violence against Women in 1994 (also known as the "Convention of Belem do Para") immediately after Vienna. This Latin American Convention was particularly lauded by feminists because of its strong language on gender hierarchy and its enforcement provisions. Some saw it as more important than the Vienna Declaration.

Europe also adopted regional measures, though weaker and later than the Inter-American Convention. Montoya (2009) notes that the EU's initiatives aimed at combating violence against women occurred after the mid-1990s (p. 333). This was partly because it was not until the late 1990s that the EU began to expand its jurisdiction beyond economic matters to social issues, especially human rights (see also Elman, 2007). The 1997 Resolution calling for a zero tolerance campaign specifically cites UN instruments (such as CEDAW and the Vienna Declaration) and the Council of Europe as motivations. This was followed by a 2000 resolution on trafficking, a 2003 resolution on domestic violence, and a 2004 resolution on honor crimes. The Council of Europe also produced a series of initiatives. For example, it promulgated a 2002 recommendation on the protection of women against violence as well as a monitoring framework.[28]

UN processes also triggered regional organizing and agreements in Africa. Following the Third World Conference on Women, held in Nairobi in 1985, there was an explosion of Africa-wide as well as sub-regional organizing, including the 1993 Kampala Prep Com and the 1994

---

[28] Note that in 2006 (after the period covered in our statistical analysis), the EU passed a more comprehensive recommendation on combating VAW (Neier, 2012, pp. 228–9). The Council of Europe also adopted a convention on violence against women on April 7, 2011.

Africa-wide UN women's conference (Tripp, Casimiro, Kwesiga, & Mungwa, 2009), both parts of the preparation for the UN's Fourth World Conference on Women held in Beijing in 1995. Violence was identified as an issue of importance in the Protocol on Women's Rights to the African Charter on Human and People's Rights, adopted in 2003.[29]

In 2005 (the last year of our study), Europe, Asia, and the Middle East lacked regional conventions that addressed violence against women. Only in Africa and Latin America were regional conventions that specifically addressed violence against women adopted.[30]

International norms on violence against women have produced the most important effects when codified in regional treaties and agreements, such as those developed in Latin America and Africa. Regional agreements strengthen international norms by emphasizing the important way that these norms apply to the specific states in question, to their identity or reference group (Omelicheva, 2011). In addition, conventions in these two regions that included specific provisions on violence against women were important in fostering and strengthening the activities of domestic women's groups working on the issue.[31] We expect that the existence of a specific regional treaty or agreement on violence against women will be positively correlated with national policy action, particularly after these norms pass a threshold of support or tipping point (see H4).

Tipping Points for Global and Regional Norms
Human rights scholars argue that there is a tipping point after which international norms begin to cascade (Finnemore & Sikkink, 1998).

---

[29] Protocol on the Rights of Women, African Commission on Human and People's Rights. www.achpr.org/files/instruments/women protocol/achpr_instr_proto_women_eng.pdf. For studies emphasizing the role of women in parliament see Kittilson (2008b); Schwindt-Bayer & Mishler (2005); M.L. Swers (2002). For studies finding party is important see Kittilson (2008b); Norris (1987); Stetson & Mazur (1995).

[30] In 2006 (again, after our study period) the fifty-seven states belonging to the Organization of the Islamic Conference named adressing VAW a priority issue for governments (OIC, 2006).

[31] We focus on conventions rather than regional service provision programs (such as DAPHNE in Europe) because such programs bypass the government agenda-setting process, and mainly involve providing resources for specific programs that do not come from national governments. As such, these programs do not require governments to make promises to address violence against women, nor do they make public statements about the importance of the issue. As a result, they neither spark government responsiveness nor provide activists with much additional leverage to challenge government agendas. In terms of diffusion, they may inspire domestic groups to apply for grants, but they do little to pressure governments to act. On DAPHNE see Elman (2007); Montoya (2009).

Tipping points reflect the point at which a given behavior or commitment is seen as "the norm" by the group in question. When only a few countries are adopting these measures, it can hardly be seen as the majority practice, but there is a point at which it becomes "the thing to do" for certain countries or groups. The existing literature suggests that this occurs around the time that the norm is adopted by about one-third of states in the system. By 1985, more than 30 percent of the countries in the system had ratified CEDAW, but the Convention itself contained little direct mention of violence. CEDAW, which did not even exist in 1975, and which did not make violence a priority in 1985 (indeed, not until 1989, as discussed),[32] would be unlikely to have a direct effect on policy making in that era. By 2005, international norms on violence in general, and CEDAW in particular, were well established in global civil society and were often invoked in discussions of domestic politics. Scholars of international law on violence against women agree that the main period of discussion of violence and the promulgation of resolutions and other measures was in the 1990s, though CEDAW still did not include specific language on violence against women until after 1992,[33] and the Optional Protocol was not adopted until 1999. By 2005, however, CEDAW incorporated new language on violence and the adoption of the optional protocol indicated even deeper support. Many accounts of national legal change, particularly in Eastern and Western Europe where changes mostly took place after 1995, point to the CEDAW and UN process as responsible for prompting action on violence against women (e.g. see chapters in Fabian, 2010). To illustrate the different effects of CEDAW before and after this tipping point, and to recognize the importance of CEDAW specifically addressing violence against women, we expect that:

H4: Any direct effects of CEDAW on violence against women policy would not be visible in 1975 or 1985, and would be most likely to be seen in 2005.

Regional conventions in Latin America and Africa would have reached their tipping points at different times. By 1995, of the thirty-five possible parties to the Convention of Belém do Pará, twenty-four (71 percent) had

---

[32] See general recommendations made by the Committee on the Elimination of Discrimination against Women, specifically CEDAW Committee General Recommendation No. 12 (8th session, 1989).

[33] For example, see general recommendations made by the Committee on the Elimination of Discrimination against Women, such as General Recommendation No. 19 (11th session, 1992).

signed and fifteen (43 percent) had ratified. By 2005, nearly all of these Latin American and Caribbean countries (thirty-two of thirty-four) had ratified. The protocol to the African Charter did not exist in 1995, but by 2005, forty-one of fifty-three states (77 percent) had signed and seventeen (32 percent) had ratified the protocol. These regional agreements reached their tipping points in 1995 (Latin America) and 2005 (Africa). No other region had a convention signed by a critical mass of states that specifically outlined action on violence against women. In such a context, it is hardly surprising that so many national governments changed their laws between 1995 and 2005.

H5: After these tipping points (1995 and 2005, respectively), international and especially regional measures of the presence of an international norm will make governments more likely to adopt or expand their policies redressing violence against women.

We measure the presence of a regional treaty using a dummy variable (Regional Agreement) that codes whether the country belongs to a region with a convention on violence against women that has passed the threshold of 30 percent support.

Regional Diffusion

International norms are also spread through regional diffusion, as nations seek to emulate and learn from those countries they view as being similarly situated in some way. Policy diffusion tends to occur between states in the same region, especially (but not exclusively) among those with similar characteristics (such as language) and who have regular contacts in other intergovernmental political and economic organizations. This occurs both through processes of elite learning and emulation of other nations and through connections in civil society. Through these connections, elites learn lessons from other countries and activists and nongovernmental organizations take ideas from proximate jurisdictions and press for government action (Berry & Berry, 1999; Boushey, 2010; Shipan & Volden, 2008; Weyland, 2005). Movements in one country tend to emulate successful movements in neighboring countries (with varying degrees of success), even when there are important differences in the history and character of regimes in the region, as the events of the "Arab Spring" demonstrate. Such neighborhood effects in the international system are likely to be closely related to the impact of regional agreements (Boushey, 2010).

H6: A country is more likely to adopt progressive policies on violence against women when other countries in the same region have done so.

We measure this effect by examining the relationship between the average score for the region (Regional Diffusion) and the score for the specific country in the region (Boushey, 2010; Mainwaring & Pérez-Liñán, 2013). The region to which a country belongs is determined using Hadenius and Teorell's (2005) database. They describe their tenfold politico-geographic classification of world regions as "based on a mixture of two considerations: geographical proximity . . . and demarcation by area specialists." This categorization roughly captures the combination of geographic proximity and political connectedness that we suggest under-lies the processes of regional diffusion we describe. Religious influences are captured in a separate measure.

Why Feminist Activism Magnifies Norms' Effects

Domestic and transnational activists magnify the effects of these treaties by highlighting the gap between ratification and compliance. In the CEDAW process, for example, governments must produce an official report for a UN committee and submit to questioning by committee members, most of who have also read the critical "shadow" reports written by civil society organizations (Baldez, 2014). Even governments that have little intention to comply are held to account for their behavior in a public, international forum (Avdeyeva, 2009). In this process, domestic activists work with international groups and organizations to increase pressure on their national governments, a pattern called the "boomerang effect" (Keck & Sikkink, 1998).[34]

Treaties thus offer normative leverage to national civil society organizations. At the same time, local activist organizations bring home the value of international and regional treaties. They raise awareness of the rights recognized by the treaties; they use them to train judges, police, and other officials; and treaties help activists lobby legislatures to change discriminatory laws. International treaties can alter the expectations of

---

[34] As we discuss in later chapters, Baldez (2014) notes that many scholars have added new analogies to capture this dynamic relationship between domestic civil society groups and movements and international actors, including the pincer effect (Friedman, 2009), the triangle of empowerment (Vargas & Wieringa, 1998), and the sandwich effect (Mazur & McBride, 2007).

domestic actors and strengthen and even spark domestic mobilization. This interaction likely produces effects that grow stronger over time (Simmons, 2009).

H7: There is an interactive effect of international norms and autonomous feminist mobilization, as each of these variables magnifies the effect of the other. This will be most visible in later periods.

The Changing Relative Importance of Movements and Institutions

Over these four decades, feminists institutionalized many of the principles they sought to advance in domestic and international institutions such as women's policy machineries and international norms. This diminished the movement's need for extensive resources. Autonomous feminist movements should still have an effect on policy, but their relative importance lessens as institutions addressing violence against women are strengthened.

H8: We expect the relative importance of institutional factors (international and domestic) to flip over the four decades of our study as autonomous women's movements play a smaller role in policy making and institutional drivers of policy change are more developed.

Controls

We control for the effects of variables hypothesized to be important in the literature. These variables reflect theoretical perspectives emphasizing the importance of women in parliament, particularly for policy changes related to women's rights, and the protagonistic role of Left-oriented or labor parties on gender equality issues (Kittilson, 2008; Schwindt-Bayer & Mishler, 2005; Swers, 2002). Using measures of parties found in the Database of Political Institutions (DPI), we also test for the effects of religious parties, since scholars have identified religious organizations as obstacles to liberalizing change on some gender-related issues, particularly family law and reproductive rights (Htun, 2003). In addition, we test for the idea that wealthier, more industrialized countries of Western Europe and North America would be pioneers in violence against women policy, as predicted by variants of modernization theory, as well as the notion that greater democracy – as measured by a country's Polity score (a common, conventional measure of degree of democracy) – would be associated with more progressive measures (Inglehart & Norris, 2003;

Wilensky, 1975). Finally, we control for path dependency to get at the enduring effects of an earlier policy process initiated by autonomous movements.

We do not control for varying rates of violence against women across countries, as data are unavailable and unreliable. Official crime data tend to reflect the effectiveness of government response rather than the rate of violence itself. Even in North America and Europe, the vast majority of incidents are never reported to the police or other authorities, and variation in reported rapes and domestic assaults tend to reflect victims' perceptions that authorities will be sympathetic and/or effective rather than the seriousness of the assault. For these reasons, our models do not include any measures of level of violence against women as controls (Weldon, 2002a).

STATISTICAL ANALYSIS: METHODS AND RESULTS

The dependent variable of this study is our original Index of Government Response to Violence against Women, described earlier in the chapter.[35] Some readers might be concerned that because the data present snapshots of years, we might not capture relationships between, for example, numbers of women in office or Left parties that would otherwise be evident. For example, large numbers of women might have been in government when a measure was adopted, but then there could be a smaller number of women in office later, when we take our measurement. This turns out not to be a major issue for our analysis, since large changes between panels that are reversed or eliminated by the time the next panel occurs are rare to nonexistent. In addition, if countries with more women or Left parties in government are more likely to adopt policies to address violence against women, this should show up in our study even if there are one or

---

[35] The fact that the dependent variable is a measure of scope and not an event count, and that the index scores are cumulative over time and comprise elements that are not independent (several areas of policy are often addressed in a single measure), mitigates against the use of a Poisson or Negative Binomial regression model (both types of regression are designed to analyze "event counts," and assume that the dependent variable tallies independent events). Nor are MLE models or Tobit appropriate, for a number of reasons – our data is not "censored" at zero, for example (for more explanation see Sigelman & Zeng, 1999). Using these other methods does not make much difference to the main findings: Our results are robust to the technique used.

two instances where there are big changes during the decade between panels or snapshots that are reversed (and are not). As our regional overviews and examples provided in this chapter suggest, examining the cases in more detail only confirms the statistical arguments offered here. This is consistent with prior studies that have not found left parties and the number of women in government to be important for this issue-area (Weldon, 2002a; Elman, 1996).

Table 2.9 presents the results of analysis of the pooled data across all cross-sections. Table 2.10 presents analyses of the individual cross-sections in particular years. Figure 2.6 presents the coefficient plots to illustrate the results of typical or the most instructive models.

Strong Autonomous Feminist Movement

As expected in Hypothesis 1, analysis of the panel data presented in Tables 2.9 and 2.10 shows that a *strong, autonomous feminist movement* is both substantively and statistically significant as a predictor of government action to redress violence against women across all models (in Model 8 in Table 2.9 it is significant as part of an interaction term). The strongest movements (value = 2) are associated with at least one additional area of action in every case while controlling for a wide variety of variables. As is illustrated by the coefficient plot in Figure 2.6, this independent variable does not have the largest association with the dependent variable (other variables are similar in size or even larger, though they often have larger confidence intervals as well (the "wings" on the point on the coefficient plot)). What is important for our purposes, though, is that this independent variable (strong, autonomous feminist movement) is consistent in size, substantively important, and the most consistently significant effect of all the predictors (has the smallest "wings"). This pattern confirms prior quantitative and qualitative evidence on violence against women showing that movements are critical catalysts for policy development in all years, though their efforts are supplemented by policy machineries, international norms, and other factors outlined in the rest of this chapter.

Though correlational findings such as these do not establish that autonomous feminist movements precede government response, we know from case evidence and previous research that autonomous movements usually predate government response by a long period of time, and are more broadly focused than just violence against women, also demanding quotas, legal reforms and other feminist policy measures (Elman, 1996; Weldon, 2002a) Perhaps most definitively, analysis of a lagged variable

TABLE 2.9 Coefficients, Violence against Women Index, linear regression with panel corrected standard errors, 1975–2005

Model number	1	2	3	4	5	6	7	8	9	10
Variable										
Strong, autonomous feminist movement	.567*** (.212)	.611*** (.219)	.545*** (.128)	.553*** (.127)	.574*** (.140)	.584*** (.128)	.530*** (.135)	.074 (.181)	.585*** (.139)	.638*** (.115)
Regional agreement on VAW	2.681*** (.514)	2.804*** (.556)	.936*** (.248)	1.630** (.644)	.937*** (.342)	.871*** (.282)	.569* (.379)	.677*** (.213)	.922*** (.336)	.987*** (.379)
Effective women's policy machinery	1.910*** (.316)	1.449*** (.360)	.618*** (.224)	1.075*** (.252)	.568* (.327)	.530** (.252)	.498* (.288)	.540** (.264)	.565* (.320)	.564** (.284)
Democracy level	.011 (.030)	.016 (.026)	.024 (.017)	.034** (.013)	.034** (.015)	.036*** (.013)	.038** (.015)	.032* (.017)	.033** (.015)	.045** (.020)
GDP (logged)	2.067*** (.717)	1.723*** (.604)	.383 (.331)	1.415** (.699)	.593* (.360)	.557 (.393)	.592 (.369)	.546 (.354)	.649** (.318)	.716 (.467)
Withdraw reservations	2.028*** (.628)	2.137*** (.584)	1.077*** (.345)	1.083** (.523)	.843** (.402)	.793** (.370)			.847*** (.396)	.780** (.363)
Women in legislature (%)		.056*** (.012)			.003 (.007)				.003 (.007)	
Regional diffusion			.703*** (.073)		.442*** (.139)	.467*** (.147)	.477*** (.150)	.732*** (.068)	.441*** (.140)	.454*** (.161)
Lagged Violence against Women Index				.697*** (.245)	.448 (.283)	.440 (.277)	.458* (.268)		.440 (.284)	.415 (.272)
CEDAW ratification							.210** (.090)	-.441* (.221)		

	(1)	(2)	(3)	(4)	(5)	(6)	(7)	(8)	(9)	(10)
Strong, autonomous feminist movement X CEDAW								.738*** (.242)		
Religious party									-.244 (.193)	.042 (.250)
Left party in government										
Observations	256	240	256	198	192	198	198	256	192	164
Overall R-squared	.621	.646	.780	.742	.801	.801	.795	.778	.802	.776
Number of countries	70	69	70	70	69	70	70	70	69	69

Notes: Estimates are from panel-corrected standard error regression models which assume heteroskedastic and contemporaneously correlated error terms. Standard errors are in parentheses. *, **, and *** denote statistical significance at the 10, 5, and 1 percent levels, respectively.

73

TABLE 2.10 *Coefficients, Violence against Women Index, linear regression, 1985 and 2005*

Model number	1	2	3	4	5	6	7
Variable	1985	2005	1985	2005	1985	1985	2005
Strong, autonomous feminist movement	.880***	.559**	.908***	.518**	.680***	.756**	1.759***
	(.281)	(.223)	(.287)	(.236)	(.220)	(.351)	(.330)
Women in legislature (%)		-.005	-.006	-.005		-.004	-.008
		(.021)	(.012)	(.020)		(.011)	(.023)
Regional diffusion	-.100	.283**	-.072	.283**	.284**	-.040	.303**
	(.246)	(.129)	(.261)	(.128)	(.109)	(.248)	(.137)
Regional agreement		.410					-.006
		(.462)					(.455)
Effective women's policy machinery	.313	1.170***	.340	1.208***	1.124***	.267	1.360***
	(.653)	(.350)	(.684)	(.364)	(.317)	(.720)	(.393)
Democracy level	.029	.112***	.020	.118***	.120***	.022	.122***
	(.018)	(.031)	(.019)	(.031)	(.031)	(.020)	(.033)
GDP (logged)	.396	.930*	.492*	.570	.767*	.446	.886*
	(.244)	(.505)	(.272)	(.450)	(.455)	(.282)	(.523)
Withdraw reservations				1.036**	.955**		
				(.392)	(.406)		
Lagged Violence against Women Index	.852***	.301**	.850***	.351***	.295**	.848***	.294***
	(.273)	(.095)	(.303)	(.102)	(.096)	(.313)	(.106)
CEDAW ratification	.387		.352			.205	1.020**
	(.268)		(.305)			(.253)	(.444)

Left party in government			-.355 (.361)			
Strong, autonomous feminist movement X CEDAW					.243 (.433)	-1.107*** (.343)
Observations	58	69	54	68	70	54	69
R-squared	.595	.809	.596	.805	.796	.599	.791

Notes: Estimates are from ordinary least squares regression models. *, **, and *** denote statistical significance at the 10, 5, and 1 percent levels, respectively.

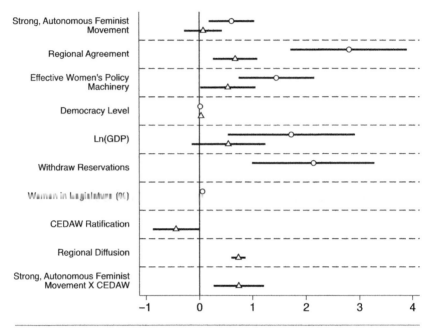

Notes: Plots depict point estimates and 95 percent confidence intervals from panel-corrected standard error regression models which assume heteroskedastic and contemporaneously correlated error terms.

FIGURE 2.6 Coefficient plot of Models 2 and 8 of Table 2.9

found that strong, autonomous feminist movements remained a strongly significant predictor of our index.[36]

More intriguing is the shift in the relative importance of feminist movements over time revealed in the single-panel analyses for 1985 and 2005 (Table 2.10) (H8). In 1985, *Strong autonomous feminist movement* and the impact of previous policy development (*Lagged dependent variable*) are the two significant determinants of policy (Models 1, 3, 5, and 6 in Table 2.10). In these models, the ratification of CEDAW (*CEDAW Ratify*) does not matter (as predicted by H3), there are no regional agreements in existence (so they are not included), and only one country out of the seventy (France) has removed a reservation to CEDAW (not included in the 1985 models). Regional diffusion has little effect. By 2005,

---

[36] In combination with qualitative data showing that autonomous movements precede and spark government action (for further explanation see Weldon, 2002a), this finding should mitigate concerns about endogeneity.

however, the coefficients for *Strong, autonomous feminist movement* are smaller (compare coefficients in Models 1 and 2, 3 and 4) and variables measuring the effects of regional and global norms have become significant. These findings confirm our predictions about changes in the relative importance of these variables over time (H8).

Women's Policy Machineries

The coefficient for *Effective women's policy machinery* was positive and significant in eight of the ten panel data analyses we ran (Table 2.9) and in most of the cross-sectional models (Table 2.10), suggesting that these agencies facilitate a more comprehensive approach to violence against women (H2).

Global and Regional Norms

Our variables capturing the diffusion of international norms (*Withdraw reservations, Regional agreement*, and *Regional diffusion*) suggest strong, substantively important effects that are statistically significant in nearly all models. Our coefficient plots show large effects (but also large confidence intervals, reflecting the difficulty of predicting the dependent variable with this variable alone). As expected (H3), the withdrawal of resolutions to CEDAW has a stronger relationship to policies on violence than does mere ratification, for which the coefficient is smaller and more weakly significant (Model 7, Table 2.9). However, the ratification of CEDAW does appear to take on more significance in the models in which an interactive variable is included, especially the later models, capturing the conditional effects of ratification on domestic mobilization (H4). The withdrawal of reservations to CEDAW is positively and significantly related to more expansive policies on violence against women, significant in all eight of the models in which it is included in Table 2.9. Although the size and significance of this effect is diminished when *Regional diffusion* and *Lagged dependent variable* are included in the model, the withdrawal of reservations is significant even when both these phenomena are included (Models 9 and 10). And *Withdraw reservations* is positively and significantly related to policies on violence in all of the single-year cross-sections we modeled, where the threshold of significance would be harder to meet due to the smaller number of cases (H3).

Also consistent with our expectations (H5), the presence of a *Regional agreement*, measured as taking effect after particular tipping points, is even more strongly related to government responsiveness than the CEDAW variables, with strong positive and significant coefficients in nine of ten models and near significance – p = .08 – in the tenth (Model 7, Table 2.9). The effects of regional agreements were particularly evident in 1995 (not shown). The effect of such regional agreements may be swamped by regional diffusion and CEDAW (as the latter came to incorporate stronger language on violence against women) in the later models (as in the 2005 cross sections). The results of exploratory modeling, though, suggest that the effects of such agreements may be temporally and causally prior to the regional cascade of policy change. These regional norm variables were far more important than dummy variables capturing the effects of regions themselves (not shown).

Regional diffusion is significant and positive in all the panel data analyses in which it is included (Table 2.9) (H6). Regional variables (*Regional diffusion* and *Regional agreements*) together account for between one and two additional areas of policy action, even controlling for the ratification of CEDAW and the withdrawal of reservations to CEDAW (Models 3 and 8), so regional influences are clearly substantively important.

We included a multiplicative interaction term to test the hypothesis that global norms have a greater impact where there is strong, autonomous feminist organizing on the domestic scene and to capture the way these two variables mutually reinforce each other (H7). The interaction of the ratification of CEDAW with a strong, autonomous feminist movement is strongly significant with a positive coefficient in a regression including both elements of the interaction as constitutive terms in the model (Model 8). Considering the effects of this interaction at the various levels of the interacting variables provides more insight into the dynamics observed (Brambor, Clark, & Golder, 2006). When a strong, autonomous feminist movement is absent (value = 0), CEDAW ratification (CEDAW Ratify) seems to have a barely significant (p = .05) negative effect (–.44). When an autonomous feminist movement is present and moderately strong (value = 1), the ratification of CEDAW has a small, positive and statistically significant effect (.67 +/– .16). But when the autonomous feminist movement is at its strongest (value = 2), ratifying CEDAW produces about one additional area of government action on violence against women (1.04 +/– .18) and is statistically significant (p = .01).

Why is the coefficient of the constitutive term *CEDAW Ratify* negative, though substantively small (and on the threshold of significance at the .05 level), when there is no strong, autonomous feminist movement? Unless pushed for and brought home by local activists, governments may ratify CEDAW merely to look good internationally and even to substitute for serious domestic policy action. This suggests that autonomous feminist movements are not merely helpful but necessary to implement international treaties, and that without them global norms create perverse incentives for governments, though this effect may be less likely in later years.

Our hypothesis was that these variables mutually conditioned each other, so marginal effects can be calculated to illustrate the way CEDAW conditions the impact of a strengthened women's movement. When CEDAW is ratified, a strong autonomous feminist movement produces an additional one to two areas of policy on violence against women (1.50 +/-.30), a strongly significant finding. There are thirty-one such cases in the dataset.[37] When CEDAW has not been ratified (when the variable is equal to zero), the impact of a strong, autonomous women's movement is statistically insignificant, though this finding likely reflects the small number of countries with strong, autonomous feminist movements that have failed to ratify CEDAW. By 2005, there were only two such countries (one of which is the United States), most likely because such movements demand ratification of CEDAW and are usually successful.

Cross-sectional analyses of the "snapshot" years of data for 1985 and 2005 show that the interaction term is significant only in the 2005 cross-sections, and not the earlier ones. We do not have space here to explore the marginal effects for each year, but this finding clearly supports our hypothesis of a shift over time (H8). This evidence of the changing effect of CEDAW over time may be due to either growing support for CEDAW (as it passes a tipping point) or the fact that CEDAW came to include language specifically about violence against women, or both. We have argued it is both, and this evidence is supportive, but cannot show conclusively that both developments matter.

Control Variables

The coefficient plots provided in Figure 2.6 provide a good sense of the importance of the control variables. The proportion of women in the legislature and democracy level both fall on the line at "0," which means they have no significant association with the dependent variable. Indeed, the effect of the proportion of women in national legislatures (Women in legislature) is insignificant in all but one (Model 2) of the 6 models in which it is included and the effect is small in all models. At its largest and

---

[37] Calculation of marginal effects and their errors follows Brambor, Clark, & Golder (2006).

most significant, Women in legislature (%) has a coefficient of .06+/–.01 (Model 2). Even in this model, this variable may be most relevant for explaining cross-national rather than over-time variation, since the variation across all countries and time periods (standard deviation = 10 percent) is much bigger than the changes over the decade in a single country (SD = 7 percent). A ten-point change would be associated with an additional one-half of an area of policy action (.5). But for our study countries, the average change in the percentage of seats in the national legislature held by women over a decade (3 points) would result in a negligible increase in responsiveness (.15 of a policy area), and a change of one whole standard deviation (7 percent) is associated with only one-third of an additional area of policy. Even this small effect drops out, however, when we control for path dependency (policies already in existence). Women in legislature (%) is statistically insignificant in both the 1985 and 2005 cross-sections (Models 2, 3, 4, 6 and 7, Table 2.10).

A measure of national wealth (*Logged GDP per capita*) is significant in four of sixteen models in which it was included (1, 2, 4, and 9, Table 2.9), but this effect mostly drops out when we control for regional diffusion, becoming much smaller and insignificant (see Model 3, for example). The *Regional diffusion* variable and *Logged GDP per capita* are collinear to some degree, making it difficult to disentangle these effects. Still, these findings are consistent with our theoretical expectations. National wealth has little bearing on whether women organize against violence within or across borders, once we control for democracy (see below) and "neighborhood" (regional diffusion) effects.

As we expected, the coefficient for religious parties (*Religious party*) is small (–.24), negative, and insignificant (Model 9). The coefficient for *Left party* is even smaller (.09) and less significant (Model 10). This conforms to our expectations that the characteristics of political parties, though sometimes thought to be important for advancing women's rights, are less relevant for this issue.

Democracy level (Polity) appears to have a much less robust, but small and positive and (in some models) statistically significant, impact on responsiveness (see Models 4–10, Table 2.9). It also appears more important in later (2005) cross-sections (Models 2, 4, 7) than in the 1985 cross-sections.[38] Using other measures of democracy (Cheibub, Gandhi, &

[38] It is possible that this might reflect the importance of international norms in this later period. This interpretation could be explored using an interaction effect, but our theoretical argument does not turn on the impact of democracy one way or the other, so in light

Vreeland, 2009; Freedom House, 2011) did not produce stronger effects of democracy (not shown). Moving through the full twenty-point range of the variable (from −10 to +10) would have some noticeable effect (about half an additional area of government action) but few countries make such transitions (the standard deviation is 7.5). A positive effect of democracy, though one that is less important than women's movements and international variables more generally, is consistent with our theoretical argument (though it does not depend on such an effect). We might expect that women are more likely to organize and be free to persuade others of feminist aims in democracies than in authoritarian regimes. Last, the *Lagged dependent variable* also showed signs and significance in the direction expected.

Overall, our approach performs well in capturing the over-time, cross-national variation exhibited in these data. Especially given the ambitious nature of this modeling exercise (capturing the dynamics of policy change in seventy countries from all world regions across four decades), the reduction of errors of prediction accomplished by these models is impressive: R-squared ranges from .60 to .83 across the seventeen models. Our approach provides greater explanatory leverage than those relying on national, legislative insiders, such as percentages of seats held by women, Left parties, or religious parties, and holds controlling for democracy and national wealth. The framework we offer, centered on the relationship between civil society and institutional change, performs far more powerfully than these conventional explanations. Social movements have political consequences, including policy change. This research helps to sort out the circumstances under which they have these effects.

CONCLUSION

Women's autonomous organizing in civil society affects state action on status issues. Autonomous movements articulate the social perspectives of marginalized groups, transform social practice, and change public opinion. They drive sweeping policy change as voters, civic leaders, and activists pressure policy makers to respond to their demands, and as policy makers themselves become sympathetic to the movement's goals.

of considerations of space and focus we leave further exploration of that variable for other analyses. We can report that a variable expressing the interaction of democracy and international norms was not significant (not shown), and leave a thorough discussion of marginal effects for future work.

These effects of autonomous organizing are more important in our analysis than women's presence in the legislature or the impact of political parties. Nor do economic factors such as national wealth trump the societal causes of policy making. Although these intralegislative and economic factors have received a great deal of attention in the study of comparative social policy and women and politics, they are inadequate to explain the significant changes in policies on violence against women. Civil society holds the key here.

While social movements are critical for catalyzing processes of policy change, the role they play changes over time as the ideas promoted by autonomous movements become encoded in new institutions, such as international agreements and declarations. New institutions begin to have independent effects and movements come to account for a smaller part of policy change, so the relative importance of institutions and movements is altered. But even in these later periods, we find that the power of autonomous movements is important to ensure that institutional reforms (such as women's policy machineries and international treaties) live up to the potential imagined by the activists who demand them. Autonomous organizing ensures that words become deeds.

In civil society, people take up the normative meanings offered by new laws and global norms and make them their own, applying them to their own contexts, giving them flesh and blood. Civic contestation and mobilization furthers the vernacularization of international law. Universal provisions are made concrete in local contexts, contributing to their legitimacy and amplifying their effectiveness (Benhabib, 2009; Merry, 2006). Those who criticize the universalist claims of human rights as neocolonial, a form of domination, or a violation of democratic sovereignty fail to account for these processes of appropriation and transformation.

Of course, as we discussed in Chapter 1, social movement activism does not determine policy change across the board.[39] Rather, the relative influence of civil society tends to vary according to the *type* of issue. Party ideology and legislator identity can be important for some issues, as we show in our discussion of parental leave and state funding for reproductive rights. Some types of issues will invoke support or opposition from organized economic interests and particular religious groups, as we demonstrate in our discussion of family law and reproductive rights.

---

[39] Though there is not space to discuss it here, we would like to note that our argument does not imply that social movements are always progressive. Some social movements push for policy changes that are conservative or that aim to undermine women's rights.

This chapter has described one path to policy change on women's rights, drawing lessons for other policies that overtly aim to transform group status. However, there may be other ways to improve group well-being, for example, through measures less overtly aimed at improving group status. For example, some women's rights issues (including access to contraception, expanded parental leave, and the modernization of family law) are championed by nonfeminist groups for nonfeminist ends. Elites promote these policies to advance technical goals or state imperatives such as national security, economic growth, population growth, and so forth. Similarly, some religious groups have supported expanded access to health care and parental leave in order to promote traditional values. Sometimes they work in concert with feminist actors, who push a feminist framing of the issue, but sometimes they do not. When autonomous social movement actors are excluded from policy processes advancing women's rights, the transformative potential of these policy changes will be muted, and the vernacularization of global norms less likely. When it comes to progressive social policies advancing group status, the roots of change lie in civil society.

3

Governing Women's Legal Status at Work

Many of the world's women are unable to earn a living and support a family in equal and dignified conditions. Women suffer from segregation in low-paying and low-status jobs, often with long working hours. Women workers are overrepresented in the informal sector and they rarely hold upper management positions, even in sectors where they are numerous (International Labor Organization, 2010). Though most governments of the world have formally committed to advancing women's economic equality, for example through support for the Declaration of Human Rights, the International Covenant on Economic, Social, and Cultural Rights (ICESCR), and the Convention on the Elimination of Discrimination against Women (CEDAW), actual state action to improve women's economic opportunities remains uneven.

Some governments have reformed overtly discriminatory laws and adopted new provisions seeking to guarantee gender equality in hiring, firing, and other employment-related matters. Others have gone even further by creating mechanisms of enforcement, proactive measures to address inequality and discrimination, and policies that seek to identify and address the unique legal problems women workers confront. On the other hand, some governments do little to combat gender discrimination at work, and keep discriminatory labor laws on the books despite adopting guarantees of formal legal equality that might seem to conflict with those laws (for example, constitutional guarantees of equality).

In this chapter, we identify patterns of cross-national variation in the laws promoting women's economic equality and analyze the politics behind these policies. We find that women's organizing and their activism on their own behalf, combined with support from the international activist and international intergovernmental authorities, have advanced women's legal status and rights in most areas, even more so than we expected when we first began studying these fields.

We define "economic equality" as a situation in which women are not disadvantaged vis-à-vis men in their efforts to gain a living and support a family. This implies that women are not discriminated against on the grounds of gender when it comes to access to work or the circumstances and structure of work (including recruitment, pay, and promotion), and that their gendered social positions – created by pregnancy, childbirth, or parental responsibilities, for example – do not stand in the way of their economic security.

Women's economic equality is inherently important as a matter of justice. In addition, women's work promotes the well-being of families and children, even in two-parent households. There is compelling evidence that women's empowerment, measured by their ability to work outside the home, education, and access to resources, improves child well-being, produces socially desirable outcomes, and is even associated with greater parenting investments by men (Agarwal & Panda, 2007; Agarwal, 1997; Belsky, Bell, Bradley, Stallard, & Stewart-Brown, 2006; Bianchi, Cohen, Raley, & Nomaguchi, 2004; Bohn & Campbell, 2004; Hobcraft, 1993; Hook, 2006; Iversen & Rosenbluth, 2010; Schuler, Hashemi, Riley, & Akhter, 1996). Not all women's work is empowering, however. Women's work in larger, more formal places of employment produces better effects for families, children, and society as a whole than work in informal, temporary, and marginal positions (Kabeer, 2012).

DISAGGREGATING ECONOMIC EQUALITY

To analyze state action to promote women's economic equality, this chapter identifies three categories of policies (see Table 3.1) (cf. Mazur, 2002, p. 82). The first category involves the eradication of state-sponsored discrimination. This involves reform of laws and policies that officially discriminate against women by preventing them from working in certain types of jobs (such as those involving heavy machinery, vehicles, alcohol, or other "hazardous" activities) or under certain circumstances (at night or overtime work, and so on). Sometimes these restrictions are justified as being protective, though it is only women who are seen as being in need of protection. At other times they are justified in language that refers to the lack of *appropriateness* of such work for women.

TABLE 3.1 *Overview of policy relating to women's legal status at work*

Type of policy	Indicators
State-sponsored discrimination	– Restrictions for women on overtime, night work, or restrictions on work in specific occupations – Restrictions on pregnant workers – Requirements for a sex-segregated workplace
Formal equality	– Equal opportunity laws – Laws prohibiting discrimination in hiring, firing, promotion, and training – Laws requiring equal pay
Substantive equality	– Enforcement mechanisms for equality laws – Policies promoting women's work in nontraditional occupations – Laws addressing women's work in the informal sector – Financial benefits or incentives for companies that hire women or for women-owned businesses – Other laws recognizing the distinctive issues and concerns confronting women at work

When governments make such distinctions among workers, they reinforce discriminatory social norms that undermine women's position in the labor market and their access to economic security.

The second category of policies involves guarantees of formal legal equality in the circumstances of work, including provisions on hiring, promotion, and training. Such policies may take the form of general statements about women's rights to equal treatment in the workplace, and sometimes these provisions specify particular areas or dimensions to which they apply (hiring, promotion, pay, training, and so forth). Antidiscrimination and equal opportunity laws signify that the state recognizes the problem of gender discrimination and has created a normative framework to combat it. Yet sometimes governments adopt commitments to combat discrimination at work while continuing to uphold laws and tolerate practices that discriminate against women. The coexistence of contradictory bodies of law can persist for years, providing judges and employers different bases on which to make decisions and guide behavior. This phenomenon highlights the importance of considering policy areas as distinct dimensions of the legal regime rather than as developmental stages.

Formal legal equality is not sufficient to advance women's status and rights. When women's de facto position in the labor market puts them at a disadvantage, an understanding of equality limited to similar treatment can prolong gender subordination. Social norms, discrimination, and occupational segregation combine to prevent women's equal access to work and equal working conditions. Many governments have thus adopted measures to promote "substantive equality," which involves addressing gender-specific problems that constitute barriers to equality at work. Substantive equality policies include the creation of agencies and mechanisms to enforce equal opportunity legislation and of policies to help women in historical and harder-to-reach areas of women's work (such as the informal sector or domestic work), as well as to increase women's presence in male-dominated occupations or in managerial ranks.

The case of Japan, where gender discrimination in the workplace has been well documented, helps to illustrate the relationship among the different policy subtypes and the behavior each policy attempts to overcome. Before the time period of our study, Japanese law explicitly endorsed and permitted sex-based differential treatment. The Labor Standards Law of 1947 banned women from certain occupations deemed hazardous, prevented women from working at night, imposed restrictions on women working overtime, and required pre- and postnatal leave as well as nursing and childcare breaks during the workday (Parkinson, 1989, pp. 608–9, fn. 1–5). Though the law prohibited wage discrimination, it permitted sex-based discrimination in hiring, promotion, training, benefits, recruitment, and job assignments. As a result, across the economy, firms treated men and women workers very differently. Men had higher status and access to superior training, promotion, and pay. It was normal for firms to require women to quit work when they married or had children. Women were rarely promoted to managerial or decision-making positions. Firms forced women to retire earlier than men (often by age thirty!) and tended to fire women workers first when downsizing (Cook & Hayashi, 1980; Parkinson, 1989; Schoppa, 2008; Weathers, 2005).[1]

It is important to note that these laws all operated in the context of the 1947 Constitution, which banned discrimination by sex. Article 14 stated: "All of the people are equal under the law and there shall be no discrimination in political, economic or social relations because of race,

---

[1] Japan was not unique in this respect. Firms in the United States also sorted workers into occupations by sex and race, and only white men had access to career ladders. These practices remained pervasive until companies were forced to change after the 1964 Civil Rights Act (Dobbin, 2009, chapter 2).

creed, sex, social status or family origin." However, judges interpreted this provision to allow "reasonable and justifiable discrimination" due to gender role differentiation based on biological differences (Knapp, 1995, p. 97).

Japan's first attempt to legislate formal sex equality in the workplace was the Equal Employment Opportunity Law (EEOL) of 1985. While feminists advocated the law, both business and unions opposed it. Unions in particular were against the removal of protective legislation (Knapp, 1995). The EEOL relaxed some (but not all) protective labor legislation; prevented firms from discriminating against women in benefits, education and training, retirement policies, and layoffs; and called on firms to endeavor to offer women equal opportunities and treatment in recruitment, hiring, job placement, and promotion. The Ministry of Labor published extremely detailed guidelines instructing firms on how to comply (Parkinson, 1989).

Notwithstanding the symbolic importance of the 1985 EEOL legislation, it was widely viewed as having failed to curb sexist practices. One problem was that there were no enforcement mechanisms to make sure that firms attempted to recruit men and women into the same jobs. Effectively, nondiscrimination in the crucial areas of hiring and promotion applied only *when women were in the same job category as men.* Firms took advantage of this loophole by designing separate job categories for men and women. Men's jobs had better pay, opportunities for promotion, and benefits than women's jobs (Schoppa, 2008, p. 59). What is more, gender-based two-track personnel systems were used in more than half of all large firms. In 1993, a group of women workers and lawyers called the "Women's Circle" submitted a shadow report, entitled *A Letter from Japanese Women,* to the CEDAW committee of the United Nations, criticizing the EEOL in light of working conditions for women in Japan (Knapp, 1995). A Ministry of Labor study group concluded in 1995 that the law had encouraged gender stratification and called for reform (Weathers, 2005, pp. 74–6).

To correct these problems, the government promulgated a major reform of the EEOL in 1997. This version prohibited sex discrimination in all phases of employment (recruiting, hiring, and job placement), required employers to take measures to prevent sexual harassment, and advocated the use of positive action to promote women. The law also attempted to strengthen enforcement mechanisms by making it easier to use mediation and allowing the government to publicize names of offenders (Weathers 2005, pp. 77–8). The reform amended the Labor

Standards Law to relax or abolish protective provisions for women except for those concerning maternity and menstrual leave. As a result, Japanese women over eighteen could work overtime and on night shifts (Hayashi, 2005).

At the same time, government officials took some action to promote substantive equality. To raise awareness about the objectives of the law, they organized meetings between managers and union officials, shared information on the lack of women managers and gender wage gaps, granted awards to progressive firms, and encouraged sharing of best practices on family-friendly policies (Weathers, 2005, p. 78). But enforcement mechanisms remained weak and most cases were resolved through mediation. Still, a few significant cases in the early 2000s made news headlines, such as when courts ruled illegal the two-track personnel system at Nomura Securities.

By the middle of the decade, the use of gender-based two-track programs had begun to decline. However, women's work remained precarious, as they constituted a disproportionate share of nonregular workers, including those working part time, on contract, and through a temporary agency. According to a government survey, women made up 64 percent of nonregular workers in 2014, who in turn made up 40 percent of the country's workforce.[2]

Japan's experience suggests that policy actions to eradicate state-sponsored discrimination, endorse formal equality, and promote substantive equality constitute necessary conditions to establish the legal basis affirming women's economic equality. Legal change in only one area is inadequate to promote equality. In fact, adoption of measures in all three areas will not lead to equality overnight. There must be mechanisms to insure compliance with equal opportunities legislation at all levels of society. In the United States, personnel managers at private companies were largely responsible for developing compliance mechanisms, and the best practices they developed for equal opportunity and diversity management diffused nationwide (Dobbin, 2009). Yet decades later, women (and minorities) still hold only a small fraction of powerful positions in major firms. The struggle for equality in the workplace and other spheres is long and arduous.

---

[2] "Plight of Irregular Workers," Editorial in *The Japan Times*, January 5, 2016. Available at: www.japantimes.co.jp/opinion/2016/01/05/editorials/plight-of-irregular-workers/#.WeQZ8a3Myu4.

MEASURING EQUAL OPPORTUNITY LAWS

To assess the degree of *state-sponsored discrimination* for each country, we asked:

(1) Are women prohibited from night work?

(2) Are women prohibited from overtime work?

(3) Are women prohibited from specific occupations by virtue of being women?

(4) Are there religious restrictions on women's work?

(5) Are there prohibitions against employment (as opposed to special rights offered) that apply to those who are pregnant or were recently pregnant, breastfeeding mothers, or mothers of young children?

(6) Are there laws segregating workers by sex?

Legal regimes are awarded one point for each measure adopted, so that the highest possible score (a "6") would reflect a regime characterized by all six prohibitions on women's work while a regime that does none of these things is coded "0." (No country discriminates on all six grounds, so the most discriminatory country scores a "4.") We do not count provisions that provide special rights or opportunities to women, such as those that enable women to combine breastfeeding with work, as state-sponsored discrimination. These provisions offer women protections that open more doors for them. This is different from denying women opportunities because they are pregnant or because they are parents of young children, especially when this does not apply to similarly situated male parents.

In order to examine the degree of *formal equality*, we examined whether the legal regime guarantees equality and prohibits discrimination in all aspects of workplace operation. These must not be general guarantees but guarantees that apply specifically to women and men. We ask:

Are there laws against discrimination against women at work? Are these laws specifically about sex discrimination? Do they (and other measures guaranteeing equality) apply to:

(1) Wages and pay?

(2) Hiring?

(3) Termination of employment?

(4) Access to training?

(5) Equal rights to participate in workplace governance? Unions?

Legal regimes that have general antidiscrimination measures that do not specifically apply to any of these areas receive a "1." Those that apply to all 5 areas, in addition to prohibiting discrimination in general, are coded "6."

In addition to these measures of formal equality, we assessed the degree of state attention to *substantive equality*. Many legal scholars and political theorists have identified limitations to the notion of equality as formally similar or equivalent treatment. Sometimes "formal" equality takes a male norm as its reference point, which implies that women must behave exactly the same as men in order to obtain equal treatment (Boling, 2015; Rhode, 1989; Young, 1990). By contrast, it may be necessary to deal with the distinctive particularities of women's and men's work and forms of life to advance equality. What is more, as noted in the discussion of Japan, equality can be understood to apply *within* occupational or status categories but not *across* them (with the consequence that equality is consistent with gender disparities). A broader, more robust perspective is necessary to expose gender inequality (Sheppard, 2010).

Finally, formal guarantees often depend on complaint-based mechanisms of enforcement, which assume that legal guarantees will mostly work and that people will identify them and bring them to the attention of state agencies or the courts. An alternative approach is for the state to assume responsibility actively to monitor compliance with equality guarantees. The burden of identifying and rectifying problems lies with the state and not the victims of discrimination. Policies that go beyond formal guarantees to address the particular character of women's work (for example, its informality or segregated character), or that seek to take an active rather than passive approach to equality guarantees, are examples of what we are looking for when we assess whether states aim to further substantive, or merely formal, inequality.

Not all governments that embrace laws on formal equality are as quick to adopt measures to promote substantive equality, such as protection for informal sector workers or enforcement mechanisms. Often, labor laws are not seen as applicable to categories of workers where large numbers of women are employed. In Nigeria, minimum wage requirements "do not apply to establishments where there are less than 50 workers or they are employed on a part-time basis or in seasonal employment" (Williams, 2004, p. 250), which means they do not apply to the agricultural, seasonal and informal sectors where most women work. In Latin America and the Caribbean, the informal sector makes up more than half of nonagricultural employment, and women constitute more than half of informal sector workers in many economies (Chen, 2001, 2005). Yet informal sector and rural workers are usually excluded from the rights and protections of national labor laws, including minimum wages, maximum working hours, social security, disability, and so forth. In Egypt, the more than three million women working in farming are excluded from the protections of the New Unified Labor Law of 2003, a fact that has been noted by the Arabic Network for Human Rights Information. Ironically, this means that the most disadvantaged women workers in both developed and developing economies (such as women working in the informal sector as domestic workers, home workers, agricultural workers, and the like) are the people most difficult to reach with regulation, suggesting that innovative policy approaches may be necessary.

Labor laws, as well as other measures promoting gender equality, tend to suffer from lack of enforcement in general. A World Bank report (2013) noted that an important reason why Turkey has not achieved substantive equality in the workplace is because it lacks enforcement mechanisms for its antidiscrimination laws. As a result, employers have found numerous ways to circumvent these laws. Though our concept of substantive equality does not include enforcement or implementation, as noted, we do study the creation of government entities to monitor enforcement, which indicates that policymakers are cognizant of the limits of formal guarantees. To be sure, whether equality-enforcing bodies devised by the law actually operate as envisaged is a question of implementation, and we do not cover that issue in this book.

Laws and policies that treat men and women differently in order to overcome gender disadvantages do not violate principles of equality. For example, in the Canadian Charter of Rights and Freedoms adopted in 1982, section 15(1) is aimed at combatting discrimination. It reads: "Every individual is equal before and under the law and has the right to the equal protection and equal benefit of the law without discrimination and, in particular, without discrimination based on race, national or ethnic origin, colour, religion, sex, age or mental or physical disability." Section 15(2), however, is aimed at ensuring that formal equality does not become an obstacle to the adoption and operation of laws intended to advance equality in practice, such as affirmative action policies. That section, which we might think of as being more oriented toward *substantive equality*, reads: "(2) Subsection (1) does not preclude any law, program or activity that has as its object the amelioration of conditions of disadvantaged individuals or groups including those that are disadvantaged because of race, national or ethnic origin, colour, religion, sex, age or mental or physical disability."[3]

This third type of government action, the area of *substantive equality*,[4] addresses the specific problems that confront women in the labor market, and seeks to translate formal legal equality into effective legal equality. We measure this third dimension of government action by asking:

(1) Are there any legal or policy mechanisms to enforce guarantees of equality?

(2) Does the government demonstrate, in its policy and rhetoric, an awareness of and attention to the problems of women working in the informal sector? Are there any efforts to address their problems?

(3) Are there any efforts or mechanisms to ensure the applicability of labor laws to the informal sector? Are there provisions for the representation of informal sector workers in formal economic planning or business consultation processes? Are there policies or incentives to facilitate the self-organization of informal sector workers?

(4) Are there provisions for positive action to promote women's work in nontraditional occupations? Job training?

(5) Does the government offer financial benefits or privileges to companies that promote women workers or to companies owned by women (such as provisions with respect to government contracting for women-owned businesses in the United States)?

Legal regimes characterized by more of these initiatives score higher; those with all five of these types of measures score a "5" while those with none score a "0."

The Indices

We created a series of indices to measure and compare government action on equality at work. One measures state-sponsored discrimination.

[3] Government of Canada, Constitution Act, 1982.
[4] Note that while this concept is informed by discussions in Canadian feminist legal scholarship, for example Shepherd (2010), there are some differences between some treatments and our concept as we outline it here. For example, in our concept we focus less on *outcomes* than does Shepherd (2010).

TABLE 3.2 *Means by year, indices of legal equality at work*

	1975	1985	1995	2005
Eradication of state-sponsored discrimination				
	1.1	1.1	1.7	.9
	(.98)	(.96)	(1.3)	(1.0)
Formal equality				
	1.8	2.7	3.9	4.7
	(2.2)	(2.4)	(2.2)	(1.0)
Substantive equality				
	.6	.9	1.7	3.1
	(.8)	(1.0)	(1.3)	(1.4)
Overall equality index				
	7.3	8.5	10.5	12.9
	(2.9)	(3.3)	(3.4)	(2.8)

Note: Higher values denote less discrimination. Standard deviations are in parentheses. *Eradication of State-sponsored discrimination* can hold values from 0 to 6. *Legal equality index* can hold values from 0 to 6. *Substantive equality* can hold values from 0 to 5. The *Overall equality index* is the sum of the *Eradication of state-sponsored discrimination*, *Formal equality*, and *Substantive equality* indices.

It ranges from 0 to 6, but relatively few countries adopt more than a few of these measures. We reverse the score here, so that states get points (maximum 6 points) when they do NOT discriminate in each of six possible areas. We call this index the Eradication of State Discrimination Index. We also created measures for formal and substantive equality. We assess formal equality by assigning one point for each aspect outlined (maximum of 6 points), and we assess substantive equality by summing the scores of dummy variables for the five items identified above (so, a maximum of 5 points for substantive equality). Our overall index of legal equality at work sums a country's score in each of these areas, producing an index of equality that can range from 0 to 17 (though no country has a score lower than 2).

Table 3.2 summarizes some descriptive statistics and shows the mean values and standard deviation for each of the three subindices (top three rows) and the overall equality index (final row). It shows that the value of all indices has grown over time, especially with regard to formal equality. Table 3.3 examines these patterns more closely, by presenting the overall numbers of countries, per year, with each type of legal provision.

Table 3.3 shows that, although the number of laws upholding state-sponsored discrimination declined overall, in some areas (such as religious

TABLE 3.3 *National laws relating to women's legal status at work. Number of countries with the legal provision in question, of a total of seventy*

Type of law	1975	1985	1995	2005
Law against night work by women	32	32	26	21
Law against overtime work by women	4	2	3	2
Law against women working in specific occupations	28	28	29	23
Religious restrictions on women's work	1	1	2	2
Ban on work for pregnant women	10	12	13	14
Law segregating workers by sex and occupation	1	2	3	3
Antidiscrimination provisions	30	44	58	68
General antidiscrimination on basis of sex	29	44	57	68
Laws requiring equal pay	24	35	50	60
Laws against sex discrimination in hiring	15	27	40	48
Laws against sex discrimination in firing	14	22	35	45
Laws against sex discrimination in training	11	20	33	42
Laws against sex discrimination in government workplace	9	11	17	25
Other laws against sex discrimination	2	4	7	13
Enforcement mechanism for equal work provisions	20	28	41	59
Policies promoting women's status at work	20	25	36	58
Policies promoting women in nontraditional occupations	2	5	22	47
Policies addressing work in informal sector	0	2	6	29
Incentives to hire women or to advance sex equality	0	1	11	23

restrictions on women's work and sex segregation at work) the number of countries with discriminatory laws grew. With regard to formal equality, the pattern is more linear. In 1975, it was most typical not to take action to outlaw discrimination. A few countries had provisions against discrimination, but most had none (the median score for formal equality in 1975 was 0). By 2005, the opposite was true: Most countries had adopted laws to prohibit discrimination in about five of the six areas we examined. A similar story may be told about substantive equality: Most countries did nothing to advance substantive equality in 1975 (the median score is 0). By 2005, most governments had adopted three distinct kinds of measures to advance substantive equality, though there was less progress here than on formal equality.

There is considerable regional variation in these trends. For example, in Latin America, state-sponsored discrimination declined, while in

Middle East and North Africa (MENA) state-sponsored discrimination increased over the period, more than doubling. Formal and substantive equality also increased more slowly in MENA than in Latin America. Overall, Latin American countries have slightly less legal protection than most countries in our study, but the MENA countries have significantly less legal equality than Latin America and the global average for the countries in our study, as well as more state-sponsored discrimination. Figures 3.1–3.4 show maps displaying the scores on the overall equality index for the seventy countries of our study.

Explanation for Historical and Cross-National Variation

What factors help to account for historical changes and cross-national variation in laws shaping women's status at work? Our typology, described in the first chapter of this book, suggests the ways in which the issue of legal status in employment is distinctive. We characterized women's economic and workplace equality in our typology as a "non-doctrinal" and "status" issue, like violence against women. Economic equality is nondoctrinal, we reason, for it fails directly to touch upon major issues contemplated in religious scriptures and other texts. Religions have a great deal to say about women's role in marriage, reproduction, and sexuality, with children, and so forth, but are quieter about women's role in the public sphere of wage work. To be sure, the fact that many religions exalt women's role as wife and mother would seem to imply skepticism about their participation in the world of wage work. But in fact, neither the Bible nor the Quran forbids women from working outside of the home. Both texts contain references to women who worked and call for their equal treatment, seemingly recognizing, as do international development agencies in the twenty-first century, that a woman's ability to fulfill motherly and familial duties often turns on her access to wage work. Our typology thus predicts that, unlike family and abortion law, religious groups will tend not to mobilize to prevent change.

In addition, the typology characterizes laws shaping women's economic equality as a "status" rather than a "class" issue. Our categorization may seem unusual, since a group's position in relation to economic resources is precisely what defines a class in the Marxist sense (Wright, 1997). The "status" provisions we study pertain to women as a category constructed by institutions of gender. This category cuts across social classes and the lines drawn by professionalization and social capital, which form the basis for modern class structures according to some

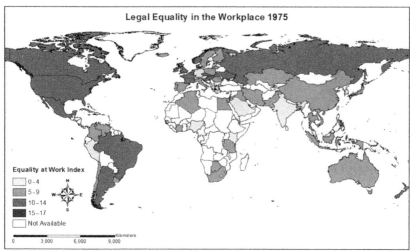

FIGURE 3.1 Legal equality in the workplace, 1975

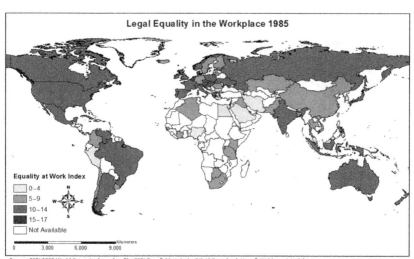

FIGURE 3.2 Legal equality in the workplace, 1985

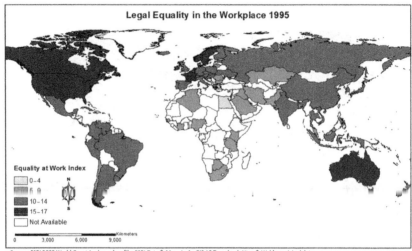

FIGURE 3.3 Legal equality in the workplace, 1995

FIGURE 3.4 Legal equality in the workplace, 2005

contemporary, Marxist-influenced scholars such as Perrucci.[5] Most salient for us is the way that laws on women's equality at work intervene in the *officially defined status of women* order to alter social roles and relations, shaping the allocation of rights and responsibilities in the workplace in the way that family law structures the balance of power in the home.

While there are several excellent works outlining differences in women's employment law around the world (see, e.g., Cotter, 2004), few scholars have undertaken to explain global, or even cross-national, variation. Mazur (2002), one of the few works to undertake a systematic cross-national study of the political processes driving these laws, provides an overview of the equal employment policies in thirteen advanced industrial states and analyzes the politics behind these policies in four countries: Ireland, Sweden, France, and Great Britain. Mazur finds that the key drivers behind equal employment policies include strategic partnerships between equality agencies, trade unions, and women in public office; authoritative equality agencies; and regional or transnational norms or initiatives (such as the European Union equality policy).

One of the only other comparative studies of policy adoption that examines sex discrimination law is Lindvert's study of Sweden and Australia (Lindvert, 2007). In general, Lindvert finds that "gendered policy logics" affect different issues in different ways, but points to specific differences in national policy regimes that shape approaches to sex discrimination. Sex discrimination law in Australia was adopted largely because of a combination of feminist activism, feminist bureaucrats, and international pressure from CEDAW. Feminist organizational skill in navigating the political system was particularly important. In Sweden, sex discrimination was advocated primarily by the Liberal Party, and neglected by Left parties and the unions. Lindvert points out, interestingly, that the gender equality unit in Sweden did not show much interest in promoting legislation on sex discrimination. To expand support for legislation, policy advocates abandoned a liberal, sex discrimination frame and adopted a more redistributive, equality

---

[5] For some scholars (e.g., Fraser, 2007) however, women resemble a "class" defined by their position in the sexual division of labor, while others, criticize this approach to materiality and gender as erasing the work women do in the public sphere and equating gender with work in the private sphere. We see the sexual division of labor as a core institution of gender (following Young, 2002) but do not claim that it is the only basis for either gender inequality, class inequality, or gender-class inequality.

frame, in addition to narrowing the focus of the bill so that it focused primarily on work, in order to secure final adoption (Lindvert, 2007, p. 250).

These two works by Mazur (2002) and Lindvert (2007) highlight the important role of feminist activists and feminist bureaucrats or agencies, while other studies have emphasized the role of women in other areas of government such as parliament (see Krook & Schwindt-Bayer, 2013 for a review). The notion of a "triangle of empowerment" (Vargas & Wieringa, 1998), in which feminist pressure in multiple venues in state and society combines to constitute an avenue for the advancement of women's rights, builds on these ideas. Feminist transnational activism has produced global treaties and agreements endorsing women's equal rights at work. Article 11 of CEDAW, for example, calls on states to insure equal rights in all areas of work, including hiring, pay, promotion, training, and benefits. CEDAW also calls for ending pregnancy discrimination, while endorsing some protections for pregnancy, such as maternity leave and work–life balance policies.

The effects of international conventions and domestic activism are intimately entwined, as the discussion of Japan earlier in this chapter suggests, and as the discussion of Canada later in the chapter also illustrates. Mazur and Stetson describe the ways that domestic and international pressures combine and produce a "sandwich effect" (Mazur & McBride, 2007), in which political pressure exerted by women at the national level interacts with political pressure from the supranational level to stimulate the development of women-friendly policies (Keck & Sikkink, 1998; Van der Vleuten, 2013). The introduction of European equal pay and equal treatment legislation between 1975 and 1985, combined with national political pressure exerted by women's movements, is an example of this "sandwich effect," which has resulted in the modification of social security policies by national governments (Vleuten, 2007, pp. 89–96). This is similar to the boomerang effect documented by Keck and Sikkink (1998), in which domestic feminist actors appeal to international bodies to pressure recalcitrant domestic governments to respect and promote human rights. Friedman similarly documents a "Pincer effect" in her work on regional advocacy (2009), while Baldez (2014) points to the analogy (coined by Javate de Dios) of a circle of empowerment as an alternative way to capture the international–domestic interaction.

The combined effect of international and domestic pressures, or the "sandwich effect," is similar to the dynamic we found in the earlier analysis of policies on violence against women. Our work in this book explains why this dynamic is particularly powerful for status issues such as violence against women and equality at work, but less crucial for family law, abortion, reproductive rights funding, and social welfare-type policies, where religion and left politics complicate the story. In the rest of this section, we explain the theoretical basis for our explanation for (and model of) cross-national variation in laws shaping equality at work.

Feminist Movements

Promoting equality for women workers involves a fundamental reorientation of women's social identities as well as normative visions of workers. What is at stake is a vision of women as full human beings and citizens entitled to equal rights in all spheres and endeavors. Put another way, equality at work requires adjusting our assumptions about human beings and workers to include women's lives and roles. Working for pay is not incompatible with motherhood; rather, working enhances a woman's ability to fulfill her motherly duties. Nor is working for pay secondary to motherhood and other traditional roles, something that women do merely to supplement family income. (Such a belief often justifies paying women less and passing them over for promotion.) Rather, working is part of being a *woman*, and being *human*. Women's advocacy on their own behalf is crucial to the success of such a revisioning of women's status (Htun & Weldon, 2010, 2012). Legal and policy changes that induce changes in the cultural and social meanings of women's roles, as well as shifts in the status ordering of society, tend to involve women's autonomous mobilization in domestic and global civil societies.

In the North Atlantic and Western European countries that were early to adopt legislation promoting equality at work, women's movements played prominent roles. The story of equality legislation in Canada illustrates this process. Established feminist groups took up issues of employment in the 1960s against the background of human rights and labor movement activism (Timpson, 2002), and began to urge the government to adopt laws to advance equality. In 1964, Canada ratified the International Labour Organization's Convention 111 on Discrimination in Employment and Occupation, which officially commits the government to developing a national policy (C111, 11.2). The Royal Commission on Equality in Employment (Abella Commission) was established in 1983; in 1984, it issued a sweeping report recommending major changes to

Canadian law and policy and introducing the term "employment equity" (Canada. Royal Commission on Equality in Employment; Abella, 1984) The Abella report acknowledged the influence of civil society groups and called for their continued involvement in the policy process. The Federal Employment Equity Act was adopted in 1986 under the conservative government of Brian Mulroney, who had made pay equity part of his electoral campaign (Mentzer, 2002; Timpson, 2002). In the same year, the Supreme Court supported a case brought by feminist organizations in Quebec (Action Travail des Femmes, or ATF) that required employers to make efforts to promote women's advancement in nontraditional jobs (*C.N. v. Canada*). The ATF argued that the Canadian National Railway hiring and promotion policies discriminated on the basis of sex contrary to section 10 of Canada's Human Rights Act (Jhappan, 2002).

In 1992, a parliamentary commission headed by a Conservative MP reviewed the Equity Act and made several recommendations for revision (Mentzer, 2002). Then, in 1995, a revised Employment Equity Act was passed under the liberal government of Jean Chrétien. The new law improved enforcement by requiring that covered employers develop an employment equity plan with timetables and numerical goals, and designated the Canadian Human Rights Commission as the enforcement agency (Employment Equity Act of 1995, sections 28–31).[6]

The origins and development of employment law in Canada show that feminist women's groups, inspired and influenced by international developments such as declarations and conventions, were influential, at least initially, in keeping economic equality for women on the public agenda. Both Conservative and Liberal administrations were responsive to these demands when movement influence was at its height. Unions and Left parties were not particularly important advocates or catalysts for policy development.

It might appear that unions played more of a role in Israel. The country's first employment discrimination case was brought by a woman flight attendant, who was supported by the working women's section of the trade union Histadrut.[7] Yet apart from this case, there was not much change in women's legal status at work in the country. Although

---

[6] The scope of federal legislation in Canada is narrower than in the United States (Mentzer, 2002), and applies only to certain industries seen as falling under federal responsibility or involving interprovincial commerce or crown corporations.

[7] *Nat'l Labor Court 33/3–25, Comm. of Airline Personnel and El-Al Israel Airline Carrier v. Edna Chazin* PDA 4:365 (1973), cited in Mlundak (2009). Some other antidiscrimination suits had been brought in the 1950s and 1960s, though mostly in the area of family law.

there was a vibrant set of women's organizations at the time, they focused more on service provision than on legal advocacy (Sharfman, 1994; Mlundak, 2009).

The main period of development of equal employment law in Israel occurred only later, in the mid-1980s, when a new focus on legal discrimination in many areas, including employment, emerged (Mlundak, 2009). March of 1982 marked the formal establishment of the organization called the Israeli Feminist Movement, founded to achieve full equality between women and men and to eliminate discrimination in all areas of life, including employment (Sharfman, 1994, p. 387). The mid-1980s saw the creation of the Legal Center for Women's Rights in the Israeli Women's Network, another major multipurpose feminist organization. With a combination of volunteer lawyers and staff, this center advocated legal change both through the Israeli Parliament (the *Knesset*) and the courts. Perhaps not surprisingly, the main developments on employment discrimination occurred in the late 1980s, with the 1987 Equal Retirement Age (Male and Female) Employees Law, the 1988 Equal Employment Opportunities Law, and the development of a more robust sexual harassment regime through amendments to the Civil Code (1990) and the 1995 amendment to the Equal Employment Opportunities Law (Halperin-Kaddari, 2003; Mlundak, 2009; Raday, 2009).

The South African Constitution, adopted in 1996, includes many guarantees against gender discrimination, largely reflecting the influence of the feminist advocates (Goetz, 1998). Women prevailed even in the face of advocacy by traditional leaders from the rural areas (Gouws & Galgut, 2016). During the process of negotiation over constitutional provisions, the Women's National Coalition wrote up an agenda for policies supporting women's rights, called the "Charter for Effective Equality," which came to be called the Women's Charter. These included guarantees against gender discrimination (Article 9 of the 1996 Constitution) and, separately, guarantees of freedom to choose a trade, occupation, or profession or join a union (Article 22) (For discussion see Cotter, 2004, pp. 126–7). Article 181 establishes, among other things, the Commission for Gender Equality, and the functions of this body are laid out in Article 187 as including monitoring, investigating, lobbying, and reporting on gender equality.

During the first five years after the adoption of the 1996 constitution, feminist activists kept up the pressure, demanding further action on their agenda. The women's section of the African National Congress (ANC)

worked to ensure that the proposals contained in the Women's Charter
were implemented by backing, for example, the 1998 Employment Equity
Act. This Act was championed by activists outside of parliament but had
a more mixed reception among women parliamentarians, who split along
party lines. Though the women's section of the ANC supported the bill,
both the opposition National Party and Liberal Party, including women
members, opposed it, seemingly due to resistance to race-based affirmative action (Hassim, 2003).

In the United States, feminist organizing has also been critical to
advancing women's rights in employment, even though the adoption of
the 1963 equal pay act and the inclusion of sex discrimination in the
1964 Civil Rights Act came before the height of feminist organizing (Hoff,
1991). Both of these early measures were linked to feminist organizing
behind the scenes and to activities by feminist bureaucrats and legislators
to some degree,[8] but the feminist movement had not coalesced around a
single set of goals at this point, and was divided or ambivalent about these
measures in their various versions. Historically, some feminist activists
and women's rights advocates had opposed the eradication of state-
sponsored discrimination in labor law, believing that the existence of
so-called protective legislation advanced women's rights. The desire to
defend protective labor legislation motivated some feminists to oppose the
Equal Rights Amendment (ERA).[9] "Protective" or "prohibitive" labor
legislation was also endorsed by male-dominated unions who wanted to
preserve their access to jobs and their higher wages (Wolbrecht, 2000).

Racial politics in the United States also complicated the discussion, as
opponents of civil rights for African Americans supported the amendment
to the Act that included language about "sex" as a prohibited basis for
discrimination. For some supporters, including sex was seen as a way to
weaken the Act (just as support for the ERA was seen as a way to weaken
unions), while for others it was outrageous to prohibit discrimination
on the basis of race but not sex, leaving "white women" in particular

---

[8] For example, the Equal Pay Act was proposed by the head of the Women's Bureau
(Peterson) under the Kennedy Administration, and the inclusion of "sex" in the civil rights
act was also linked to women's organizing, specifically the behind-the-scenes efforts of the
National Women's Party (NWP), an organization of a few hundred mostly white, privileged women with connections to conservative politicians, as well as a handful of feminist
women representatives and senators (Bird, 1997; Brauer, 1983; Freeman, 2008; Rupp &
Taylor, 1987).

[9] In Japan, some women's groups similarly opposed the government's proposals to revise
some protective labor legislation in the late 1970s.

without any basis for complaining of discrimination. In some ways, passage of this important measure was as contingent on particular personalities (Howard Smith, Martha Griffiths) as on feminist organizing.

This pattern changed in the following decade, however. Governmental reluctance to follow through on the promise to eradicate sex discrimination represented by the Civil Rights Act spurred a wave of protest by feminists that led to important improvements in the legal regime governing women's work. Indeed, in 1966, the National Organization for Women was formed to demand implementation of these laws, and waged a decade-long battle to give the Equal Employment Opportunities Commission (the EEOC, the enforcement mechanism for the Civil Rights Act) the teeth needed to ensure compliance with prohibitions on sex discrimination. In 1967, the first "women's liberation" group formed in Chicago and hundreds of local consciousness-raising and radical feminist groups began to organize. The same year, the Johnson Administration issued Executive Order No. 11375, which added "sex" to the categories upon which discrimination by federal contractors was not permitted. 1968 saw the formation of the Women's Education and Action League (WEAL), the organization that filed the first ever sex discrimination lawsuit against the University of Maryland (Hoff, 1991, pp. 236–8). The creation of the President's Commission on the Status of Women in 1969, and its report, strengthened the feminist movement, bringing disparate regional groups together to form a national movement (Duerst-Lahti, 1989; Hoff, 1991).

This ascendant second-wave women's movement demanded action on women's rights, creating political pressure that led to the "spate of women's rights legislation endorsed by the Ninety-Second Congress (1971–3)" (Hoff, 1991). In 1971, then Labor Secretary Shultz issued guidelines requiring all firms doing business with the government to create action plans for hiring and promotion of women. In the same year, Presidential Executive Order No. 11478 condemned sex discrimination by government agencies. Litigation over Title VII increased in the late 1960s, and "numerous lower-court decisions by 1970 not only approved changed EEOC guidelines but also voided a half-century of protective legislation, with Title VII interpretations expanding equal treatment of women in the workplace" (Hoff, 1991, p. 235).

Women's movements were similarly important for the development of equal opportunity legislation in other advanced democracies. In Norway, a coalition of women's groups pushed for the adoption of the Equal Status Act of 1978. Initially opposed by unions, and ultimately adopted under the rule of a conservative party, the Act was an important step toward legal equality for women in the workplace (Weldon, 2011). In Australia, the Women's Electoral Lobby (WEL) was important to the passage of sex discrimination legislation such as the 1976 Sex Discrimination Act (Sawer & Unies, 1996). Swedish women's groups were also important, alongside other groups, in influencing sex discrimination legislation (Lindvert, 2007).

In each of these contexts, then, women's independent organizing was an important part of the story of generating public attention and policy proposals related to women's legal status at work, prompting the expectation that;

H1. The presence of strong feminist movements should be associated with more expansive legislation on women's equal status at work.

International Norms

Our discussion of the role of feminist movements showed that they often drew inspiration and support from international forces. Women's movements working transnationally ensured that principles of equal rights were reflected in global treaties and agreements. As mentioned earlier, CEDAW addresses women's legal status at work in Article 11, which calls on states parties to "take all appropriate measures to eliminate discrimination against women in the field of employment in order to ensure, on a basis of equality of men and women, the same rights." Similarly, the Beijing Platform for Action, endorsed by the world's governments in 1995, calls on states to "Promote women's economic rights and independence, including access to employment, appropriate working conditions and control over economic resources" (Strategic objective F.1) and "eliminate occupational segregation and all forms of employment discrimination" (F.5).

CEDAW ratification provided the impetus for the first EEOL adopted in Japan, mentioned earlier. The Japanese government had originally not planned to sign CEDAW, but eventually caved to pressure and protests from women politicians, women's groups at home and abroad, and the media (Knapp, 1995). The need to comply with the Convention helped overcome domestic political opposition, particularly from business interests (Simmons, 2009).

Australian feminists were similarly inspired by international events surrounding CEDAW in pursuing an expanded sex discrimination law in 1984 (Lindvert, 2007). Similarly, as the earlier discussion of Canadian activism suggests, feminists often shaped their domestic legislative priorities in concert with, or relying on, international commitments made by their governments. Such commitments give feminists standing to demand that the government meet its promises.

In Chapter Two, we showed that regional norms and pressures were especially strong mechanisms for the diffusion of international norms on violence. Regarding work, regional mechanisms have been strongest in Europe. As early as 1975 and 1976, the European Economic Community adopted directives calling for equal pay for women and men and for their equal treatment in employment, working conditions, and vocational training, respectively. As European Union law and regional institutions gained strength, states were compelled to modify their domestic institutions to comply with equal rights directives and their progress was monitored by EU agencies (Council Directive 2000/78/EC).

In other regions, transnational mechanisms developed later. For example, the Organization of African Unity member states adopted the African Charter on Human and People's Rights in 1981 in Nairobi, but the original text lacked specific measures addressing gender discrimination at work. These were affirmed only in 2003, when the Organization of African Unity adopted Article 13 of the Protocol on Women's Rights.[10] Though it comes just at the tail end of our study, and therefore was not as well established as the European norms, we consider whether this regional norm in Africa also makes a difference.

Our discussion of international norms suggests that:

H2. National ratification of international and transnational conventions, agreements and declarations, such as CEDAW ratification, should be associated with more expansive legislation on women's equal status at work.

H3. The presence of regional agreements, like those that apply to EU members and the African Protocol, should be associated with more expansive legislation on women's equal status at work.

We expect CEDAW to become more powerful in later decades of our study period. Baldez (2014) argues that the effects of the Convention gradually increased as CEDAW gained legitimacy, its interpretation

---

[10] Protocol on the Rights of Women, African Commission on Human and People's Rights, www.achpr.org/files/instruments/womenprotocol/achpr_instr_proto_women_eng.pdf; see also Cotter (2004), pp. 122–3.

and application grew clearer, the intrusion of external political considerations (such as the Cold War) diminished, and NGOs became more
explicitly involved in the treaty compliance review process. As this suggests, CEDAW ratification is not a single event with immediate impact,
but rather triggers a political process that develops over time.

Women's Policy Agencies

Various studies have identified the role of women's policy agencies in
promoting equal employment legislation. Stetson and Mazur (1995, p. 3)
define women's policy machineries as "any structure established by government with its main purpose being the betterment of women's social
status." These agencies, often founded in response to feminist demand,
are theorized to be influential because they "allow the entrance of feminist
ideas into the political debate, promote women's interests, and give access
to the women's movement" (see also Bleijenbergh & Roggeband, 2007,
p. 440; Mazur & McBride, 2007; Stetson & Mazur, 1995; True &
Mintrom, 2001; Weldon, 2002a). During the United Nations Decade
for Women (1976–85), approximately two-thirds of member states
adopted women's policy agencies (though of varying strength and prominence) to recommend and promote legal and bureaucratic reforms, and
to administer public policies helping women (Sawer & Unies, 1996, p. 1).

The work of these agencies helped put women's equality on national
agendas. Often, directors and staff of women's agencies lobbied legislators and state officials about women's concerns. In Brazil, for example,
the women's policy agency in the 1980s (called the National Women's
Council) organized women delegates to the country's constituent assembly into a "lipstick lobby" to make sure the new constitution upheld
women's rights in a variety of areas (Pitanguy, 1996). They were successful: One of the first articles upholds the principle of equal rights for
men and women and another article (point 20 under Article 7) calls
for affirmative action in the form of "protection of the labor market for
women through specific incentives, as provided by law."[11]

The impact of women's policy agencies has been particularly visible in
Australia. Australian feminists formed the WEL, a nonpartisan

---

[11] The translated text of the Brazilian Constitution is available at the Political Database of
the Americas, a service of the Center for Latin American Studies of the Edmund A. Walsh
School of Foreign Service. http://pdba.georgetown.edu/Constitutions/Brazil/english96
.html#mozTocId847721.

organization to press women's policy demands, in 1972. They succeeded in getting a women's advisor to the prime minister appointed, and then successfully pushed for the creation of the Office of the Status of Women (Sawer & Unies, 1996, pp. 4–5). Australian "femocrats" were able to secure numerous policy changes, primarily during periods of Labor governments. In 1975, the Sex Discrimination Act was passed, which created a complaints-based enforcement process. Ratification of CEDAW gave the government a basis for federal legislation on women's rights (Sawer & Unies, 1996, p. 9). The 1984 Federal Sex Discrimination Act (Cotter, 2004, p. 96) created a Sex Discrimination Commissioner to oversee implementation. This year also saw the first women's budget, and public service reforms introduced equal opportunity programs. The enforcement agency (HREOC) was charged with inquiring into complaints and carrying out research and education. In 1993, the provisions on sex discrimination were strengthened in the Commonwealth Sex Discrimination Act.

In some countries, as we noted in Chapter 2, women's policy agencies are poorly designed, lack resources, and wield little influence or expertise. They may be mere window dressing or symbolic reforms aimed at making it look like action is being taken, when in fact nothing is being done. But elsewhere, agencies are important centers of expertise and resources, providing support to women's advocacy groups and offering concrete policy proposals (Stetson & Mazur, 1995; McBride & Mazur, 2010, 2011; Weldon, 2002a). Sometimes, they are given cross-sectoral influence and have access to political leaders. Again, we suggest, drawing on the literature, that policy agencies that are well-positioned and supported are the ones that are most likely to make a difference.

These experiences suggest that:

H4. Effective women's policy agencies should be associated with more expansive laws on women's equal status at work.

Left Parties

Whereas the political strength of unions and Left parties may be associated with class policies and other redistributive efforts, it is not likely to be the principal factor behind change in gender status policies such as legal equality for women at work. In fact, unions in some countries have opposed sex equality in the workplace, particularly the eradication of "protectionist" labor legislation. By banning women from certain occupations, such legislation reduced competition for male union members' jobs (Wolbrecht, 2000). Labor unions have sometimes been criticized for being poor advocates for working women, and Left parties have sometimes failed women more generally, failing to prioritize sex equality when it seems like other considerations may prevail. Both unions and Left parties have become important allies for women's movements in many places, and on some policies, but on status issues Left parties have not been the instigators of change, and have even at times been opponents of advances in women's rights.

H5. The strength of Left, labor, or union-backed parties should not be associated with the more expansive legislation on women's equal status at work.

STATISTICAL ANALYSIS

To explore these relationships and hypotheses, we analyzed the relationship between several independent variables and the dependent variable, our Index of Sex Equality in Legal Status at Work, which sums the index for state discrimination (coded so that less discrimination is better), formal legal equality, and substantive equality measures. Values range from 0 to 17 (though no state has a score lower than 2).[12] Our models included the factors mentioned earlier (feminist movements, CEDAW ratification, women's policy agencies, Left parties) as well as several controls, including economic development, degree of democracy, a communist legacy, the presence of religious legislation, women in parliament, and women's labor force participation. We used random effects regression analysis to take the panel structure of the data into account.[13] The results of the analysis are reported in Table 3.4.

---

[12] This sort of variable is not an event count variable and the assumptions behind analytic techniques designed to handle count variables (for example, Poisson regression) are often violated by these data. To take just one example, the index does not sum events that are *independent*. For more on Poisson regression and the assumptions required see Winkelmann, 1997. For more on why this specific type of index of policy scope is not an event count, see Weldon 2002a, 2006a; Htun and Weldon 2012.

[13] The two main panel data analysis techniques are known as fixed effects (FE) and random effects (RE). FE models absorb the time-invariant differences and drop out those explanatory factors that do not change over time, making them inappropriate for a study like ours that aims to take into account both relatively static features (such as religious type) and more dynamic variables (such as feminist movement strength). RE models are appropriate when it seems that differences across entities have some influence on the dependent variable and they can include time-invariant variables (Clark & Linzer, 2015).

TABLE 3.4 Coefficients, Overall Legal Equality at Work Index, GLS random effects models, 1975–2005

Model	1	2	3	4	5	6	7
Variables							
Strong, autonomous feminist movement	.530**	.490**	.639***	.492**	.650**	.660***	.644***
	(.224)	(.223)	(.247)	(.224)	(.255)	(.248)	(.246)
CEDAW ratification	.303			.160			
	(.364)			(.372)			
Regional agreement	1.615***	1.493***	1.009**	1.509***	.980**	.869*	.994**
	(.425)	(.434)	(.436)	(.429)	(.453)	(.446)	(.430)
Effective women's policy machinery		.773**	.098	.645*	.141		
		(.373)	(.373)	(.382)	(.377)		
Left party strength (cumulative)						.007	
						(.004)	
Official Religion	-1.190***	-1.383***	-1.211**	-1.256***	-1.024**	-1.274***	-1.198**
	(.446)	(.447)	(.486)	(.448)	(.515)	(.477)	(.484)
High Religiosity					-.076		
					(.632)		
Muslim Majority					-.786		
					(.770)		
Catholic Majority					.149		
					(.581)		
Women in Parliament (%)	.088***	.094***	.068***	.080***	.068***	.073***	.068***
	(.019)	(.019)	(.019)	(.020)	(.019)	(.019)	(.019)
Former Colony	2.002***	1.729***	1.651**	1.844***	1.529**	1.442*	1.577**
	(.595)	(.550)	(.704)	(.603)	(.739)	(.652)	(.681)
GDP (logged)	4.451***	4.368***	4.816***	4.289***	4.508***	4.443***	4.727***
	(.562)	(.496)	(.738)	(.570)	(.783)	(.755)	(.718)

(continued)

TABLE 3.4 (continued)

Model	1	2	3	4	5	6	7
Variables							
Communist	1.064*	1.521**	.862	1.251**	.905	1.290**	.920
	(.618)	(.627)	(.663)	(.629)	(.694)	(.653)	(.641)
Female labor force participation rate	.026*			.023			.022
	(.014)			(.014)			(.015)
CEDAW ratification (Lagged)			1.275***		1.335***	1.316***	1.313***
			(.328)		(.332)	(.326)	(.316)
Female labor force participation rate (Lagged)			.023		.016		
			(.015)		(.017)		
Observations	254	258	196	254	196	199	196
Overall R-squared	.620	.608	.645	.624	.655	.637	.648
Number of Countries	69	70	69	69	69	70	69

Notes: Estimates are from random effects regression models. Standard errors are in parentheses. *, **, and *** denote statistical significance at the 10, 5, and 1 percent levels, respectively.

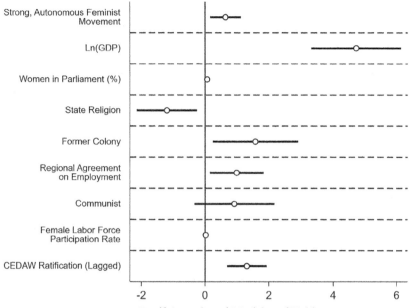

FIGURE 3.5 Coefficient plot of Model 7 of Table 3.4

Table 3.4 reports seven models, designed to examine the effects of the various modeling strategies employed. Model 1 includes all the factors we explicitly theorized to be important as well as controls that are necessary to capture the relevant impact in this area (female labor force participation, logged GDP). All models include those factors we have argued were important earlier in the book (religious variables) whenever they are statistically significant. Model 2 introduces those factors thought to be important in the literature (women's policy machineries) and Models 3 and 4 combine these elements, showing how they perform together. Model 5 demonstrates the impact of a range of religious variables, and Model 6 shows the (non-)impact of Left parties. Model 7 is the same as the first except that the CEDAW ratification variable is lagged. We discuss and compare these models and the variables in the models below. Figure 3.5 presents a coefficient plot of Model 7 in Table 3.4.

As we expected, the sandwich model of strong, autonomous women's movements and international and regional instruments working together to drive policy adoption is consistent with the patterns we see here. The strong, autonomous feminist movement has small but significant and positive impacts in each model. Other variables (such as GDP) have larger effects, but the direction and reliability of the association with women's movements is important. Exploratory modeling revealed that the association with feminist movements was strongest in developed countries and for the range of policies we call "substantive equality." This is precisely what we would expect, given our theoretical approach that focuses on movements as uniquely able to articulate women's distinctive needs, and as key catalysts (but not the sole determinants) of government action to advance women's legal status at work.

The impact of international norms and regional conventions is also part of the story. The discussion above pointed to CEDAW as particularly relevant, but especially over the longer term. Looking at the relationship between CEDAW ratification and immediate policy change revealed only small, positive but insignificant associations. Going back to our theoretical expectations, as well as the patterns observed in the case we discussed, suggests that CEDAW ratification took some time to have an effect. Our analysis of violence against women in Chapter 2 also suggested that CEDAW had a greater impact over time. Given this lag, we also examined whether looking at CEDAW ratification a decade out made more of a difference. We found that it did, and the lagged CEDAW ratification variable (in Models 6 and 7) proved to be a strong predictor of government action to promote women's legal status in the workplace, adding additional areas of legal equality.

Regional conventions and agreements can sometimes be even more powerful drivers of women's rights than international ones, especially when there are strong transnational networks of transnational activists (Htun and Weldon 2012). The literature points to EU agreements as being very influential for member states, and we find that EU membership has a small but positive and significant association with increased action to promote sex equality, as expected (not shown).

On the African continent, the Charter might also be thought of as an emergent norm. The protocol on women's rights specifies several legal principles relating to equality at work. While the Charter itself had not reached a "tipping" point, and was not as well established as the EU mechanisms discussed, states that had signed on to the Women's Rights protocol to the Charter might be thought of as early adopters, or norm-givers in the region. Our coding for regional agreements, then, also captures participation in the African protocol. The presence of a regional norm is associated with greater scope of action promoting women's rights in employment, and controlling for regional influences helps refine the impact of CEDAW as a specific measure.

In several models (3, 5, 6, 7), both feminist activism and international norms (*CEDAW ratification*, lagged) are strongly associated with progressive policies. This result is consistent with either additive effects of CEDAW ratification (as we modeled them here) or interactive effects (as we modeled them in Chapter 2). In an additional model (not shown, but available in the replication files), we did not see the powerful effect of mutual magnification so clearly manifest.[14]

Our analysis also offers some insights into why women's policy machineries sometimes seem to matter and at other times do. The literature would lead us to expect that an *Effective women's policy machinery* would be a good predictor of the likelihood of reform, but this relationship did not seem to hold consistently in the data (H2, Models 2, 3, 4, 5). The strength of the relationship (as reflected in the level of significance) between women's policy machinery and legal equality varied across models, as did the size of the coefficient. Particularly when we controlled for the longer-term effects of CEDAW ratification (CEDAW ratification lagged), the relationship between policy machineries and legal equality appeared to be weaker, with smaller coefficients, suggesting that the effects of CEDAW ratification over time are tapping the same processes leading to establishment of women's policy machineries, which is entirely possible. As we discussed, many such agencies were established as part of the process of complying with CEDAW, and so may be understood as part of the same phenomenon. Where CEDAW or other regional norms are already exerting an effect, the impact of women's policy machinery may be less dramatic.

Our framework also leads us to expect that Left and labor parties are not associated with action on sex equality in this area. To explore this hypothesis, we investigated whether the strength of Left parties was associated with greater sex equality in laws governing women's work (H4). Many scholars have used the strength of Left parties as a proxy for labor mobilization (e.g., Esping-Andersen, 1990). We found only statistically insignificant associations between Left parties in government and greater sex equality, whether we used a dummy variable for presence of a Left party (not shown), a measure of union density (available only for

---

[14] Since using the lagged ratification variable cuts down the number of cases, we are left with few degrees of freedom to explore the interaction, producing less robust analytic results. Interested readers can explore these nonfindings in Model 8 in the replication files. We hope that further research can explore whether the "circle of empowerment," mutually reinforcing model has better purchase in another context or dataset.

a smaller number of countries) (not shown), or a more refined measure of Left-party power capturing all the seats controlled by Left parties in the legislature and the cumulation of such influence over the decades (Model 6). None of these specifications revealed stronger relationships. We also tried other measures (such as potential labor power) and still failed to find a relationship (not shown).[15] As this suggests, there is no strong or statistically significant relationship between Left parties and sex equality laws, especially compared to the effects of women's movements and international institutions. This result conforms to our expectations about women's movements mattering more than Left parties for "gender status" policy issues.

We also expected religious factors to be less important here. This was true for most religious variables, but the impact of a constitutionally established religion did appear to have a consistently and significantly negative effect, being associated with about one fewer area of government action. Other religious factors, such as religiosity or religious denomination, had no association, as expected. This is in sharp contrast to other areas we have examined, where religious factors, regardless of the specific operationalization, showed consistently negative and frequently significant associations – effects that were robust across a variety of types of religious indicators and regardless of measure. The impact of constitutionally established religion here may be more reflective of the continuity of general institutional legacies associated with lack of change in the area of women's rights, rather than religion per se.

The analysis of the variable for communism is even weaker. In the case of VAW, we found that communism suppressed women's organizing and indirectly delayed action on women's rights. For doctrinal policies, we expect (and find, in Chapter 4) that communist efforts to reduce the influence of religious institutions produced lasting effects on women's rights. Such powerful, large, and consistent effects are not in evidence here, even though one might think that a communist legacy would be more direct for a work-related area like women's legal status at work. We would think that communism would have had a mixed impact in this area, associated with the greater likelihood of reform of religiously inspired restrictions on women's rights, but with support for formal egalitarian measures, and more weakly associated with

---

[15] Some measures (for example, a dummy variable for Left parties or a measure of ideology) produced barely significant (p = .05 or .06) results in this analysis, but these were not robust and effects were small.

substantive equality. The experience of communism was mostly associated with legal reforms in the expected direction (positive), but effects were small compared to the associations observed in other areas (see our analysis of family law) and the variable was significant in only a few models (Models 2, 4, and 6).

The percentage of parliamentary seats occupied by women was consistently significantly and positively associated with greater equality in laws governing the workplace. Differences over time and across countries of one standard deviation are associated with a bit less than one additional point on the scale. This suggests that a change of one standard deviation (ten percentage points more parliamentary seats occupied by women) would be associated with almost one additional sex equality measure, or area (or a bit less: .09*10= .9). Changes of such magnitude are rare, however, even over a decade, perhaps accounting for why the literature rarely points to women in government as a key element driving sex equality law in this area. A larger proportion of women in the legislature may make policy processes more amenable to the adoption of laws promoting women's rights in the workplace (or vice versa), especially together with other actors and influences advocating such change, such as feminist movements, women's policy agencies, and international and regional norms.

Some of the control variables exhibited less expected, if significant, results. A colonial experience was associated with greater sex equality as well, which was not expected. Perhaps this is the other side of the effect of constitutionally established religion, suggesting that discontinuities create opportunities for reform while continuities impede them when it comes to women's rights in the workplace. Democracy level, using Polity measures, had no relationship at all with sex equality in workplace laws (not shown).

Although the positive impact of logged GDP was in the expected direction, the impact was more significant than one might have expected. National wealth, per capita, appears to have the strongest and largest association with legal equality than any other variable in the model. With a standard deviation of 1.09, a one-SD change in the variable is associated with about four or five additional areas of sex equality. For a dependent variable with a range of 17, this is a sizable effect (though clearly, other factors are also involved). Functional explanations are tempting to explore. Greater wealth translates into more economic opportunities for women and more demand for legal reform. Such a relationship should be picked up by the measure of female labor force participation, but that variable does not add much. Modernization explanations are also tempting, but one would expect to see stronger associations with religiosity and female labor force participation on that score. Also, the most prevalent legal barriers to women's work are in the MENA region – a wealthier, if more religious, region. One conclusion might be that in wealthier countries, more women are in the paid labor market and so women's movements focus more on these guarantees, while in developing countries, the informal nature of women's work makes legal guarantees pertaining primarily to formal work less of a priority. Still, one would think that women's labor force participation would be a proxy for this explanation as well. Nor can GDP be seen as a proxy for state capacity, which also seems to perform poorly in our models (not shown).

In the main, then, the results of statistical analysis for this issue-area conform to our expectations about the importance of autonomous feminist movements for a "gender status" policy issue such as women's legal status at work. Since legal status is an issue affecting all women, regardless of their class background, ethnic identities, and other affiliations, and since it involves change in the meaning of women's roles, we expected that autonomous feminist organizing would be associated with more expansive policies. We do not expect this to be the case with issues such as parental leave and childcare, which we will turn to in a later chapter. Though feminist movements care about, and have mobilized around, these issues, a broader coalition and more conducive contextual factors are necessary to initiate welfare state expansion and other changes in state–market relations.

CONCLUSION

Although this area of women's rights relates to their economic autonomy and well-being, it is primarily a question of legal status and less one of class. For this reason, autonomous feminist organizing is a key driver of change, with international conventions adding weight to women's claims. In addition, especially over the long term, international and regional norms as expressed in conventions and other agreements strengthen domestic actors seeking change and are particularly influential in those contexts where dependence on the international community is greater (for example, those countries more dependent on foreign aid). As we will see, however, when advancing gender equality fundamentally challenges the organization of state–market relationships, the story becomes quite different. We turn to this next dimension of economic rights in Chapter 5.

Are legal reforms sufficient to achieve economic equality? In Western countries, equal opportunity policy was perceived "simultaneously as a success and a failure" (Mazur, 2002, p. 82). Though equal legal status was achieved on the books, women did not gain parity with men in pay, organizational hierarchies, or meaningful work. This suggests that change in women's legal status alone has not been enough to create conditions for economic equality. Though such policies shape the rights and circumstances of women in the workplace, they do not address the social conditions *outside* of wage work that shape women's choices and employer decisions. To address such conditions, feminist activists have lobbied for an expansion of those social policies that help to make wage work and caregiving more compatible (work–life balance or reconciliation policy). In the next chapters, we focus more on the family, studying both family law (Chapter 4), which we characterize as a "doctrinal policy," and publicly funded parental leave and childcare (Chapter 5), which we characterize as "class policies" that allocate public resources to alleviate the reproductive labor the gender system assigns to women as a class. Such policies alter state–market relations to help women (and men) simultaneously meet their caregiving and wage-work responsibilities.

4

Doctrinal Politics

Religious Power, the State, and Family Law

Family law is an essential dimension of women's citizenship in the modern state.[1] The rights established in family law shape women's agency and autonomy; they also regulate access to basic resources – such as land, income, and education – that determine a citizen's ability to earn a living independently (Agarwal, 1994; Deere & Leon, 2001; Halley & Rittich, 2010; Kabeer, 1994; Okin, 1989; World Bank, 2012). Yet the family law upheld by the state is a notorious site of inequality. Legal unification and codification during periods of state building and Western colonization tended to produce patriarchal outcomes in many places, even in contexts where a diversity of family forms and even women's freedoms had flourished (Ahmed, 1992; Dore, 2000; Glendon, 1989; Tucker, 2008). The Napoleonic Code, Muslim personal status laws, the Hindu Code Bill, and Anglo-American common law, for example, upheld the notion that men were in charge of family life: They controlled property, were the legal guardians of children, and had the right to restrict their wives' public activities. Women were obliged to obey their husbands and had limited access to divorce and, in many traditions, fewer inheritance rights than men.[2] (For a description of the evolution of family law in most of the world's legal traditions, see Appendix B at the end of this book.)

[1] An earlier version of this chapter was published as Mala Htun and S. Laurel Weldon, Religious power, the state, women's rights, and family law. *Politics & Gender*, 11 (September 2015), 1–27.
[2] To be sure, other family forms and social orders around the world deviate from patriarchal models. For example, polyandry (wives taking multiple husbands) was practiced in the Ladakh region of India before being banned in the 1940s by the government of Jammu and Kashmir. Traces of the practice can still be encountered today. In addition, polyandry

Many countries liberalized their family laws over the course of the twentieth century to promote equality and expand individual rights. Communist countries in the West and East reformed family law to eliminate religious and traditional influences, promote women's participation in the labor force, and encourage broader social transformation (Berman, 1946; Massell, 1968; Molyneux, 1985a). Most European and North American countries expanded women's freedoms in the mid- to late twentieth century (Glendon, 1989, 1987). Several East Asian countries eliminated patriarchal provisions in family law, though at different times: Japan was earlier to change than Korea, for example (in 1948 and 1990, respectively). Meanwhile, other countries held onto restrictive laws, including many – but not all – states in the Middle East and North African (MENA) region, as well as many postcolonial states with multiple legal systems of statutory, customary, or religious law (Cohen, 2012; Halperin-Kaddari, 2003; Musawah, 2009; Williams, 2006; Women Living under Muslim Laws, 2006). Into the twenty-first century, family law in a significant number of countries continued to discriminate against women, denying them the rights held by men and contributing to their disadvantaged social positions.

Why do some countries have family laws that uphold women's rights, while others do not? This chapter shows that the state's approach to religion is a major factor associated with the degree of sex equality in family law. As argued in Chapter 1, gender issues have different histories, activate distinct conflicts and political cleavages, and involve different sets of actors. Whereas other women's rights issues conform to logics of status politics and class politics, we argue that family law, abortion, and other reproductive rights conform to a logic of doctrinal politics. Doctrinal politics involves expanding the realm of deliberative and accountable politics vis-à-vis the domains of religion and culture.

---

has been observed in precontact Polynesian societies (Goldman, 1970) and among the Masai (a highly patriarchal society). Turning to a different dimension of variability, some societies are matrilineal, including the federation of societies known as the Iroquois. These groups also reserved some governing functions for women: The clan mothers of the Oneida selected those who served on the governing council and made all decisions about land, property, and family. Some customary laws in Africa granted women more rights to land than the colonial laws that replaced them. Our review focuses on the world's most influential (and patriarchal) legal traditions. The fact that we do not focus on these alternative traditions should not be taken to imply that other historical and cultural patterns did not exist. There are many other examples of societies that upheld special roles for brothers, uncles, and other male and female kin.

Many scholars of gender and politics have emphasized religion's influence over family law (and women's rights more generally) (see, e.g., Blofield, 2013; Charrad, 2001; Htun, 2003; Kang, 2015; Moghadam, 2003,
2009; Razavi & Jenichen, 2010; Williams, 2006). There is less consensus
about *what it is about religion* that matters, and why and how it matters.
Some scholars working with a broad cross-national perspective focus on
particular religions, such as Islam or Catholicism (Alexander & Welzel,
2009; Castles, 1998; Cherif, 2010, p. 1154; Donno & Russett, 2004; Fish,
2002); others connect gender equality to the degree of religiosity of a society
(Inglehart & Norris, 2003). In this chapter, we stress the importance of the
institutionalized relations between state and religion for family law outcomes, which vary considerably across countries. Some states resist intervention in religious affairs, while others confer official status on particular
religions through constitutional establishment, funding, and enforcement of
religious legislation, among other measures (Fox, 2008, 2013).

Our statistical analysis reveals a strong association between the political
institutionalization of religious authority and sex equality in family law. In
countries where political and ecclesiastical power are tightly linked, family
law tends to discriminate against women. In the context of a separation
of secular and religious institutions, family law tends to be more egalitarian. When religion is institutionalized, patriarchal interpretations – and
interpreters – of family law gain greater authority and more immunity to
contestation, and are increasingly insulated from external influences. What
is more, these patriarchal versions of religious tradition get more closely
linked to the public status of religion. Challenges to particular versions of
family law are seen as challenges to the entire church–state relationship.

We do not argue that any and all religions are patriarchal. Religions are
best understood as "multivocal" (Stepan, 2000): Doctrinal interpretations
of women's rights vary within faiths and over time. For example, though
state officials and conservative clerics often invoke Islam to defend patriarchal laws, most contemporary movements for egalitarian family law in
the Muslim world also present their claims within a religious framework
(Abu-Odeh, 2004; Badran, 2009; Balchin, 2009; Mir-Hosseini, 1999,
2006; Othman, Anwar, & Kasim, 2005; Singerman, 2005).[3] People have
justified practices of sex discrimination *and* legitimized projects of gender
equality in the name of religion. As this suggests, religious doctrine is not a

[3] Scholars of Islamic constitutionalism claim that pluralism originates in earlier traditions,
but that citizen contestation over religious law was stymied by the state (Quraishi, 2008,
2012).

thing; it is a site of struggle (Bayat, 2007, p. 4; see also Hajjar, 2004; Mir-Hosseini, 2006). We show in this chapter that the political institutionalization of religious authority – not the hegemony of a particular religion, the strength of religious beliefs, or the assertion of spiritual values by a political party – is a key religious factor associated with differences in discriminatory outcomes across countries.

This chapter stresses the importance of historical experiences of colonialism and communism, which shaped the contemporary contours of family law by establishing a legacy of state–religion relations. Colonialism tended to enhance religion's importance: Colonial rulers of many countries empowered traditional and religious rulers to administer family and other customary laws, while usurping their authority to govern other areas of social and political life. In addition, many colonial powers codified diverse and variable practices of family law, thereby inventing not just the traditions but also the communities they applied to (Kang, 2015; Ranger, 1983; Williams, 2006). These moves linked the status of religious and cultural identities to the fate of family law. The experience of communism had the opposite effect. Communist governments sought to reduce religious power and expand women's rights. They replaced conservative family laws with egalitarian models, which endured for the most part into the postcommunist era.

Institutionalized state–religion relations set the stage for more and less egalitarian family laws, but did not determine the outcome. Organized social forces shaped the degree to which laws upheld women's rights. For example, many states that separated from religion – including the United States, France, and Turkey – continued to uphold male dominance and privilege in family law for decades, reflecting and contributing to sexist ideas and practices in the broader society (Landes, 1988; Glendon, 1989; Kandiyoti, 1991b; Kerber, 1998; Cott, 2000). The mere absence of religious obstacles was not enough to guarantee legal equality in these countries. The global growth of the feminist movement and the consolidation of international norms on women's human rights (embodied in the Convention on the Elimination of All Forms of Discrimination against Women – CEDAW – and other agreements) inspired local coalitions to mobilize around egalitarian reform of family and civil codes. As we see in this chapter, the presence of strong feminist movements is linked to more egalitarian family law. Feminists have forged alliances to push for reform, even in otherwise inauspicious contexts. However, reformist coalitions were more likely to succeed when they did not have to face the additional hurdle of challenging the religious orientation of the state.

FAMILIES AND FAMILY LAW

Family law consists of legal norms governing the formation and internal relations of families, which we define as "social units created by biological or affective ties among people who commonly contribute to one another's economic, moral, and psychological well-being" (Minow, 1987, pp. 959–60). Family law includes rules about marriage and its dissolution; the respective rights, obligations, and capacities of spouses; the relationship between parents and children; marital property; child custody or guardianship; and inheritance. These rules are usually – but not always – codified in national civil or family codes and expressed in judicial decisions. In this chapter, we do not consider the myriad other ways that modern states affect women and families, including, but not limited to, maternity and parental leave, childcare provision, tax credits, rules on part time and flexible work, sick leave, and family allowances. These family policies are wrapped up in discourses about budgets and redistribution in a way that family law is not, while family law tends to touch upon religious doctrine more directly than other family-related policies (Htun & Weldon, 2010; Lowi, 1964). We analyze parental leave and childcare in Chapter 5.

Families are crucial to politics. The earliest political institutions grew out of family and kin networks (Adams, 2005; Weber, 1978), and family relations historically supplied normative models of political authority (Cott, 2000).[4] At the same time, politics constructs the family. Its definition and boundaries – not to mention the roles, relations, and identities of its members – are constituted by political processes and especially by the modern state (see, e.g., Halley & Rittich, 2010; Nicholson, 1986; Okin, 1989; Olsen, 1985; Rhode, 1989). Families do not exist prior to politics; rather, notions of the family as primordial and prepolitical are the result of politics.[5] Diverse political actors invoke the family to advance their political agendas and the family is the site of ideological and distributional battles (Minow, 1987; Mohamad, 2009; Strach, 2006; Thomas, 2011).

---

[4] To be sure, not all political theorists have argued for the alignment of familial and political authority. This was the subject of Locke's classic response to Filmer's identification of monarchical and patriarchal authority (Locke, 1988). Still, many political, legal, and philosophical discourses identify the family as the basic unit of social and political organization and the primary arena for the moral development and education of citizens (Hegel, 1999; Okin, 1989; Rawls, 1971).

[5] As Butler argues with regard to the subject, it is "perhaps *most* political at the point in which it is claimed to be prior to politics itself" (1994, p. 163).

Leaders of many religions and cultures historically used family law to demarcate the present and future membership of their communities. Family law provisions – especially relating to marriage and birth – have determined who can become a member of a group and who is responsible for maintaining its values and ways of life. Sexuality in general, and women's sexuality in particular, has figured prominently: By regulating how, when, and with whom a woman bears children, family law controls entrance into the community. In this way, Shachar notes, family laws "fulfill a task similar to that of citizenship law for a state ... [they] provide the bonds which connect the past to the future, by identifying who is considered part of the tradition" (2001, p. 45). As deployed by (usually male) cultural authorities, family law connects the status of individual women to the construction and maintenance of group cultural identity (Cohen, 2012; Okin, 1999; Razavi & Jenichen, 2010; Shachar, 2001, 2008).[6]

Family law also has a distributive function. It allocates rights, responsibilities, and privileges between men and women, parents and children, brothers and sisters, and so forth (Shachar 2001, pp. 54–5). These rules have tended to put women at a disadvantage relative to men and perpetuated their dependence on other family members. For example, most legal traditions historically granted husbands greater – if not exclusive – control over common property during (and often after) marriage and limited women's ability to seek independent work and obtain divorce. Women, who play such an important role demarcating the boundaries of the cultural community, are the ones most often disabled by its family law.

Modern states are relative newcomers to family law (Glendon, 1989; Charrad, 2001). Historically, family law consisted of rules, norms, and decisions over kinship and reproduction that were interpreted and administered by traditional rulers including chiefs, heads of clans, and religious officials. The decision to impose central power over family law, or to delegate its administration to traditional and religious authorities, marked a crucial juncture in the state building process. In North Africa, for

---

[6] The connection between religion, culture, and family law is the product of politics, not a transhistorical condition. As Halley and Rittich (2010) put it: "Family law did not always exist; rather, it was invented" (p. 755). And one crucial reason it was invented was to separate a domain of group status and community ties from the more universal, global domain of the world capitalist economy.

example, weaker central leaders preserved traditional Muslim family laws to appease clan groups (Morocco) and stronger central leaders broke clan power by secularizing the law in national family codes (Tunisia) (Charrad, 2001). In India, Nehru, following British policy, opted not to secularize family law but to preserve separate personal laws for the main religious groups so as to ease Muslim fears about their domination by Hindus in Independent India, particularly after partition (Williams, 2006).

When it became an independent state, Israel left largely intact the personal status components of the Ottoman *millet* system it inherited through the British mandate (Sezgin, 2013, pp. 77–9). Religious courts of fourteen officially recognized communities have exclusive jurisdiction over marriage, divorce, and other family matters, and they regularly apply provisions that contradict constitutional principles of equal rights. Preservation of the *millet* system enabled Israeli leaders to promote the religious identity of the state and a unification of Jewish identities, while simultaneously differentiating Jews from non-Jewish groups. Sezgin characterizes the Israeli policy as a nation-building project of "vertical segmentation and horizontal homogenization" (Sezgin, 2013, pp. 93–8).

Often, states pursued their political projects through family law. The Khmer Rouge regime in Cambodia (1975–9), for example, used family law – in particular through a policy of forced marriages – as a tool to organize society. As Jacobs describes, state officials in many regions matched spouses themselves, often on the spot at community meetings, and presided over group weddings. The regime's objective was to become the "rightful 'parent' of the nation" (p. 18), to assemble society into rural collectives, to stimulate population growth (which included close monitoring of sexual intercourse among couples), and to promote social homogeneity (since people were paired with similar "types") (Jacobs, 2017).

Communist governments in West and East adopted secular and egalitarian family laws to build national power while marginalizing traditional religions, premodern cultures, and tribal mores (Berman, 1946; Glendon, Gordon, & Osakwe, 1985; Hazard, 1939; Molyneux, 1985a). In addition, liberating women was a means to achieve other ends, such as expanding the labor force. Improved rights were also intended to mobilize women in support of the new social order.

Some state-building projects preserved religious and customary family law in bargains to consolidate their power, while others suppressed traditional religions and customs. For both types of projects, women's status in family law served as an instrument of state consolidation. State elites aimed to improve their power and position, not improve women's autonomy, dignity, or rights. As a result, official efforts to "emancipate" women were rarely accompanied by moves to create the space for autonomous women's organizations to formulate and represent their own interests (Kandiyoti, 1991a, p. 13; Molyneux, 1985a; Najmabadi, 1991, pp. 60–3). State officials could quickly take rights away depending on what they deemed to be in the nation's interest.

Although egalitarian family law tends to correlate *today* with greater official secularism (while discrimination is associated with greater official religiosity), secular states have not *always* promoted women's rights. Secular codifications of family law were often as discriminatory as those of a more explicitly religious nature. For example, the Swiss Civil Code and the Turkish Code that copied it –adopted in 1907 and 1926 respectively – were secular *and* sexist. Women's legal status in those countries differed little from the religiously inspired laws codified around the same time in Egypt.

Nor is religion always bad for equality. Religious perspectives on women's rights vary depending on which representation of the religion one encounters. Religious traditions are always contested. Some groups of men currently privileged by a religious tradition may be particularly keen to defend that tradition, ignoring alternate interpretations or precedents. Other groups of men and women may find a different tradition more compelling. Some religious traditions honor spaces for reflective deliberation by all participants about the nature of tradition itself. As we show in this chapter, the association between the political institutionalization of religious authority and discriminatory law is more a function of patriarchal control of religion than of innate doctrines or traditions. The interpretation of religious doctrine depends on who speaks in religion's name.

GLOBAL VARIATION IN FAMILY LAW

We measured women's rights in family law by studying formal, codified legal provisions. To compare across countries and over time, we created a new index of sex equality in family law ("Index"), which constitutes the dependent variable of this chapter's analysis. The Index assesses formal legal equality in thirteen areas, including marriage, property, parenting, inheritance, and divorce. Values range from 0 to 13. The higher the value of the Index, the more a country's legal regime has approximated formal equality. (See Table 4.1.)

Each element of the Index is coded (0, 1) to indicate whether or not the provision in question disadvantages women or promotes equal rights. The maximum score, 13, indicates that a country's family laws are free from discrimination in all thirteen areas, while the minimum score, 0, means that a country discriminates against women in all thirteen dimensions analyzed. Cronbach's alpha for these thirteen items is .91. Each element of the Index is weighted equally.[7]

In countries with single, national legal regimes, we coded the Family Code or the Civil Code. In federal countries without national family codes, we were often able to code federal court decisions establishing parameters constraining state laws, and model laws adopted in influential states (such as the Mexican Federal Civil Code). In countries with multiple legal systems (India, Israel, Kenya, Malaysia, Nigeria, and so forth), we tended to follow two rules: (1) we opted to code codified, statutory law and not customary law and (2) we opted to code the law governing the largest population group (such as the Hindu Code Bill in India). Our coding method is similar to that used by the World Bank's Women, Business, and the Law group, which coded the law applying to a woman residing in the country's primary business city (World Bank, 2013).

The formal equality measured by our Index signals an elimination of legal gender discrimination. Some scholars are critical of those who focus on formal equality (Rhode, 1989), and we agree with many of these critics that eliminating official discrimination is not sufficient for the achievement of full, substantive equality. (We argued this same point in the previous chapter.) Nevertheless, formal equality is an important component of gender equality more generally and is more variable globally and over time than many people realize. Our Index captures the degree to which states have upheld the value of equality by eliminating the most egregious and disadvantageous gender differences in family law, setting the stage for more nuanced legislation and jurisprudence to promote substantive equality.

---

[7] Our measure provides a sense of the extent of equality across many areas of family law. We do not claim that each area is equally salient in all national cases. Equal weighting offers simplicity and transparency, important features of a new measure. The detailed item scores are available on Htun's personal website for people who wish to try other weighting schemes.

TABLE 4.1 *Family Law Index*

Element	Description	
Inheritance	Men (sons, brothers, widowers) inherit more than women of equal status by law or in the event of intestate succession	0 = yes; 1 = no
Spousal rights and duties	Men have more power than women: The law stipulates, for example, that wives must obey their husbands	0 = yes; 1 = no
Guardianship	The father holds or exercises parental power or legal guardianship over minor children	0 = yes; 1 = no
Marital property regime	The marital property regime gives women fewer rights, for example, by naming the husband as executor of community property	0 = yes; 1 = no
Right to work	Wives need their husbands' permission to work, or husbands can legally prevent their wives from working	0 = yes; 1 = no
Name	The law requires a common marital name	0 = yes; 1 = no
Minimum marriage age	No minimum age of marriage, or different minimum ages for women and men	0 = yes; 1 = no
Consent	Marital consent discriminates against women, for example by accepting the consent of people other than the spouses to validate a marriage	0 = yes; 1 = no
Marriage ban	The law forbids people (or only women) from marrying certain categories or groups besides relatives	0 = yes; 1 = no
Divorce	Men and women do not have equal rights to divorce or the country does not legally permit divorce	0 = yes; 1 = no
Custody after divorce	The law gives fathers guardianship or custody of children following divorce, even if the mother has temporary custody	0 = yes; 1 = no
Property after divorce	The division of property after divorce favors the man, for example by presuming that he will keep common property such as the marital home, even if the wife keeps her own property	0 = yes; 1 = no
Adultery	Laws on adultery are more favorable to men, for example by judging men's adultery by more lenient criteria from those used regarding women's adultery	0 = yes; 1 = no
TOTAL	13 = highest sex equality score; 0 = lowest score	

The Index does not include information about postdivorce alimony and maintenance for women. This reflects our (and general scholarly) ambivalence about the implications of protective legislation for women's equal rights. On the one hand, these provisions advance women's de facto status by reducing their vulnerability. On the other hand, the mere existence of protective legislation may reinforce the idea – and the practice – of women's dependency. Most gender-equitable legislation makes support provisions gender neutral and permits judges to determine the need for support on a case-by-case basis. Yet this approach may not do enough to protect vulnerable groups in countries with extreme gender inequalities, where families (and even judges) may want to punish women by withholding main-tenance. Nor does our Index reflect attempts to deal with problems arising from cohabitation (also known as common law marriage), a salient issue across many countries and increasingly prevalent in Europe, where marriage rates have dropped in recent decades (Sayare & de la Baume, 2010).

Figures 4.1 to 4.4 show maps depicting values of the Family Law Index for the countries of our study at all four points in time. Appendix B at the end of this book offers a more detailed description of the evolution of family law in most of the world's legal traditions.

The figures and maps presented here depict very different patterns than those for violence against women, a nondoctrinal status issue. By the beginning of our time period (1975), many countries in the West had already reformed family law in an egalitarian direction. With violence against women, by contrast, scores were low across the board in 1975. Second, family law appears overall to be much stickier than violence against women. Regional differences remain pronounced over all four decades. By 2005, the level of the Index remained low in many countries, particularly in the MENA region. However, as we note below, simply being a Muslim-majority country is an inadequate guide to the degree of discrimination in family law.

Why do some legal regimes disadvantage women across many areas, while others treat women and men relatively equally, and still others uphold a mix of provisions? In the next several sections of this chapter, we present hypotheses about the association between egalitarian family law and several factors, including religion, colonialism, communism, feminist movements, and feminist international law.

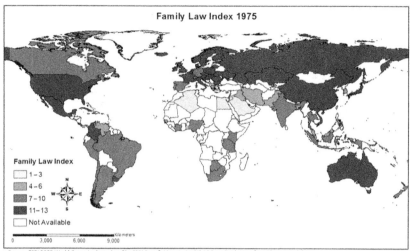

FIGURE 4.1 Map of Family Law Index, 1975

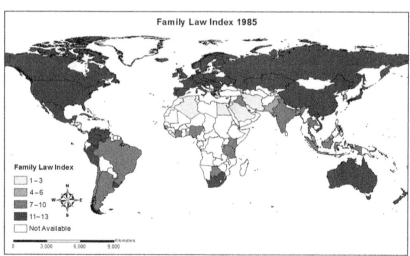

FIGURE 4.2 Map of Family Law Index, 1985

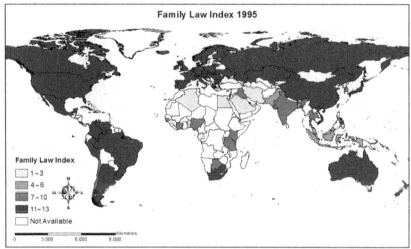

FIGURE 4.3 Map of Family Law Index, 1995

FIGURE 4.4 Map of Family Law Index, 2005

THE ROLE OF RELIGION

Understanding global variation in family law requires examination of the role of religion.[8] As we explained earlier, provisions on marriage, inheritance, and parenting are major components of most ecclesiastical doctrines. Within the contours of contemporary politics, religion has the potential to influence family law in myriad ways. Which aspects matter most? Our primary hypothesis focuses on state–religion relations, though we also assess the relationship between family law and variables emphasized by scholarship on religion and public policy such as religiosity, confessional or denominational type, and religious parties (see, e.g., Castles, 1998; Esping-Andersen, 1990; Hagopian, 2009; Kahl, 2005; Kerbsbergen & Philip, 2009; Minkenberg, 2002, 2003; Scheve & Stasavege, 2006a, 2006b; Stadelmann-Steffan & Traunmuller, 2011).

Today, there is significant variation in the extent to which state power grants public status to religious doctrines, symbols, and ideas, with configurations ranging from near fusion (Saudi Arabia) to virtual separation (United States).[9] Most countries lie between these two extremes, producing variation in what we call the *political institutionalization of religious authority*. At one end of the spectrum, the state upholds religious education, holidays, and practices, provides funding for religious institutions, and appoints ecclesiastical officials, among other measures (Fox, 2008). The public legitimacy of religion in such contexts tends to promote "sacralization," a process in which "the primary aspects of life from family to politics, are suffused with religious rhetoric, symbols, and rituals" (Stark & Iannaccone, 1994, p. 234). Religious doctrine, rather than public or universal reasons, serves as the normative basis of law making (cf. Weber, 1978, p. 226). At the other, secular end of the spectrum,[10] the state maintains a normative basis that is at least

---

[8] In this chapter, we define religion as "a system of beliefs and practices oriented toward the sacred or supernatural, through which the life experiences of groups of people are given meaning and direction" (Smith, quoted in Gill, 2001, p. 120). This encompasses the world's major faiths as well as the spiritual traditions upheld by smaller cultural groups.

[9] Many scholars of religion and politics disaggregate two dimensions of state–religion relations: restriction and favoritism. The former refers to limitations on the practice of religion and religious organizations and the latter to privileges and subsidies to a particular religion or group of religions (Driessen, 2010; Fox, 2008; Grim & Finke, 2006; Traunmuller & Freitag, 2011). As will be discussed in this chapter, our measure is closer to the favoritism dimension.

[10] Our understanding of *secular* here is a political one. We refer not to the intensity and pervasiveness of religious beliefs and practices but to the political separation of the state

formally independent of religious institutions and doctrine. Public
reasons, not particular religious beliefs, supply the rationale for political
decisions (Creppell, 2010, pp. 24–35; Rawls, 1993).

Though religious doctrine is not *necessarily* patriarchal, it was *historically* so. Religions can and do change, but the state affects the timing and
pace of this process. State institutionalization of ecclesiastical doctrine tends
to freeze patriarchal understandings of religion and link them to the public
status of religion more generally. State intervention enhances the authority
of certain religious interpretations – and interpreters – rendering them less
liable to contestation and less exposed to broader societal influences.
Political institutionalization reduces religious pluralism, suppressing cur
rents of religious thought that are more supportive of sex equality.[11]

It can be hard to reform family law in these contexts. Challenges to the
religious interpretations supported by state law come to be seen as challenges to the entire institutional configuration linking state power to
religious authority (and vice versa). Family law becomes a referendum
on the role of religion in the polity and on the public and legitimizing
character of religious doctrines. To uphold patriarchal family law is to
defend religion's role; to favor egalitarian reforms is to challenge the
historic bargain between church and state. As a result, opponents of
change often brand critics of family law as heretics. The greater the degree
of political institutionalization of religion, the more likely it is that criticism will be suppressed and critics maligned.

For example, religious conservatives denigrated those Egyptian women
who contested sex discrimination in family law as Western and immoral
(Singerman, 2005). Opponents of legal divorce in Brazil in the 1970s
criticized proposals for reform as sinful, and Roman Catholic bishops
declared to legislators that "no good Catholic" could vote for the bill
legalizing divorce (Htun, 2003). In Niger, conservative activists declared
that a proposed secular family code was part of a "wind of subversion
and blasphemy blowing across [the] country that seeks to suppress or

from religion. As many scholars since Marx and Tocqueville have pointed out, political
secularization is compatible with a religious society (Cassanova, 1994; Gill, 2001; Jelen
& Wilcox, 2002; Katznelson & Stedman-Jones, 2010; Stark & Iannaccone, 1994).
[11] Political institutionalization tends to create religious monopolies. Religious officials author-
ized by the state seek to protect their position from external and internal challengers. Such
monopolies tend to make religions top-heavy and resistant to change, posing a barrier to
reformers seeking to update religious doctrines. This may be why some scholars have found
that state involvement depresses religious vitality (Chaves & Cann, 1992; Gill, 1998;
Iannaccone, 1991; Iannaccone, Finke, & Stark, 1997; Stark & Iannaccone, 1994).

even destroy Islam" (cited in Kang, 2015, pp. 60–1). Conservative religious activists referred to those Malaysian feminists who defended women's rights in the name of Islam as "traitors," accused them of insulting Islam, and declared they were "not qualified enough" to discuss religious topics (Mohamad, 2009; Moustafa, 2012; Neo, 2003, p. 70). Zainah Anwar, founder of Sisters in Islam in Malaysia, opined that the debate over family law is not so much about women's rights but "about the place of Islam in the public space and the place of Islam as a source of law and public policy."[12]

Since political institutionalization links patriarchal family law to the public status of religion more generally, reforms are difficult, and family law will often remain discriminatory. We propose that:

H1: In countries with official state religions, family law will be less egalitarian than in polities without official religions.

H2: Family law will be less egalitarian in countries where the government upholds religious practices and principles in law.

Institutionalized state–religion relations may not have the same effect across all contexts, as they are shaped by beliefs and practices in society. As Grzymała-Busse (2015) shows, churches gain moral authority when religious and national identities are fused. This fusion developed historically as a result of church responses to national conflicts and grows out of societal religiosity, but does not always correspond to the legal separation of church and state.

We also consider other aspects of religious life. In their analysis of dozens of countries, Inglehart and Norris (2003) found a negative association between religiosity – measured by beliefs in God and attendance at religious services, among other factors – and beliefs about gender equality. Since degrees of societal religiosity are related to support for women's rights and church intervention on these issues, we must explore the relationship between religiosity and the degree of sex inequality in family law. Specifically, we consider the following hypothesis:

H3: Countries with higher degrees of religiosity have less egalitarian family law.

We anticipate that, on its own, religiosity will not be so consequential for women's rights. Religiosity will have a stronger association with women's rights in the context of official, legal support for particular religions. The main impact of religiosity will consist in the ways it

---

[12] Interview, Petaling Jaya, Malaysia, April 26, 2011.

conditions the effect of state–religion relations on women's rights. In countries where everyone is a believer, official religious institutions and doctrinal interpretations are widely perceived as legitimate (Hagopian, 2009; Htun, 2009). In societies where no one believes in God, institutionalized religion has less influence over public policy (Minkenberg, 2002). This may be why some studies of family policy and abortion in Europe argue that religion–state relations have the opposite effect of that which we describe here. For example, Scandinavian countries with public, official religions but very low religiosity preside over Europe's most expansive family policies and most liberal abortion regimes, and were early liberalizers of patriarchal family laws. In the Netherlands, where church and state are institutionally separated but religiosity is higher, family policies and abortion laws have historically been more conservative than in Nordic countries (Minkenberg, 2002, 2003; Morgan, 2006). This suggests that:

H4: High degrees of political institutionalization of religious authority, combined with high degrees of religiosity, are associated with sex inequality in family law.

In addition, several studies link particular religions to women's low status. For example, large groups of people in Muslim-majority countries, particularly in the MENA region, have attitudes that are relatively unsupportive of gender equality. There are fewer women in positions of power in MENA, lower rates of female labor force participation, and discriminatory laws on citizenship and nationality (Alexander & Welzel, 2009; Cherif, 2010; Donno & Bruce, 2004; Fish, 2002; Inglehart & Norris, 2003, 2004; Ross, 2008). Some scholars have argued that Roman Catholicism endorses gender hierarchy, and connected the Catholic countries of Europe to less feminist policy outcomes in social welfare and abortion policy (Castles, 1998; Esping-Andersen, 1990; Minkenberg, 2003). In addition, government officials seeking to defend sexist laws and practices have invoked the doctrines of Islam, Judaism, Hinduism, Catholicism, and indigenous African customs to support their positions.[13]

Yet in light of the variation in the interpretation and use of religion, it is difficult to attribute causal power to the singular doctrines of "Islam," "Catholicism," or "Hinduism." Once institutionalized and codified by state

---

[13] For example, Israel referenced respect for religious traditions in its reservations to Article 16 of CEDAW (UN Women n.d.). India also introduced reservations to CEDAW for similar reasons (Sezgin, 2009, 2011). In Kenya and Uganda, traditionalist activists opposed family law reform as inconsistent with local custom (Baraza, 2009; Tripp et al., 2009).

power, certain versions of religion may be patriarchal, but this owes to contingent historical factors, not the nature of religion. In fact, countries dominated by the same religion show varied patterns of family law. Consider the difference in timing in the legalization of divorce in Catholic countries in Europe (France 1884; Ireland 2002) and in Latin America, where Mexico legalized divorce in 1917 while Chile waited until 2004. Even in 2013, women in Chile lacked equal rights to marital property. Laws vary across Muslim-majority countries as well: though many countries remain conservative, Tunisia, Turkey, and Morocco have embraced egalitarian approaches, while others such as Iran and Indonesia become more discriminatory during the period of our study.[14] We therefore propose that:

H5: The political institutionalization of religious authority is more powerfully associated with discriminatory family law than confessional or denominational type.

The other religious factor to take into account is the presence of religious parties. They have been important actors in debates on family law in many countries, notably including Italy, Chile, Israel, and India (Clark, Hine, & Irving, 1974; Hagopian, 2009; Halperin-Kaddari, 2003; Hasan, 2010; Htun, 2003). Yet the presence of religious parties does not always correlate with the existence of religious cleavages or otherwise signal the importance of religious actors in political life (Kalyvas, 1996; Minkenberg, 2002). Due to the internal evolution of religious doctrine – especially among Christian churches – and the potentially moderating effects of political inclusion (e.g., Schwedler, 2011; Wickham, 2004), religious parties do not always oppose family law reform. We therefore believe that the relationship between religious parties and family law will be more ambiguous than the relationship between state–religion relations and family law.

H6: The political institutionalization of religious authority will have a more powerful association with discriminatory family law than the presence of religious parties in government.

In summary, our primary hypothesis is that religion is connected to discrimination in family law primarily through the character of

---

[14] Variation in the approach of Muslim-majority countries characterizes other gender issues as well. Kang, for example, describes differences among African Muslim-majority countries concerning gender quotas, women's representation in parliament, and support for international human rights treaties (Kang, 2015).

state–religion relations. The political institutionalization of religious authority is negatively associated with egalitarianism, especially in devout societies. Other religious factors, such as religiosity on its own, confessional or denominational type (such as being a Muslim-majority polity), and confessional parties, are less important.

COLONIALISM

In many societies, the experience of Western overseas colonialism helped to tie religious and cultural identities to the fate of family law. Colonial powers often codified patriarchal versions of local kinship rules, and endowed traditional leaders with authority to apply these rules while denying them power over other areas of social life. British policy, for example, was based on the principle of "noninterference" in the personal laws of subject communities, including provisions on marriage, divorce, guardianship, and inheritance. As Warren Hastings, then Governor-General of India, put it in 1772: "the laws of the Koran with respect to the Mussalmans, and those of the Shasters with respect to the Hindoos, shall be invariably be adhered to" (quoted in Williams, 2006, p. 6). "Noninterference," however, was politically and selectively interpreted, if not a misnomer altogether. As numerous scholars have shown, the British – and other European colonial rulers – did not leave family laws alone, but wrote down the rules and bolstered the power of the customary authorities who applied them.

Often, colonial policies replaced more egalitarian practices with patriarchal provisions. In South Asia, Hindus and Muslims had been internally diverse and overlapping categories, not distinct communities. Many practiced local customary laws – some of which were more advantageous to women – instead of Hindu or Muslim religious law (Williams, 2006). In Malaysia too, the British, when faced with diverse and fluid customary practices, invented homogeneous doctrines. As Hussin notes, "The matriarchal laws of the *Minangkabau* of West Sumatra began to be replaced by more patriarchal *adat temenggong*, and British interpretations of Islamic law from India came to be accepted legal practice for some areas of Malay religion and custom" (2007, p. 779). The British reified fluid social norms and practices by inscribing oral languages, codifying customs, and introducing categorical ethnic distinctions (Ranger, 1983; Vail, 1989).

Though the French colonial emphasis on cultural assimilation and national unity is often contrasted to the British policy of indirect rule and multiculturalism (Mamdani, 1996), customary law was preserved in many former French colonies. Unwilling to risk the tribal rebellions they feared national codification would trigger, the French tolerated customary laws in colonial Algeria (Charrad, 2001). In Niger, the French created a parallel legal system, which applied the Napoleonic Code to French citizens and customary and Muslim law to locals. This relative autonomy of customary law boosted the power of traditional leaders, who later blocked adoption of a secular, national family code after the country achieved independence (Kang, 2015).

The legacy of these colonial policies, albeit with important variations across countries, implies that:

H7: Being a former colony inclines a country to more discriminatory family law.

Postcolonial states were not discriminatory for all women's rights issues. Many former colonies were quicker to introduce gender quotas than established democracies in the West. In addition, former colonies in the Americas and Africa adopted regional agreements on violence against women, which motivated countries to modify national legislation to combat the practice and protect survivors, as we discuss in Chapter 2.

COMMUNISM

Whereas colonial nation building connected religious and cultural identities to gender subordination in family law, the experience of communism had the opposite effect.[15] Strong currents of socialist thought endorsed sex equality. Alexandra Kollontai, a prominent Russian communist revolutionary, called in 1909 for "No more inequality within the family," arguing that "The woman in communist society no longer depends upon her husband but on her work. It is not in her husband but in her capacity for work that she will find support" (1977; see also Engels & Morgan, 1978).

Communist leaders saw the liberation of women as a means to break up kin-based and traditional societies and install a new social order (Massell, 1968). In addition, they believed that women's emancipation from the patriarchal family would increase the size, quality, and skill of the labor force, help modernize the rural economy, and transform the family into a unit of socialization to the new regime (Molyneux, 1985a, p. 53; see also Molyneux, 1985b, pp. 245–6).

---

[15] To be sure, religious revival has characterized many postcommunist societies, but thus far has not led to a rollback of egalitarian family law (though it has produced greater restrictions on abortion in some countries, such as Poland).

Communist governments – including those of the Soviet Union, China, Cuba, and Vietnam – launched an assault on religious and traditional cultural practices, often using women's roles as a weapon (Massell, 1968).[16] Most communist governments adopted secular and egalitarian family laws as part of this strategy. The Soviet law on marriage and divorce of 1917 and the Family Code of 1918 aimed to break the power of the Eastern Orthodox Church by requiring that marriages be registered with the state and invalidating religious unions (Hazard, 1939, pp. 225–6). These laws banned polygamy, introduced equality between the spouses and between parents, made divorce easy to obtain, and eliminated the stigma of illegitimacy (Berman, 1946, pp. 39–48). Communist states of the Global South followed the Soviet example and introduced egalitarian family laws. Codes adopted in North Korea in 1946, China in 1950, North Vietnam in 1959, South Yemen in 1974, and Cuba in 1975 introduced the principle of formal legal equality between spouses and eliminated religious or traditional practices associated with the old regime (Molyneux, 1985a, pp. 48–9). These experiences suggest that:

H8: A communist past (or present) creates a legal legacy of sex equality and should be associated with family laws that conform to principles of equal rights.

We do not mean to suggest that sex equality was a feature of all spheres of life under communism, or that communism affected all areas of women's rights equally. With the exception of the North Vietnamese law of 1959, communist leaders generally refused to acknowledge the reality of male dominance in the family and of problems of domestic and sexual violence. As we showed in Chapter 2, communist and postcommunist countries on average were more reluctant to adopt legislation to combat violence against women. Communist leaders defined national priorities according to men's needs and rarely women's. Occupational segregation by sex, wage gaps, high rates of divorce and abortion, and a persistent sexual division of labor put women at a disadvantage in most socialist states (Molyneux, 1985a, p. 51). What is more, feminist movements have tended to be weak. Communist governments created organizations to mobilize women, but these were (by definition) officially

---

[16] Though ecclesiastical influences were marginalized from foundational family laws, in practice religious authorities were not completely excluded from participation in socialist societies. State–religion relations under communism were complex and included moments of cooperation as well as conflict (Mirescu, 2011).

mandated and not voluntary organizations, and therefore not social movements (Domínguez, 1978; Howell, 2003).

FEMINISM AND WOMEN'S MOVEMENTS

The political institutionalization of religious authority and the legacy of colonial rule created obstacles to family law reform and empowered opponents of gender equality. This raises the question: What motivated attempts at reform in the first place? Religious factors posed a barrier insofar as political actors demanded that discriminatory family laws be modified. Where religiously based obstacles did not exist, the motivation to pursue reform of family law might not exist either. Explaining the chances for reform in nonreligious contexts, the possibility for change after ruptures in the religion–state relationship, and the impetus behind innovations in religious doctrine requires that we take into account the protagonistic role of feminist movements and the codification of their ideas in international treaties.

Strong feminist movements. Feminist movements have been the key actors challenging male dominance in multiple spheres. Feminist movements have drawn attention to women's subordinate status in education, the economy, the family, and public decision making, though with varying degrees of success. Reforms to combat violence against women, end discrimination at work, promote access to childcare, and deal with a range of other issues were placed on public agendas by these movements (see, e.g., Alvarez, 1990; Banaszak, 1996; Basu & McGrory, 1995; Costain & Majstorovic, 1994; Mansbridge, 1986; Weldon, 2002b). In some places, feminist mobilization was robust and widely supported. In others, movements remained weak or were crushed by governments.

Along with the right to vote, family law was one of the earliest targets of organized activists. In Europe and the Americas in the nineteenth century, feminists criticized how women lost their civil rights upon marriage and family laws institutionalized male domination (Cott, 1987; Deere & Leon, 2001; Dore, 2000; Lavrin, 1998). As the Declaration of Sentiments, endorsed by U.S. feminists at the Seneca Falls Convention in 1848, put it, man has "made [woman], if married, in the eyes of the law, civilly dead" (Stanton, 1848).

In the twentieth century, prior to the emergence of the second-wave feminist movement, elite feminists – often working in coalition with male lawyers, progressive politicians, and other modernizers – pressured governments to expand women's rights in family law. In Brazil in the late 1940s and 1950s, for example, Rio de Janeiro lawyer Romy Medeiros da Fonseca began lobbying elite circles of lawyers and politicians to remove the legal handicaps suffered by married women under the 1916 Civil Code. Thanks to her efforts, the 1962 *Estatuto da Mulher Casada* (Married Women's Statute) granted married women full civil capacity, and eliminated husbands' authority to prevent wives from working, traveling, or engaging in routine financial transactions (Htun, 2003, pp. 62–7).[17]

Where feminist movements have been strong and have not faced the barrier of official religious favoritism, reform of family law has been more comprehensive and easier to accomplish. In Canada, the United States, and the United Kingdom, the strength of the feminist movement was the primary factor behind family law reforms from the 1970s to the 1990s. These movements were more successful when their efforts were supplemented by international pressure (such as campaigns in the European Union) or legitimized by widely accepted norms and institutions (such as the Canadian Charter of Rights and Freedoms) (Bashevkin, 1998). In many cases, feminist activism prompted governments to create official commissions to investigate the status of women and offer policy recommendations. Implementation of these recommendations led to family law reform in Canada (Bashevkin, 1998; Boyd & Young, 2002) and in New Zealand (Committee on Women, 1978). By contrast, in Pakistan in the 1950s, Chile in the 1970s, and Kenya in the 1990s, opponents alleging that reforms undermined Islam, the family, or traditional customs blocked the recommendations of expert commissions (Baraza, 2009, p. 1; Htun, 2003, pp. 73–4; Ihsan & Zaidi, 2006, p. 214).

Given the importance of feminist movements in prompting national discussions about women's rights in family law, mobilizing allies for change, and raising public awareness about discrimination, we propose that:

H9: The presence of strong feminist movements is associated with more egalitarian family laws.[18]

---

[17] Romy and her allies (including Senator Nelson Carneiro) were unable to promote a full agenda of family law liberalization (which would have included the legalization of divorce) merely through political pressure applied among elites. More profound change came in Brazil when the military government of General Ernesto Geisel signaled its willingness to confront the Roman Catholic bishops, thus opening the door for reformist coalitions to change the Constitution to eliminate the principle of marital indissolubility and legalize divorce (Htun, 2003, pp. 85–95).

[18] See Chapter 2 for more on our approach to feminist and women's movements. We argue there that autonomy is important to some gender issues, such as violence against women, which are almost never prioritized by nonfeminist political parties and groups (Weldon,

As the examples just given show, feminist efforts to reform family law may span many years and even decades. When they were weak or confronted opposition to egalitarian reforms, feminist movements have sought allies in the state and in transnational networks and have leveraged international conventions such as the Convention on the Elimination of All Forms of Discrimination against Women (CEDAW), to which we now turn.

Feminist international law: CEDAW. Feminist movements have influenced domestic policy making by seeking to institutionalize their demands in international conventions, declarations, and other agreements, as we argued in previous chapters. The Convention on the Elimination of All Forms of Discrimination against Women (CEDAW) is the most important document for family law. Adopted by the United Nations General Assembly in 1979, CEDAW calls on states to "eliminate discrimination in all matters dealing with marriage and family relations," mentioning in particular the freedom and consent to marry, rights and obligations during marriage, divorce, parental rights, names, property, and the right to work.[19] These family law provisions have been controversial: many states that ratified the treaty included reservations pertaining to them (Ihsan & Zaidi, 2006; Musawah, 2009).

CEDAW reflects and magnifies the feminist movement's influence in global and local politics. Transnational feminist networks mobilized for the treaty, which codifies feminist ideas about nondiscrimination and equal rights (Baldez, 2014). Ratification of CEDAW, in turn, strengthens domestic movements. Ratification lends support and legitimacy to feminist claims, while transnational and regional organizing around CEDAW gives local groups ideas, resources, and templates to leverage the treaty to promote change (Baldez, 2014; Freidman, 1995; Liebowitz, 2002).[20] As this suggests, domestic activism is critical to the enduring impact of CEDAW and other international agreements on women's rights (Benhabib, 2009; Htun & Weldon, 2012). We propose:

H10: Ratification of CEDAW will be associated with greater equality in family law.

2002b, 2011). Family law, by contrast, has been on the policy agenda for a very long time and demands legal and technical expertise available in elite networks connected to parties and the state. In addition, women's distinct perspectives and experiences – which can be developed in the context of an autonomous movement – are less relevant for achievement of formal, legal equality than are issues addressing the distinctive needs of women or the ways that formal equality falls short of substantive equality.

[19] The full text of the convention is available at www.un.org/womenwatch/daw/cedaw/text/econvention.htm#article16.

[20] Interview, Kuala Lumpur, Malaysia, April 29, 2011.

ANALYSIS

In this section, we explain our statistical analysis, and explore the degree to which it supports our theoretical approach. Our analysis pools four cross-sections, or yearly snapshots, of data (1975, 1985, 1995, 2005) into a single dataset encompassing seventy countries. As this suggests, we aim to address cross-national variation as well as variation over time in each country in one analysis. This type of dataset is analogous, in its structure, to survey data in which individual subjects (people) are studied in many waves or points in time. The set of people studied in such an analysis are called "panels." For this reason, this type of data is called "panel data." This type of data offers some challenges and opportunities not covered in a standard, ordinary least squares regression analysis, so where possible, analysts use techniques designed to take the "panel-like" structure of the dataset into account. The random effects regression analysis we employ here is one of the typical approaches to such analyses.[21] The panel we use in this analysis is "balanced," meaning there is the same number of observations in each wave or time period.

Our analysis reveals considerable support for our theoretical approach to explaining the degree of sex equality in family law. Overall, our models improve our understanding of cross-national variation considerably. R-squared varies from .54 to .83 across the ten models. Breaking the overall R-squared into within and between components, we see that the latter is generally higher, meaning our model performs better in capturing variation across countries than it does variation over time within each country. For this type of analysis, coefficients represent the average effect of the independent variables on the Family Law Index when the variable changes both across time and across countries by one unit. Negative coefficients indicate that a variable is associated with less equality (more discrimination) while positive coefficients indicate an association with greater equality (less discrimination).

Religious Factors

Though the maps seen in Figures 4.1–4.4 show that Muslim-majority countries of the MENA region had lower average values on the index than other countries, our analysis reveals that type of religion is very

---

[21] For an explanation, see footnote 13 of Chapter 3 and Clark & Linzer (2015).

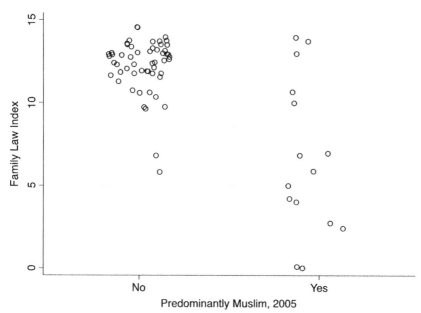

FIGURE 4.5 Family Law Index in Muslim-majority and non-Muslim-majority countries

limited as an explanation for discriminatory law. Figure 4.5 shows that there are few non-Muslim countries among those with the lowest values for the Family Law Index countries (the bottom left side of the panel is empty). At the same time, the figure also shows that Muslim-majority countries have scores across the entire range of the index (the right side of the panel). On its own, simply knowing that a country is Muslim-majority does not help us predict what the degree of equality in family law will be in that country. Explaining the range of outcomes with respect to family law across Muslim countries is not at all a simple matter.

Rather than focusing on type of religion, our approach emphasizes the connection between state–religion relations and the degree of sex equality. Specifically, we posited a negative association between the political institutionalization of religious authority and sex equality in family law. We measured political institutionalization in two ways: through the presence of an *Official religion* and the degree to which the state upholds *Religious legislation*.[22] We adapted *Religious legislation* from Jonathan Fox's

---

[22] In other analyses (not shown) we also used Fox's *Government involvement in religion* (GIR) variable, which does not perfectly map onto our conceptualization, as well as the

TABLE 4.2 Coefficients, Family Law Index, GLS random effects models, 1975–2005

Model number	1	2	3	4	5	6	7	8	9	10
Variables										
Official religion	-1.726*** (.430)	-1.497*** (.497)			.088 (.434)					
Religious legislation			-.275*** (.039)	-.198*** (.041)	-.183*** (.046)	-.187*** (.042)	-.175*** (.043)	-.176*** (.044)	.238 (.149)	.198 (.139)
Religiosity scale			-.012 (.012)	-.018 (.013)	-.002 (.012)	.001 (.012)	-.010 (.013)	-.010 (.013)	.031* (.017)	.029* (.016)
High religiosity	-.586 (.511)	-.138 (.586)								
Former colony	-1.363** (.532)	-1.408** (.577)	-1.077* (.566)	-2.821*** (.794)	-.797 (.543)	-.967* (.520)	-2.365*** (.708)	-2.318*** (.816)	-.677 (.539)	-.622 (.505)
Communist	2.948*** (.629)	2.733*** (.676)	2.059*** (.565)	1.594*** (.558)	1.874*** (.526)	1.770*** (.505)	1.497*** (.514)	1.519*** (.550)	1.822*** (.530)	1.681*** (.493)
Strongest feminist movement	1.157*** (.361)									
Strong feminist movement	.366 (.262)									
Strongest feminist movement (lagged)		1.446*** (.419)	.963** (.472)	1.085** (.450)	.927** (.445)	.853** (.433)	.94** (.425)	.983** (.445)	.862* (.448)	.807* (.424)
Strong feminist movement (lagged)		.633** (.284)	.225 (.342)	.492 (.325)	.072 (.328)	.159 (.328)	.16 (.327)	.414 (.333)	.075 (.329)	.003 (.317)

	(1)	(2)	(3)	(4)	(5)	(6)	(7)	(8)	(9)	(10)
CEDAW ratification	.324 (.242)					1.208* (.666)	1.080* (.644)	1.074* (.648)		
CEDAW ratification (lagged)		-.001 (.226)	.342 (.341)	.466 (.317)	.413 (.327)				.407 (.327)	.423 (.315)
Women in parliament (%)	.040*** (.013)	.037*** (.014)	.056*** (.016)	.040** (.016)	.048*** (.015)	.047*** (.015)	.038** (.015)	.038** (.016)	.039** (.016)	.037** (.015)
Democracy	.094*** (.021)	.097*** (.024)	.137*** (.037)	.036 (.042)	.083** (.038)	.098*** (.037)	.047 (.040)	.045 (.041)	.127*** (.035)	.087** (.036)
Muslim majority					-2.817*** (.829)	-2.509*** (.784)	-1.366 (.832)	-1.362 (.842)		-2.070*** (.787)
Catholic majority					.567 (.450)	.521 (.423)	.185 (.459)	.175 (.471)		.574 (.410)
Africa				1.823* (1.062)			1.505 (1.040)	1.522 (1.063)		
Asia				-2.255*** (.862)			-1.736** (.864)	-1.746** (.873)		
Latin America				2.490*** (.833)			1.792** (.875)	1.776** (.893)		
Middle East				-2.330*** (.760)			-1.735** (.784)	-1.744** (.793)		
GDP (logged)				.057 (.341)			.039 (.338)			

(continued)

147

TABLE 4.2 (*continued*)

Model number	1	2	3	4	5	6	7	8	9	10
Variables										
Religious legislation X religiosity scale									$-.007^{***}$ (.002)	$-.005^{***}$ (.002)
Observations	277	209	114	114	114	114	114	114	114	114
Overall R-squared	.541	.540	.729	.817	.781	.789	.8⎯8	.828	.786	.816
Number of countries	70	70	64	64	64	64	6⎯	64	64	64

Notes: Estimates are from random effects regression models. Standard errors are in parentheses. *, **, and ⁂ denote statistical significance at the 10, 5, and 1 percent levels, respectively.

Religion and the State database (Fox, 2008, especially pp. 54–5).[23] Capturing the ways in which political authority upholds religious principles across multiple spheres (education, diet, dress, political participation, and so forth), it is a count of legislation on religious holidays, religious education, government funding for religion, blasphemy laws, religious requirements for public office, and others. The existence of religious laws in many areas reflects a significant fusion of ecclesiastical and political authority. The adapted measure covers thirty-seven types of religious legislation, and our countries present a wide range of variation, with Saudi Arabia scoring 31 and the United States scoring 1. The mean is 8 and the standard deviation is 5.8. The establishment of an *Official religion* was measured as a dummy variable, available for all four time periods (1975, 1985, 1995, and 2005). *Religious legislation* was available for only 1995 and 2005. In order to capitalize on the availability of a more refined measure and also to use our entire database, we used both of these measures in our analyses.[24]

As Figure 4.6 shows, we find a negative relationship between *Religious legislation* and the Family Law Index. Countries with lower values of *Religious legislation* (those where the government adopts fewer religious laws) tend to have higher values on the Family Law Index (to be more egalitarian). Countries with higher values on *Religious legislation* (where the government adopts more religious laws) tend to be less egalitarian.

According to the analysis presented in Table 4.2, *Religious legislation* is associated with a change in the Family Law Index of 1.6 fewer areas of equality ($5.8^* -.28 = -1.6$). This effect holds up controlling for region (Model 4, 7, 8), for religiosity (Models 3–8), and for those countries where Islam was the dominant religion (Models 5–8). Similarly, when a country has an *Official religion*, our models estimated that it will have one to two fewer areas of equality in family law (out of thirteen possible areas), a finding that is statistically as well as substantively significant (Models 1 and 2, Table 4.2).

To show this another way, Figure 4.7 plots coefficients and their 95 percent confidence intervals from our first three random effects

religious legislation measure. The results are mostly the same, supporting our claim that the relationships we report here are robust and not dependent on particular measures.

[23] We adapted Fox's index for our purposes by excluding his elements that related to the situation of women and the family (e.g., "personal status defined by clergy," "laws on inheritance defined by religion").

[24] In other analyses (not shown) we imputed the missing data to see what difference missing the early years made. This only strengthened our analysis (available on request).

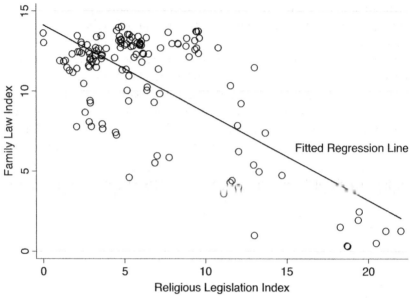

FIGURE 4.6 Family Law Index and Religious Legislation Index, pooled 1995 and 2005

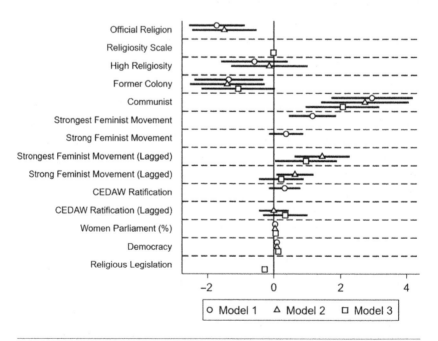

Note: Point estimates and 95 percent confidence intervals from random effects models are shown above.

FIGURE 4.7 Family Law Index coefficient plot of models 1, 2, and 3 of Table 4.2

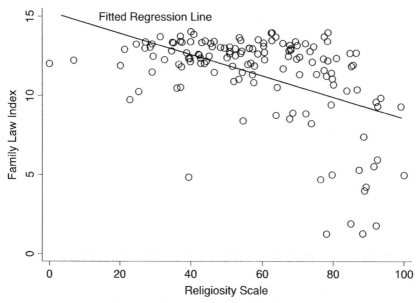

FIGURE 4.8 Family Law Index and religiosity scale, pooled 1995 and 2005

models. Recall that when a 95 percent confidence interval includes zero, that explanatory variable is not statistically significant at the five percent level. All coefficients for both *Official religion* and *Religious legislation* are negative and statistically significant.[25] In and of itself, this suggests a strong negative relationship between the political institutionalization of religious authority and sex inequality in family law, as we expected.

What about the degree of religiosity? We measured societal religiosity with Inglehart and Norris's *Strength of Religiosity Scale*. Examining a scatterplot of religiosity plotted against our Family Law Index reveals that religiosity, on its own, is a poor predictor of sex inequality in family law (Figure 4.8). Particularly at high levels of religiosity, the Family Law Index values vary widely (see the right side of Figure 4.8). The coefficient plot in Figure 4.7 similarly shows that *Religiosity scale* was not a significant correlate of sex equality in family law.

However, since the more refined measure of *Religiosity scale* was available for only a subset of our dataset, we also used a simpler measure –

---

[25] The one exception observed across our ten models is the coefficient for the *Official religion* variable in Model 5, which includes all religious variables for comparison, and where some multicollinearity seems to account for the reversed sign.

the World Values Survey question about "importance of God" – to explore whether examining religiosity over a larger span of time and in more countries might better reveal its effects.[26] Our analysis found no statistically significant association between *High religiosity* and sex inequality in family law. (See the large confidence intervals in Figure 4.7 that cross the zero line.)

We expected that the effects of the political institutionalization of religious authority would vary with the degree of societal support for dominant religious institutions. Exploring this expectation requires an analysis that goes beyond an examination of additive effects – specifically, an analysis of the interaction between these variables. Accordingly, we examined the interaction between *Religiosity scale* and *Religious legislation* and found support for our argument (Models 9 and 10 in Table 4.2).

Before examining marginal effects over the whole range of our independent variables, let us first examine what the coefficients of the constitutive terms tell us. In an analysis of interaction effects, constitutive terms are the part of the interaction examined but that are also included separately in the model (as is necessary to explore interaction effects) (Brambor et al., 2006). The coefficient of the constitutive term *Religiosity scale* in Models 9 and 10 of Table 4.2 is .03 and .03, respectively, but is not significant. This suggests that when *Religious legislation* is zero, religiosity has no reliably predictive effect on sex equality in family law. Similarly, the coefficient of *Religious legislation* in Models 9 and 10 is also positive but not significant (.24 and .20, respectively). This suggests that when religiosity is nonexistent (equal to zero), a fusion between church and state has little predictable effect on sex equality in family. Because no country has a complete absence of religious legislation (that is, no country is 0 on the religiosity scale), this prediction is of little practical use (it is outside the range of actually existing observations). To analyze the effects of the political institutionalization of religious authority at different levels of religiosity, we examined the adjusted predictions of increasing *Religious legislation* at three different levels of religiosity: *Religiosity scale* at its median value (59) and religiosity at one standard deviation above (79) and below (39) this value (Figure 4.9). This figure shows the relationship between the institutional relationship and sex equality in family law at each of the levels of religiosity specified.

---

[26] We are grateful to Pippa Norris for suggesting this measure.

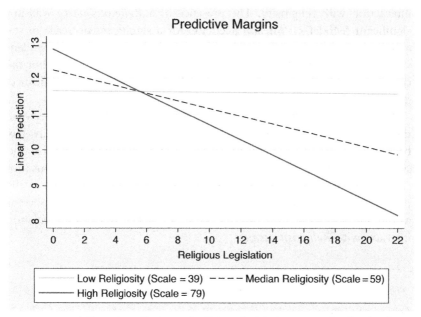

FIGURE 4.9 Adjusted predictions of religious legislation at varying levels of religiosity scale

At the median value for religiosity (*Religiosity scale* = 59, the dashed line), our model estimates a negative relationship with sex equality in family law. Examining this relationship at values one standard deviation above and below the median brings our argument into sharper relief. Our model estimates that at low levels of religiosity (one standard deviation below the median), religion–state fusion has little effect on sex equality in family law (see the light gray line in Figure 4.9, *Religiosity scale* = 39). In a condition of high religiosity (*Religiosity scale* = 79, the black line), greater political institutionalization of religious authority has a more dramatic, negative relationship. This negative relationship between political institutionalization and equality becomes even more pronounced the higher one goes on the religiosity scale. At the highest values of religiosity, the combination of church–state fusion and a devout population is a potent mix that obstructs reform of family law. Egypt, for example, has one of the highest scores on religious legislation and scores 90 on the Religiosity scale. Its score on the Family Law Index is 1, one of the three lowest (least egalitarian) in our entire sample.

Other mechanisms of religious influence on law did not seem nearly as important or reliable as the religious legislation variable, especially in interaction with religiosity. The presence of a *Religious party* was not significant (Model 5). *Muslim* accounts for a significant decrease in sex equality – the change associated with the entire range of the independent variable is between 1.3 and 2.8 fewer elements of sex equality – but the coefficients in Models 5 and 6 vary in both size and statistical significance, depending on controls.

Our analysis shows, then, that the negative relationship between the political institutionalization of religious authority and family law becomes sharper in a context of high religiosity. Examining the size and significance of these effects when the variables are held at their means (not shown) reveals that other mechanisms of religious influence, such as the presence of a religious party or the type of religion, are not as important as the religious legislation variable, especially when *Religious legislation* interacts with *Religiosity scale*.

Colonialism and communism

Our analysis showed that being a *Former colony* – a dummy variable indicating the experience of Western overseas colonialism – is associated with greater inequality in family law. The coefficient is negative across all ten models and statistically significant in half of them (see Table 4.2 and Figure 4.7). By contrast, we expected that the experience of communism, because it promoted an ideology of formal sex equality and marginalized religion, would have the opposite effect and create a legacy of sex equality in family law. Indeed, the effect of *Communist* is positively and significantly associated with sex equality in all ten models. (See Table 4.2 and Figure 4.7).

Feminist Movements and CEDAW

Our analysis showed that feminist movement strength, entered as a factor variable,[27] has a small but statistically significant effect on sex equality in family law. As Table 2.10 shows, a very strong feminist movement was significantly associated with egalitarian family law, while a strong

[27] We show this variable in Table 4.2 entered as a factor variable, which treats each value as a category, to show the distinct effect at different levels of feminist movement strength. Analyses treating the variable as a continuous variable (not shown), entered simply as a regular variable, similarly found a significant effect of a strong feminist movement, and a substantively important effect at the highest levels of strength.

feminist movement was not a significant predictor, although the direction of the coefficient is positive. Our case studies suggested that feminist movements might produce changes in family law over a longer period of time as they mobilized allies, raised awareness, and built on international conventions. In order to test this idea we employed a measure that lags *Feminist movement strength* by a decade. Even lagged, we still find that the strongest feminist movements added about one area of sex equality in law (see Figure 4.7 and Models 2–10 in Table 4.2), with stronger effects in earlier periods. This lagged indicator was significant in about half the analyses, but further analysis showed that these effects were stronger and more significant for earlier periods than later ones.

Our variable indicating whether or not a country ratified CEDAW was significantly associated with greater equality in family law in the models that captured the later periods of our dataset (1995 and 2005, Models 6, 7, and 8). This seems to suggest that CEDAW had a relationship with family law primarily in the later periods. However, a lagged version of this variable was not significant, perhaps because of the absence of the earlier years of data (1975 and 1985), inclusion of which would make the over-time impact of CEDAW most visible. The statistically significant association of CEDAW ratification with greater equality in family law in these later years suggests that adoption and ratification of an international convention, on its own, may be inadequate to influence domestic law making in an immediate sense. The correlation between CEDAW and egalitarian law may be most visible in later periods, or when analysis of lagged variables is possible (as our prior analysis suggests).[28] Global treaties need to be brought home and "vernacularized" by local actors, requiring additional time to be put to work (Benhabib, 2009; Htun & Weldon, 2012). This delayed effect might be even more pronounced in areas where women's rights reform requires reforming long-established law or where reform faces vigorous and entrenched domestic opposition.

---

[28] Note that the final models (9 and 10) use this lagged specification of CEDAW and it is not statistically significant in these models. Running these models with the nonlagged variable shows that CEDAW ratification is significant. We continue to use the lagged version in these final two models because this is what is most consistent with our interpretation of the data and our theoretical approach in earlier chapters. It is not significant in these models, on our interpretation, mostly because of the temporal domain of the dataset for those models, which does not provide an adequate empirical base to make lagged effects visible.

Controls

We found that *Women in parliament* had a statistically significant effect on sex equality in family law that was fairly consistent in size, if very small, regardless of specification and other model variations (see Figure 4.7 and Table 4.2). While women in parliament might prevent rollbacks, they tend not to be major instigators of family law reform, a finding that has also been suggested by research in other areas of women's rights (Weldon, 2011). *Democracy* has a statistically significant relationship to family law when examined over three or four decades (Figure 4.7), but this effect is less robust in the analysis focusing on 1995 and 2005 (Models 3–10 in Table 4.2).

CONCLUSION

This chapter has demonstrated a powerful association between sex discrimination in family law and the political institutionalization of religious authority. When state power and religious power are fused, particularly in highly devout societies, it is difficult to reform family law and patriarchal norms endure. Qualitative evidence suggests that, in these contexts, patriarchal family law becomes linked to the public status of religion. Feminist movements and secular activists have a hard time demanding reform without questioning the historical arrangements between church and state. Their challenges to patriarchal family law come to be seen as threats to the entire apparatus of state and religious authority, breathing new life into older struggles over the boundaries and nature of the state–religion relationship. Ecclesiastical hierarchies defend discriminatory family law in order to protect their broader institutional privileges and normative legitimacy. Whereas international norms and transnational movements have helped compel national policy making on gender issues such as violence against women, participation in decision making, and workplace equality, family law has a greater tendency to remain sealed off from political contestation and external influences.

Religion is important to understanding family law, but not in the ways often depicted in scholarly literature (especially cross-national statistical analysis). Previous work has a tendency to identify Muslim-majority countries and religious societies as environments conducive to legal gender discrimination. Instead, here we focused on the institutionalized fusion of religious and political authority and the rigidities this introduces into both religious and state law. The key factor associated with discriminatory family law is not any particular religion, the degree of religiosity, or the presence of religious parties, but the institutional role states have crafted for religions and the frequent presence of these structures in Muslim-majority polities.

Religion is a field of contestation. Religious beliefs can be deployed for multiple causes, and religious actors have assumed conservative and progressive stances on social issues such as family law as well as human rights, poverty, social insurance, and democratic governance (see, e.g., Cassanova, 1994; Hagopian, 2009; Mainwaring, 1986; Scheve & Stasavege, 2006b). Depending on the institutional and political environment in which they are embedded, religious actors from the same denomination may behave differently. Braun's work on the role of religious rescue networks during the Holocaust in the Netherlands and Belgium shows that Catholic and Protestant churches reacted in opposite ways depending on whether they were the majority or minority religion. It was not Catholicism or Protestantism per se that shaped the actions of religious communities toward Jews, but their institutionalized status as religious minorities (Braun, 2016).

Religion can and has been repurposed as a force for gender equality in family law and other areas of social life, but repurposing religion is harder when the state props up particular religious interpretations and actors. Political institutionalization seals off family law from political deliberation and mechanisms of accountability. Equality advocates should seek not to marginalize religion or erase its influence from the polity, but to delink religious power from state power. Though religions in civil society are not always egalitarian or progressive, they are compelled to be responsive in order to remain relevant (Gill, 1998, 2001). The state, not religion, thwarts advances in women's rights.

5

Class Politics

Family Leave and Childcare Policy

In previous chapters, we argued that altering gender institutions that disadvantage women involves creating new patterns of cultural value and expanding the realm of democratic politics to encompass religious authority. In this chapter, we argue that achieving gender equality, particularly across class lines, also requires defining new institutional roles for, and relationships between, state, market, and family with respect to caring and providing for children and other family members (Fraser, 1997; Lewis, 1992; Orloff, 1993).[1] We focus particularly on policies of family leave (including gender-specific *maternity* leave, gender-neutral *parental* leave, and the gender-role-changing "use it or lose it" provision of *daddy* leave) and childcare, which enable mothers and fathers to participate in the paid labor force and, often, to have access to higher education and a career (Gornick & Meyers, 2003; Morgan, 2006). By adopting these policies, the state recognizes that (at least some) care work is a public responsibility, a move that is essential for women's rights and gender justice.

Public provision of family leave and childcare is deeply inflected by class, providing economic benefits to women and men of the middle and working classes. Expansive policies are therefore associated with a different constellation of actors and conditions than those correlated with policies on violence against women, workplace equality, family law, and

---

[1] At times, we refer to such work as *reproductive labor*. This involves the work required for the survival of the human species, including caring for children, elders, and extended family members; cooking, cleaning, laundry, repairs, transport, shopping, and financial management; and plant and animal husbandry.

the legality of reproductive rights. Whereas those gender issues were characterized by status politics and doctrinal politics, respectively, family leave and childcare conform to a logic of *class politics*. The expansion of paid family leave and public provision of childcare involves the provision of public services and supports to promote equality between women and men as well as equality among women of different classes. We hypothesize that more generous family leave and childcare should be associated with the power of actors advocating social policies that address issues of class equality more generally, such as Left parties and labor unions, as well as with the activism of feminist movements, women's policy agencies, and women in parliament. We also expect economic development and the breadth of the state's tax base to be important, since this determines the resources available to promote social welfare (Esping-Andersen, 1990; Huber & Stephens, 2001; Korpi, 2006, 1983).

This chapter analyzes the variation and development of family leave and childcare policies across the seventy countries of our study, helping to fill some gaps in the literature on gender and welfare states. Many scholars have analyzed the impact of welfare regimes on women's lives, though mostly in advanced economies (see, e.g., Daly & Rake, 2003; Gornick & Meyers, 2008, 2003; Iversen & Rosenbluth, 2010; Leira, 1992, 2002; O'Connor, Orloff, & Shaver, 1999; Sainsbury, 2001). A growing literature explores social policies in the Global South (see, e.g., Franzoni, 2008; Garay, 2016; Haggard & Kaufman, 2008; Huber & Stephens, 2012; Mares & Carnes, 2009; Niedzwiecki, 2014, Forthcoming; Pribble, 2013; Rudra, 2007; Segura-Ubiergo, 2007), but only a small part of it analyzes policies on care work (for exceptions see Blofield, 2012; Blofield & Franzoni, 2014; Gerhard & Staab, 2010; Molyneux, 2007). Very little scholarship seeks to explain gendered social policies globally, in a way that encompasses both developed and developing countries and crosses regions (for exceptions, see, e.g., Razavi & Staab, 2012). Since even the poorest countries are adopting policies to combat poverty and promote inclusion, studies on whether and how developing welfare states in the Global South incorporate concerns about gender equality and recognition of care work is a priority.

SOCIAL PROVISION AND GENDER JUSTICE

Unless the state supports care work, it is difficult to imagine how societies will help women overcome historical gender disadvantages and evolve toward greater equality and justice. Cultural and political systems in most contemporary societies fail to recognize, and to compensate, the labor involved in caring for family members as work. When societies do compensate such work, they do so primarily at lower wages or in the informal sector. Whether paid or unpaid, women typically dominate the care-work sector.

Contemporary systems of public social provision in many places, especially Northern and Western Europe, were originally developed to support male breadwinners in unemployment, at old age, and in the event of disability. Their dependents were supported only indirectly (Lewis, 1993). In these very same welfare states, and in other countries too, social provision was premised on distinguishing between deserving and undeserving women (Abramovitz, 1996; Skocpol, 1992), rewarding military service (Skocpol, 1992), or encouraging fertility among certain groups to combat nativist fears about race suicide (Koven & Michel, 1993). In Eastern Europe, it was assumed that women would work in the paid labor market while also bearing the brunt of care work at home, and social policies were designed to support women's assumption of this "double burden." In these ways, welfare states have constructed and upheld gender regimes: constellations of rules that structure, and are shaped by, ideas about masculinity and femininity, and the relations between raced and classed categories of masculinity and femininity (Connell, 1987; Williams, 1995). Though the specific form of these regimes has varied, the position of disadvantage that women have occupied has not.

The normative family arrangement of male breadwinner and female caregiver upon which some Northern welfare states were premised is not universal today, and likely never was, even in Northern and Western European states (Coontz, 2016; Duncan, 1996; Lewis, 1993). Indeed, the form of the "gender contract" varied widely across Europe, with several distinct and identifiable forms (Duncan, 1995, 1996). This idea seems to have even less purchase across the Global South. In Africa, for example, some 26 percent of households are headed by women (including divorced women, widowed women, and women with migrant husbands), though there are differences between regions. In Southern Africa, 43 percent of households are headed by women, while in West Africa, about one in five households is headed by a woman (Milazzo & van de Walle, 2017, p. 9). Households headed by single women are common in the Global North as well: In the United States, for example, single mothers headed up 23 percent of family households with children in 2016, while single people living alone without children made up more than a quarter (28 percent) of households (US Bureau of the Census, 2016). Households headed by single women are disproportionately poor, since women tend to be paid less than men and experience more career interruptions due to the care work they perform. In many countries, lone mothers have astoundingly high rates of poverty (Chant, 2007; Pearce, 1978).

For many families navigating the contemporary world, the traditional family form is both infeasible and unwise. Maintaining a minimum standard of living often requires that both parents earn wages at work (though many families live in poverty even when both parents work). Women who choose – or are forced – not to participate in the paid labor force are highly vulnerable in the event of divorce or abandonment. Access to wage work enables women to support themselves and their families. What is more, studies show that women who are economically independent or potentially independent have greater bargaining power at home and are less susceptible to domestic violence (Agarwal & Panda, 2007; Iversen & Rosenbluth, 2006; Panda & Agarwal, 2005).

Labor force participation may be desirable for women for many reasons, but women's "second shift" (Hochschild & Machung, 1989) of housework and care work poses an obstacle to their equitable participation in wage work. The fact that men have fewer responsibilities for care work makes them more available for the labor market, and grants them higher incomes and recognition, more opportunities for advancement to leadership positions, and more leisure time. Recent studies show that many employers place a premium on "round the clock" availability, which puts caregivers at a disadvantage (Goldin, 2014). For all women, but especially those without the ability to outsource care work to nannies and maids, gaining higher wages and more opportunities requires that men (or other caregiving partners) assume a greater share of care work and housework, or what Gornick and Meyers (2008) refer to as "halving it all."

Similarly, in many Global South contexts, a practice and assumption of "familialism" has prevailed into the twenty-first century. Care work and reproductive labor are performed largely by women, either in the home or via kinship networks (Razavi & Staab, 2012). What is more, women's participation in the formal labor force – disproportionately in informal, irregular, seasonal, part-time, and lower-paid jobs – is rarely accompanied by a reduction in their "second shift" of care work. A significant group of working women enter wage work out of desperation (which Kabeer calls a "distress sale" of labor), to insure the survival of their families, and to cope with poverty and other crises. Their decision to work does not result from an active choice and the conditions of work are hardly empowering (Kabeer, 2012, pp. 21–3). Women's work begins to generate more positive externalities for children, families, and societies in general when they work on a regular basis in formal-sector enterprises, primarily in the public but also in the export-oriented sector (Kabeer, 2012, pp. 20, 39).

One way the state can help to alleviate the double burden is by guaranteeing the availability of family leave and childcare for women and men who lack the resources to rely on the market or do not have help from caregiving partners or family members. State provision thus has the potential to promote equality not only between women and men but also among women of different socioeconomic classes and social groups. In addition, some states have used care policies to support changes in gender roles. To offer men financial incentives to assume more responsibility for parenting, Norway in 1993 and Sweden in 1995 introduced "daddy leave," a nontransferable leave period. Studies show that the policies contributed to a significant increase in the number and proportion of fathers who took parental leave, shifted the sexual division of labor, and benefitted children and families over the longer term (Cools, Fiva, & Kirkebøen, 2015; Haas & Hwang, 2008; Kotsadam & Finseraas, 2011).

All contemporary welfare states have policies that shape work–life integration, or reconciliation, to varying degrees, with differing emphases, and with diverse consequences for gender and class equality (cf. Blofield & Martínez Franzoni, 2015; Esping-Andersen, 2009; Gornick & Meyers, 2003; Mazur, 2002; Martínez Franzoni & Voorend, 2012; O'Connor, Orloff, & Shaver, 1999). Whereas some welfare states have developed policies to enable parents to take time off work to care for young children, provided childcare for working families, and promoted flexible work schedules and part-time employment, others have done less to mitigate work–family conflict or tension. Whereas some welfare states explicitly aim to alter the sexual distribution of labor and encourage men to assume a greater share of care giving, others do not.[2] The key questions are: Does social policy enable women to maintain an autonomous household (Orloff, 1993; Young, 2002), or does it reinforce a male breadwinner model of the family (Connell, 1990; Lewis, 1993)? Does social policy push poor women into the low-wage labor market without regard to their or their families' well-being (Abramovitz, 1996), or does it empower women to

---

[2] Welfare states differ along another crucial dimension: their age orientation. Whereas some welfare states bias their spending toward children and the young, the spending pattern of others is biased toward the elderly (Lynch, 2006).

pursue work or family-related responsibilities as needed? Do women of different social classes have equal chances at economic independence and gender equality?

THE LOGIC OF CLASS POLITICS

Up to this point, this book has focused on policy areas that involve questions of women's status, such as violence against women and workplace equality, and those that also touch upon religious doctrine, such as family law. We showed that change to policies involving women's status depends on the mobilization of feminist movements outside of political parties and the state. Doctrinal sex-equality policies challenging religious traditions, by contrast, are closely associated with the power of religious forces and the institutionalized relations between the state and organized religion. The social policies we analyze in this chapter conform to a different logic. To a much greater degree than other policies analyzed in this book so far, parental leave and child care provision rely upon, and form part of, the institutionalized relationship between state, market, and family. By adopting these policies, the state assumes a greater responsibility for social provision and care work in particular. This expansion in the state's role in many cases represents a significant increase in state budgets (cf. O'Connor, Orloff, & Shaver, 1999; Orloff, 1993). Since the form and degree of state spending is already the subject of contestation in most welfare states, efforts to expand or reshape state policies related to the family become part of this broader struggle in a way that policies on violence against women, divorce, or sex discrimination in the workplace do not.

Left Party Power

The prospect of enlarging the welfare state to encompass care work animates actors and interests invested in particular patterns of state spending. Typically, Left parties and labor unions favor particular types of expansion while Right parties and business associations resist those same policies. We therefore expect that expansive family policies (by which we mean generous, publicly paid parental leaves aimed at both women *and* men and state support for childcare) should be associated with the strength of Left- or union-backed political parties as well as the strength of other "usual suspects" of gender equality policy, including feminist movements, women in parliament, and women's policy machineries. By extension, the association between Left parties on the one hand and parental leave and childcare on the other should be stronger than the relationship between Left parties and other gender issues such as abortion legality, family law reform, or violence against women, all of which trigger welfare state expansion more weakly or indirectly.

This emphasis on Left parties builds on a long scholarly tradition. Classical approaches to Left parties emphasized egalitarian values in general (Duverger, 1954), and scholars have extended these arguments to state action on women's rights, claiming that the egalitarian values of Left parties make them more likely to support sex equality (Rule, 1987; Stetson & Mazur, 1995). Particularly relevant to the discussions of social policy and its connection to class inequality on which we focus here, the classic power resources theory approach posits that variations in the size and form of the welfare state owe to differences in the degree of the political mobilization of the working class across countries. When strong labor movements mobilize, and social democratic and other Leftist parties have political power, the government is more likely to adopt universal, generous, and comprehensive welfare policies (Esping-Andersen, 1990; Huber & Stephens, 2001; Korpi, 2006, 1983).

Studies of postcommunist countries add further support for this connection. Carreja and Emmenegger (2009) find that party composition of government, and especially the role of Left parties, is the most robust factor accounting for total public and social expenditures. In a study of welfare states in lesser developed countries (LDCs), Rudra (2002) argues that the weakness in labor power in developing countries (in contrast to the greater political power of labor in advanced industrial countries) accounts for the inability of workers to prevent the erosion of welfare states, as government spending in LDCs declined in the face of globalization from 1972 to 1995.

On the other hand, cross-national and over-time analysis of Latin American countries in recent decades has found that Left party strength is not associated with greater social expenditures (Niedzwiecki, 2015), though historically the power of Left parties was important for the development of the region's most generous welfare regimes (Huber & Stephens, 2012). The connection between Left parties and welfare state expansion may be more tenuous in the developing world, and also in emerging democracies, where parties lack deep roots in society and connect with voters through personalistic (rather than programmatic) appeals, and where electoral volatility is high (Mainwaring, 1999; Mainwaring & Scully, 1995). In the context of more weakly institutionalized party systems, Left parties may be only inconsistently committed to redistributive and social democratic agendas (Kitschelt, Hawkins, Luna, Rosas, & Zechmeister, 2010). In Latin America, for example, many Left parties elected in the 1980s and early 1990s violated their mandates and introduced austerity policies (Stokes, 2001), while Left parties elected later in the 1990s and the 2000s were more supportive of redistribution to reduce social inequalities (though not always for women or other disadvantaged groups) (Levitsky & Roberts, 2011).

Some scholars have linked Left parties directly to advances in women's rights and representation (Jenson, 1995; Norris, 1987; Stetson & Mazur, 1995; Wängnerud, 2009). Kittilson found that Left parties were associated with expanding maternity leave but not parental leave (Kittilson, 2008), while Grey found that party ideology mattered more than gender in promoting expansive parental leave (Grey, 2002). Democratic party strength in the U.S. states is associated with expanded childcare (Weldon, 2011).

Other scholars, however, have contested the idea that labor mobilization would advance women's rights in light of the male-dominated nature of unions (Elman, 2001; Gelb, 1989; Wolbrecht, 2000). In the United States, unions and their Democratic Party allies objected to reforms that would eliminate so-called protective labor legislation and open male-dominated professions to women (Wolbrecht, 2000). Elman emphasizes that Left parties have not been advocates for government action on VAW in general, nor on sexual harassment in particular (see also Weldon 2002a; 2011). Henderson and White (2004) found that social democratic governments were not associated with longer maternity leave. Finally, there is some research suggesting that the impact of Left parties on gender equality may depend on the specific ideology of the party (whether the party is "old" or "new" left) and on its organization (Grey, 2002; Kittilson et al., 2006).

As this suggests, the literature on Left parties, social policy, and sex equality contains some seemingly contradictory findings. At least some of the confusion in the literature can be resolved, we argue, by examining the type of gender issue and the form of the welfare state already in existence where advocates press for expansions of the welfare state to encompass greater gender equality. Some of the disagreement about the role of Left parties in relation to gender equality relates to the type of gender issue at hand. Prior chapters found that Left parties were not key catalysts for policies on VAW, employment law, or family law reform. But we would expect that they do matter for this particular issue, where class politics is more salient, and where Left parties would traditionally advocate for the kinds of policies feminists support.

In addition, we would argue, Left parties may play different roles in different contexts: Earlier policy decisions may shape the role of Left parties in later periods. As Pierson notes, new policies create a political constituency of those who benefit from the policy. This means the politics of welfare state expansion may be different than welfare state retraction (Pierson, 1994). Policy advocates confront a different political landscape depending on the policies adopted in prior periods. It may also be that Left parties are less important in developing countries where party systems are less institutionalized.

The strength of Left parties and a bigger redistributive coalition may be more important when a particular policy amounts to a major change in approach, pushes the state into new areas, and intervenes in the market in new and more aggressive ways. When state intervention in the market is already a well-established tradition, by contrast, a new policy may not require backing by a large coalition or civic mobilization. As Kamerman and Moss note: "What is radical in one historical period becomes conservative in the next" (Kamerman & Moss, 2009, p. 203). For example, policies such as public provision of maternity leave have a long history in Scandinavian social democracies and in former communist countries. In these contexts, feminist activists and women in parliament may have sufficient strength, without a bigger coalition, to promote greater public provision of care work, because their aim involves an expansion of a familiar policy rather than a radically new role for government.

National Wealth

Though there is little dispute that welfare states exist across the Global South, there is more contention about how and why welfare states in less developed countries are different from those in advanced industrialized states, and from each other (Rudra, 2007). Some argue that emerging democracies and other polities in the Global South lack the preconditions of an expansive welfare state: a broad tax base; a legitimate, central governing authority; a national labor market providing for the livelihood of most citizens; and financial markets offering insurance and instruments for savings. A developed form of capitalism, as well as an autonomous state, enabled the evolution of welfare states in the richer countries (Gough, 2004, p. 21). In poorer countries, when the state provides any social benefits, large sectors of the population, including informal sector workers, domestic workers, agricultural workers, and women who are economically inactive, tend to be excluded. In many countries of the Middle East and North Africa, for example, the benefits of social policies such as maternity leave, health care, and pensions have been limited primarily to urban residents and government workers (Karshenas & Moghadam, 2009, p. S54). The oil-rich states of the Persian Gulf had more generous policies than other countries in the region, but they were "essentially handouts from the rentier state" rather than "entitlements accruing to tax paying and gainfully employed citizens" (Karshenas & Moghadam, 2009).

The welfare states of most contemporary developing states tend not to offer social policies as generous as those of advanced industrial states. Historically in sub-Saharan Africa, social insurance programs such as pensions applied to formal sector workers; other assistance programs were temporary and targeted to specific groups, such as food subsidies and agricultural inputs (fertilizer, seeds) for farmers (Oduro, 2010, p. 5). As part of structural adjustment programs introduced in the 1980s, schools and hospitals began to charge user fees, thwarting many people's access to basic services. In the late 1990s and 2000s, some countries began to introduce more comprehensive social programs in order to reduce poverty, such as old age pensions in Botswana; a conditional cash transfer to the extreme poor in Ghana and South Africa; cash transfers to vulnerable households and individuals in Kenya, Malawi, Mozambique, and Uganda; and a universal noncontributory pension for the elderly in Lesotho (Oduro, 2010, pp. 11–12).

While increased national wealth is unlikely to translate seamlessly or automatically into more expansive policies (as the history of contestation over social provision in the advanced industrial states attests), it is reasonable to think that greater national wealth makes it more likely that such policies will be adopted, and they need not compete directly with other policy priorities. When more funding is available, there are fewer sharp trade-offs between different policy priorities. Wealthier states are better able to afford a wide array of forms of social provision.

As this discussion suggests, we would expect the overall level of economic development to be associated with more extensive family leave and child care provision, as it is with the size of the welfare state in general. On the other hand, there may not be a single, unified account of family leave and childcare provision that spans the diverse experiences of emerging and established democracies. Fortunately, we do not aim to provide one; our analytical objective in this chapter is more modest.

We seek merely to show that the patterns of variation are different for class issues as compared to other areas of women's rights. Since the histories, coalitions, and ideas in family leave and childcare differ from those behind status issues such as VAW and doctrinal issues such as family law, empirical trends will also differ.

This is not to suggest that the dynamics driving family leave and childcare will be exactly the same, just because they are both class issues. Indeed, childcare is an issue that challenges the assumption that children will be cared for at home, in the private sphere, most likely by a mother or other female family member. At the same time, childcare workers tend to be women, and the cost of childcare is an issue that pits middle class and other families who pay for center-based childcare against the women who work in these centers, who benefit from higher wages. No such conflict arises from maternity leave, which affirms the importance for children of parental (and often maternal) care and sometimes reinforces the idea that women's primary responsibilities are at home rather than in the world of paid work. Feminists have historically been more ambivalent about maternity leave policies than they have been about support for childcare. In addition, maternity leave has often been cast as a labor issue, and many maternity leave initiatives predated modern feminism. Indeed, states may solve the work–family reconciliation problem by relying more on one of these strategies than the other.

In spite of these differences, we anticipate that class politics animates these two issues more than it does status or doctrinal issues. In the rest of this chapter, we first describe patterns of family leave provision and then turn to an analysis of childcare, concluding with a combined discussion of how our findings relate to our contention that gender issues that are class issues are distinct from the other types of issues we explore in this book.

PART I. FAMILY LEAVE: A GLOBAL OVERVIEW

In most countries, public policy provides for time off for workers who give birth or care for children, a policy we call "family leave." Leave may be guaranteed in labor law, provided for by specific legislation, or introduced as part of an unemployment insurance or social security program. Leave takes different forms: *maternity* leave, *parental* leave, and *daddy* leave (more formally known as nontransferable parental leave for fathers). Paid leave may be funded by government, the employer, or a combination of the two. In addition, leave policies vary in terms of the length of the leave provided and the conditions of eligibility.

Maternity leave, intended for women only, is important to ensure that the biological exigencies of childbirth do not jeopardize women's ability to support themselves and their families by participating in the labor market. However, such leave, especially when understood to encompass not only these biological or health dimensions of childbirth but also the socially prescribed parenting responsibilities, can reinforce the traditional sexual division of labor in the home and can help maintain occupational segregation in the workplace (cf. Becker & Becker, 2009). Laws that require employers to assume the entire cost of leave (employer mandates) place responsibility for children squarely in the private sphere, and fail to enunciate the public value of care work. Such systems represent little challenge to existing gender roles and leave in place existing redistributive arrangements. What is more, in the absence of strong protections for discrimination against women, these systems tend to aggravate women's disadvantaged position in the labor market. To avoid costs associated with maternity protections, for example, employers in Mexico often demand periodic pregnancy tests as a condition of employment (Bensusán, 2007; Htun & Jensenius, 2016a).

Parental leave, by contrast, is gender-neutral and may be taken by anyone, including adoptive parents, mother, father, or someone standing *in loco parentis*. The concept thus incorporates a distinction between the biological needs that result from childbirth and the social and practical needs that stem from care giving and parenting. It is important to distinguish between parental leave and *paternity* leave, a gender-specific leave for fathers to enable them be present at the time of a child's birth and for a short period thereafter.

Daddy leave, meanwhile, is a special kind of parental leave designed to help bend the social norms that had precluded many men from taking up gender-neutral parental leave. If fathers do not use the leave, they may not transfer the time to the other parent. In some Scandinavian countries, as already mentioned, daddy leave has led to increased numbers of men taking time off to care for infants and helped to normalize men's expanded role in parenting.

Overall, there has been a steady, global growth in the number of countries offering any *maternity* leave (to encompass all the seventy countries in our study), as well as paid maternity leave (to include *almost* all countries, with only a few laggards, including the United States[3]).

---

[3] Other countries without paid maternity or parental leave in 2011 included Lesotho, Papua New Guinea, and Swaziland (International Labor Office, 2010). Australia introduced paid leave in 2011.

There has been a dramatic expansion in *parental* leave in Europe and in some of Asia, but not in other world areas, where parental leave is virtually nonexistent, with some minor exceptions (International Labor Office, 2010, p. 49). In addition, the length of maternity leave has grown from a global average of 2.4 months to 3.7 months, as have international norms with respect to the ideal length of leave (International Labor Office, 2010).[4] The MENA region tends to have the shortest legally mandated maternity leave, followed by Latin America and Asia (International Labor Office, 2010, p. 6).

Mechanisms to supply paid maternity leave vary dramatically across countries, though there has been a slow trend toward greater public participation. Richer countries of Europe tend to pay maternal salaries out of social insurance funds; poorer ones of sub-Saharan Africa, South Asia, and the Middle East and North Africa (MENA) tend to require employers to pay (though 34 percent of African countries finance leave through social security and 24 percent through a mixed system). In Latin America, most countries pay from social security, though a significant number (around 40 percent) require cost splitting between employers and the government (International Labor Office, 2010, p. 25, Figure 2.4).

The countries of the MENA region have offered paid maternity leave for several decades, though often in the form of employer mandates. For example, government-supported maternity leave was offered in Iran before the revolution; in Egypt and Turkey, maternity leave policies date from 1964 and 1971, respectively (Hatem, 1992). In other parts of Africa, paid maternity leave is offered through a mix of employer mandates, public financing, and mixed regimes (cost splitting). In Nigeria, the employer mandate model prevails. The Labor Act of 1990 granted women the right to leave six weeks prior to birth and prevented women from working for six weeks after, but required that employers pay women at least 50 percent of their wages. There is no gender-neutral parental leave policy, and no pressure to create one. People whom our team interviewed for this book, including government officials, nongovernmental organization (NGO) representatives, activists, and members of the news media, reported a complete absence of discussion about paternity leave for men in Nigeria and in Africa more broadly. What is more, our questions about the possibility of parental leave for men were met

---

[4] The ILO Maternity Protection Convention of 2000 mandates fourteen weeks of leave; the 1951 Convention mandated twelve. For its part, the 1919 Convention stated only that women should not be permitted to work for six weeks after birth.

with chuckles. The civil service tends to enforce maternity leave provisions, but coverage is much spottier outside the public sector.[5]

In 2012, MENA, South Asia, and sub-Saharan Africa were the regions most likely to uphold employer mandates for the payment of maternity leave salaries.[6] Employer mandates were also common in South Asia, with the policy in force in Bangladesh, India, Pakistan, and Sri Lanka. In Southeast Asia, the situation was more mixed: Indonesia and Malaysia had an employer mandate but in Burma (Myanmar), Laos, and Vietnam, the cost of leave was paid through social insurance. In Thailand, the law mandates cost splitting.[7]

Latin American governments enforce maternity leave and most legislation provides for around three months, though Brazil and Costa Rica require sixteen weeks and Cuba eighteen, while Chilean law was reformed in 2011 to mandate six months of *parental* leave (four and a half months for the mother and six weeks more for either parent, at the mother's discretion) (Blofield & Martínez Franzoni, 2014). Most countries in the region (and all ten in our database from Latin America) require paid leave, though the sources of funding vary from place to place. In some countries, such as Brazil and Mexico, leave is financed entirely through social insurance funds, while in others, such as the Dominican Republic and Ecuador, the cost is split between the government and employers (50/50 in the former; 75/25 in the latter). Only in El Salvador is the cost of leave financed entirely by employers.[8]

Differences in reimbursement mechanisms are loosely associated with the size of the tax base. Employer mandates have generally been more common in poorer countries, while generous publicly paid leave has been more common in wealthier countries. Yet there are some exceptions to this general trend: the oil-rich Gulf states such as Saudi Arabia, the United Arab Emirates, Qatar, and Kuwait, for example, uphold employer mandates.[9]

---

[5] Interviews conducted by Cheryl O'Brien in Lagos and Abuja, 2008.

[6] Employer mandates prevailed in Botswana, the DRC, Eritrea, Iraq, Kenya, Kuwait, Lesotho, Malawi, Mauritius, Nigeria, Qatar, Saudi Arabia, Sudan, Syria, the United Arab Emirates, Tanzania, Yemen, Zambia, and Zimbabwe (United Nations Statistics Division, 2012).

[7] There are some discrepancies between these data on policy and the ILO (2010) dataset. For example, the description of the policy in Tanzania in inconsistent across these two sources. Further research is required to settle this question.

[8] United Nations Statistics Division (2012), Statistics and Indicators on Women and Men, Table 5g. Maternity Leave Benefits, http://unstats.un.org/unsd/demographic/products/indwm/default.htm.

[9] In the Gulf, rates of women's employment (at 25–30 percent, except Saudi Arabia, where FLFP was only 7 percent in 2011) are considerably lower than OECD averages but

A growing number of countries have begun to require maternity leave coverage for domestic workers. South Africa grants domestic workers four months of maternity leave, paid out of social insurance funds. In at least 53 other countries in the ILO's study of 167 countries, domestic workers were covered by maternity leave legislation (International Labor Office 2010, p. 38).

Breastfeeding has been an important theme in discussions about leave policies in several countries. In Gulf and other Arab states, though maternity leave times tend to be short, various laws require that employers grant women one to two hours of time per day to breastfeed, for between eighteen months and two years following a child's birth. The United Arab Emirates' Child Rights Law, adopted in January 2014, requires mothers to breastfeed for the first two years of a child's life.[10] In Chile, many of the bills to expand maternity leave since the return to democracy in 1990 were sponsored by representatives who emphasized the importance of breastfeeding (Blofield & Martínez Franzoni, 2014). Advocates justified the 2011 reform expanding parental leave to six months (paid) on the grounds of allowing working women to breastfeed for a longer period of time as well as increasing female labor force participation (since Chile has one of the lowest rates of the region) (Blofield & Martínez Franzoni, 2014).

Fertility rates are another factor linked to variation in leave policies (Blofield & Lambert, 2008; Boling, 2015; Rosenbluth, 2007). In advanced democracies, other things being equal, fertility rates are higher where the structure of the labor market and care policies does not force women to choose between work (or economic independence) on the one hand and having more children on the other (Rosenbluth, 2007). In countries where social policies are less generous, women must often make a choice between wage work and children, and many choose work. Such strategic considerations preceded, and continue to supplement, the gender justice arguments supporting family policies such as daddy leave and paid parental leave (Koven & Michel, 1993; Boling, 2015).[11]

---

growing, and there is evidence of societal pressure to expand the length of leave. See for example Mohannad Shawari, "It's time Labor Ministry reviewed laws concerning maternity leave," *Arab News*, May 4, 2013; Editorial, "Longer maternity leave is welcome in the UAE," *The National*, March 7, 2013.

[10] Emma Graham-Harrison, "UAE law requires mothers to breastfeed for first two years," *The Guardian*, July 2, 2014; Salem Ola, "FNC passes mandatory breastfeeding clause for child rights law," *The National*, January 21, 2014.

[11] The equation cuts in the opposite direction in much of the Global South, where women's status is inversely related to fertility rates.

In Europe and East Asia, declining fertility rates have motivated governments to adopt a range of policies intended to make work and motherhood more compatible, including longer leave time, protection and support for part-time employment, and expansion of child care centers.[12] Japan's Child Care Leave Law of 1991, for example, mandated one year of job-protected parental leave, which, after a 2001 reform, included payment of 40 percent of salary funded by social insurance. A 2005 reform extended parental leave benefits to contract workers, many of whom are women (Hayashi, 2005). Later, the reimbursement rate was raised to 67 percent of salary for a six-month leave, and the law permitted men whose wives were full-time housewives to take leave. Arguably as a result of these efforts, the country's fertility rate rebounded after reaching a low of 1.26 in 2005.

In Korea as well, the government has progressively expanded parental leave benefits: A 1987 law granted (unpaid) parental leave to women, followed by a 1995 reform expanding the leave to men. A 2001 reform began to subsidize leave (at far lower than average wages, however) and throughout the decade Congress regularly expanded the size of the income replacement. Though the government's intention was to incentivize men to take parental leave, without higher replacement rates, few men are willing to take advantage of the policy.

In the Netherlands, a 1996 reform gave part-time workers equal status with their full-time counterparts and a 2000 law granted workers the right to determine their own working hours. A 2009 reform expanded parental leave to twenty-six weeks for each parent (nontransferable). As a result, rates of women's employment are high – in 2011, 76 percent of mothers with children under six worked – and the fertility rate exceeds the EU average (though at 1.8 it continues to be below the replacement rate).[13]

---

[12] The number of live births in the European Union declined fairly dramatically between 1960 and the 2000s. In 2011, fertility rates in virtually all of the twenty-seven EU countries were below replacement rates (except for France, Iceland, and Ireland), dramatically so in some large economies such as Germany (1.36), Italy (1.41), and Spain (1.36). See European Commission, "Fertility statistics," Eurostat, October 2012, http://epp.eurostat.ec.europa.eu/statistics_explained/index.php/Fertility_statistics.

Among the five East Asian "tigers" (Japan, South Korea, Hong Kong, Taiwan, and Singapore), fertility rates are well below replacement levels (1.4 in Japan and Korea, 1.3 in Singapore and 1.07 in Hong Kong). At 0.9, Taiwan's fertility rate is held to be the lowest in the world. See Ralph Jennings, "Taiwan birthrate falls to world's lowest," *Voice of America*, August 16, 2011.

[13] European Union, n.d., "Netherlands: Reconciliation of work and family life through part time work," European Platform for Investing in Children, Country Profiles, http://europa.eu/epic/countries/netherlands/index_en.htm.

While declining fertility provided a context for advocates to frame
generous family policies, this did not mean that they were always framed
this way or that declining fertility was a necessary precondition for policy
adoption or expansion. Access to maternity leave predated the fertility
crisis in Italy and Spain, while daddy leave was adopted amid conditions
of relatively low fertility (Sweden) and relatively higher fertility (Norway).
As this suggests, there is considerable variation in leave policies among
the wealthier countries and among countries with low fertility.[14] This
variation suggests that we need to look at political variables – including
the role of Left parties and feminist movements – for an explanation of the
contours of policy on family leave.

MECHANISMS BEHIND LEAVE POLICY:
THE UNITED STATES AND NORWAY

Comparing the experiences of the United States and Norway sheds light
on the respective roles of historical legacies, Left party power, strategic
framing, and feminist activism behind family leave policy. In addition,
analysis of the path toward daddy leave in Northern Europe illuminates
how policy legacies can create conditions for expansion, even in more
radical directions.

First, we probe the puzzle of why the United States is the only advanced
democracy with no national, publicly paid parental leave. Why has the
strong, autonomous feminist movement that pushed for enactment of the
Pregnancy Discrimination Act (PDA) of 1978 not secured a leave policy?
Instead of the paid parental leave characteristic of other advanced societies, the United States guarantees only twelve weeks of gender-neutral,
unpaid, family or medical leave, the result of the Family and Medical
Leave Act of 1993 (FMLA). The FMLA was first introduced by representatives Patricia Schroeder (Democrat, Colorado) and William Clay
(Democrat, Missouri) in 1985. Feminists were part of the original effort
to get some kind of leave policy on the political agenda and framed
their proposals in gender-neutral terms, as medically necessary or family
leave. Yet the original advocates of the leave policy had to make many
compromises, leading to strategic and ideological divisions (Bernstein,
2001). Feminists were sidelined as other interests took over, and women's

[14] In general, however, virtually all the advanced economies have adopted a minimal version
of paid maternity leave. The United States is currently the only advanced democracy with
no publicly paid parental leave (except in a few states).

organizations ultimately did not play a major role in the development or passage of the FMLA (Mazur, 2002, p. 114). The initial framing stuck, however, and the bill that ultimately became the FMLA was widely seen as a labor or "family"-related bill (Stetson, 1997, pp. 270–1). Labor unions and conservative groups supported the proposal, viewing it as a prolabor and profamily idea. Business interests framed the legislation in terms of labor rights and opposed it, as did states' rights groups, which resisted federal mandates.

As with many initiatives seen as prolabor, the bill to create unpaid family leave was supported by Democrats and opposed by Republicans. Some Republican legislators broke ranks and supported the Act, arguing it was a profamily measure that would help workers cope with demands of work–life balance. After delays owing primarily to business-based opposition, the bill passed both houses of Congress in the spring of 1990. But Republican President Bush vetoed the bill in 1990 anyway. In 1991–2, both houses passed the FMLA and the President vetoed it again. The Senate overrode the veto (but the House did not) and the FMLA became an election issue in the presidential campaign of 1992. While campaigning, Bill Clinton pledged to sign the law. Congress once more passed the bill and it was signed into law in 1993 by President Clinton (Bernstein, 2001). This means that the Act passed with the support of the left-wing party and in spite of opposition from the right-wing party (if the Democrats count as left).[15]

The FMLA requires that employers grant up to twelve weeks of leave (which can be unpaid) in a twelve-month period for the purposes of caring for a child or sick family member, or for personal medical reasons. Coverage is limited, as the Act applies only to private employers with more than fifty employees and to public agencies. Studies estimate that the FMLA covers some 60–65 percent of employed people, and an even smaller share of women workers (Ruhm, 1997, p. 177). What is more, most workers who stood to benefit from the FMLA already were able to take time off from work to care for children, due to provisions of the PDA, disability benefits, maternity leave laws in some states, sick leave, and firm-specific policies. A survey conducted in 1995 revealed that

---

[15] Whether or not the Democratic party is a Left party is controversial for some, since, especially in the South, Democratic legislators can seem more conservative than labor or Left parties in other nations (say, according to Canadian or European standards). Nevertheless, the Democratic Party does have close ties to labor, and is certainly more left than the other major party, so for labor issues the partisan divide between Democrats and Republicans remains relevant, as this discussion reveals.

merely 17 percent of workers reported taking leave for a reason included in the FMLA, and only 7 percent of the 17 percent (1.2 percent total) claimed the leave was taken under federal provisions (Ruhm, 1997, pp. 182–4). Overall, the effects of the Act on patterns of leave taking were modest, though there is evidence that the FMLA improved child health outcomes (Rossin, 2011).

Significantly, few women were present in Congress when the FMLA was passed, although the original bill was strongly supported by a woman legislator. Though record numbers of women entered Congress in 1992 (dubbed the Year of the Woman), they still amounted to merely 11 percent of members of the House and 14 percent of the Senate.

The U.S. experience suggests that a country's overall level of economic development may be an enabling condition for generous leave policies, but that the strength of Left parties is a crucial factor determining whether governments actually offer leave. Indeed, the power of the Democratic Party has been important not only at the national but also at state levels in advocating for paid family leave, while Republicans have opposed it. In the 1990s, the Clinton administration introduced a scheme that allowed states to augment their unemployment insurance programs to provide paid leave to new parents. Several states were also developing or had developed their own paid leave schemes. Democratic state legislators, women's groups, and unions all pushed for such measures. In Massachusetts, an expansion of unemployment insurance to cover maternity leave (so-called Baby-UI) was championed by a coalition of union groups, women's groups, and Catholic groups. Early in his first term (2002), however, Republican president George W. Bush repealed provisions offering federal support to states with paid leave. Repeal was supported by state and federal chambers of commerce, and opposed by unions and women's groups.[16]

In Norway, family leave developed much earlier than in the United States, and Left parties played an important role in policy developments. Policies date from the late nineteenth century, in the context of the class

---

[16] Three states – California, New Jersey, and Washington – still provide an average of 10–12 weeks of paid maternity leave through temporary state disability insurance. Political dynamics similar to those at the federal level drove state action. In New Jersey, for example, a Democratic governor and mostly Democratic legislators strongly supported the measure, with additional support from the unions and women's organizations. Business interests were opposed, and Republicans were split on the issue (Raghunathan, 2001; Parmley, 2001). Democrats have framed leave policies as "family issues," "children's issues," or "family values" policies, not as women's rights or labor policies.

struggle over social reform and the nationalist struggle to be free of Swedish domination (Leira, 1993; Sainsbury, 2001). Indeed, maternal support policies have roots in nationalist movements and civil war in several national contexts (Koven & Michel, 1993; Skocpol, 1992). Norwegian working women have had access to paid maternity leave since 1909, well before women won the right to vote and stand for parliamentary elections (in 1913) (Leira, 1993). Norway was the first of the Scandinavian countries to provide economic compensation to mothers, twenty years before both Sweden and Denmark (Melby, Ravn, & Wetterberg, 2009; Sainsbury, 2001).

Norwegian feminists tried to expand maternity leave in the late 1970s, after the 1971 "women's coup" that brought many more women into government and the successful subsequent campaigns to expand women's political representation in 1977 and 1979.[17] The women elected as a result of this mobilization report that they immediately began to work to change policies on childcare, equal pay, and shelters for battered women. By 1978, there were 37 women in the Storting (national parliament), constituting about 24 percent of the total. This was the biggest change in women's representation across the Nordic world at that time (Raaum, 2005). Still, efforts to expand maternity leave were unsuccessful, although Norwegian men and women obtained the right to shared maternity and paternity leave for childbirth (Weldon, 2011).

In the 1980s, the discussion of maternity leave again rose to prominence, and the government adopted a series of expansions toward the end of the decade.[18] Then, in 1986, the Labour government established a government commission to examine men's gender roles and aspects of maleness and masculinity, including fatherhood. In 1989, this commission recommended extending parental leave to twelve months, and reserving three months of leave for the father. Notably, the division of unpaid care was framed as a gender equality issue.

The Labour-controlled legislature adopted a scaled-back version of the commission's proposal. The three months reserved for the father was cut to four weeks, and the father's right to care was made conditional on the mother's employment. With these changes, the Labour government

---

[17] Norwegian feminists emphasized the importance of organizing to elect more women to government. They were very successful at exploiting particular features of the Norwegian electoral system (organizing campaigns to cross out the names of men and write in the names of women), and the large number of women elected in the 1971 local/county elections has come to be called the "Women's Coup" (Bystydzienski, 1995, p. 45).

[18] "Daddy leave," which had been discussed publicly earlier, was not part of these reforms.

introduced the "fedrekvote" (father's quota or daddy leave) that came into effect in 1993 (Leira 2002, p. 95). Norway was the first country in the world to introduce this kind of policy.

Wide-ranging public discussion about the importance of father involvement for child well-being paved the way for the new policy. There was little opposition to the final version of the measure, probably because it was seen as a modest expansion of existing leave provisions and did not take any time from the mother. Both Conservatives and Labour ultimately supported parental leave expansions (Kamerman & Moss, 2009). Parliament granted fathers the right to parental leave independent of the mother's employment status in June 2000.

Over the following two decades, daddy leave was adopted in four additional countries (but rescinded in one by 2005): Sweden, Denmark, Italy, and Iceland. Though daddy leave had long been discussed in Sweden, which may have motivated adoption of the policy in Norway, it was actually adopted only in 1995. While it had been championed by the women's caucus in the Social Democratic Party in the 1970s, the party leadership rejected it (Melby et al., 2009). However, the party did appoint a "Daddy Group" in 1982 to consider the measure. More than a decade later, a center-right coalition government introduced the policy, with support from the opposition. When the government expanded daddy leave to two months in 2002, all the conservative parties opposed the expansion (Melby et al., 2009).

In Denmark, daddy leave was introduced under a social democratic government in 1997. In 2001, however, daddy leave was revoked with the election of a liberal–conservative government coalition, though the overall amount of parental leave was extended by a year. Danish conservatives were more supportive of the extension of parental leave than of a policy that promoted gender role change (Borchorst & Siim, 2002). They were able to revoke daddy leave because of division over this measure within the Social Democratic Party (Borchorst & Borchost, 2006; Melby et al., 2009). No commission on fatherhood or public discussions of men's role as fathers led up to the law's adoption.

These stories suggest that Left parties have been very important for the development of daddy leave proposals. In each case, daddy leave was championed by social democratic parties, while repeal or reduction was accomplished only by more conservative parties. It is worth noting that Left parties were not always dominant when the leave was adopted, which may obscure the central role that Left parties play. It also suggests that public discussion and debate about fathers' roles, men, and masculinity was important to build societal support for the policies.

STATISTICAL ANALYSIS

In this section, we explore the factors associated with more generous family leaves. Our dependent variable is an index of *overall leave generosity*, a measurement of the structure and generosity of leave policies that taps the degree to which they promote equality. Examining maternity and parental leave individually may produce unusual outcomes, since these provisions are related to each other and may change in ways that do not reflect the overall aims of leave. Those governments that offer daddy leave, for example, may offer less parental or maternity leave. Or governments may reduce gender-specific maternity leave while expanding parental leave. For these reasons, it makes sense to examine all three kinds of leave together. The combined index allows us to address the big question of how the three policy subtypes combine to create an overall leave regime.

We created the index using the following formula:

- Maternity leave generosity = Duration of leave + (Duration of leave*publicly paid)[19]
- Parental leave generosity = Duration of leave + (Duration of leave*publicly paid)
- Daddy leave generosity = 2 points
- Overall leave generosity = (maternity leave generosity/5) + (parental leave generosity/5) + Daddy leave generosity

This weighting provides about equal weight to each of the three dimensions of family leave in most cases. The Index ranges from 0 to 7.7 and has a mean of 1.9 and a standard deviation of 1.8. Figure 5.1 depicts the ways that the regional averages of overall leave generosity have changed over time. Leave expanded significantly in Europe, North America, and East Asia, but far less in the Global South (including Latin America).

To explore the covariates of the generosity of leave policy, we considered several hypotheses. First, we explored the role of *Left parties*, the primary factor associated with welfare state expansion in the advanced democracies according to power resources theory. Due to ideological commitments to social justice and equality, and to please working-class and union constituencies, Left parties often use their position in government to expand redistributive social policies.

---

[19] Both of these indices norm the duration of leave to be out of 10.

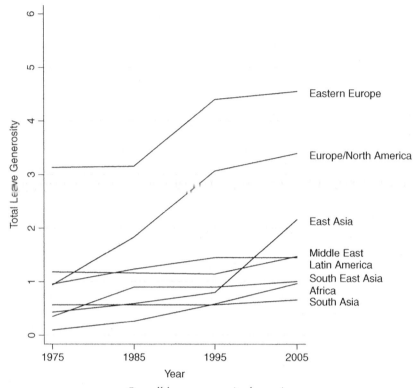

FIGURE 5.1 Overall leave generosity by region, 1975–2005

H1: The presence of Left parties in power should be associated with more expansive family leave.

In light of the importance of greater national wealth for a more expansive welfare state, we expect that:

H2: National wealth should be associated with more expansive leave.

Communist governments worldwide sought to increase women's participation in the labor force and enacted social policies to facilitate work–life balance, including family leave. We would therefore anticipate that the experience of communism would incline a country toward more generous leave.

H3: The experience of communism should be associated with more expansive family leave.

Our fourth hypothesis concerns the role of *feminist movements*. We would expect feminist movements to play less of a role for maternity leave policies, which uphold the traditional gender division of labor, and more of a role for gender-neutral parental leave and daddy leave, which modify gender roles. Adoption of daddy leave in particular is likely to require both civil society support and the support of Left parties, as well as a legacy of state intervention in the market. Yet because of its rarity, the adoption of daddy leave is ill-suited to statistical analysis. Reflecting the distinction between class issues involving redistribution and status issues contesting women's cultural subordination, we would also expect that the relationship between feminist movements and generous leave policy should be weaker than between feminist movements and status issues such as violence against women and legal status at work.

H4: There may be an ambiguous relationship between feminist movements and the overall generosity of family leave.

International agreements such as the Convention on the Elimination of All Forms of Discrimination against Women (CEDAW) should not bear as much relation to family leave as other women's rights areas. Feminists mobilizing around CEDAW are less focused on family leave than on violence against women, equality at work, family law, and other issues. Though most feminists recognize the importance of work–life balance to gender equality, the preconditions for family leave policies (such as an extensive formal labor market, broad tax base, and the like) are absent in much of the world. Regional agreements or networks that lead to the sharing of policy ideas across borders and that create regional pressures for conformity may be more influential. This is particularly likely in the case of the European Union.

H5: EU membership will have a stronger association with generous family leave than CEDAW ratification.

Finally, as in our analysis of other women's rights issues, we consider the relationship between family leave and other factors, such as women in parliament (we expect a positive association), religious factors (no association), fertility rates (no association), the presence of women's policy machineries (positive association), the degree of democracy (positive association),[20] and women's labor force participation rates (positive association).

---

[20] Numerous studies from Latin America, for example, have found that democracy exerts a positive influence on the level of social spending, particularly more progressive social

Findings

As in previous chapters, we used generalized least square (GLS) with random effects. Table 5.1 presents our full results. Overall, the results support our first hypothesis about the association between Left party power and more generous leave. *Left party power* is a measure of the cumulative strength of Left parties over the study period.[21] As noted in previous chapters, measuring Left party power as the share of seats held by Left parties is fairly standard. Here we added a cumulative dimension to the measure to capture the enduring effects of Left party dominance on social policy. The idea is that if Left parties were present in each of the earlier three data points, then one might see more generous policies in the fourth time period even if Left parties are not in power at that time. It therefore makes sense to measure the impact of the cumulative presence of Left parties, not just the impact of Left parties at the specific time point when the policy is measured.[22]

The relationship between Left party power and overall family leave generosity was larger and more reliable (as the higher level of statistical significance indicates) than the association between Left party power and maternity and parental leave (not shown). Each standard deviation of change in cumulative Left party power was associated with about half a point increase (.01*53) in leave generosity. This may suggest that Left parties are more reliably associated with expansion of leave policies in general than with any particular form of leave policy.

National wealth is strongly and significantly associated with overall leave generosity across all models, confirming Hypothesis 2. The coefficients are larger, and the association is stronger, than when we looked at only maternity leave (analysis not shown). This suggests that economic development is more closely associated with overall spending than with any specific form of spending. Institutional and political factors determine the shape of social spending, while national wealth generates the revenue to enable spending in the first place.

---

spending (Avelino, Brown, & Hunter, 2005; Brown & Hunter, 1999; Huber & Stephens, 2012; Kaufman & Segura-Ubiergo, 2001).

[21] Specifically, it is the total of the share of Left party power at each of four measurement points, that is, Left party power in 1975 plus Left party power in 1985 plus Left party power in 1995 plus Left party power in 2005.

[22] This approach to measurement makes even more sense in light of the difficulty of rolling back social policies once they are enacted (cf. Pierson 1994, 1996), as well as the enduring influence of earlier policy choices, as illustrated in the discussion of daddy leave.

TABLE 5.1 Coefficients, overall family leave generosity, random effects linear models, 1975–2005

MODEL	1	2	3	4	5	6	7
Variable							
Left party strength (cumulative)	.007***	.008***	.008***	.008***	.008***	.007***	.007***
	(.002)	(.002)	(.002)	(.002)	(.002)	(.002)	(.002)
GDP (logged)	.886***	.983***	1.094***	1.114***	1.094***	1.046***	1.094***
	(.254)	(.237)	(.312)	(.325)	(.312)	(.313)	(.315)
Communist	2.019***	2.007***	2.118***	2.116***	2.118***	2.123***	2.020***
	(.381)	(.350)	(.375)	(.370)	(.375)	(.374)	(.386)
Strong, autonomous feminist movement	-.366***	-.347***	-.339***	-.339***	-.339***	-.337***	-.346***
	(.103)	(.103)	(.107)	(.108)	(.107)	(.107)	(.107)
Women in parliament (%)	.019**	.022***	.023***	.023***	.023***	.023***	.020**
	(.009)	(.008)	(.008)	(.009)	(.008)	(.008)	(.009)
CEDAW ratification				-.029			
				(.164)			
EU member						.331	.343
						(.226)	(.226)
Effective women's policy machinery	.055						
	(.159)						
Democracy level	.013						
	(.014)						
Fertility		.074	.074	.069	.074	.069	.092
		(.078)	(.078)	(.079)	(.078)	(.078)	(.080)

(continued)

TABLE 5.1 (*continued*)

MODEL	1	2	3	4	5	6	7
Variable							
Female labor force participation							.010
							(.008)
Official religion	.067						
	(.258)						
High religiosity	.415						
	(.288)						
Observations	255	257	253	253	253	253	253
Overall R-squared	.481	.473	.465	.466	.455	.479	.480
Number of countries	70	70	69	69	69	69	69

Notes: Estimates are from random effects regression models. Standard errors are in parentheses. *, **, and *** denote statistical significance at the 10, 5, and 1 percent levels, respectively.

The experience of communism is significantly associated with leave generosity, as Hypothesis 3 proposed. The size of the coefficients suggests a substantively important role as well: A communist legacy is associated with about two additional points on the generosity scale. The analysis given in this section suggests that this association is mainly driven by the impact of communism on parental rather than maternity leave, though communism shapes both areas substantially and significantly. It may be surprising to see the communist legacy extend to gender-neutral parental leave, which is more of an equality-promoting measure. Our analysis finds that the effects of communism trump many other factors, including religion.

Our measure of the strength and autonomy of feminist movements is significantly, and negatively, associated with leave generosity. We expected a more ambiguous or insignificant effect. By contrast, the presence of women in parliament seems to have a significant and positive association with overall leave generosity. This important role for women in parliament is striking compared to the smaller role that we see for women office holders in other areas of sex equality policy.

Table 5.1 shows the full range of models we used to test our hypotheses. We found that global and regional influences (CEDAW ratification and EU membership) were not significant, nor were religious variables, level of democracy, or women's labor force participation. We did not find a statistically significant relationship between fertility and overall leave generosity, which may suggest that fertility rates are relevant mainly when they are seized upon as a rationale for policy expansion (Kingdon, 1984). It may also be that the response to fertility rates is more complex than a mere functional approach would suggest, with actors choosing different types of policy responses to the pressures they perceive. It is important to remember, however, that our analysis combines both developed and developing and high- and low-fertility countries. We would expect fertility to exert diverse effects across these contexts.

In summary, we found that the institutionalization of Left values, whether via the historical experience of communist government or the presence and power of Left parties, exerted a significant influence on the generosity of family leave in general. Contextual factors such as GDP per capita were also important, suggesting that in contexts where there is more of a revenue base, publicly paid family leave (as opposed to unpaid, mandated, or mixed sources of funding) is more likely, since such initiatives need not compete with other basic policy priorities. Finally, the presence of autonomous feminist movements was not a significant correlate of more generous policy; in fact, feminist movements had a small negative effect.

PART II. CHILDCARE

In many countries and among many social groups, it is primarily family members who care for the children of working women. In other countries and social groups, women tend to rely on institutional child care centers supplied by the market, the state, or a combination of the two. The quality and affordability of market-supplied childcare can vary dramatically, however. In countries such as the United States, rich women have access to excellent childcare while poor women are often compelled to rely on substandard services (for horrifying examples, see Cohn, 2013). State supply of childcare is therefore important to promote greater class equality among women and families, and to make sure that economically disadvantaged children do not fall farther behind (cf. Putnam, 2016).

CROSS-NATIONAL TRENDS IN CHILDCARE POLICY

Our analysis focuses on national child care policies.[23] For each country, we first asked whether there was a national or federal child care policy. If there was one, we asked whether it was provided through:

- Government-run child care centers
- Cash transfers to parents to pay for childcare
- Tax credits for money spent on childcare
- Subsidies to child care centers
- Employer mandates – that is, requirements that firms with a certain number of workers provide child care services for their employees
- Other child care provision

   Table 5.2 shows that, among the countries included in our study, the most common approach to providing childcare (for those that did provide it) on the part of the national government was to offer a program of government-run day care. The other common option was to offer subsidies to the operators of the centers. Though access to day care expanded dramatically over our period, most countries still lacked accessible childcare by 2005.

   Patterns of policy development vary considerably by region. For example, although we saw a broad expansion of access to childcare over our study period, access has decreased or remained roughly the

---

[23] Our dataset focuses only on national policy, not implementation, enforcement or effectiveness.

TABLE 5.2 *Government action on childcare (seventy countries)*

(Seventy countries)	1975	1985	1995	2005
National day-care policy	46	50	52	57
Government-run day care	25	25	27	30
Cash transfers	8	8	8	9
Tax credits	5	6	10	13
Subsidies to centers	17	18	19	22
Employer mandates	6	8	8	13
Other day-care policies	5	7	9	8
Countries with restricted eligibility for day care	24	25	31	37
Countries with greater access to day care	16	19	19	24

same in Eastern Europe, and has remained unchanged in every region except for Western Europe and Asia.

Cash transfers to families seem to have been a popular policy in Western Europe in the 1970s and 80s but are not common in other regions and seem rarer today. Tax credits, in contrast, have become more popular, particularly in Western Europe (but are virtually nonexistent in Eastern Europe). Employer mandates are more common in the developing world (especially in Asia and the Middle East and North Africa) than they are in Europe.

In the Global South, laws in many countries uphold employer mandates requiring companies with a minimum number of women workers to provide onsite child care centers. Such laws are common in Latin America, even though many countries also introduced public child care programs in the 2000s. In Ecuador, for example, the labor law requires businesses with more than fifty women workers to offer day-care centers.[24] In Egypt, similarly, the New Unified Labor Law (2003) obligates the employer who hires 100 workers or more to provide workplace childcare (Global Network, 2009).

Often, these laws are designed to facilitate breastfeeding of infants and young toddlers. Chile's laws require companies with twenty or more women workers to provide care for children under two so women can breastfeed, while in Brazil, companies with thirty or more women workers must provide onsite childcare for children up to six months old (Blofield & Martínez Franzoni, 2014). Overall, around one-third of the

---

[24] *El Universo*, February 13, 2013, www.eluniverso.com/2013/02/14/1/1356/trabajador-recibira-pago-directo-guarderia.html.

167 countries – including countries from a wide variety of world regions – studied by the ILO for their 2010 report had legislation on the books requiring employers to provide facilities for breastfeeding, though not always in the form of a child care center. In some cases, employers unable to provide onsite facilities were required to reimburse employees for the cost of care elsewhere (ILO, 2010, p. 85).

The Nigerian government, in a partnership with UNICEF that began in 1991 and lasted at least until the late 1990s, committed several million Naira to a child care program. The program initially had some trouble with implementation because it applied Western standards for quality care to the Nigerian context, with little attention to local conditions. For example, some guidelines called for grassy spaces, which few providers could arrange given the Nigerian climate and context. The guideline was changed to permit sandy spaces instead, and the program was more successful. Although ultimately considered a success, UNICEF withdrew its funding and the government no longer offers this program (Alemika, Chukwuma, Lafratta, Messerli, & Souckova, 2005). There are new initiatives and programs to support childcare in Nigeria, funded by a combination of federal government, state, and international donor funds (UNESCO, 2006).

It is important to distinguish between day care for infants and toddlers and care for older children (age three and older). Many countries offer preschool and other forms of early childhood education for the latter group but lack comprehensive coverage for infants and toddlers. In Sweden, for example, a total of only thirty children under the age of one were in publicly funded childcare in 2005. The country's generous leave provisions come with the expectation that most babies will be cared for at home by their parents (Morgan, 2008). In Latin America, coverage rates are considerably higher for the 4–6 age group (though participation varies from a low of 30 percent in Paraguay to a high of 80 percent in Bolivia, Chile, and El Salvador) than for children aged 0–3, for whom coverage is well under 20 percent in most countries (Blofield & Martínez Franzoni, 2014).

Even when childcare is of the highest quality, it can sometimes be difficult to find because eligibility is restricted, because the number of spaces is limited, or because of the geographical location of centers. In several advanced countries, and in Europe in particular, childcare is intended to promote early education and child well-being, not women's work or independence. As a result, the hours of care provided are not designed to accommodate the schedules of working parents: Programs may be for half a day or every other day, and coverage may not be provided during holidays. Programs with limited hours are less likely to advance the economic independence of most women. Rather, such programs tend to presume that someone – such as a mother or a wealthy woman's nanny – is available to care for children during those frequent times when the program is out of session.

Quantity of childcare is usually measured by looking at the numbers of children currently using day-care slots or other child care arrangements and the size of waiting lists. Related measures include the number of working mothers who cannot work longer hours or cannot work at all because they cannot get access to childcare. Quality of day care is usually measured in terms of child-to-caregiver ratios, the qualifications of caregivers, and safety and other regulations affecting the physical facilities. Both quality and quantity are difficult to ascertain precisely, especially in ways that facilitate cross-national analysis.

A good example of these trade-offs is child care policy in France. France is often thought of as the model for excellent government child care provision. Though child care quality is judged to be very good, there are actually comparatively few slots. In the United States, there are a comparatively large number of day-care slots (giving working women more access to day care) but the quality of the care is relatively low and public funding limited to people whose income falls below specified levels. What is more, even though the quantity is large in cross-national terms, the supply of day care still fails to meet the need for it.[25]

ACCOUNTING FOR CHILDCARE POLICY

What explains these variations in child care policy? Much of the literature on the politics of childcare policy centers on the advanced economies (Henderson & White, 2004; Kamerman & Moss, 2009; Morgan, 2008), and adopts a functional approach focused on needs or demand for care. In this view, the characteristics of the population affect the services that governments provide. For childcare, needs have been difficult to operationalize in quantitative terms given the issue of reverse causality between child care availability and women's numbers in the workforce. Does women's growing labor force participation lead to an increase of

---

[25] In the United States, regulation of childcare centers varies by state, but the main mechanisms for funding childcare (tax breaks, the Community Development Block Grant, and Temporary Assistance to Needy Families (TANF)) are federal.

child care policies (needs precede policy) or does a greater supply of childcare enable women to join the workforce (policy precedes need)? Could childcare expansion prompt women to seek more demanding, career-oriented jobs (cf. Skorge, 2016)? The problem of reverse causality can be handled in several different ways in quantitative analysis, including the use of lagged variables, an approach we take here. Qualitative research suggests that demand comes before the adoption of policies (Ellingsæter & Leira, 2006). However, it also suggests that needs by themselves are not enough to cause policy changes. Needs can be met in multiple ways. What is more, given the multitude of demands a state faces at any given time, a need must be brought to the attention of government officials before it can inspire policy change (Estevez-Abe, Iverson, & Soskice, 2001; Hall & Soskice, 2001). Accounting for different policy configurations requires analyzing the role of advocates and opponents, and their interactions amid diverse institutional and developmental contexts.

We would expect women's organizing to be more important for the expansion of childcare than for the generosity of parental leave. Child care centers challenge the idea that women must care for their own children all the time, and government provision of, or support for, these centers signals that children are a public responsibility, not a private one. Our first hypothesis is:

H1: Strong feminist movements will be associated with national childcare policies.

As above, we would expect public provision of childcare also to trigger a Left–Right conflict over the role of the state in social provision. The role of actors promoting socioeconomic redistribution (such as Left parties) will still be important. Hence:

H2: The strength of Left parties will be associated with national childcare policies.

Finally, national wealth may shape the likelihood that states provide or support childcare outside of the family or kin networks:

H3: National wealth will be associated with childcare policies.

As in the other chapters, we control for a wide range of factors (degree of democracy, religious factors, women in parliament, and so on). Rather than recapitulating the reasons for those controls here, we refer the reader to our earlier chapters and discussion of our framework. Perhaps it is worth paying particular attention to the numbers of women in parliament in this issue-area. A few studies have found that women in parliament are associated with more expansive childcare policy, as noted. Still, a growing number of scholars cast doubt on the notion that women politicians will advocate shared women's interests, especially across the lines of class and race, and especially when it comes to women leaders from parties of the Right (O'Brien, 2004; Smooth, 2006, 2011; Weldon, 2011). Other scholars are skeptical of the impact of sheer numbers, and focus instead on the "critical acts" of legislators (Celis, Childs, Kantola, & Krook, 2008). What is more, legislators' support for childcare may also be a function of their membership in Left parties. Our argument neither stands nor falls on the role of women in this particular issue. We contend that feminist movements, Left parties, and national wealth should drive policy on this issue more than religious factors or other control variables.

STATISTICAL ANALYSIS

This analysis focuses on the factors associated with governmental adoption of a national childcare policy. Since this dependent variable is dichotomous (1 = national childcare policy; 0 = no policy), we use random effects logit to take this dichotomous structure and the panel-like structure of the data into account.

The results depicted in Table 5.3 reveal a surprisingly significant, positive relationship between strong, autonomous feminist movements and the existence of a national childcare policy. While this relationship is not especially strong in the global analysis, it is much stronger than we found in the area of family leave and much stronger than we expected to find for a redistributive social policy area. This finding was fairly robust to different specifications of the model, different methods of analysis, and other methodological variations.

Left parties are also statistically significant and substantively important in some specifications of the model. This finding is much less robust, disappearing in some specifications (see the first few models in Table 5.3). Women in parliament do not have a robust association with the adoption of a national day-care policy, contrary to at least some existing literature, and an effective women's policy machinery is weakly significant in only one of three models in which it is included. It may be that women in government and Left parties work to prevent rollbacks of policies where they exist. This may explain why our descriptive statistical analysis found that access to day care declined as Eastern European nations moved from communist regimes providing more generous day

TABLE 5.3 *Coefficients, national childcare policy, random effects logistic regression models, 1975–2005*

Model number	1	2	3	4	5
Variable					
Strong, autonomous feminist movement	3.136* (1.602)	2.536* (1.419)	1.003 (1.478)	1.111* (.571)	1.152* (.637)
Left party strength (cumulative)	.051 (.034)	.025 (.026)	.038 (.034)	.023** (.011)	.030** (.015)
Women in parliament (%)	−.033 (.170)	−.028 (.119)	−.201 (.133)	−.033 (.043)	−.038 (.046)
Effective women's policy machinery	4.398* (2.478)	3.605 (2.551)	−.324 (1.706)		
GDP (logged)	13.349*** (3.507)	11.557*** (4.242)	3.905 (3.719)		
EU member	−7.451** (3.202)				−2.536* (1.423)
CEDAW ratification	−3.124 (2.477)	−2.359 (2.385)			
Withdrawal of reservations CEDAW					2.544 (1.553)
Female labor force participation (%)	−.154 (.108)	−.162 (.101)	−.088 (.130)		
Fertility rate			−3.363** (1.507)		
Democracy level	−.615*** (.226)	−.446** (.226)	−.251 (.166)		
Former colony	−7.852** (3.983)	−3.391 (3.955)			
Official religion	1.589 (2.577)				
Religious party	2.658 (2.500)	1.885 (2.635)			
Communist	−7.108* (4.054)	−1.629 (3.315)	−1.958 (3.055)		
Muslim majority	−3.691 (4.354)	−4.837 (3.986)	−5.059 (4.193)		
Catholic majority	−2.311 (3.330)	−2.802 (3.342)	−1.752 (3.446)		

Model number	1	2	3	4	5
Variable					
Proportional	4.316*	4.588			
representation	(2.460)	(2.844)			
Observations	196	196	252	276	276
Number of	65	65	69	70	70
countries					

Notes: Estimates are from random effects logistic regression models. Coefficients are unadjusted. Standard errors are in parentheses. *, **, and *** denote statistical significance at the 10, 5, and 1 percent levels, respectively.

care to market-driven systems. This nonfinding was obtained in the vast majority of specifications of the model.

Economic conditions – measured here as the log of GDP per capita – have a significant and positive effect in Models 1 and 2 but are insignificant in Model 3, which controls for fertility. Regional agreements and organizations may also have some effect. For example, EU membership was positively related to the development of a national day care policy (Models 1 and 5). On the other hand, being committed to the economic and social rights treaty (ICESR) or to CEDAW did seem to matter in some specifications (not shown) and seemed to matter in some of the cases of policy change discussed in these chapters, though it did not rise to the level of significance in the models shown (Table 5.3). We expected that international treaties and norms would be weaker in the area of redistributive class policy than in the area of status and doctrinal policies, though different specifications or more data might reveal more influence here.

Also, perhaps surprising to those who adopt a more functional view of public policy responsiveness, there was little relationship between need or demand (female labor force participation) and the development of a day-care policy (Models 1, 2, 3). This was true even in an analysis using a lagged variable for female labor force participation (not shown).

Included in only one model, fertility was negatively associated with the development of a national day-care policy (and also negatively associated with female labor force participation, GDP, and several other variables). Indeed, fertility was so closely correlated with nearly every other variable in the model, and especially with all of them together, that it made it impossible to run the analysis with that variable included and get meaningful results.

In our parental-leave analysis, it seemed that fertility was not a primary factor. It is hard to tell if it is a factor with respect to childcare, because fertility and GDP are so closely related, and both are significant and potentially theoretically relevant. In order to explore the relationship between fertility and childcare policy, we divided the dataset into high- and low-fertility countries to see what difference that would make for the analysis, finding that perhaps Left parties and a policy legacy of generous parental leave mattered more in low-fertility countries, while women's movements might be more important in high-fertility countries. This may expect the lack of robust findings on Left parties in the global analysis (see discussion in the Appendix and Table 5.A.2).

In summary, strong, autonomous feminist movements were far more important as a correlate of childcare policy than we expected. Though childcare policies are often seen as prochildren and profamily, they are still premised on the idea that someone other than a child's mother provides the bulk of the childcare. Nonmaternal care poses a greater challenge to gender roles than the idea that mothers should be able to put their children first and stay home from work to care for young ones. Feminist movements were essential to promote such a reconceptualization of women's lives and roles. Left parties were also important, especially in established democracies, but the effects were not global or uniformly strong, suggesting that we need more theorizing and study of the conditions under which Left parties promote redistributive gender policy issues, especially in developing countries and nondemocracies. Contextual factors such as fertility and national wealth create conditions that are highly conducive to policy development, but the choice of how to respond to these pressures is political and path dependent.

CONCLUSION

Family leave and childcare policies, which involve state assumption of some responsibility for social provision, help to further gender and class equality, though in different ways. Such policies can help promote women's economic independence, have the potential to trigger changes in gender roles, and may also reduce socioeconomic disparities among women and families. Since family leave and childcare often require an expansion of the state's role in social provision, they touch upon state–market relations and may pose a challenge to existing economic interests. Policy expansion may therefore require a big political coalition anchored by the strength of Left parties, especially where such policies must be introduced de novo, rather than expanded or altered. By contrast, when social provision for reconciliation is already an established tradition, a broader coalition may not be necessary to promote change. Left parties play a particularly decisive role in leave policies, especially daddy leave, while autonomous feminist movements seem more likely to play a decisive role in promoting childcare. While feminist movements and international agreements are of particular importance for status issues, and religion–state relations and religious power for doctrinal issues, economic factors and actors matter more here.

Our statistical analysis found that the relationship between Left power and the overall generosity of family leave was strong, and the impact of a communist legacy was also important. Yet the relationship between Left power and childcare was less significant. The varying importance of Left parties may suggest that parental leave and childcare function as substitutes. To promote women's work–life balance, a country may opt either to extend family leave or to expand access to childcare, but not both. If a working woman has access to a long period of paid parental leave, she does not need childcare for the early period of a child's life. Conversely, if childcare is readily available, then a working woman has less need for extended family leave. What is more, family leave – which allows women to stay home to care for children – poses less of a challenge to ideas about traditional motherhood than childcare provision, especially infant care.

The configuration of political actors and interests in a given country will shift policy choices in one direction or the other, working within the institutional legacies of past policy decisions and political transformations (such as communism and colonialism). Left party strength in the Scandinavian countries contributed to the extension of family leave there, and the virtual nonexistence of infant care (though Left parties have also supported childcare, and clearly play a role in that area as well, even if it is less decisive). In the United States, where the political Left is weaker but feminist movements are strong, infant and childcare is more widely available through the market, and is also supported by government funding for low-income women (through the Child Care Development Block Grant). Government funding for both childcare and family leave in the United States, however anemic, has been supported more by Democrats than by Republicans at both the federal and state levels (Weldon, 2011).

While both of these issues are class issues with distinctive political dynamics related to the clash between labor and business, between those favoring a greater state role in social provision and those opposing it, it also suggests that within a single policy domain, policies often thought of as distinct may in fact be related to each other. Early choices may set states on a path that conditions later responses in the same field (Boling, 2015; Pierson, 2004; Skocpol, 1992). This only strengthens our efforts to expand the range of policies feminist analysts analyze, and pushes us to consider the relationships, and differences, between and among these policies.

Chapter 5 Appendix

Fertility and Childcare Policy

To analyze the relationship between fertility and childcare policy in greater depth, we analyzed high- and low-fertility countries in separate analyses. As mentioned earlier, governments of countries with low birthrates in the Global North have expanded parental leave and improved childcare policies in order to make work and motherhood more compatible for women. These states may see fertility as a strategic problem relating to a core imperative of the state (Boling, 2015; Dryzek et al., 2003; Koven & Michel, 1993). Indeed, the qualitative literature on family policy makes a strong link between low fertility in Europe and other rich countries and the development of measures to encourage childbearing for working women. This effect may be so strong that other factors that might make a difference (such as EU membership) are overwhelmed by this much stronger effect. On the other hand, it could be that the coupling of fertility and wealth has a particular significance for childcare that is less visible for parental leave.

In low-fertility states (mostly more developed states), the strongest predictor of adoption of a day-care policy, more than feminist movements or Left parties, was the overall generosity of leave policy (lagged), which had a strong negative effect. States with generous leave policies were less likely to also adopt a national day-care policy. This suggests that when states confront low fertility, they may respond either by adopting generous leave policies or by developing a national day-care policy, but they generally are not equally likely to do both. Perhaps coincidentally, many of these low-fertility states were on the track to a leave-focused family policy long before the second-wave feminist movement put women's

TABLE 5.A.1 *National childcare policy, by region*

Western Europe (fifteen countries)	1975	1985	1995	2005
National day-care policy	13	13	14	14
Government-run day care	4	4	4	4
Cash transfers	4	4	3	3
Tax credits	3	3	6	8
Subsidies to centers	8	8	9	10
Employer mandates	0	0	0	0
Other day-care policies	2	2	3	3
Countries with restricted eligibility for day care	7	7	10	9
Access to day care	3	4	8	10

Eastern Europe (fourteen countries)	1975	1985	1995	2005
National day-care policy	10	10	8	9
Government-run day care	8	8	6	7
Cash transfers	0	0	0	0
Tax credits	0	0	1	1
Subsidies to centers	2	2	2	2
Employer mandates	1	1	0	0
Other day-care policies	1	1	2	1
Countries with restricted eligibility for day care	7	7	6	6
Access to day care	7	8	6	7

Latin America (ten countries)	1975	1985	1995	2005
National day-care policy	6	8	9	9
Government-run day care	4	5	7	7
Cash transfers	0	0	1	2
Tax credits	0	0	0	0
Subsidies to centers	1	1	1	2
Employer mandates	2	3	3	3
Other day-care policies	2	3	3	3
Countries with restricted eligibility for day care	2	2	3	4
Access to day care	0	0	0	0

MENA (eight countries)	1975	1985	1995	2005
National day-care policy	3	4	4	6
Government-run day care	3	2	3	2
Cash transfers	0	0	0	0
Tax credits	0	0	0	0
Subsidies to centers	0	0	0	0
Employer mandates	0	1	2	5
Other day-care policies	0	1	0	0
Countries with restricted eligibility for day care	0	1	2	5
Access to day care	1	1	0	1

Africa (five countries)	1975	1985	1995	2005
National day-care policy	0	1	2	2
Government-run day care	0	0	0	0
Cash transfers	0	0	0	0
Tax credits	0	0	0	0
Subsidies to centers	0	1	1	1
Employer mandates	0	0	0	0
Other day-care policies	0	0	1	1
Countries with restricted eligibility for day care	0	0	1	1
Access to day care	0	0	0	0
Asia (fourteen countries)	1975	1985	1995	2005
National day-care policy	10	10	11	13
Government-run day care	6	6	7	10
Cash transfers	2	2	2	2
Tax credits	1	1	1	2
Subsidies to centers	3	3	3	3
Employer mandates	3	3	3	5
Other day-care policies	0	0	0	0
Countries with restricted eligibility for day care	4	4	5	8
Access to day care	4	4	3	4

workplace equality on the agenda. Perhaps the association of fertility, development, and parental leave is more of an artifact, and childcare is more similar to parental leave than in fact was initially suggested.

In high-fertility (mostly developing) countries, strong, autonomous feminist movements appear to have a stronger, positive relationship with the adoption of childcare policies, and policy legacies appear to have a weaker association with the adoption of childcare policies. Perhaps these countries respond to work–family reconciliation in this way because the revenue base for more generous leave policies so prevalent in the North is not present. In this case, the coupling of low fertility and childcare is, again, just an artifact of the link between national wealth and high fertility.

Since the difference between high and low fertility maps roughly onto the difference between wealthier and less wealthy countries, the association between fertility and childcare policy adoption could mainly be capturing the effect of EU membership and national wealth in spurring more and earlier policy development favoring parental leave. In postcolonial countries with less established policy traditions, prior policies may

TABLE 5.A.2 *Coefficients, random effects logit, national childcare policies, high- and low-fertility countries, 1975–2005*

Fertility level	Low	Low	High	High	High	High
Model number	1	2	3	4	5	6
Variable						
Strong, autonomous feminist movement	.247 (1.831)	−1.241 (3.105)	1.358** (.648)	.963 (.677)	1.226 (1.287)	1.007 (1.364)
Women in parliament (%)	−.137 (.117)	−.158 (.179)	.019 (.051)	.008 (.054)	−.040 (.061)	−.186 (.119)
Left party strength (cumulative)	.018 (.034)	.130* (.079)	.023 (.014)	.019 (.013)	.033 (.028)	.044 (.029)
CEDAW ratification (lagged)						3.573** (1.812)
Leave generosity (lagged)		−1.988** (.976)		.039 (.380)		
GDP (logged)		−8.240 (16.840)			6.762* (3.496)	7.922 (4.865)
Former colony					−3.133 (2.447)	−1.137 (3.505)
Observations	63	62	211	141	194	135
Bayesian information criterion	53.095	54.831	206.886	163.870	188.681	153.805
Number of countries	35	35	69	63	67	62

Notes: Estimates are from random effects logistic regression models. Standard errors are in parentheses. *, **, and *** denote statistical significance at the 10, 5, and 1 percent levels, respectively.

exert less effect. In the absence of a national fertility crisis, perhaps both parental leave and childcare policies seem less pressing, unless raised by feminists. This would be especially true for childcare, which tends to have more support from feminists than maternity leave.

6

Reproductive Rights

Class, Status, and Doctrinal Politics

Improvements in reproductive and sexual health services, including access to contraception and safe abortion, are linked to the health of women, the well-being of children and families, economic development, and a reduction in government expenditure on health care, sanitation, and education. Local and global feminist movements, as well as public health practitioners, have advocated a loosening of legal restrictions on abortion and an expansion of public funding for reproductive health services. Yet the promotion of reproductive and sexual health often triggers political resistance. Religious organizations tend to oppose liberalizing and expansive change on these issues, though to different degrees across contexts. In many countries, including countries where a majority or significant minority of the population is Catholic, conservative and traditional politicians, social movements, interest groups, and religious organizations have sought to introduce greater restrictions on access to abortion and contraception. They have also raised objections to the dissemination of scientifically accurate information about reproductive and sexual health (Gerntholtz et al., 2011; Grzymała-Busse, 2015; Htun, 2003; Viterna, 2012).

Why does reproduction incite controversy? What shapes differences in reproductive rights across countries? This chapter explores two distinct but related areas of government action that relate to the intimate politics of reproduction: the legal status of abortion and the degree of state funding for abortion care and contraceptive methods. Our objective is to show that the category of women's reproductive rights consists of different issues. Though reproduction challenges religious claims to govern kinship in most places, some aspects of reproductive politics affect women as a "status" group while others invoke "class" differences among women. Within the context of doctrinal politics, this status–class distinction implies that factors associated with more liberal abortion law differ from the factors associated with greater state funding for abortion and contraception. Whereas religious variables and the experience of communism are related to differences in abortion's legal status, the strength of Left parties is more important for the extent of state funding for abortion and contraception.

POLITICS OF REPRODUCTION: DOCTRINE, STATUS, *AND* CLASS IN ABORTION AND CONTRACEPTION POLICY

In most places, pregnancy and motherhood are central to constructions of femininity and women's identities as women, albeit deeply inflected by race and class (Collins, 1990; De Beauvoir, 1953; Mottier, 2013; Ruddick, 1995). The vast majority of women become mothers, and many find the experience to be among the most meaningful and rewarding of their lives. But pregnancy and motherhood can also be associated with disadvantage and injustice. Every year, hundreds of thousands of women die from preventable causes related to pregnancy and childbirth. Almost all of these deaths take place in the Global South, with about two-thirds of these deaths occurring in sub-Saharan Africa (Gerntholtz, Gibbs, & Willan, 2011; World Health Organization, 2015). Pregnancy and motherhood also have implications for women's economic security and the realization of their potential and dreams. Especially in contexts with limited social and public support for working families, motherhood – particularly single motherhood – can be associated with women's disproportionate representation in lower-paid jobs and the ranks of the poor (Godoy, 2004; Pearce, 1990).

Public health practitioners, human rights advocates, and the international development community endorse the widespread provision of reproductive and sexual health services so that women are able to control whether and when they become pregnant. The availability of contraception reduces rates of maternal mortality, infant mortality, unplanned pregnancy, sexually transmitted disease (STD), deaths from HIV/AIDS, and unsafe abortion (World Health Organization, 2016a). The World Health Organization estimates that more than 20 million unsafe abortions occur each year around the world, and that 5 million women in the Global South are admitted to hospitals for complications from these unsafe abortions. Treating these complications costs some 700 million dollars annually (World Health Organization, 2016b).

Yet in many countries, people frame the expansion of reproductive rights and health services as a threat to religion and the moral order, not as a matter of public health. Why do these groups oppose abortion and contraception? Discursive frames connecting human reproduction with the tenets and status of religious doctrine accounts for the thorny controversy in many countries – although the content and dynamics of these frames vary across societies (Ferree, 2002). While many actors, including feminist movements, medical practitioners, and international development organizations, have framed reproduction as a matter of women's autonomy and public health, religious organizations and social conservatives have argued that both contraception and abortion – albeit to varying degrees – are matters of community values, the status of religion, and the human rights of unborn life (Htun, 2003).

In other contexts, dominant religious traditions place less emphasis on opposing abortion in order to protect fetal life. Though inflected with moral concern, abortion does not carry the same doctrinal significance for Hinduism as for Catholicism, for example. In India there is broad societal acceptance of abortion, even among conservatives, when performed for certain reasons, such as to end a pregnancy considered shameful or when prenatal testing reveals that a fetus is female (Sibasish, 2013). Indian feminists are more concerned with promoting the value of female babies and children, as well as women's choice and consent with respect to abortion and contraception, than with legal access to those services.[1]

As this discussion suggests, abortion and contraception take on different meanings for different groups. For some, religious doctrine weighs heavily, while others are concerned with women's lives, health, and opportunities. Other factors, including the wealth of the state, the balance of power between political parties, and the strength of civic movements, are also likely to shape public discourse and policy. How do we sort out these different variables? In this chapter, we argue that reproductive politics encompasses doctrinal, status, *and* class issues. We show how disaggregating law and policy into those gender-status issues which are primarily doctrinal (abortion legality) and those gender-status issues which are *both* doctrinal and class-related (funding for reproductive rights) enhances our understanding of government action in this critical area. Representing the fourth, bottom right cell in

---

[1] Interviews between Laurel Weldon and women's rights experts and reproductive rights activists in New Delhi, 2010.

our typology presented in Table 1.1, reproductive policies may be the most complex issue we study in this book.

Doctrine

Who has the right to govern the process of reproduction: the woman who has the potential to bear the child, the men concerned for their genetic and financial legacies, or the broader family and community who claim that their future, and honor, are at stake? Does human life begin at the moment of conception? Is there a balance between the woman's life and the fetus's potential? If so, how should this balance be struck? Do decisions about reproduction fall within a zone of privacy immune to public authority? Or does the state have an interest in upholding the value and sanctity of life?

The world's two biggest organized religions have said a great deal about questions of reproduction in general, and about contraception and abortion in particular. In Roman Catholic theology from Augustine and Aquinas, and affirmed in the *Humane Vitae* encyclical, sexual activity – or the "marital act" – had to be open to the possibility of procreation. Intervening in reproduction with contraceptive methods has therefore been prohibited. For its part, abortion is a crime, tantamount to murder. Historically, however, Catholic positions on abortion have been more varied. Though abortion was always condemned, it was not considered to be homicide until after the fetus had acquired a soul.[2] Only after 1869, when papal references dropped the distinction between the ensouled and unensouled fetus, did it become clear that abortion was a crime starting from the moment of conception (Htun, 2003, pp. 33–4).

The Muslim tradition has historically been more open to contraception as well as to abortion. In classical Islam, marriage was a civil contract, polygamy was endorsed, divorce was easy to obtain (for men), and sexual pleasure was a legitimate end in its own right, even for women (Musallam, 1983). The *hadith* – compilations of early teachings of Muhammad and the key texts of early centuries of Islam – contain numerous references to contraception. The *hadith* indicate that the Prophet knew about contraception and permitted the practice, at least in some circumstances, and always within the context of God's infinite power (Musallam, 1983, pp. 15–16).

---

[2] Before 1869, most Catholic thinkers endorsed the Aristotelean notion that ensoulment occurred 40–80 days after conception (Htun, 2003).

In subsequent centuries, prominent Muslim jurists affirmed the lawfulness of contraception. Ghazali, for example, endorsed economic reasons for practicing contraception, which included the cost of supporting dependents and the desire to limit family size, as well as protecting the value of female slaves and concubines. The desire to avoid pregnancy to protect nursing infants was also widespread (Musallam, 1983). However, jurists usually based their endorsement of contraception on a woman's consent, since she had the right to have children as well as a right to sexual pleasure (which coitus interruptus was believed to reduce) (Musallam, 1983, pp. 28–34). Classical Muslim positions on abortion were also permissive, at least in some interpretations.[3] Arabic medical texts contained instructions on how to perform abortions and indicated the conditions under which abortion becomes necessary (Musallam, 1983, p. 69).

More recently, Muslim religious leaders in countries such as Algeria, Egypt, Iran, and Saudi Arabia have issued *fatawa* declaring that abortion is permissible under certain circumstances such as fetal anomaly, rape, and if the pregnancy poses a threat to a mother's life and health (Hessini, 2007, pp. 77–8). Muslim discourse on abortion tends to place greater value on the life of the pregnant woman and her existing children than on that of the fetus. Rather than tackling the question of when life begins (as in the case of Christian discourse), it considers stages of fetal development and the circumstances of the pregnant woman (Hessini, 2007, p. 77). On the other hand, decision making on abortion does not rest with the woman but with the physician, and it is expected that the father will give his consent to abortion, in recognition of his rights regarding the unborn child (Bowen, 1997, p. 168).

In summary, the world's two biggest organized religions – the Catholic branch of Christianity and Islam – have a lot to say about abortion and contraception. Their positions are different, however. Islam is more permissive. And the values and priorities invoked vary. Catholicism emphasizes the absolute value of human life, the sanctity of the marriage bond, and the procreative purpose of the "marital act," or sexual intercourse.

---

[3] The Hanafi school, which made up the majority of orthodox thinkers, permitted abortion until the end of the fourth month, at which time the fetus was believed to be ensouled or fully "formed." Shafi and Hanbali jurists also tended to permit abortion (though up to differing time periods). Maliki jurists prohibited abortion completely. Abortion was not approved of by any of these schools (by contrast, it was frowned upon), but was justified to protect the mother's health and the well-being of her existing children. Under the classical principle of respect for plurality of legal opinion, all of these positions were considered legitimate by orthodox Muslims (Bowen, 1997; Musallam, 1983, p. 58).

Islam seems to place greater value on the circumstances and implications of pregnancy, the idea of marriage as a civil contract, and the sexual pleasure of husband and wife. This suggests that policies that seek to extend women's access to abortion and contraception will present greater challenges to established Catholic doctrine than to tenets of the Muslim faith, at least in classical interpretations.

To be sure, there is a significant gap between the evolution of religious doctrine in scholarly texts and papal encyclicals on the one hand and the invocation of religious beliefs by political actors on the other. As we saw with debates on family law, the interpretation of religion is a political struggle. In a multivocal tradition, power determines who speaks in the name of religion (Bayat, 2007; Stepan, 2000). When the state adds its strength to empower some religious actors at the expense of others, pluralism declines and certain religious ideas – often the most patriarchal – gain hegemony.

Struggles over doctrinal interpretation also characterize political debates on abortion and contraception. There are a variety of religious positions, even within Catholicism. Catholics for a Free Choice (CFC), for example, is a religious organization that defends the right of women to decide whether to carry a pregnancy to term. They believe that Catholic values and doctrine support this choice, and seek to help individual women find religious justification and comfort for their position. CFC's publications state that "many ... theologians have said that abortion can be a moral choice" and that "Catholicism is based on a deep respect for the conscience, which each person must follow above all else when making a moral decision," and offer women exercises and meditations (Catholics for Choice, 2015). Yet the church hierarchy has not recognized, and has even condemned, these and other dissident positions on reproductive health. In 2014, for example, the Vatican publicly rebuked the Leadership Conference on Women Religious, an organization representing nuns in the United States, for the "prevalence of certain radical feminist themes incompatible with the Catholic faith" in the group's programs and presentations, among other offenses.[4]

To be sure, as discussed previously in the chapter, reproductive rights are not controversial doctrinal issues everywhere. Abortion, for example, triggers a "clash of absolutes" in the United States (Tribe, 1992), and is merely the "tip of the iceberg," connected to profound worldviews about

---

[4] www.usccb.org/loader.cfm?csModule=security/getfile&pageid=55544.

motherhood, women's roles, science, reason, and the nature of society (Luker, 1984). But abortion has ceased to be a matter of daily controversy in much, but not all, of Europe (Outshoorn, 1996). The Japanese government began to permit easy access to abortion through the Eugenics Protection Law of 1948, but did not legalize the low-dose birth control pill until 1999 (Norgren, 2001).

Nor has access to abortion provoked opposition on religious grounds in India, where the practice has been legal since 1971. The lack of controversy may owe to the fact that the issue of "personhood" as it relates to fetal life has not been a matter of much debate for Hindus, or perhaps it is because classical religious texts provide exemptions for threats to a woman's life, making opposition to abortion less of an absolute (Coward, Lipner, & Young, 1989). Unlike the debate in Christian contexts, the "sanctity of life" has not been a salient part of the Indian debate, which has focused more on questions related to the "relief of suffering" (Chitnis & Wright, 2007).

In India and other parts of Asia (particularly in China), abortion is becoming more controversial for other reasons. The desire to have sons motivates families to abort female fetuses at disproportionate rates. Sex-selective abortion, combined with infanticide and the neglect of girls, has generated a crisis of "missing women" (Nie, 2011; Sen, 1990; World Bank, 2012). The 2000 Chinese census presented a distorted sex ratio: There were 120 males for every 100 women nationwide, and 150 men per 100 women in some areas (Nie, 2011). The oversupply of men across the region undermines social stability and has the potential to threaten international security (Hudson & Den Boer, 2004). Though various laws in China prohibit prenatal sex testing and sex-selective abortion, these regulations have been largely ineffective, and 30–40 million women are missing in the country (Nie, 2011).

Status

In addition to their religious significance, the legal status of abortion and contraception reflects the cultural valuation of women as a status group. Legal restrictions permitting – or denying – women to make choices about the reproductive processes of their own bodies are intimately connected to women's standing as full and equal persons. Are women rights-bearing individuals of equal status as men, entitled to make decisions that shape the fundamental conditions of their lives without the consent or oversight of others? Whether or not the state imposes its will over the decision to get pregnant and to carry a pregnancy to term is a crucial barometer of women's status as citizens. State involvement in such an intimate decision implies that women are lesser citizens, the violation of whose right to privacy and bodily autonomy is easily accepted.

Not everyone frames abortion and contraception issues in these ways. For some social conservatives, it is precisely women's ability to gestate and birth a child that marks their uniqueness and difference from men. Society should therefore value and celebrate this singular feminine characteristic. Proponents of this view often believe that abortion and, to a lesser extent, contraception undermine women's rights by allowing men to exploit women as sexual objects and circumvent their reproductive power. By making abortion impossible, the state affirms women's uniqueness and thereby their equal status (cf. Luker, 1984).

Though these pro- and antichoice positions have opposing political implications, they commonly see abortion as a marker of women's status. For the first, feminist view, legal access to abortion is a sign of higher status. For the second view, legal abortion is associated with lower status. Analogous arguments can be made about contraception.

Class

Legality, however, is not all there is to the politics of abortion and contraception. Abortion's legal status, for example, does not always correlate with its accessibility and availability (Blofield & Haas, 2013; Githens & Stetson, 2013). In fact, access to abortion may depend more on the health-care system than on the law (Lovenduski & Outshoorn, 1986). Is access to health care widespread and affordable? Is abortion available in public clinics and hospitals? The same point holds for contraceptives more generally. Contraceptives may be legal, but they must be located and paid for. While such costs may be negligible for middle-class women, other women might have to choose between paying for birth control pills on the one hand or paying rent and feeding their children on the other. This dilemma may be particularly acute in contexts where political opposition has reduced state funding for contraceptives, so they are no longer accessible and affordable.

As this suggests, whether or not the state offers financial support for women's access to abortion and contraception may be crucial to some women's reproductive lives. The availability of public funding may make a difference between women's ability to take advantage of legal rights or the practical irrelevance of these legal rights.

Our analysis treats state funding for abortion and contraception as a separate dimension from the issue of whether abortion and contraception are legally available. Whether the government commits financial support to women's reproductive rights is as much a question of women's class as it is of their gender status. State funding affects women differentially according to their class position. What is more, whether or not the state offers funding is shaped by the relationship between the state and the market, and the array of forces determining the degree to which the state intervenes in the market. Whereas status issues invoke an array of actors struggling over the cultural valuation and recognition of women, class issues invoke a different set of struggles over the respective roles of state, market, and family in social provision.

COMBINING CLASS, STATUS, AND DOCTRINE

Abortion, contraception, and state funding are doctrinal gender issues. Yet whereas abortion and contraception legality are doctrinal *status* issues, funding for abortion and contraception are doctrinal *class* issues. We expect that religious authorities will oppose liberalizing change on both legal norms and state funding. On the other hand, we expect the social and political conditions associated with more liberal legal norms to differ from those associated with more generous state funding. Specifically, we expect the array of factors that we identified as shaping doctrinal policies – communism and colonialism, religiosity, church–state fusion, dominant religion – to be more decisive in shaping abortion legality. Class-politics actors, such as Left parties, and institutional legacies, such as patterns of social provision, should be more influential in shaping funding for reproductive rights than they are for abortion legality. After explaining how we measure legality and funding, we describe the dimensions of global variation, and then turn to an assessment of how much explanatory leverage our approach provides in accounting for the wide variations in government action, both in laws and in funding.

INDICES OF REPRODUCTIVE RIGHTS

We constructed two indices. The first measures the ways abortion law varies across countries, and the second measures the extent of state funding for reproductive rights. We do not measure and analyze the legality of contraception in this chapter. By the time period we study, there was very little variation in the legality of contraception. Historically, however, some countries did criminalize the distribution, manufacture, and even use of contraception – including the United States, until the Supreme Court decision of *Griswold* v. *Connecticut* in 1965. What is more, not all contraceptive methods have been legal in every country. In Japan, as mentioned earlier in this chapter, the low-dose contraceptive pill was not approved for sale by the Health Ministry until 1999 (Norgren, 2001). But for our study period in the statistical analysis (1975–2005), the legality of contraception in general varied little.

By contrast, abortion legality varied significantly over the same period, and continues to differ in important ways around the globe. Some countries permit elective abortion (at the request of the pregnant woman), others criminalize the practice completely, and yet others enable women to seek abortions under certain, specified conditions. Various bodies of law regulate abortion, including the constitution, the criminal code, the health code or codes of medical ethics, and jurisprudence. In a few federal systems such as the United States, Mexico, and Australia, laws on abortion vary by state, but in the vast majority of countries there is one national law.

We treated the national law as the level responsible for women's rights, even in federal states. If federal law did not permit legal access to abortion, we asked if women's access varied significantly across the states or provinces and, if it did, whether the federal government took action to address women's legal status (by developing model policies, taking states to court, using funding mechanisms, or otherwise using the powers of the federal government to advance women's rights). If they did not, we coded federal policy as that of the worst state, since this was the level of legal access tolerated by the federal government by their inaction. This reflects the standard understanding of policy as encompassing both action and inaction.

There are at least two axes along which abortion legality can vary: the period of time in which abortion is available and the range of reasons that are seen as permissible grounds for abortion. Sometimes, access to abortion is restricted on the basis of how far along the pregnancy is. This legal approach is often called a term model.[5] Other laws focus on the cause or reason for

[5] For example, pregnancy may be divided into time periods (such as trimesters) and different criteria are applied in each trimester. Laws that offer differentiated access across the term of pregnancy tend to create more legal barriers later in the term. For example, they may allow elective abortion in the first trimester and apply more restrictive criteria in the second and third trimester.

TABLE 6.1 *Abortion Law Index*

Legal status of abortion	Score
Elective abortion in first and second trimesters, no restrictions[6]	10
Elective abortion in first trimester with no restrictions *or* elective abortion in first and second trimester with some restrictions	9
Elective abortion in the first trimester, with some restrictions	8
Abortion permitted on soft grounds (economic necessity, mental health) in addition to various hard grounds (including, at a minimum, rape and threat to the mother's life)	4–5
Abortion permitted when a woman has been raped in addition to other hard grounds (including, at a minimum, threat to the mother's life)	3
Abortion permitted for more hard grounds (health, fetal abnormality, incest, but not rape)	2
Abortion permitted when mother's life is in danger (ONLY)	1
Abortion forbidden under all circumstances	0

abortion.[7] They tend to criminalize abortion but also to specify certain causes or conditions under which abortion is exempt from punishment. These causes include "soft grounds," when abortion is permitted for reasons of health, financial hardship, and large family, among others, and "hard grounds," including abortions performed to save the life of the mother, when the pregnancy results from rape, or in the event of fetal abnormalities.

In addition to measures aimed at making abortion more or less legal or accessible, laws may contain rhetorical preambles that exhort women and others not to participate in abortion. Such provisions may define abortion as a "crime against life" or "crime against morality," or state that the purpose of the law is to "protect life" (Glendon, 1987). Some countries have adopted so-called "conscience clauses," permitting physicians opposed to abortion to opt out of performing the procedure. While these measures, strictly speaking, do not affect the legal status of abortion, they may affect abortion access, a separate question.

To compare abortion law across countries and over time, we created a ten-point Abortion Law Index. Countries with a score of 10 are the most

---

[6] Note that "elective abortion" includes those laws that require the woman to be in a condition of "distress" from her pregnancy to obtain an abortion, but when the woman is the only one who determines whether or not she is in distress (such as the French law discussed in note 7).

[7] Sometimes laws combine these approaches or models. The French law, for example, permits abortion up to twelve weeks if for women who claim to be in distress (Glendon, 1987). The woman is the only judge of her distress. It is therefore a "cause" model in theory but a term model in practice.

TABLE 6.2 *State Funding Index*

Legal and policy measures on funding	Score
Funding for *both* contraception and abortion	10
Funding for *either* contraception or abortion	5
No government funding for contraception or abortion	0

permissive; those with a score of 0 are the most restrictive (see Table 6.1). In addition, we analyzed the extent of state funding for abortion and contraception. We coded countries according to whether the state provided funding for both abortion and contraception, some funding, or no funding (10, 5, 0 respectively).[8] Higher values indicate more generous public funding, lower values less generous funding (see Table 6.2).

GLOBAL VARIATION

Table 6.3 depicts the mean scores on the Abortion Law Index over time. It shows that in 1975, the vast majority of countries had laws that placed some restrictions on abortion (mean of 3.8). By 2005, more countries had liberalized (mean of 5.4). Figure 6.1 depicts the trends in the Abortion Law Index over time in different regions. It shows that Eastern European countries consistently had the most liberal abortion laws, while North American and European laws grew more liberal over time, with some exceptions, such as Ireland. In East Asia, abortion laws are moderately permissive and have remained stable, or slightly liberalized.

In the Global South, patterns of change were more varied. Abortion laws in some African countries liberalized steeply after 1995, perhaps because of the Beijing conference. In the Middle East we have seen slight movement toward liberalization over our study period, while more restrictive policies in South Asian and Latin American countries changed the least. In no region did we see an overall movement toward stricter abortion policies, though there were rollbacks in individual countries such as Poland.

This regional discussion masks some interesting intraregional trends. Our examination of the country-level data revealed that intraregional variation has grown over time. Consider Latin America. In the 1970s,

[8] We mainly used the 0, 5, and 10 values (three different values) in Chapter 7, focused on comparing models across issues areas. For the ordered logit analysis in this chapter, we recoded this as having values 0, 1, 2.

TABLE 6.3 *Mean value of Abortion Law Index, by year*

Year	Mean value of Abortion Law Index, seventy countries
1975	3.8
1985	4.5
1995	5.1
2005	5.4

TABLE 6.4 *State funding for reproductive rights, by year*

Year	Mean score on State Funding Index, seventy countries
1975	5
1985	6.35
1995	6.35
2005	6.85

Latin American countries were similar in permitting abortion on hard grounds only. But by the second decade of the twenty-first century, some countries had rolled back abortion laws to ban it completely (Chile, El Salvador, Nicaragua), while others (Uruguay, Colombia, as well as Mexico City) had significantly liberalized access to abortion. Patterns of abortion legality across Latin America suggest that while a Catholic heritage may incline a country toward stricter rules, political institutions and actors ultimately intervene to shape the possibilities for reform. As we argued in Chapter 4, the political institutionalization of religious authority, not religious denomination or religiosity alone, is the critical factor shaping women's rights on doctrinal issues.

Government funding for abortion and contraception also changed over our study period. In 1975, governments across much of North Africa and South and Central America funded neither abortion nor contraception, while funding of some kind was provided across much of the Global North, especially the former Soviet Union. By 2005, nearly every country in South and Central America had adopted funding for either abortion or contraception. In the Middle East and North African (MENA) region, a few governments still failed to fund reproductive rights of any kind, and two of the independent Baltic states eliminated funding altogether in the postcommunist era (Estonia and Lithuania). But overall, most

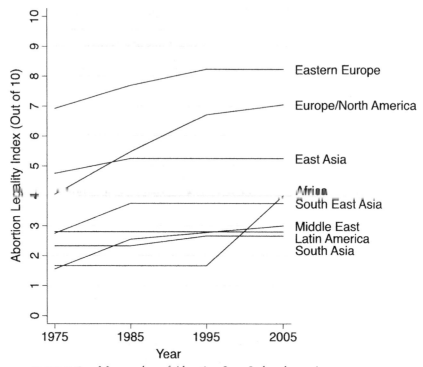

FIGURE 6.1 Mean value of Abortion Law Index, by region, 1975–2005

governments moved toward expanding or maintaining government funding, with the biggest wave of change happening between 1975 and 1985. Variation around the mean also became smaller: The standard deviation decreased by 20 percent from 1985 to 2005. This decline implies that the countries as a group became more likely to expand funding for reproductive rights over the study period, and also that variation among the countries decreased (see Table 6.4).

EXPLAINING GOVERNMENT ACTION

This chapter aims to establish that, even within the broader category of doctrinal issues, it is worthwhile to distinguish status from class politics. This implies that the set of explanatory factors associated with permissive abortion law is not the same as those associated with generous state funding. Our framework suggests that the importance of religion, and institutional characteristics, such as communism and colonialism, that reduce or enhance religious influence, should be evident in both abortion legality and reproductive rights funding. In contrast, distinctively class-politics actors and institutions, such as Left parties, should matter more for the funding issues. The actors relevant for status issues such as feminist movements should play a role in both issues.

In this section, we present the factors that we study in the empirical analysis, focusing on Left parties and religious factors. We also spend some time discussing feminist movements, to illustrate how feminist movements came to focus on reproductive rights issues in so many places.

Religion

As noted above, abortion and contraception touch upon the doctrines of many of the world's religions, and policy making on these issues animates religious organizations in most, but not all, countries (Blofield, 2013; Htun, 2003; Razavi & Jenichen, 2010; Htun & Weldon, 2010, 2015). Scholarship has identified numerous mechanisms of religious influence on politics, including the content of specific religious traditions or doctrines, degree of overall social religiosity, and church–state relations. As in Chapter 4 on family law, we test for these different types of religious influence here.

While the established doctrine of dominant religions plays an important role in our account, it is important to note that there is significant variation in abortion policy even among countries with the same religious tradition. Majority Catholic Italy and France permit elective abortion and fund it fully, while Ireland and Chile, also majority Catholic states, prohibit it. In some countries where Islam is the dominant religion, abortion is restricted unless performed to save the mother's life, while other Muslim-majority countries permit abortion to preserve mental and physical health and others have at times permitted it more broadly, for example Iran between 1976 and 1979.

The intensity of religious belief may lead citizens to prefer more restrictive abortion policies and increase the public support and legitimacy of political projects seeking to ban or curtail legal permission for abortion. Inglehart and Norris's (2003) analysis of the World Values Survey revealed a strong correlation between religiosity and skepticism about women's rights. On the other hand, there are grounds to doubt a direct association between religiosity and abortion or contraception policy. The United States, for example, is the most religious of advanced democracies, but presides over broad legal access to abortion and provides funding for contraceptives, although such funding is controversial.

As we argued in Chapter 4, state–religion relations shape policy. We showed that the political institutionalization of religious authority – the involvement of the state in propping up particular religions' views and practices – enhanced the power of religious voices and shaped intrareligious debates about women's rights, equality, and reproduction. The more the state is involved in religion, the more discriminatory is family law, especially in polities with high degrees of societal religiosity.

By contrast, scholars of Europe found that close relations between church and state (such as in the Scandinavian countries with established religions) were associated with more liberal laws on abortion and more expansive family policies. Countries with more "secular" arrangements had stricter abortion and family policy regimes (Minkenberg, 2003; Morgan, 2006). To explain these findings, Minkenberg (2003) argued that churches are more effective when they have "room for maneuver" independent of the state. Northern European countries with close church–state relations also have extraordinarily low levels of religiosity.

H1: Religious factors, especially the political institutionalization of religious authority, should be associated with restrictive policies on abortion and a lower level of funding for abortion and contraception.
H2: Since these religious factors share the stage with class-based actors and institutions for reproductive rights funding, the relationship between religious factors and funding for reproductive rights may be weaker than it is for abortion legality.

Communism

The historical experience of communism should exert an important influence on doctrinally -related policy making. As we argued in Chapter 4, communist regimes sought to reduce the influence of religion on public life, and often promoted sex equality as a means to undermine traditional cultural practices. Communist regimes also tended to preside over permissive abortion policies and to provide for contraception, with some exceptions, such as Romania under Ceausescu. The rationale for liberal measures did not derive from a belief in women's bodily autonomy and respect for reproductive choices. Rather, communist governments sought to promote women's participation in the labor market. When reproductive freedom came into conflict with the goals of the state, reproductive rights were curtailed. In the Soviet Union, for example, abortion was liberalized in 1920 but then banned in 1936 under Stalin, who wanted to increase the birth rate (Htun, 2003, p. 45). For the most part, countries have maintained the state funding established under these communist regimes, with only a couple of exceptions, for example Estonia and Lithuania. Because of this role of communism in religious politics, we anticipate, as in Chapter 4, that:

H3: Countries with experience of communism will have more permissive abortion policies.

Reproductive rights funding, however, is not just a doctrinal issue. It is also a class issue. In this area, religious actors and institutions compete for influence with Left parties. When Left parties are strong, feminist activists and international norms have an additional foothold in domestic politics and make the effects of religious actors and institutions less clear. In addition, communism may also be seen as a class-based factor, since it establishes a legacy of state intervention in the market to promote socio-economic redistribution.

H4: The role of communism in relation to funding for abortion and contraception may be attenuated and complex, and thus weaker than it is in comparison to legality alone.

Left Parties

In previous chapters, we analyzed the complicated relationship between Left parties and women's rights advocacy. Some classical analysis connected Left parties to sex equality, which suggests that Left party strength should be associated with more liberal laws on abortion and more expansive funding for reproductive rights. Yet other scholars have focused on tensions between Left parties, feminists, and gender justice. The ambiguous relationship between Left parties and women's rights suggests that Left parties will be important for change on some gender issues, but not all issues. In particular, we would not expect Left party strength to be associated with issues related to women's status, such as legal permission for abortion and contraception. As argued in the previous chapters, we theorize that autonomous feminist movements are the main actors working to reframe women's status and put status changes on the policy agenda (more on this later in this chapter).

We would expect Left parties to matter in the expansion of the state's role in funding reproductive rights. As we argued in Chapter 5, we expect to find an association between Left party strength and expanding social welfare provision more generally. Since funding for abortion and contraception can be cast as a question of class equality among women, Left parties are likely to be champions of this dimension of reproductive rights. Public funding involves social spending to empower citizens and intervene in the market. Hence, we hypothesize that the strength of Left parties should be positively correlated with more generous state funding for abortion and contraception.

H5: The strength of Left parties should be associated with more robust funding for women's reproductive rights.

H6: Left parties should be more weakly associated or unassociated with the degree
of liberalization of abortion laws.

Feminist Movements

The political agenda of the second-wave feminist movement has emphasized the importance of access to abortion and contraception. Feminist activists in particular have framed the liberalization of laws on reproductive rights as a question of women's rights. More generally, autonomous feminist movements have often succeeded in pushing neglected aspects of gender equality into the dominant political discourse, providing new frames to old issues that were not previously perceived as marginalizing women (Htun & Weldon, 2012; McAdam, Tarrow, and Tilly 2001; Weldon 2002b; 2011). By bringing salience to the problems and perspectives of women, feminist movements have promoted cultural change and mobilized allies for the cause of reproductive rights reform, among other issues.

To be sure, a variety of other political actors and groups have demanded changes to law and policy on contraception and abortion. Advocates of family planning, partisans of population control, lawyers seeking to reduce the size of the black market, liberals favoring personal freedom, secularists wanting to limit religious influence, and medical professionals with an interest in improving public health have pushed for liberalization of abortion laws and to legalize and provide contraception across many societies.

In the United States, for example, the influential American Legal Institute (ALI) produced model laws in many areas, including abortion. The American Medical Association pushed for better access to abortion in the aftermath of birth defects caused by thalidomide and the rubella (German measles) epidemic. In 1967, twelve states adopted the ALI-supported abortion reform, which extended to doctors the right to perform an abortion in cases of danger to the mother's physical or mental health, likely deformity of the child, or where the pregnancy resulted from rape, incest, or other "felonious intercourse" (Stetson, 1998). Yet these legal reforms were directed more at empowering doctors than women themselves.

Only when women's rights activists joined the fight for abortion law liberalization did it come to be seen as an issue of women's rights. Rather than pushing for the empowerment of doctors, the National Organization for Women (NOW) and other groups demanded the complete repeal of laws criminalizing abortion. They succeeded in many states, the first of which was New York in 1970. Through civil disobedience and litigation, feminist movements pushed for the repeal of laws criminalizing abortion at the state-by-state level, until the 1973 *Roe* v. *Wade* Supreme Court decision ruled that abortion fell within the realm of a constitutional right to privacy (Ibid).

The same pattern of feminist reframing of public health initiatives characterizes global discourse on family planning. Although there were many advocates of better access to birth control in the 1960s, including the ABCL (the forerunner of International Planned Parenthood Federation) and groups concerned about population growth, the women's health movement acted decisively to frame reproduction as a matter of women's self-determination.[9] Likewise, it took concerted organizing by women in the Global South and women of color to point out that sterilization and other population control policies treated women "instrumentally" and often violated their rights to bodily integrity and autonomy (Corrêa & Reichmann, 1994).

While women's activism on their own behalf was not the only force that pushed for liberalization of reproductive rights, feminist organizing has been the main source of arguments that *reforms are needed to advance women's autonomy*. In addition, once these laws have been liberalized, feminist activism has been active in preventing efforts to roll back or undermine these rights. In 2016, protesters took to the streets in

---

[9] In the United States, government funding for contraceptives dates from 1970, and did not result initially as much from feminist activism as it did from advocacy by social reformers interested in family planning and addressing concerns about "overpopulation." The Food and Drug Administration (FDA) approved the first oral contraceptive in 1960. Proposed by President Nixon, and passed with bipartisan support, the Family Planning Services and Population Research Act of 1970 "sets the standards for publicly funded family planning services in the U.S.," including providing funding for contraception. The Title X statute requires that programs are "voluntary, confidential and include a broad range of contraceptive methods" (Office of Population Affairs, 2015).

Poland to oppose a proposed measure to restrict abortion rights. These "massive" protests "forced lawmakers to abandon that proposal."[10]

Where feminist movements are strong and autonomous from other organizations, we would expect to see more liberal reproductive rights policy. This suggests that:

H7: The presence of stronger, autonomous feminist movements should be associated with more permissive abortion policy.

H8: The presence of stronger, autonomous feminist movements should be associated with greater public funding for abortion and contraception.

International Norms on Women's Rights

International law, agreements, and global norms influence domestic policy on women's human rights. Many scholars have identified the Convention on the Elimination of All Forms of Discrimination against Women (CEDAW) as an important mechanism for advancing women's rights across multiple contexts (Baldez, 2014; Htun & Weldon, 2012; Simmons, 2009). CEDAW was the first, and is the only, human rights treaty to specifically affirm the reproductive rights of women (Amnesty International, n.d.; Simmons, 2009). The transnational feminist reproductive rights movement worked to see that agreements endorsed at the International Conference on Population and Development (Cairo, 1994) and the Fourth World Conference on Women (Beijing, 1995) recognized women's reproductive rights (Htun, 2003, p. 149). The Beijing document also called on governments to review laws that contained "punitive measures against women who had undergone illegal abortions" (Htun, 2003, p. 150).

We would therefore expect that:

H9: Ratifying CEDAW should make abortion legality and reproductive rights funding more likely, as they are both status issues.

H10: Ratifying CEDAW will relate more closely to greater state funding for contraception and abortion than to the degree of legal permissiveness of abortion.

Control Variables

We also take into account the relationship between the presence of women in legislative office – operationalized as the percentage of parliamentary seats held by women – and reproductive rights. Some scholars

[10] www.theguardian.com/world/2016/oct/24/polish-abortion-law-protesters-march-against-proposed-restrictions.

have argued that a larger presence of women legislators makes women-friendly policies more likely in general (Schwindt-Bayer & Mishler, 2005), while others have argued that party ideology mediates the impact of gender (Htun & Power, 2006; Swers, 2002). Increasingly, however, the literature on women and politics has moved away from explanations relying on numbers of women toward accounts that focus on particular leaders as critical actors (Celis et al., 2008; Childs & Krook, 2006; Weldon, 2002a). This new literature takes account of the complexity of women's interests and women's policy issues.

What is more, research on abortion in the United States suggests that women representatives act mainly to curb rollbacks on women's rights instead of as advocates for new areas of action (Berkman & O'Connor, 1993; Hansen, 1993). These findings suggest that social movements are the main protagonists of contentious issues. Yet experience shows that movements have been more successful at pushing policy when they have allies within the state that help them transcend protest as their only means of influence (Blofield, 2012; Kingstone, Young, & Aubrey, 2013). On this basis, then, there could be a positive association between women's presence in the legislature and more expansive policies on women's reproductive rights. This may be particularly salient in national contexts such as the United States, where a strong feminist movement strengthens politicians who aim to defend women's rights. Since our argument does not turn or depend on this association, we include it primarily as a control variable. We examine both direct effects and effects that are conditional on the presence of a strong, autonomous feminist movement.

We also control for whether the country was colonized by a Western power. As we argued in Chapter 4, former colonies tend to be weaker states that allow for religious authorities to gain greater influence in the political system, which implies that reproductive rights could be more difficult to obtain. Finally, we control for the level of democracy, which implies a political system that is more open and more attentive to the demands of organized groups. This may enable either feminist movements or religious organizations to develop a greater influence in the policy-making process. However, the specific mechanism through which groups in favor of reproductive rights may influence politics is largely captured by our model in the form of feminist movements and Left parties.

ANALYSIS

We analyze two dependent variables, one mapping onto *legality* of abortion and one capturing *funding* for contraception and abortion, and find support for our hypotheses. We present two distinct models aimed at capturing the distinct political logics affecting each of these two areas of reproductive rights reform. As in previous chapters, we use multivariate regression techniques appropriate for panel data. For abortion legality, we use random effects to account for the autocorrelation between panel observations. For reproductive rights funding, which has only three levels, we used ordered logit.

Table 6.5 presents the results for both of our dependent variables. Note that for the ordered logit models, we present odds ratios in the table. Recall that odds ratios equal to one suggest no effect, odds ratios less than one suggest a negative effect, and odds ratio greater than one signal a positive effect. Models 1 and 3 in Table 6.5 are the most basic models for abortion legality and reproductive rights funding, respectively. They do not include any interactions, but still offer some preliminary support for our hypotheses. Models 2 and 4 represent our best models for each issue.

Religious variables were more powerfully associated with the permissiveness of abortion law than with expansive reproductive rights funding, but in both cases, the coefficients are predictably negative. For abortion legality, for example, the significant coefficient is negative for all four religious variables (*Catholic majority*, *Muslim majority*, *Official religion*, and *High religiosity*) in Models 1 and 2 (Table 6.5). Official state religion is associated with lower scores on our ten-point scale, about 1 point lower.

For reproductive rights funding these results are a bit weaker, but still in the same direction. Catholic majorities made funding for reproductive rights much less likely. With an odds ratio of 0.059 this suggests that governments in Catholic majority countries are about 94 percent less likely to increase funding for reproductive rights than their Protestant or other counterparts. (Muslim majority is not so significant or robust.) The odds ratio for high religiosity ranges between 0.412 and 0.449 for the two models for reproductive rights funding, meaning that in each case, greater religiosity makes reproductive rights funding less likely. But it is not statistically significant in all cases, so there is not as strong or robust a relationship as there is with abortion legality.

The variables with the most explanatory power are different for abortion legality than for reproductive funding, as expected. The establishment of an official religion shapes abortion legality but is not significantly associated with reproductive rights funding. Similarly, a communist legacy was positively and very significantly correlated with abortion legality, but not significantly associated with reproductive rights funding.

TABLE 6.5 *Abortion legality and reproductive rights indices, various regression techniques, 1975–2005*

Dependent variable	Abortion legality		Reproductive rights funding	
	Coefficients		Odds Ratios	
Model	1	2	3	4
Catholic majority	−.685	−.807	.059*	.066*
	(.563)	(.573)	(.094)	(.101)
Muslim majority	−.622	−.745	.092	.117
	(.710)	(.721)	(.181)	(.221)
Official religion	−.976**	−1.055**	.186	.199
	(.469)	(.474)	(.229)	(.236)
High religiosity	−.617	−.719	.412	.449
	(.539)	(.542)	(.525)	(.564)
Communist	3.763***	3.866***	4.407	4.030
	(.662)	(.670)	(7.783)	(6.898)
Former colony	−1.504**	−1.456**	.153	.163
	(.625)	(.632)	(.251)	(.258)
Left party strength (cumulative)	.008**	.006	1.108*	1.019**
	(.004)	(.004)	(.009)	(.009)
Women in parliament (%)	.024	−.001	1.080*	1.113**
	(.017)	(.021)	(.044)	(.059)
Strong, autonomous feminist movement X women in parliament (%)		.045		.921
		(.032)		(.070)
Strongest, autonomous feminist movement X women in parliament (%)		.068**		.972
		(.034)		(.086)
CEDAW ratification	.199	.196	6.584**	6.180**
	(.327)	(.325)	(5.188)	(4.812)
Strong, autonomous feminist movement	−.418	−.839*	.719	1.545
	(.332)	(.462)	(.513)	(1.542)
Strongest, autonomous feminist movement	.510	−.326	7.863*	9.443
	(.432)	(.608)	(8.407)	(13.757)
Polity	−.032	−.033	1.067	1.082
	(.028)	(.028)	(.065)	(.067)
GDP (logged)	.392	.467*	.701	.635
	(2.088)	(2.084)	(.422)	(.386)
Observations	252	252	252	252
R-squared	.520	.517		
Bayesian information criterion			388.203	398.121
Number of countries	69	69	69	69

Notes: Models 1 and 2 are estimated using linear regression (re). Models 3 and 4 estimate ordered logistic models. Standard errors are in parentheses. *, **, and *** denote statistical significance at the 10, 5, and 1 percent levels, respectively.

Being a postcolonial state (having a colonial experience) similarly seems to be associated with more expansive laws on abortion but not with more generous reproductive rights funding.

Interestingly, this means that the full complement of religious factors – including not only official religion (a measure of the political institutionalization of religious authority) and high religiosity, but also those institutional factors more indirectly associated with religion such as communism and colonialism, identified in Chapter 4 in relation to family law – are also associated with abortion legality, but not with reproductive rights funding to the same degree, if at all. This supports our argument that abortion legality and family law follow a similar doctrinal logic. It is also worth noting that institutional aspects of religion, in this case the state's designation of an official religion, have the strongest relationship with women's rights in any model.

These results support the claim that policies expanding women's control of reproduction inspire ecclesiastical opposition when they challenge the doctrine of the majority religion. The institutional fusion of church and state tends to be associated with more restrictive abortion laws. These variables seem less important, and have a weaker association, if any, with reproductive rights funding (though they are consistently negatively associated, if at all), perhaps because Left parties and class politics are complicating the picture. Religious concerns about funding may also be somewhat muted where legality restricts access to reproductive services. On the whole, though, this research is consistent with prior studies showing that religious factors dampen the effect of international norms and women's activism, exerting a negative effect that restricts the expansion of women's rights and inspires rollbacks in some contexts (Blofield, 2013; Htun & Weldon, 2015; Simmons, 2009).

Left Parties

Left parties matter for reproductive rights funding, and in the expected direction. The odds ratio in Model 4 suggests that for each one-unit increase in cumulative Left party power, the odds of a country providing a higher level of funding increases by about 2 percent. In other words, holding all other variables at their means, a country with an increase of one standard deviation in cumulative Left-party power (53 percent of the seats) is more likely to fund reproductive rights (one additional point out of ten). In contrast, Left parties did not rise to the level of statistical significance for abortion legality once other considerations were taken into account (Model 2). At most, if significant, we would expect an increase half as large (.5 out of 10) for this area (Model 1). In summary, Left parties play a larger and more significant role for reproductive rights than they do for abortion legality. These differences do not depend on different analytic techniques, and are even sharper if one uses GLS or OLS for both dependent variables.

Feminist Movements

The association between feminist movements and reproductive rights is weaker than we expected, especially with respect to abortion legality, but not entirely inconsistent with our approach. The odds ratio in Model 3 suggests that a strong, autonomous women's movement (value = 2) is substantively (see the large coefficient) and significantly associated with more funding for reproductive rights. We report the weaker level of significance here since degrees of freedom mean that only one factor, CEDAW ratification, is significant at the .01 level, and the strong autonomous feminist movement variable just barely misses the threshold with p = .05. The size and direction of this relationship are also visible in Model 4, though here the variable is not significant. In Model 1, feminist movements are not significantly associated with expanding abortion rights. However, analysis (not shown) using a lagged version of the feminist movement variable shows a significant association, suggesting that abortion politics may be similar to family law. With both issues, feminist movements work to change long-established law and struggle against entrenched opposition, which may require a greater lag time for us to see impact.

In addition, examining an interaction between feminist movements and women legislators (Model 2) shows that movements are significantly and positively associated with expanding abortion legality in their interaction with women in parliament. This suggests that the effects of feminist movements may be more contingent on the presence of insider allies in an area like abortion, where the opposition is established and entrenched and institutional legacies are so powerful. It may also reflect the weaker impact of feminist movements in Eastern Europe, where legalization, at least initially, did not reflect the initiatives of feminist activists but rather the goals of communist regimes seeking to marginalize religious influences and promote women's labor force participation.

The effects of feminist movements, then, are weaker than expected here, especially as they relate to abortion, where they are dwarfed in relation to the central role played by religion and communism. Especially when confronting entrenched opposition, feminist movements may be even more important in combination with other political actors such as women in parliament and Left parties.

The association between feminist movements and abortion legality was magnified when there was a larger share of women in the legislature. This effect was not necessarily expected, but, as noted, there is some support for it in the literature. Indeed, the "triangles of empowerment" literature points to the power of connecting women in civil society with women in government (Vargas & Wieringa, 1998). The interesting thing, from our perspective, is that the association between women politicians and women's rights did not extend to class issues such as reproductive rights funding. Perhaps women in the legislature are poor advocates for working-class women, as was the case of women in the U.S. Congress who voted for welfare reform measures that were punitive against poor women (Mink, 1998). When it comes to class-based gender issues, autonomous feminist movements may find more powerful and reliable partners for policy advocacy in Left parties than among women in parliament.

It is important to note that the coefficient for our variable indicating the presence of a weaker feminist movement (that is, when our measure for strong autonomous feminist movements takes on a lower value) is negative, especially with respect to abortion legality. This is likely a reflection of the politics of abortion in postcommunist countries, where abortion legality was fairly uniform across the region, but where the emergence of democracy, and weaker feminist movements, was associated with rollbacks in legal access to abortion in some places. Analysis of data comparing communist to postcommunist countries shows a strong association between feminist movements and abortion legality in countries without a communist legacy, and a strong negative association in the postcommunist countries. Controlling for the communist legacy should take this into account to some degree, but may not be capturing the entire effect of communism on women's movements and women's rights.

International Norms

International agreements did not call on countries to liberalize their abortion laws, but they did commit countries to improving women's reproductive health, to greater education about sexuality, to prevention of HIV/AIDS and other STDs, and to preventing unwanted pregnancies. Though the text of CEDAW does not mention abortion, the Beijing Platform for Action called on countries to recognize and deal with the health impact of unsafe abortions, which it framed as a "public health concern." Lack of attention to abortion in the text of CEDAW may explain the differential relationship between CEDAW and our two different reproductive rights indicators – abortion legality and state reproductive rights funding.

CEDAW ratification proved to have a positive association with expanded rights for women for both abortion legality and reproductive rights funding, but was statistically significant only for the funding variable, and with a sizable impact. If we see funding as a class-based issue, this is especially interesting, since some have argued that international norms are weaker when it comes to social and economic rights than when it comes to civil and political rights (O'Brien, Goetz, Scholtem, & Williams, 2000).

There is more disagreement about how CEDAW and other international norms apply to the legality of abortion than there is regarding funding for reproductive rights. The transnationalization of the abortion discussion offered opportunities for both the feminist reproductive rights movement *and* the anti-abortion movement to organize, and to circulate financial and discursive resources (Htun, 2003). Discussions about reproductive rights in general, and abortion in particular, at global conferences in Cairo and Beijing were rife with conflict. A coalition of the Vatican and conservative governments in the Middle East and Latin America tried to eliminate reproductive rights provisions from the final documents and to backtrack on what was achieved in Cairo and Beijing at follow-up meetings years later. Our analysis suggests that conservative countermobilization was more successful with regard to the legal status of abortion than it was with state funding on reproductive rights.

Control variables such as national wealth (GDP) and democracy (Polity) appeared to have little notable effect across the two models. Democracy was significant in neither, and GDP was significant in only one model, with a small, positive effect.

CONCLUSION

The analysis presented in this chapter confirms that abortion and reproductive rights funding are complex issues spanning multiple dimensions of women's rights. On the one hand, the issue of reproductive rights – especially as reflected in abortion legality – conforms to a doctrinal dynamic similar to family law. More religious societies and countries with close state–religion relations have less liberal policies. Communist regimes that marginalized religious power have more liberal policies, as do advanced democracies where religiosity is relatively low.

On the other hand, reproductive rights – as reflected in state *funding* for abortion and contraception services – invoke questions of class. The legality of abortion and contraception does not necessarily mean that people have access to means of family planning, or that safe abortions are available in public hospitals. Social and economic status shapes women's de facto access to contraception and abortion. Government funding for reproductive rights can help to close this gap. As is the case with government supply of family leave, the strength of Left parties is associated with the expansion of the state's role in combatting class inequalities among women and families.

We framed reproductive rights as a status issue, and hypothesized that the logic of status politics – feminist movements leveraging international norms to promote the idea of women as full citizens – would be important here. While we did not find a significant association between the strength of feminist movements on their own and more liberal abortion laws, we did find that such movements made a difference to reproductive rights over the long term (lagged with respect to abortion legality) and when acting with women in parliament (with respect to abortion legality), and that they seemed to be more strongly and directly associated with reproductive rights funding. In addition, the ratification of CEDAW was positively correlated with state funding for reproductive rights.

Overall, the countries of the world vary considerably with regard to the legal status of abortion. Some countries ban the practice completely, others allow it under a limited set of circumstances, while still others permit elective abortion. National governments show a greater tendency to converge toward offering more funding for contraceptive and abortion access. The complexity of the area of reproductive rights suggests that feminist activists may need to make use of additional support represented by international norms and Left parties, especially where opposing forces are institutionalized and strengthened by state power.

7

The Multiple Logics of Gender Justice

Feminist movements are the main drivers of comprehensive policies to combat violence against women, but not of generous parental leave. Religious factors are related to discriminatory family law but not to class policies, such as parental leave or childcare, to the same degree. Left parties are associated with parental leave but not action on employment law. As we have been analyzing each policy issue, these cross-issue comparisons have remained largely implicit. Comparisons across issues have motivated the analysis in each chapter but we have not addressed them directly. Why are feminist movements more important for some types of issues than other types? Why does religious opposition present an obstacle to change on some women's rights but not all women's rights? Why are some religions – such as Islam or Catholicism – associated with patterns of variation on some doctrinal issues but not others?

We have defined four different types of women's rights issues. For each of these four types, we identified actors and institutions that are most salient, and offered theoretical accounts of *why* it should be those actors and institutions that matter for that specific issue-type. In our issue-focused chapters, we offered analysis that was confined mostly to the specific issue at hand to show how the actors and institutions we posited as important were in fact the ones that mattered for that type of issue. Our overall approach has implications for comparisons between these issues, suggesting that there should be similarities among issues of the same "type" and differences between issues of different types.

By comparing our explanations for each policy *type*, and by comparing issues according to whether they adhere to the classification we have proposed (for example, are all doctrinal issues the same?), we can assess the extent to which they adhere to different logics of change that we outlined at the outset of the book, and then developed and refined in the issue-specific chapters. Are we on the right track in our account of the specific patterns of differences across issue types? We can also assess whether this approach adds anything to traditional approaches in comparative politics and gender and politics. To what degree are women's rights driven by a singular process, such as economic modernization, democratization, demographic changes, or changes in cultural attitudes (cf. Inglehart & Norris, 2003)? What does our approach add to traditional theories of gender and politics that focus mainly on women in parliament, feminist movements, or how to create more "women-friendly" states?

THE THEORETICAL FOUNDATION FOR CROSS-ISSUE ANALYSIS

In the first chapter, we presented our typology of gender-equality policy issues. Table 7.1 duplicates the typology, with the policies examined in each of the previous chapters highlighted in bold text. We also identified particular actors and institutions that we expected would be the most salient for each issue-type (we reproduce that table here, as Table 7.2, for ease of reference).

We turn now to asking whether the expectations we laid out in that first chapter seem to obtain, and whether the approach we have outlined helps to understand the variations we have seen across the issues of gender

TABLE 7.1 *Typology of policies to promote gender justice and equality*

		Do the policies challenge the doctrine of religious organizations or the codified tradition or sacred discourse of major cultural groups?	
		No: Nondoctrinal	Yes: Doctrinal
Does the policy advance women's rights primarily as a status group or as a gender-class group?	Status	Violence against women Gender parity/quotas Constitutional equality **Legal equality in the workplace**	Family law **Abortion legality** Reproductive freedom
	Class	**Maternity/parental/ daddy leave** **Public funding for childcare**	**Public funding for abortion and contraceptives**

Source: Htun & Weldon, 2010(modified from its original version).

TABLE 7.2 *Most salient actors and institutions for each policy type*

	"Nondoctrinal" policies	"Doctrinal" policies
Gender status policies	Feminist movements (+)	Religion (–)
	International agreements (+)	Feminist movements (+)
	I	II
Class policies	Left parties (+)	Religion (–)
	Socioeconomic conditions (+)	Left parties (+)
	III	IV

justice considered in this book. As we tackled each issue in the issue-specific chapters, we adapted our measures and analyses to the particular issue. Here we aim to compare issues to each other, so we take a different approach. To ease cross-issue comparison, we apply the same model – the same variables, measures, and so forth – to each of the dependent variables in the study, to compare whether and how the same set of independent variables is associated with each type of policy. We apply these findings side by side in a single analysis, which produces insights that are not available when we take an issue-by-issue focus.

The results, which we elaborate in this chapter, show that the same model, with equivalent measures for each independent variable, performs differently for each type of women's rights issue when we change only the dependent variable. In addition, we show in a side-by-side analysis of a series of statistical models that each type of policy has distinct dynamics, and we demonstrate that different combinations of contextual variables and actors drive each policy area. Our objective is to demonstrate that our framework helps to understand the cross-issue variation and explains *why* the different actors and contextual factors that matter have the effects (or noneffects) that they do. We illustrate the mechanisms and relations behind these observed patterns with examples drawn from our fieldwork and prior research. The chapter shows the power of our approach within and across national contexts.

The Rationale for the Model

The base model most closely approximates an overall approach to gender justice, incorporating refinements and insight generated by the preceding chapters in this book. It includes all the actors and contextual factors in our framework as well as variables aimed at capturing the principal perspectives of comparative politics and gender and politics. The factors include feminist movements, international treaties and conventions (such as CEDAW), religion (including church–state relations, the degree of societal religiosity, and religious parties), economic conditions, and Left parties, as well as variables such as women's agencies in the state, numbers of women in parliament, the experience of Western overseas colonialism, the experience of communism, the degree of democracy, and the dominant religion. Our focus here is to contrast issues with each other. By contrast, in our issue-specific analyses, we were able to go beyond this single model to explore the unique characteristics of each issue more fully.

The base model uses the lagged version of the feminist movement variable. For some areas, movements took longer to exert their effects, since legal codes were entrenched and harder to change. In other areas, it might not be necessary to lag this variable, but here we apply a lagged variable in all models. Similarly, we use the measure for the cumulative strength of Left parties, rather than the dummy variable for whether a Left party is present in government. In some issue areas, it seemed that the cumulative effect of Left parties over time best captured the influence of Left parties. We do not use the measure for political institutionalization of religious authority (count of religious legislation, from the Religion and the State Database) that we used in Chapter 4, because that would restrict our comparative analyses to only two of our cross-sections. Instead, we use the establishment of an official state religion (available for all time periods), as well as an array of other variables aimed at capturing religious influence, such as religious parties, predominantly Muslim or Catholic country, high religiosity (measured by the World Values Survey question about belief in God), and so on. We use the lagged version of the CEDAW ratification variable, since approaches that emphasize learning and the growing influence of CEDAW over time best capture the treaty's impact. We include standard variables for comparative politics (measures for GDP and democracy) as well as gender and politics (proportion of parliamentary seats held by women, effective women's policy machinery) as control variables, and we have some conclusions to offer about these approaches as well.

Table 7.3 presents OLS with panel-corrected standard errors for the whole dataset of dependent and independent variables for 1985 to 2005. (We lose 1975 because of the use of lagged variables.) With our replication files, interested readers can generate the same table using random effects, to see that the choice of one or the other of these methods does not change the findings significantly. As we noted in Chapter 3 (footnote 13),

TABLE 7.3 *Multiple areas of women's rights, linear regression with panel-corrected standard error, seventy countries, 1985–2005*

Issue-area	Violence against women	Equality at work	Family law	Abortion legality	Leave generosity	RR funding
Issue-type	Status	Status	Doctrinal	Doctrinal	Class	Class and doctrinal
Variable	1	2	3	4	5	6
Strong, autonomous feminist movement (lagged)	.707***	.526***	.270**	.493***	−.556***	1.209***
	(.118)	(.183)	(.122)	(.058)	(.195)	(.233)
Effective women's policy machinery	.716***	.148	−.333	−1.145***	−.329*	.491
	(.233)	(.259)	(.268)	(.400)	(.188)	(.371)
Democracy level	.023	.036**	.139***	.056	.063***	.037
	(.019)	(.016)	(.031)	(.052)	(.016)	(.034)
GDP (logged)	2.614***	1.306***	−.739***	1.069**	.956***	−1.845***
	(.765)	(.418)	(.276)	(.436)	(.263)	(.564)
CEDAW ratification (lagged)	1.604***	1.036***	.158	.006	.647**	.479
	(.583)	(.227)	(.155)	(.417)	(.256)	(.332)
Communist	−1.274**	.533***	1.480***	3.523***	1.954***	1.037***
	(.629)	(.178)	(.196)	(.216)	(.256)	(.332)
Former colony	1.496**	.252	−.832***	−1.304**	−1.169***	−2.385***
	(.686)	(.318)	(.281)	(.532)	(.194)	(.644)
Official religion	−.718**	−.732***	−.376**	−1.113***	.443***	−.345*
	(.310)	(.214)	(.155)	(.255)	(.163)	(.199)
High religiosity	−.164	−.059	.178	−1.015***	.560***	−.101
	(.364)	(.192)	(.201)	(.319)	(.213)	(.355)

(continued)

233

TABLE 7.3 (continued)

Issue-area	Violence against women	Equality at work	Family law	Abortion legal	Leave generosity	RR funding
Issue-type	Status	Status	Doctrinal	Doctrinal	Class	Class and doctrinal
Variable	1	2	3	4	5	6
Catholic majority	.064	.401**	.788***	-.731**	.029	-.735***
	(.350)	(.194)	(.210)	(.325)	(.225)	(.191)
Muslim majority	-.053	-.230**	-2.329***	.631	.917***	-.308
	(.366)	(.104)	(.506)	(.441)	(.191)	(.602)
Religious party	-.112	.265**	-.937*	-.497	-.732**	-1.300**
	(.428)	(.115)	(.517)	(.319)	(.334)	(.644)
Left party strength (cumulative)	.009***	.004***	.001	.006**	.007***	.006***
	(.003)	(.001)	(.002)	(.002)	(.001)	(.002)
Women in parliament (%)	.027***	.036***	.066***	.076**	.042***	.070***
	(.009)	(.005)	(.012)	(.013)	(.012)	(.015)
Observations	198	198	198	198	198	198
R-squared	.653	.665	.771	.573	.531	.387
Number of countries	70	70	70	70	70	70

Notes: Standard errors are in parentheses. *, **, and *** denote statistical significance at the 10, 5, and 1 percent levels, respectively.

234

fixed effects are not appropriate for the type of variables and analyses we undertake here. The Hausman test tends to produce poor results in assessing the analytic approach best suited to the kind of data we are working with, so we do not use it to determine whether random effects is appropriate (Clark & Linzer, 2015). Since OLS is more robust to violations, and more intuitive to interpret, we present those results here. Note that for this analysis, all dependent variables are measured on a scale adjusted so that the maximum value is 10. This means we normed both family law and the leave generosity variable to be out of 10 for this analysis. We discuss the results in the following sections.

ANALYSIS

Our analysis shows that the same model does not have the same results in each issue-area, with different variables being significant and offering different degrees of explanatory power (Table 7.3, Models 1–7). No single variable is statistically and substantively significant in all models, and even the most consistently important variables vary to some degree in their importance in these different analyses.

Status Issues: Quadrant 1

Policies that we classify as nondoctrinal "status" policy issues (Quadrant 1 in Table 7.1) include violence against women and women's legal status at work. We would expect these "status" policies to be ones where feminist movements, and international norms such as CEDAW, had particular relevance. Indeed, looking at Models 1 and 2 in Table 7.3, we can see that strong, autonomous movements are positively and significantly associated with both of these issues, and that they are not so associated with every issue-area (every model) in the table. Feminist movements appear to be negatively associated with parental leave policy, and more weakly associated, and perhaps associated with smaller effects, with at least some doctrinal policies (such as family law).

Similarly, CEDAW ratification is singularly important for nondoctrinal status policies. CEDAW ratification may also be important for some of the other policy areas discussed here. In Table 7.3, it appears to be more weakly associated with both parental leave (perhaps reflecting the long-standing impact of the International Labor Organization's recommendations and long-established conventions related to maternity leave) and the adoption of a national childcare policy. In addition, some of the issue-specific analyses suggest interactive relationships that would be complicated to explore comparatively in this chapter (since different issues suggest different interactions are most important). These relationships would not be evident where interactive analyses are not explored (as in Table 7.2, compared to, say, Table 2.9). Still, CEDAW ratification appears to have a strong, robust, and positive direct association with the two policy issues the book's introduction identified as nondoctrinal status issues.

We also expected religious variables and class-based actors (such as Left parties) to matter less for these issues. Left parties have no discernible effect (the coefficient is zero, even if the relationship is significant) on these issues, something amplified in the issue-specific analyses we presented in previous chapters. Similarly, religious variables such as religiosity, Catholic or Muslim majority, and religious party have no statistically significant impact for VAW. The weak relationship with official religion does not hold up in our issue-specific chapters once other variables are taken into account. There does appear to be some weak relationship with some religious variables for the employment law issue, but again, these are not very robust as they are not significant once we control for more variables and use different specifications (as demonstrated in Models 3 and 5 in Table 3.4 in Chapter 3). There is certainly not the strong, consistent impact of religious institutions we see in relation to doctrinal issues (something we return to later in this chapter).

Our expectations for this issue-type, then, are largely borne out. We argued that because these issues relate to women's status as women, feminist movements would play a particularly important role. We also argued that international norms might have more impact where they did not confront opposition from domestic groups (such as religious groups or business groups) or have to confront longstanding institutional barriers to change, such as religious institutions or social policy legacies. If we are right, similar dynamics are likely to apply to gender quotas, provisions for constitutional equality, or other status issues. We return to this point in the conclusion.

Doctrinal Issues (Quadrant 2)

Our analysis includes two issues that are gender status, doctrinal issues (see quadrant 2 in Table 7.1). We expected that when women's rights initiatives challenged the established doctrine of the dominant religion, and where levels of religiosity are high, religious factors will be important. We also expected strong, autonomous feminist movements to still have some effect.

We did see a positive and significant effect of feminist movements on doctrinal issues (Models 3 and 4, Table 7.3), if not as large, strong, or robust as the effect on status policies. This may reflect the greater importance of religious variables here.

Turning to the religious variables, having an official religion has a negative association for doctrinal issues, though it varies in strength. We know from our earlier chapters that this is not robust for VAW or equality at work, and is more robust for family law than even our analysis here suggests, especially when we use the more refined religious law measure. The strongest negative relationship seen in Table 7.3 concerns the association between official religion and abortion legality, and both doctrinal issues (abortion and family law) have more robust relationships with this variable and concept (on robustness, see the issue-specific analyses in the chapters). In contrast, official state religion and other religious variables have little salience for class-based issues.

We see the particular doctrinal significance of family law in Muslim majority countries in Model 3, an effect that is much weaker for abortion, which does not have the same religious significance in Islam as in Christianity. For Catholics, abortion is much more clearly politicized as a doctrinal issue, while family law as a whole (which encompasses far more than just divorce) is much more complicated. For both doctrinal issues, however, the denomination of the dominant religious group matters.

Interestingly, it seems that CEDAW ratification has a weaker association with doctrinal policies than other areas. We anticipated that domestic opposition would blunt the impact of CEDAW, and that this would be especially keen with doctrinal issues. International forces may not be so powerful where national identity, as expressed in religion, seems to dictate resistance. This may explain why increasing pressure placed on Ireland by Europe has produced a strengthening of opposition to abortion.

While there are differences between doctrinal issues, then, in the main they conform to our expectations that religion would be the most important factor.

Class Issues: Quadrant 3

Family leave policies (such as maternity and parental leave), on which so many cross-national analyses of women's substantive representation rest, are clearly different from most other areas of equality policy. For example, the importance of feminist movements, women in parliament, and religious factors seem to have different relationships with the other areas of women's rights. This can be seen by contrasting Model 5, focused on overall leave generosity, with other models in Table 7.3.

We expected economic conditions to have a particularly great effect on class-based issues. For example, we expected level of development or national wealth to have a strong relationship with the generosity of parental leave, as it does with overall welfare state size. In fact, logged GDP did not appear to have its strongest relationship with class issues. If anything, GDP seemed more strongly associated with status issues, such as VAW and Equality at work. It may be that a more refined measurement of economic conditions is necessary to capture their impact. For example, Annesley, Engeli, and Gains (2015) use our framework to show how the business cycle affects policy decisions. It may also be that economic conditions interact with other variables (such as fertility rates) and require more detailed analysis to reveal their effects.

We expected Left parties to be especially important for class issues such as family leave, childcare, and funding reproductive rights. Left party strength is strongly significant, and is positively related to the generosity of family leave in this table, but the effect is small and may not seem substantively important. With a coefficient of .004 and an SD of 53, a standard deviation change in the cumulative strength of Left parties would be associated with only a .20 change in the dependent variable (about 2 percent of the range of the variable). A change from the value at the minimum to the maximum value on cumulative Left party power would be associated with a one-unit change in the dependent variable, which is more significant. Perhaps the small steady impact of Left parties over time eventually adds up to more generous leave. These effects are somewhat larger when a model tailored to class-based issues is constructed (see Chapter 5). Overall, there is some support for the idea that Left parties are positively associated with class issues. Our issue-specific chapters showed that Left parties had little relationship with policy on VAW, equality at work, or abortion legality in the period that we studied.

Surprisingly, CEDAW appears to have a relationship with overall leave generosity, something we did not expect. Indeed, we may have underestimated the importance of CEDAW, and the impact of international norms, for these class-based issues in general. We anticipated that opposition from business groups and national policy styles would prove formidable obstacles for international influences, but it may be that with domestic support, for example, from social movements and Left parties, the iterative process outlined by Baldez (2014) makes CEDAW powerful enough to influence policy making. This becomes particularly salient in discussing the last type of policy issues, to which we now turn.

Doctrinal, Class-Based Issues: Quadrant 4

Ironically, doctrinal, class-based issues may be easier to make progress on than doctrinal status issues, because they create the potential for a coalition with Left parties. We anticipated that feminist movements, Left parties, and religious variables would matter here. Left parties appear to be particularly important (a finding we amplify in the issue-specific chapter) because of the combined effects of women in parliament, feminist movements, and international norms. Religious variables do seem to matter, as we expected, though perhaps differently than we thought, with religious parties becoming important and confessional type (Catholicism) also being important. The factors we thought were important do actually matter here, suggesting that it is worth considering the religious, class, and status elements of this issue in order to understand it fully.

Women in Parliament and Feminist Movements

Larger proportions of women in parliament appear to have some relationship with women's rights across most of these issues, although the effects are much less robust than some other factors, less significant, and substantively very small. Overall, our analysis suggests a much smaller role for women in parliaments in promoting women's rights than one might expect, given the overwhelming focus – at least in political science – on the role of women in office and measures designed to put more women there (such as gender quotas).

The weak relationship between women in parliament and women's rights becomes even more evident when one gets into the more detailed analysis of each issue-area. Our chapters showed that a host of factors (religion, institutional legacies, civil society actors, and political parties) are just as, or even more, important than women in parliament when it comes to understanding state action on women's rights. Though numbers of women in parliament are significantly and positively associated with more advanced policies in most (but not all) models, they are far from the only or most important factor. In some of these cases, it may be that women in parliament have a small but significant effect, but in others the seeming statistical association masks a different causal relationship, as we showed in the chapter on VAW (Chapter 2), for example. In that chapter, we showed through more granular qualitative analysis that the role of women in parliament is negligible in many cases. In most models, the size and significance of the coefficients suggests that larger proportions of women in the legislature are unlikely to have much of a substantive effect on their own, without movements, parties, and international pressures to catalyze policy change.

Our analysis suggests that the focus on women's representation in politics as a causal driver of women's rights (a focus justified by much of the scholarship on maternity leave) may have colored our conventional wisdom and established ideas about politics. The comparative studies in this book show that family leave differs from other women's rights issues and also that women's presence in parliament may not be as important as other drivers of equality policies. Feminist movements are key fighters for new visions of women's rights, while women politicians serve as critical actors or bulwarks against rollbacks in reforms. Institutional factors and other contextual variables may far outweigh the role of women in parliament in shaping policy outcomes (cf. Weldon, 2002b). This does not mean that women's legislative presence makes no difference. On the contrary: Women's presence in power helps to erode the cultural status hierarchy associating masculinity with power (Htun, 2016; Mansbridge, 1999).

Nor do we argue that feminist movements always matter in the same way or degree for every issue. Our cross-issue analysis suggests insights into the conditions under which women's movements matter most, and when they matter less. Feminist movements appear to be more strongly associated with status issues. For violence against women and equality at work, feminist movements seem to have a more direct, immediate impact. However, for issues requiring extensive reform of existing legal regimes (family law, abortion), the lagged variable seems to have a stronger association. Feminist movements have a direct impact on newer issues where law and doctrine are silent or conflicted, whereas they take time to register effects on long-salient issues where laws are well established. On the more family-focused issues, particularly those that may challenge traditional gender roles to a lesser degree (maternity leave), feminist movements may be less important.

Comparative Politics and Variation across Policy Issues

As this suggests, any explanation for the politics of gender justice must be able to account for cross-issue variation, as is the case with comparative and international politics or even politics more generally. Analysts of comparative politics and policy have developed many typologies of issues, including Lowi's foundational typology distinguishing between regulatory, distributive, and redistributive issues (Lowi, 1964) and Nancy Fraser's more recent distinction between remedies promoting either redistribution or recognition as distinct, irreducible dimensions of social justice (Fraser, 2003). Gochman (1998) emphasizes the importance of the particular issue at hand to understanding militarized interstate disputes, while Sanbonmatsu points out that the politics of women's rights vary by issue within the United States (Sanbonmatsu, 2004). Indeed, policy studies has long been organized (perhaps too much) by issue, as the ways in which problems are structured (what kind of an issue is this?) determine many important questions that policy analysts wish to consider (Dunn, 2011). But the main approaches to comparative politics vary in their ability to accommodate the political differences of these different issue types. In the sections below, we consider the purchase of existing approaches to comparative politics to the cross-issue variation we see in this chapter.

Institutions and Issues: New and Old

Our analyses support the power of institutional approaches to the analysis of politics, and illustrate the ways in which institutional approaches may be adapted to take account of cross-issue variation. In the models in Table 7.3, institutional legacies are powerful determinants of women's rights for many areas. For example, the experience of communism was particularly important (the strongest predictor) for doctrinal policies such as family law and abortion legality (Models 3 and 4) due to communist regimes' efforts to marginalize religion. Communism was also associated with policies related to traditional class equality, as socialist doctrine supported working mothers but did not challenge gender roles (Leave generosity, Model 5). By combatting religious authority, communist governments reduced the influence of major obstacles to reform. Communist projects, which also tried to push women into the workforce, provided a template for legal reforms in the workplace based on a formal model of legal equality. Communist legacies did not shape policies on VAW, which did not involve a struggle against religious doctrine so much as a struggle over the regulation of women's bodies and personal privacy. Personal privacy, individual self-determination, and bodily integrity were values that animated feminist campaigns of recent years but did not drive communist reforms.

In addition, the antidemocratic nature of communist regimes stunted the development of civil society movements, including feminist movements. Official state feminism under communism, which involved the mobilization of women into the service of the regime and often had nothing to do with feminism, tainted postcommunist efforts to organize women and advance women's rights. This antifeminist legacy has hobbled policy development in areas where women's autonomous organizing is especially important, such as VAW.

The institutional legacy of colonialism also had varying impacts. Former colony status is significant to at least a weak degree and has a sizable association for five of the six areas in the first set of models. It has negative associations with sex equality for all of the doctrinal areas (though levels of significance vary somewhat). Postcolonial states present special obstacles to advancing women's rights on family law, abortion, equality at work, and parental leave: Postcolonial states seek to make up the legitimacy deficit they encounter as relatively new institutions, often with contested origins, by relying on religious institutions and actors for support.

At the same time, we find that the impact of institutions and the restrictiveness of institutional legacies, such as the impact of path dependency, varies across issues. For example, a past policy decision to emphasize childcare (as in the United States) or parental leave (as in Sweden) may limit the later development of the alternate path in addressing work–family reconciliation (Chapter 5). Similarly, past policies on violence against women pave the way for future policies (Chapter 2). In this way, our analysis suggests that there is tremendous path dependency for those areas already defined as part of a set of power relations between the state and other major institutions (such as the market or organized religion). For example, when equality policies form part of, or challenge, the institutionalized set of state–market relations, path dependency seems to be important for explaining cross-national variation. For family leave policy, such path dependency is critical for getting a handle on cross-national variation. It seems less important in newer areas such as reproductive rights funding and VAW, though as these policies become established, they do shape later policy developments as well.

New institutions, such as international norms and women's policy machineries, may also exert an influence, but this seems to depend more on the animating influence of civil society movements. These institutions seem to have less of a visible effect in areas where institutional patterns of response to an issue are already well established (family law, abortion, and so forth). As much of the literature suggests, older, more established institutions, even if they persist at an informal level, can undermine the effects of new institutions layered on top (Streeck & Thelen, 2005). On the other hand, it does suggest that even new institutions can, in some cases, exert an effect when they are reinforced by civil society actors and opposition is minimal or disorganized.

Development and Democracy

National wealth, while clearly an important factor and correlate of greater women's rights in many cases, varies dramatically in its impact and importance in our analysis. Coefficients are large and positive in some areas (nondoctrinal status areas such as VAW and women's legal status at work – Models 1 and 2 respectively), but in others the associated coefficient is smaller or even negative. And, as the analysis in the prior chapters shows, even the strength of the relationship, as reflected in the statistical significance of the association, disappears in the specifications that control for the most important determinants of each issue-area.

Similarly, higher democracy levels do not seem to be strongly associated with promoting women's rights in most models. They have only positive, significant effects in two models of all those shown – family law (Model 3), legal status at work (Model 2), and leave generosity (Model 5) – and these are not at all robust findings (see Chapters 2, 3, and 5).

The study of comparative politics often takes both level of development and experience with democracy as foundational, dividing fields of study along these lines at major conferences, and baking these factors into research designs as elements that make countries comparable or not. Our analysis suggests these factors may be less important than such approaches assume, or at least that we need to consider the possibility that the degree and kind of impact may vary considerably.

CONCLUSION

Gender equality policies cannot be considered part of a single basket. Each challenges fundamental values and institutions set by the status order, class inequalities, and the power of religious and cultural doctrine. Whether or not a policy involves women's status with respect to men, class positions, or the authority of the state against religious and cultural groups sets in motion distinct political dynamics. Understanding which social identities are activated and which institutions are challenged by a given equality initiative helps to understand the forces arrayed for and against the initiative, and what it will take to make change. Much of the conventional wisdom about gender equality policy and comparative politics and social policy more generally may not hold equally well for all areas of women's rights (and maybe for all areas of social policy, comparative politics, and international affairs).

The approach presented here reveals a way out of the puzzles with which we began this book. Why did Latin America surpass Europe in the mid-1990s with respect to the innovative nature of policies on VAW? Our analysis suggests that on status issues such as violence against women, regional agreements are critical to diffusing model policies across the region, and this regional agreement (demanded by a transnational feminist network in Latin America) emerged earlier in Latin America than in Europe. Why has law and policy in the United States been innovative with respect to violence against women, but lagging the rest of the developed world with respect to family leave? Our approach suggests that the difference lies in the contrast between the logic of status policies and the logic of class politics. Specifically, the answer lies in the weakness of labor mobilization, and especially the lack of a real Left party. Why have legal barriers to abortion increased in Catholic Ireland, while women in Italy, the seat of the Vatican, enjoy fully funded, legal abortion? Here, the logic of doctrinal politics helps shed light on the subject. The difference in legality is driven mainly by the role of the Irish state in promoting the Catholic religion, while the difference in funding is likely driven by the strength of Left parties in Italy, as well as the lack of an official religion. Similarly, the difference between Muslim countries where family law has been successfully reformed (such as Morocco) and those where they have not (such as Iran or Egypt) lies in the combination of high religiosity and the degree of the political institutionalization of religious authority. Our approach helps to unravel these puzzles and, on the way, provides insight into the field more broadly.

Conclusion

In recent decades, feminist activists have worked to transform states and societies to advance women's rights. Social movements and transnational networks have mobilized to advocate legal changes, new public policies, and governmental compliance with international treaties and declarations. These efforts have helped to reshape state action in diverse areas including the family, reproduction, sexual violence, the economy, and public life. At the same time, feminist activists and scholars have long been skeptical of the state. Both directly and indirectly, state action has upheld gender institutions that put women at a disadvantage, through mechanisms of social provision, family law, the regulation of reproduction, employment law, criminal justice, obligations for military service, and instruments of organized violence.

Recognizing the multifaceted nature of state power, this book tackled the question of whether, to what extent, and under what conditions states can be harnessed as forces for gender justice. Though the answers are as complex as the phenomena of states and gender themselves, this analysis revealed some significant relationships and patterns that advance our understanding of gender and politics as well as the politics of social justice more generally. Our approach helps to solve conundrums at the heart of comparative gender politics, and suggests new directions for political analysis.

At the outset of the book, we identified a series of puzzles. The global movement toward gender equality was propelled by international organizations, transnational and domestic feminist movements, and human rights networks, as well as major attitudinal and behavioral changes in many societies – changes to which those movements contributed. But trends toward gender equality were also uneven, progressing in fits and starts, and advancing in different ways across issues. In some countries and regions, gender equality seemed to improve quickly on many fronts, while equality initiatives seemed barely to gain ground in others. National governments could be progressive on some issues and laggards on others. State action to promote the rights and dignity of women has been anything but a simple, linear, or unidimensional process.

Major theories of comparative politics have accounted for these processes in terms of economic development, secularization, democratization, the power of socialist and Leftist parties, or women's presence in politics, among other factors. These perspectives, which imply we should see big differences across countries and over time, are less able to explain variation in women's rights *within* countries and *across* issues. Understanding the possibilities for gender justice requires that we unpack the institutions of gender and the different ways that the state upholds these gender orders. States can move in contradictory directions, simultaneously granting and denying rights, because gender is multidimensional, and states and societies intersect along multiple pathways. State action is contested in different arenas, involving diverse sets of actors and invoking distinct, though related, historical conflicts.

Our analysis in this book helps to unravel these surprising phenomena. We disaggregated women's rights into different dimensions, mapped out which policies combat disadvantage along each dimension, and then identified the *logics* – the distinct histories, conflicts, actors, and ideas – surrounding each area of gender justice.

By emphasizing that gender is multidimensional, we draw a contrast with unidimensional approaches that reduce gender inequality to a single dimension such as patriarchy, material inequality, or sexuality. Our book conceptualizes gender as an institution that has many facets and that varies along more than one axis. The dimensions of gender that we define in this book turn on the relations between gender and other social institutions that affect how equality initiatives are interpreted and processed politically. These include social status hierarchies, class relations, and the historical claims of religious groups to govern kinship and reproduction.

Advancing gender justice entails a change in social status hierarchies. In most places, these hierarchies divide people into binary sex categories that privilege dominant forms of masculinity and denigrate women and the many forms of the feminine. In this sense, all gender issues are status issues. But some gender equality policies primarily address these status issues while others involve challenges to other dimensions as well. We identify two other dimensions of gender issues: (1) whether they were targeted at shifting responsibility for social provision from the family and market to the state, and thus promoting greater class equality and (2) whether they involved expanding the sphere of accountable and deliberative politics against domains of kinship and reproduction governed by religious doctrine and codified cultural traditions. This framework identifies at least four different kinds of women's rights issues, each of which corresponds to a different history, triggers a distinct conflict or cleavage, and activates a distinct set of protagonists. On this basis, we hypothesized that different women's rights issues would exhibit different patterns of variation across time and space and that different explanatory factors would be prominent in each type of policy area.

In order to assess the utility of our approach, we developed a multiissue dataset with global reach and cross-temporal scope. Our data covers seven policy areas in seventy countries at four points in time, from 1975 to 2005. We developed an index for each issue-area that enabled us to compare over time and across countries, purposively designed to capture countries from every region of the world and over the period in which organized feminism has had its major impact. We combined our original data on policy with existing data on political, economic, and social conditions, all at the national level. In addition, we did fieldwork consisting of elite interviews and participant observation in a smaller group of countries. Our experience with previous research projects also helped develop our intuitions.

The empirical analyses in this book provided support for our approach but also revealed some surprises. We uncovered four distinct logics of gender justice corresponding to each of the four categories in our typology: *status politics, doctrinal politics, class politics*, and a *status-doctrinal-class* combination. We found that cross-national patterns of policy on violence against women and legislation promoting equality at work conformed to a logic of status politics. The impetus for change came from feminist movements, who helped to consolidate international norms, which they leveraged to pressure for greater changes in domestic contexts. Family law and the legality of abortion, by contrast, followed a logic of doctrinal politics. Religious groups clashed with secular and feminist coalitions over who governed kinship and reproduction and on what terms, and the outcomes of their conflicts were shaped by the historical legacy of state–religion relations. Class politics, which involved an expansion of the state's redistributive role to assume responsibility for care work vis-à-vis markets and families, helped account for cross-national patterns of family leave policy.

Economic conditions and the power of actors endorsing redistribution –
such as Left parties – were important components of class politics. In our
final quadrant, which combined elements of status, doctrine, and class, we
found that feminist movements, international influences, Left parties, and
religious groups were significantly associated with variation in policy
patterns, due to their historical roles supporting and opposing the legality
and accessibility of reproductive rights.

In the rest of this conclusion, we propose that the power of our
approach extends beyond the specific issues to which we have applied it
in this book. The study of public policy is often broken down by issue-
area (for example, women's rights, environmental policy, health policy,
transportation policy, and so forth). Our approach suggests that scholars
may benefit from analyzing commonalities across these sectors, and from
disaggregating issues within these sectors to gain greater insight. In particular, our dimensions of disaggregation (pertaining to status, class, and
doctrine) may offer explanatory power for a wider range of issues than
just those pertaining to women's rights. For example, group status is
relevant for other dimensions of disadvantage, including race, ethnicity,
and sexuality, and status politics inflects a wide range of issues including
education, access to the labor market, immigration, health-care policy,
national security, and science policy. What is more, religious support and
opposition characterizes a wide range of policies, including medical
research, often thought of as a health-politics issue, and attitudes toward
technology that are thought of as science and technology policy issues.

QUOTAS AND SAME-SEX MARRIAGE

Our disaggregated approach can help account for patterns of policy on
issues not considered in this book, such as gender quotas in politics or the
struggle for gay marriage. Gender quotas, for example, conform to a logic
of status politics. Quotas change the face of power, helping to promote the
recognition of women as a status group and erode discriminatory beliefs
and patterns of gender bias (Htun, 2016; Ridgeway, 2001). Policy change
originated with women's mobilization and involved the influence of international norms. Though women in parliament and in political parties were
more important in pushing for quotas than for policies on violence against
women, autonomous feminist activists were the ones who originally raised
the question of women's exclusion from political decision making and
worked to create international norms reflected in intergovernmental agreements such as the Platform for Action developed in Beijing in 1995. In

coalition with women politicians, feminist activists authored bills to present in legislatures, lobbied male politicians, and raised public awareness of women's exclusion (Baldez, 2004; Dahlerup, 2006; Dahlerup & Friedenvall, 2005; Htun, 2016; Krook, 2009; Paxton, Hughes, & Green 2006). Once the example was set in certain countries, quota laws spread to others in the same region with astonishing speed, as activists learned from the successful strategies of their colleagues elsewhere (Crocker, 2005; Krook & O'Brien, 2010).

The recognition of gay marriage – which we would classify as a gender-status, doctrinal issue – also originated in social movement mobilization. Like the movements to combat violence against women, campaigns for gay marriage tend to be autonomous from parties and the state, engage in a high degree of transnational networking, and leverage the experiences and resources of other countries (Díez, 2015; Friedman, 2012). While gay marriage has inspired a wide array of opponents, in a significant number of places, activists have convinced the broader public that the issue is fundamentally about equality and that gay marriage advances, rather than contradicts, family values and human rights.[1] In the case of both quota and LGBT rights, international and regional norms have been important forces driving policy diffusion (Ayoub, 2016; Krook, 2009) – a distinctive aspect of the logic of status policies, as we showed in our chapter on violence against women.

Unlike quotas and violence against women, however, gay marriage is a doctrinal issue. Changing the definition of marriage to include same-sex unions poses a challenge to the principles of various religions. In many countries, religious organizations and their allies in civil society and national parliaments have mobilized to oppose the legalization of same-sex marriage (Ayoub, 2016; Corrales & Pecheny, 2010). It is therefore not surprising that change in countries with powerful religious forces, such as the evangelical caucus in the Brazilian Congress, has occurred via the judicial route and not through legislation approved by parliament. The judiciary is more insulated from societal pressures and its members are not subject to reelection. Influence over believers among the electorate is a mechanism that enhances the power of religious groups, especially in contexts with weak countervailing forces in civil society (Hagopian, 2008; Htun, 2009).

---

[1] Some opponents from within the LGBT movement include those who question the value of marriage rights for any group (Chasin, 2001; Murray, 2012) and those who argue instead for destabilizing marriage as a site of rights (Butler, 2004; Warner, 2002). Our point here, though, is that this is a type of issue that was pushed to prominence by autonomous activism.

Cross-nationally, parliamentary enactment of gay marriage has occurred mostly in richer countries where societal religiosity is low, such as in countries in Western Europe and in Uruguay, as well as in places where transnational networks have brought their influence to bear (Ayoub, 2016). In more religious countries, the politics surrounding same-sex marriage has been contentious. The *approval* of gay marriage in Mexico City, for example, triggered a backlash, as multiple other Mexican states changed their constitutions to *ban* same-sex marriage (Lozano, 2010, 2013). Ayoub (2016) identifies "religious nationalism" as a key domestic factor that explains the uneven diffusion of international norms on LGBT rights across Europe, though Ireland, which legalized same-sex marriage through a public referendum in 2015, is an important exception to this pattern. Crucially, however, the archbishop of Dublin issued a public statement of noninterference prior to the vote.[2]

In summary, though religious forces are crucial actors in same-sex marriage in many countries, they have been nearly absent in discussions surrounding gender quotas. Both quotas and gay marriage touch upon patterns of cultural value that encode the relative worth of social groups. But unlike marriage, quotas do not touch upon questions of kinship and reproduction, the historic domain of religious doctrine. Gay marriage reconsiders the historic, doctrinal construction of marriage as heterosexual, and thus invokes considerable, though not universal, religious opposition. We need a different analytical toolkit to understand patterns of variation and change on both issues.

RACIAL INEQUALITY

Issue disaggregation is a potentially useful tool to understand obstacles and constraints to change on other matters of social justice. Consider racial equality. Scholars have long debated the relationship between race and class, with some arguing that the main effects of race can be collapsed with class (Wilson, 2012) or arguing that cross-class solidarity is a key element of racial identity (Dawson, 1994). Others, meanwhile, emphasize the processes of identification, vulnerability to violence, and other aspects of embodied African American experience (Coates, 2015). Both perspectives are correct in that "race" is both a structural principle of political economy as well as a source of cultural stereotypes and biases. Ending

---

[2] www.pewforum.org/2015/06/26/gay-marriage-around-the-world-2013/#ireland.

racial disadvantage therefore involves questions of recognition as well as redistribution. Racial justice entails modifying the status hierarchy that codes some groups as subordinate, as well as promoting their greater access to resources and economic opportunities (Fraser, 2000, 2003).

Race, like gender, is a multidimensional phenomenon (Collins & Chepp, 2013; Crenshaw, 1993; Hancock, 2007),[3] and the relations between these dimensions vary across national contexts. The "house of race" is constructed differently in different places (Appiah, 1993, 1997; Harris, 1990). Diverse institutional legacies make different issues and identities more and less salient (Marx, 1998; Skocpol, 1992). As a result, our multidimensional, cross-national approach may also offer insights into comparative analysis of racial politics and policy. Our approach would predict that states need a range of measures to address the many distinct dimensions of racial disadvantage, and that different political logics would characterize each policy area.

Consider the distinct governmental approaches to combatting the racial disadvantage suffered by Afrodescendants in the Americas. Countries of the Americas share a common legacy of slavery, colonialism, and racial oppression. As President Obama put it in his historic 2016 visit to Cuba: "we live in a new world colonized by Europeans. Cuba, like the United States, was built in part by slaves brought here from Africa. Like the United States, the Cuban people can trace their heritage to both slaves and slave-owners."[4] The same claim applies to Brazil, Venezuela, Colombia, Mexico, and numerous other American countries. Yet different political conditions have given way to different emphases in policies to combat racial disadvantage, to the extent that policy has targeted race at all, which has been a relatively recent phenomenon in most places (See, e.g., Htun, 2004; Loveman, 2014; Paschel, 2010; Telles, 2004). Patterns of variation are somewhat analogous to the approach to women's rights we developed in earlier chapters of this book.

In Colombia, the mobilization of indigenous movements and the consolidation of international norms of indigenous rights brought the frame of ethnic status to prominence (Jung, 2008; Van Cott, 2005; Yashar, 2005). Afro-Colombian movements, the state, academics, and

---

[3] Indeed, social theorists have argued that these dimensions are characteristic of oppressed or marginalized social groups in general. Young (1990; 2002), for example, delineates five aspects of group oppression that characterize various kinds of groups, including oppressed racial groups: violence, cultural imperialism, economic marginalization, political powerlessness, and the scaling of bodies. See also Williams (1988).

[4] www.whitehouse.gov/the-press-office/2016/03/22/remarks-president-obama-people-cuba.

nongovernmental organizations (NGOs) framed black demands in the same ways that worked for efforts to gain rights for indigenous people: as claims for the recognition of culturally distinct groups. Until relatively recently, the state has treated Afrodescendants as an ethnic status group meriting greater cultural autonomy, collective title to land for rural communities, and access to political decision making (Hooker, 2005; Paschel, 2010; Wade, 2009, 2011). Afrodescendants and their rights were "ethnicized" (Restrepo, 2004). A discourse of racial disadvantage, discrimination, and marginalization, rather than a problem of cultural recognition, has been slower to materialize (Htun, 2016, chapter 5). Colombia's initial approach to racial disadvantage followed the same sandwich pattern of international and domestic forces prompting policy action that we observed with gender status policies such as violence against women.

In Brazil and Cuba, countries where Left parties and ideology are strong, the state's approach to race has focused more on the class-based dimensions of racial equality than on the group-based, status dimensions. State and social actors' efforts to address racial equality have primarily emphasized the mechanism of redistribution. The Cuban Revolution, for example, combatted racial disparities in well-being and the official discrimination upheld by the previous Batista regime: It ended formal segregation in public beaches and parks, and opened up public service employment and schools to everyone (De la Fuente, 2001, pp. 259–85). It focused on the redistribution of resources by improving access to health, education, income, and opportunities for work. Yet the class approach did not diminish entrenched racial prejudices and stereotypes, such as the association of blackness with criminality and inferiority and the aesthetic valuation of whiteness. This status hierarchy continues to justify differential treatment, and while racial gaps have grown after market reforms introduced in the 1990s, government policy has done little to redress these inequities (De la Fuente, 2001; Domínguez, 1978; Sawyer, 2006).

Brazil's approach to racial disadvantage has also, to a certain extent, been modeled on class, especially under the administration of the Workers' Party (Htun, 2016, chapter 6). For example, the 2012 Law of Social Quotas, aiming to expand access to public universities for poor people and Afrodescendants, mandates an admissions quota for public school students. The public school quota contains a subquota for racial groups according to their proportion of the population in each state. To be sure, the introduction of any racial quota in Brazil marks a watershed change over the state's historic approach, which was to deny the salience of race altogether. Yet it is significant that in the federal law promulgated by the Workers' Party, racial quotas were nested within social class quotas, not given an independent basis and justification (Htun, 2016). By contrast, the relatively more conservative (but still center-Left) administration of Fernando Henrique Cardoso (1994–2002) had begun to adopt a more status-oriented approach to race, such as by adopting quotas in public service employment and affirmative action for the diplomatic corps (Htun, 2004).

In other regions as well, policies to bend the racial status hierarchy such as affirmative action, legislative quotas, and the like have been adopted in response to agitation in civil society by autonomous groups. The United States government introduced affirmative action and other measures to end discrimination and promote equal opportunities largely in response to the civil rights movement, but international influences also contributed to creating an environment conducive to reform (Layton, 2000). In South Africa, the oppressed African majority and other racialized groups and their allies mobilized to demand an end to Apartheid, a campaign that was strongly reinforced by an international campaign to diffuse the norm of racial equality (Klotz, 1995; Marx, 1998).

Different policies address different dimensions of racial disadvantage, in the same way that different policies tackle distinct dimensions of gender. In the examples in this chapter, some measures focused more on class and redistribution while others focused more on status and recognition, encompassing a wide range of issues from police brutality to political participation. In each country, the different political conditions, legacies, actors, and ideologies characterizing each polity help shape the types of approaches governments adopted. Socialist revolution and Left power tended to emphasize class, while contexts of participatory democracy and inclusion, such as the Colombian constitutional process, emphasized status. We can account for these different outcomes by unpacking the policy problem into different dimensions, singling out those policies that combat disadvantage along each dimension, and then examining the logic and facilitating conditions of each policy.

HEALTH POLICY

Our theoretical approach offers a guide to understanding policies in areas that are less obviously analogous to gender equality. Consider health policy. The United States is a world leader in biomedical research, a policy that makes the National Institutes of Health the largest funder of health research in the world. But the country is a laggard in providing health care to all its citizens, and only recently expanded the government-sponsored health-care program beyond means-tested, targeted programs such as Medicaid and Medicare via the Affordable Care Act. Disaggregating health care into policies that tackle class inequality to some degree (such as the Affordable Care Act) and those that do not (funding for NIH, physician-assisted suicide) may help explain why the United States has been slow to develop policies in some areas while being a leader and innovator in others. The same weak actors that cannot secure paid parental leave have been too weak to push through significant, comprehensive government-provided health care for citizens.

Our approach suggests that disaggregating areas such as "health policy" or "science policy" according to the dimensions we have outlined (whether the policy affects group status, class-based inequalities, or doctrinal issues) suggests insights about policy processes that might not otherwise come to light. Health policy issues that inspire religious opposition (such as stem cell research using fetal tissue) are likely to be influenced by church–state relations and societal religiosity as well as institutional legacies of colonialism and communism. The structure of government-provided health care, by contrast, is likely to be shaped by Left parties and unions as well as institutional legacies of communism, while access to technology might be affected by civic contestation by marginalized groups.

To understand patterns of change and variation, we can disaggregate policy issues not just by topic (health, transportation, and so forth) but also by the types of institutions challenged (market, religion, status hierarchy) and the social identities of the groups affected. Disaggregating issues along these dimensions reveals that the usual divisions of comparative politics and international relations (regions, wealth, democracy, labor mobilization, norms) do not necessarily influence all dimensions of women's rights or human rights in the same way or to the same degree, not to mention other important political phenomena.

THE IMPLEMENTATION OF GENDER JUSTICE POLICIES

This book analyzed policies formally adopted by governments, including laws, constitutions, Supreme Court decisions, and policy documents. We argued that a study of policies on the books is critical for political scientists, feminists, and others concerned with human rights and democratic policy making. Policies themselves violate women's human rights when they discriminate against, disadvantage, and silence women, and treat them as less than fully human. Government action sends a signal about national priorities, social equality, the contours of citizenship, and who counts, and doesn't count, as a member of the polity (Phillips, 2012). As Mary Ann Glendon put it, the law tells a story "about who we are, where we came from, and where we are going" (Glendon, 1987, p. 8).

Though an important story, our analysis of variation and trends in the laws on the books is not the whole story. Patterns of policy implementation can shape the extent to which rights earned on the books are actually felt on the ground. Variation in the efficacy of rights may be a function of state capacity, unequal access to resources, civic organizing, or deliberate political choices (Brinks, 2007; Holland, 2017; Levitsky & Murillo, 2009; Putnam, Leonardi, & Nanetti, 1994). Whereas this range of analysis fell outside the scope of this book, our approach may facilitate exploration of these questions in a way that other approaches to measurement may not. The distinction between status politics, doctrinal politics, and class politics may offer some understanding of the different opportunities and obstacles to the institutionalization of women's rights. Applying our approach to this area of policy studies would require a substantial theoretical extension and elaboration of our approach, and may be a promising avenue for future research.

GENDER JUSTICE AND THE STATE

Our analysis has revealed some important insights into the obstacles faced by advocates of women's rights. There are no silver bullets or easy answers. Many of the barriers to gender equality are deep, historic, and involve some of the most powerful actors in society, such as religious organizations, business groups, and political parties. We should not expect too much in the way of societal transformation from solutions that focus on only one dimension of the problem of gender equality, or even on one small part of one dimension, such as getting more women into positions of power. The project of gender justice operates on many fronts, including reconstructing the status hierarchy that subordinates women and femininity, redistributing the sexual division of labor that devalues care work and relegates women to lower-paying jobs, and expanding the domain of deliberative and accountable politics vis-à-vis protected realms of religion and culture.

What is the best option for advocates of gender equality and justice for women? Our book supports the sophisticated, pragmatic view that many activists take toward the state. Since gender equality is not a project that can be pursued in a single domain or at a single point in time, it does not make sense to pursue only comprehensive solutions. Even major transformations of the economy and society brought about by revolution, war, economic growth, technological change, or secularization may leave gender hierarchies largely intact. Sometimes, incremental changes are all that is possible, which may require a narrower and more tactical focus. Our analysis helps to illuminate the obstacles and opportunities for both narrower and broader initiatives, so advocates may better understand the strategies that are most likely to prompt opposition and those which are most likely to succeed in a given context. Gender equality is not a one-shot deal. It is a long game. The logics of status, doctrinal, and class politics shape the multiple and complex pathways to gender justice.

Appendix A

Data and Methods

This appendix contains material on research design, data, and methods. Some of this information is repeated from the empirical chapters of the book, but we have included it all together here for the convenience of readers looking for these kinds of details.

CASE SELECTION FOR STATISTICAL ANALYSES: COUNTRIES IN THE STUDY

The countries (seventy in total) included in this study are: Algeria, Argentina, Australia, Austria, Bangladesh, Belgium, Botswana, Brazil, Bulgaria, Canada, Chile, China, Colombia, Costa Rica, Croatia, Cuba, Czech Republic, Denmark, Egypt, Estonia, Finland, France, Germany, Greece, Hungary, Iceland, India, Indonesia, Iran, Iraq, Ireland, Israel, Italy, Ivory Coast, Japan, Jordan, Kazakhstan, Kenya, Lithuania, Malaysia, Mexico, Morocco, Netherlands, New Zealand, Nigeria, Norway, Pakistan, Peru, Poland, Portugal, Romania, Russia, Saudi Arabia, Slovak Republic, Slovenia, South Africa, South Korea, Spain, Sweden, Switzerland, Taiwan, Tanzania, Thailand, Turkey, Ukraine, United Kingdom, United States, Uruguay, Venezuela, Vietnam.

These countries represent 85 percent of the world's population. Though this set of countries was not selected randomly, there is no compelling reason to think that the findings discussed here would not apply to most national settings. From what we know of the set of all countries in the world, our dataset is reasonably representative. For example, 55 percent of our cases are democracies, compared to 59 percent of countries in the world. However, we find some lack of representativeness at the extremes of wealth, poverty, and despotism. The poorest 20 percent of countries represent only 7 percent of our dataset, and the richest 20 percent of countries represent 14 percent of our dataset. The two groups that are missing entirely include the handful of countries that are the most despotic in the world (North Korea, Eritrea, Sudan, Burma until 2015) and chronically failed states (Libya, Somalia, Congo, Yemen). Still, we believe our findings should be widely applicable since there are no compelling counterfactuals suggesting that they would not be. These considerations are similar to those raised by the World Values Survey and most other cross-national datasets.[1]

STATISTICAL METHODS: RATIONALE AND APPROACH

The statistical analyses presented in this book explore the relationship between various areas of government action (our dependent variables) and various explanatory factors (the independent variables) for all seventy countries. The dataset includes single-year cross-sections of all countries in 1975, 1985, 1995, and 2005. In some cases, we examine "snapshots" (cross-sections) of particular years, but in most cases we use regression analysis techniques that take into account both the cross-sectional and over-time nature of the dataset. This type of data is sometimes called "panel data" because it is analogous to studying the same people in different waves of a survey, or panel, over time.

This larger, over-time dataset provides more explanatory leverage than standard cross-sectional studies, as we are able to incorporate repeated measurements of the same countries at different times. Panel data analysis most commonly uses either fixed or random-effects regression models to improve on pooled OLS. Random effects is a type of regression suited to panel data as it takes into account the over-time and cross-sectional nature of the data. It is to be preferred over fixed effects when there are slow-moving variables and over regular OLS regression, which assumes independence of observations, a presumption that is violated by the structure of panel data.

In most cases we were unable to make use of fixed effects because of the large number of countries relative to panels, because we want to estimate the effects of relatively time-invariant variables, and because we expect the relationships to change over time. In any event, recent research suggests that such techniques may be particularly poor for some

---

[1] For a discussion of these issues in panel data more generally see Woolridge, 2010; specifically for cross-national studies see Hug, 2003; Jackman, 1985; Kohn, 1989; Livingstone, 2003; Bauer and Ameringan, 2010.

of the types of explanatory variables we wish to examine (institutional and macro-level variables that are slow, but not impervious, to change). Since we did not use fixed effects, and the Hausman test is unsuited to a determination of which analytic technique is best suited for our type of data, we do not report the Hausman test in most of our analyses (for more on this point see Clark & Linzer, 2015).

Some readers might be concerned that because the data present snapshots of years, we might not capture relationships between, for example, numbers of women in office or Left parties that would otherwise be evident. For example, large numbers of women might have been in parliament when a measure was adopted, but then there could be a smaller number of women in office later, when we take our measurement. When it comes to women in parliament, this really is not a threat to our analysis since large changes between panels that are reversed or eliminated by the time the next panel occurs are rare to nonexistent. In addition, if countries with more women in parliament are more likely to adopt certain policies, this should show up in our study even if there are one or two instances where there are big changes during the decade between panels or snapshots that are reversed (and there really are not). For Left parties, the situation is a little more complicated because there are situations where Left parties are dominant in one panel and then are not so dominant in the next. To try to take account of these cases, we have also examined our countries to see if we are modeling the impact of parties and women in parliament in the ways that existing theoretical and qualitative literature would support for that specific issue. In some cases (for example, the chapter on family leave policy) we adopt a measure that takes into account the cumulative effect of Left parties. The change between panels is not the issue here so much as the delayed or cumulative effect of Left party dominance in earlier periods, which matters only for one or two issue-areas. Examining the cases in more detail (which we have done elsewhere, as well as in the specific chapters to some degree) tends to confirm the statistical arguments offered here (Htun & Weldon, 2010, 2012, 2015).

DEPENDENT VARIABLES: INDICES OF WOMEN'S RIGHTS AND GENDER EQUALITY POLICIES

We develop indices for each of our analyses of women's rights. They are measures of the degree to which the government promotes equality and autonomy in the areas of violence against women, family law, abortion law, funding for reproductive rights, equality at work, parental leave, and child care. While the indices vary in several respects, none of them are what might be called an "event count," that is, a count of how many events occur in a fixed time period. The assumptions behind analytic techniques designed to handle count variables (for example, Poisson regression) are often violated by our measures. To take just one example, our indices do not sum events that are independent, as it is not unusual for one piece of legislation to address several of the areas considered.[2] Our measures are better conceived as capturing scope, comprehensiveness, or degree of gender equality rather than number of events, pieces of legislation, or any other type of "count" as is conceptualized by "count" models.

Our measures are not intended to capture policy enforcement, implementation, effectiveness, or other social practices. The difference between adoption and implementation is conceptually clear and well established in the policy literature (see, e.g., Pressman & Wildavsky, 1979) and varies across types of policies, as not all measures are well funded and executed. The study does not examine effectiveness, which is conceptually distinct from both implementation and adoption and depends on sound policy design, state capacity, political will and myriad other factors (Weldon, 2002a; Franceschet, 2010). Even well-intentioned administrations sometimes adopt ineffective policies (and in fact, some have argued that effectiveness conflicts with responsiveness: see, e.g., Rodrik & Zeckhauser, 1988).

VAW Index

The index of government responsiveness to violence against women is coded out of a total of ten points as follows:

3 points for *services to victims* (1 for each of the following):
  – Government funds domestic violence shelters/establishes special courts or police stations
  – Government funds rape crisis centers/ establishes special courts or police stations
  – Government provides crisis services for other forms of violence (stalking, FGM, eve-teasing [street harassment], *sati*, and so forth);
3 points for *legal reform* (1 for each of the following):
  – Government has adopted specialized legislation pertaining to domestic violence (for example, specifying that rape in marriage

---

[2] For more on Poisson regression and the assumptions required see Winkelman, 1997. For more on why this specific type of index of policy scope is not an event count, see Weldon, 2002a, 2006a; Htun and Weldon, 2012.

is a crime, or that violence in a domestic situation is a crime, or specifying the penalties for such crimes)
  – Government has adopted specialized legislation pertaining to sexual assault/rape (for example, rape shield laws)
  – Government has adopted specialized legalization pertaining to other forms of violence;
1 point for *policies or programs targeted to vulnerable populations of women* (allocate one point for any of the following programs/policies):
  – Government provides specialized services to women of marginalized communities, ethnicities, and so forth (bilingual hotlines, specialized crisis centers, specially trained nurses and police, and so forth)
  – Government recognizes violence against women as a basis for refugee status (gender persecution)
  – Government protects immigrant women in abusive relations from deportation;
1 point for *training professionals who respond to victims of any type of violence against women*:
  – Government provides training for police, social workers, nurses, and so forth;
1 point for *prevention programs*:
  – Government funds public education programs
  – Other preventative measures;
1 point for *administrative reforms*:
  – Government has a coordinating body/government agency to provide research, policy analysis and coordination of government response on violence against women.

Family Law Index

Each element of the Index is coded (0, 1) to indicate whether or not the provision in question disadvantages women or promotes equal rights. The maximum score, 13, indicates that a country's family laws are free from discrimination in all thirteen areas, while the minimum score (0) means that a country discriminates against women in all thirteen dimensions analyzed.[3]

---

[3] Although we can report that Cronbach's alpha for these thirteen items is .91, we do want to note that we are not relying on Cronbach's alpha to tell us that divorce law and marital property regimes are related to each other. They are included in the index because conceptually, they are important elements of family law. We merely report Cronbach's alpha here for interest.

TABLE A.1 *Family Law Index*

Element	Description	
Inheritance	Men (sons, brothers, widowers) inherit more than women of equal status by law or in the event of intestate succession	0 = yes; 1 = no
Spousal rights and duties	Men have more power than women: The law stipulates, for example, that wives must obey their husbands	0 = yes; 1 = no
Guardianship	The father holds or exercises parental power or legal guardianship over minor children	0 = yes; 1 = no
Marital property regime	The marital property regime discriminates against women, for example by naming the husband as executor of community property	0 = yes; 1 = no
Right to work	Wives need their husbands' permission to work, or husbands can legally prevent their wives from working	0 = yes; 1 = no
Name	The law requires a common marital name	0 = yes; 1 = no
Minimum marriage age	No minimum age of marriage or different minimum ages for women and men	0 = yes; 1 = no
Consent	Marital consent discriminates against women, for example by accepting the consent of people other than the spouses to validate a marriage	0 = yes; 1 = no
Marriage ban	The law forbids people (or only women) from marrying certain categories or groups besides relatives	0 = yes; 1 = no
Divorce	Men and women do not have equal rights to divorce or the country does not legally permit divorce	0 = yes; 1 = no
Custody after divorce	The law gives fathers guardianship or custody of children following divorce, even if the mother has temporary custody	0 = yes; 1 = no
Property after divorce	The division of property after divorce favors the man, for example by presuming that he will keep common property such as the marital home, even if the wife keeps her own property	0 = yes; 1 = no
Adultery	Laws on adultery are more favorable to men, for example by defining men's adultery as different from women's	0 = yes; 1 = no
TOTAL	13 = highest sex equality score; 0 = lowest score	

As Table A.1 shows, each element of the Index is weighted equally. Our measure provides a sense of the extent of equality across many areas of family law. We do not claim that each area is equally salient in all national cases. Equal weighting offers simplicity and transparency, important features of any new measure. The detailed item scores are available on malahtun.com/data. Table A.2 provides a guide to the legislation we coded in countries with multiple legal systems.

TABLE A.2 *Guide to family law coding in countries with multiple legal systems*

Country	Ethnoreligious composition[4]	What we coded
Bangladesh	Muslim 90%; Hindu 9%	1961 Muslim Family Law Ordinance
Botswana		Civil statutes including Matrimonial Causes Act of 1973, the Marriage Act of 2001, and the Abolition of Marital Power Act of 2004
India	Hindu 80%; Muslim 13%; others include Christians, Sikhs, Buddhists	Hindu Code, including the including the Hindu Marriage Act; Hindu Succession Act; Hindu Minority and Guardianship Act; and the Hindu Adoptions and Maintenance Act
Israel	Jewish 76%; Muslim 16%; others include Christians, Druze	Orthodox Jewish law
Kenya	Christian ~78%; Muslim ~10%	Civil Statutes, including Marriage Act, the Matrimonial Causes Act (of 1941), the Married Women's Property Act (of 1882), and the Children's Act of 2001
Malaysia	Muslim 60%; Buddhist 19%, Christian 9%, Hindu 6%	Islamic Family Law (Federal Territories) Act of 1984
Nigeria	Muslim (50%); Christian (40%)	Marriage Act; 1970 Matrimonial Causes Act; 1882 Married Women's Property Act
South Africa		Marriage Act of 1961 and its amendments

---

[4] Statistics on religious composition come from the CIA World Factbook.

Workplace Equality

To measure laws governing women's rights and opportunities in the workplace, we created three indexes. The first is a measure of the extent of state-sponsored discrimination, such as laws excluding women from particular occupations or types of work. The second index is a measure of state action to promote formal legal equality by prohibiting discrimination in wages, hiring, promotion, and the like. The third index measures state action on substantive equality to combat de facto disadvantages facing women in the labor market.

To assess the degree of *state-sponsored discrimination* for each country, we asked:

(1) Are women prohibited from night work?
(2) Are women prohibited from overtime?
(3) Are women prohibited from specific occupations by virtue of being women?
(4) Are there religious restrictions on women's work?
(5) Are there prohibitions against employment (as opposed to special rights offered) that apply to those who are pregnant or were recently pregnant, breastfeeding mothers, or mothers of young children?
(6) Are there laws segregating workers by sex?

The highest possible score (a "6") would reflect a regime characterized by all six prohibitions on women's work while a regime that does none of these things was coded "0." No country discriminates on all six grounds so the most discriminatory country scores a "4." We did not count provisions that provide special rights or opportunities to women, such as those that enable women to combine breastfeeding with work, as state-sponsored discrimination.

In order to examine the degree of *formal equality*, we investigated whether there were laws against discrimination against women at work, and if they (and/or other measures guaranteeing equality) applied to:

(1) Wages/guarantees of equal pay for equal work?
(2) Hiring?
(3) Termination of employment?
(4) Access to training?
(5) Equal rights to participate in workplace governance? Unions?

Legal regimes that have general antidiscrimination measures that did not specifically apply to any of these areas received a "1." Those that applied to all five areas, in addition to prohibiting discrimination in general, were coded "6."

This third type of government action, *substantive equality*, addresses the specific disadvantages women face in the labor market to promote equal opportunities. We measured this third dimension of government action by asking:

(1) Are there any legal or policy mechanisms to **enforce** guarantees of equality?

(2) Does the government demonstrate, in its policy and rhetoric, an awareness of and attention to the problems of women working in the informal sector? Are there any efforts to address their problems?

(3) Are there any efforts or mechanisms to ensure the applicability of labor laws to the informal sector? Are there provisions for the representation of informal sector workers in formal economic planning/business consultation processes? Are there policies or incentives to facilitate the self-organization of informal sector workers?

(4) Are there provisions for positive action to promote women's work in nontraditional occupations? Job training?

(5) Does the government offer financial benefits or privileges to companies that promote women workers or to companies owned by women (such as provisions with respect to government contracting for female-owned businesses in the United States)?

Legal regimes characterized by more of these initiatives have higher scores; those with all five of these types of measures score a "5" while those with none of these measures score a "0."

TABLE A.3 *Summary of three workplace equality indices*

State-sponsored discrimination	0–6
Formal equality	0–6
Substantive equality	0–5
Overall equality (sum of formal and substantive)	0–17

Again, the distinction between these elements, and their grouping in this way, is based on a conceptual and not an empirical argument.

Index of Abortion Law

The Abortion Law Index is intended to capture the circumstances under which abortion is legally permitted. It is not meant to capture de facto access to, or availability of, abortion (see Table A.4).

TABLE A.4 *Abortion Law Index*

Legal status of abortion	Score
Elective abortion[5] in first and second trimesters, no restrictions	10
Elective abortion in first trimester with no restrictions OR elective abortion in first and second trimester with some restrictions	9
Elective abortion in the first trimester, with some restrictions	8
Abortion permitted on soft grounds (economic necessity, mental health) in addition to various hard grounds (including, at a minimum, rape and threat to the mother's life)	4-5
Abortion permitted when a woman has been raped in addition to other hard grounds (including, at a minimum, threat to the mother's life)	3
Abortion permitted for more hard grounds (health, fetal abnormality, incest, but not rape)	2
Abortion permitted when mother's life is in danger (ONLY)	1
Abortion forbidden under all circumstances	0

Reproductive Rights Funding

We coded public funding for reproductive rights in the following way:

- No government funding for contraception or abortion = 0
- Funding for EITHER contraception or abortion = 5
- Funding for BOTH contraception and abortion = 10

---

[5] Note that "elective abortion" includes those laws that require the woman to be in a condition of "distress" due to her pregnancy when the woman is the only one who determines whether or not she is in distress.

Family Leave

Our index combines parental leave generosity, maternity leave generosity, and the provision of "daddy leave" into an index called *total leave generosity*:

- Maternity leave generosity = Duration of leave + Duration of leave* publicly paid
- Parental leave generosity = Duration of leave + Duration of leave* publicly paid
- "Daddy leave" generosity= 2 points if present
- Overall leave generosity = maternity leave generosity/5 + parental leave generosity/5 + Daddy leave generosity

This weighting provides about equal weight to each of the three dimensions of family leave in most cases, and reflects the importance of "daddy leave" in adding additional months of paid leave to the overall amount of paid leave provided and in making leave available to both parents. The Index ranges from 0 to 7.7 and has a mean of 1.9 and a standard deviation of 1.8.

Childcare

We investigated the existence of a national or federal childcare policy. Our main measure used in the analyses is a dichotomous one, reflecting whether or not a national childcare policy exists. If there is one, we code whether it was provided through:

- Government-run day-care centers
- Cash transfers to parents to pay for day care
- Tax credits for money spent on day care
- Subsidies to day-care centers
- Employer mandates – requirements that firms with a certain number of workers provide day-care services for their employees
- Other day-care provision

INDEPENDENT VARIABLES

In Table A.5, we summarize how we operationalize and obtained sources of data for our independent variables. Many of the same independent variables are used from chapter to chapter, but there are also differences.

TABLE A.5 *Independent variables*

Variable	Description	Data source
Official religion	Presence of an official state religion (dichotomous)	Barro and McCleary (2005)
Religious legislation	Number of religious laws enforced by the state	Religion and the State Dataset, round 2 (Fox, 2008, 2013)
High religiosity	Whether the average ranking of God's importance is high or low (dichotomous)	World Values Survey Association (2009) question F063 on the importance of God in one's life
Religiosity scale	Strength of religiosity scale (0–100)	Teorell et al. (2011) (see Inglehart & Norris, 2003)
Religious party	Whether a religious party is one of the three largest parties in government and/or the party of the chief executive (dichotomous)	Database of Political Institutions from Teorell et al. (2011)
Former colony	Experience of overseas Western colonial rule (dichotomous)	Teorell et al. (2011)
Communist	Current and former communist countries (dichotomous)	Teorell et al. (2011)
Feminist movement strength	A three-point ordinal scale. 0 = no autonomous feminist movement; 1 = strong and autonomous movements; 2 = strongest, autonomous movements are coded as 2. (Coding for strength and autonomy can be used separately too)	Htun and Weldon (2012)
CEDAW ratification	Ratification of CEDAW (dichotomous)	UN Treaty Database (2011)
Withdrawal of reservations to CEDAW	Coded 1 if a country withdrew a reservation to CEDAW in the preceding decade	UN Treaty Database (2011)
Women in parliament	Percentage of seats occupied by women in the lower house of parliament (0–100)	Interparliamentary Union (2011)

Variable	Description	Data source
Women's policy agency	Measure of women's policy machinery effectiveness. Coded 1 if policy machinery	True and Mintrom (2001), supplemented by additional data sources for missing countries and years (UN, 1993; 1998; Avdeyeva, 2009; Rai, 2007)
Democracy	Combined Polity score (–10 to 10)	Teorell et al. (2011)
GDP	Log of GDP per capita	Heston, Summer, and Aten (2006)
Left party presence	Dummy Variable	Data from the Database of Political Institutions (augmented by other sources for a few specific countries and years)
Left party strength	The percentage of seats assigned to Left parties in the lower legislative chamber	Data from the Database of Political Institutions (DPI). Missing data for five countries filled in based on data from the Interparliamentary Union (IPU) data archive
Cumulative Left party Power	The proportion of parliamentary seats held by all Left parties summed across all four cross-sections.	As above, the data is primarily from DPI, with missing data filled in based on Interparliamentary Union (IPU) data
Women's labor force participation	Rate of female labor force participation	World Bank. Gender Statistics
Fertility	Number of children per woman	World Bank. Gender Statistics

Each chapter includes more discussion of the specific variables and the reasons for including them in each analysis.

In some cases, we modified existing datasets. Below we provide additional information about these changes.

Official Religion

From Barro and McCleary (2005). Barro and McCleary's data on official state religions covers 1900, 1970, and 2000. We used their 1970 data for our 1975 time point and their 2000 data for our 2005 time point (after verifying and correcting for any changes in state religion in intervening years). In order to fill in our 1985 and 1995 data points, we investigated cases of change in state religion between 1970 and 2000. There were two: Ireland abandoned its state religion in 1972 and Sweden its state religion in 2001. In addition, we recoded three cases in which Barro and McCleary report disagreement with their data source (Barrett's *World Christian Encyclopedia*): Spain (1978 constitutional change disestablishing Roman Catholicism), Portugal (1976 constitution), and Italy (1984 concordat).

Religious Legislation

From Religion and the State (RAS) Dataset Round 2 (Fox, 2008, 2013). We modified the RAS index of "Specific Types of Religious Legislation." According to the 2012 codebook, "This category refers to laws or government policies which legislate or otherwise support aspects of religion. This includes diverse laws and policies including the direct legislation of religious precepts, funding religion, religious monopolies on aspects of policy or law, and giving clergy and religious institution official powers or influence." For our measure, we deleted laws related to family, personal status, and women's rights in order to avoid endogeneity.

High Religiosity

From the World Values Survey, question about the importance of God. To maximize the availability of comparable data across countries and years, we created a dichotomous measure that captures whether or not the average respondent reported that God was very important in her/his life (average self-reported score of 8 or greater). Any remaining missing values were estimated based on analysis of secondary sources on individual countries.

Cumulative Left Party Power

Left party power refers to the percentage of seats assigned to Left parties in the lower legislative chamber. We took data from the Database of Political Institutions and filled in missing data with election data from the Interparliamentary Union, supplemented by secondary sources on the specific Left parties in question to determine whether a party should be characterized as Left. We looked for a close relationship to organized labor or other national or international socialist organizations, as well as for statements about the priorities and ideology of the party. *Cumulative Left party* merely summed the Left party variable over the four cross-sections (that is, 1975 value plus 1985 value plus 1995 value plus 2005 value).

Appendix B

Family Law in the World's Legal Traditions

In this Appendix,[1] we describe the evolution of family law in the legal traditions affecting the majority of the world's citizens, especially in the global South: Muslim family law; multiple legal systems (common in former British colonies, these systems promote the coexistence of religious, customary, and civil and/or common law); civil law, upheld in Europe, Latin America, and parts of Asia; and socialist or communist law, which shaped Europe, parts of Asia, and parts of Latin America. Socialist law is a subset of civil law but merits a separate section since its ideological orientation is distinct, and relevant, for family matters.

RELIGIOUS LAW: MUSLIM FAMILY LAW

Of the legal traditions considered in this book, Muslim family law has had the most enduring influence. Most countries with Muslim family law have changed very little since national laws were codified throughout the twentieth century, as early as the 1920s in Egypt and as late as 1984 in Algeria. Only one country of our study – Morocco – has thoroughly overhauled its family law to conform to principles of gender equality. Turkey, also a Muslim-majority country, did not adopt classical Muslim family law but instead introduced a European-style civil code modeled on

---

[1] An earlier version of this appendix was published as part of Mala Htun and S. Laurel Weldon, "Sex equality in family law: historical legacies, feminist activism, and religious power in 70 countries," Background Paper for the 2012 World Development Report, World Bank, Washington, DC, 2011.

the Swiss Civil Code, inspired by the Napoleonic Code of 1804. This family code, also patriarchal, was significantly modified in 2001.

It is widely believed that women are disadvantaged by classical Islamic provisions on marriage, divorce, inheritance, and other areas. Many scholars argue, however, that the Quran's rules represented an improvement in women's status over previous practices. Under the tribal customary law prevalent in ancient Arabia, for example, only male relatives (agnatic heirs) inherited property. Men had an unlimited right to polygamy and unrestricted rights to divorce, with no waiting period (Esposito & DeLong-Bas, 2001; Jawad, 1998; for a more nuanced perspective highlighting the diversity of social practice prior to Islam, see Ahmed, 1992). According to Kabyle customary law – operative among the Berbers of Algeria until the national Family Code was codified in 1984 – women had no rights to inheritance and were considered part of a man's inheritance. The dower paid at the time of marriage belonged to the male guardian and not to the woman. Mothers had practically no custody rights over their children (Charrad, 2001, p. 47).

Quranic family law modified these practices in several respects. Instead of denying women any inheritance, it ordered fixed shares to go to wives, children, and other female relatives. Among these "Quranic heirs," women received about half the amount of male shares, a discrepancy justified by men's legal duties to maintain their wives and families. The remainder of the estate would go mostly to male relatives on the male line, so-called "Class 2 agnatic heirs" (Esposito & DeLong-Bas, 2001, pp. 37–41). Women were permitted to own and manage property and to retain control of their personal property even after marriage. The dower – or *mahr* – was explicitly named as the woman's property. Intended to safeguard their position in marriage, a portion of the *mahr* is usually paid at the time of the marriage contract; in the event of divorce, the husband is required to pay the remaining amount to the wife.

Unlike the Roman Catholic tradition, which views marriage as a sacrament or an institution authored by God, Muslim marriage is a contract. The law assumes that the marital bond is fragile. Far more stable and durable are ties among agnates (male kin). The fragility of marriage is evident in the way Islamic law facilitates divorce (at least by the man), separation of property between spouses (in contrast to the community of property characteristic of most civil and common law systems), and polygamy (Charrad, 2001, pp. 31–40).

What is more, marriage is a purely private matter, a contract between families, not a question of public order or responsibility. Until the twentieth century – when laws requiring marriage registration and, later, notification of divorce and additional marriages were adopted – the state had no purview over marriage.

A male guardian (*wali*) contracts – and consents to – the marriage on behalf of the woman, while men contract their own marriages. A woman need not even be present at the marriage ceremony (Charrad, 2001, p. 33). Though men were permitted to marry women of other religions, women could marry only other Muslims. Under classical Islamic law, men and women reaching puberty were considered eligible for marriage, usually at the age of nine for girls and twelve for boys.

Men and women have distinct rights and obligations. Women are required to obey their husbands, care for children, and maintain the home. A woman who does not fulfill these obligations is considered "disobedient" (*nusyuz* in Indonesia and Malaysia) and can lawfully be denied maintenance in some countries (Musawah, 2009).

Men, in turn, are obliged to support their wives and children financially and to provide the marital home. (In the Hanafi school dominant in the Middle East and South Asia, however, a husband's failure to maintain was not considered grounds for divorce until twentieth-century reforms.) Men also have the right to restrict their wives' activities, such as preventing them from working and going out in public. The law considers men to be the legal guardians of children – a status they retain even after divorce, though mothers are entitled to temporary custody.

Men enjoy far greater rights to divorce. They may divorce their wives by order (*talaq*), unilaterally and automatically: They do not need any grounds, nor do they need to notify the court. In less frequent (and officially disapproved of) divorces (*talaq al-bidah*), men can utter an irrevocable declaration of divorce at a single point in time. If a man makes three declarations of divorce, it is final and irrevocable: The couple may not be reconciled or remarried unless the woman marries another man and then divorces him (Esposito & DeLong-Bas, 2001, pp. 29–37).

After divorce, men are required to give their wives the remainder of the *mahr* (dower). Yet remarriage is prohibited until the end of the *iddah* period (typically three months). In the case that the woman was pregnant, *iddah* would help determine parentage. It also offered time for reconciliation (and revocation of an *ahsan* divorce) and payment of maintenance.

Women's ability to initiate divorce under classical Muslim law is heavily restricted and differs across the four schools. A judicial divorce is available to women under Maliki law, the most liberal, on the grounds of cruelty, desertion, or lack of maintenance. Hanafi law, by contrast, permits the woman to initiate divorce under far more limited circumstances, such as if one spouse renounces Islam or if the husband is unable to consummate the marriage (Esposito & DeLong-Bas, 2001, pp. 33–4).

After divorce, mothers have custody rights of boys until age seven and girls until age nine, after which time children are returned to their father as the legal guardian and his relatives. Crucially, whereas women may retain their individual property after divorce, common property – including the marital home – is considered to be the husband's.

The distributive functions of classical Muslim family law disadvantage women relative to men. Various provisions, however, were intended to protect them, including the dower (*mahr*), the husband's legal responsibility to maintain his wife and children, and the waiting period (*iddah*). Women and men had asymmetrical rights and obligations, but the law was not completely inattentive to the vulnerable situation it placed women in (Esposito & DeLong-Bas, 2001).

Most modern Muslim countries codified family law, though late by global standards. Prior to codification, many countries had multiple and overlapping legal systems. Often, colonial authorities tolerated the coexistence of Muslim law, tribal law, and other customary laws in order to divide and rule (Charrad, 2001). In this context, the state had little authority over family matters. Marriages were not even required to be legally registered until the twentieth century.

Whereas the Napoleonic Code dates from 1804, the first modern codification of Islamic family law was the Ottoman Law of Family Rights, promulgated in 1917. It legislated aspects of family life previously left entirely to religious authorities. The Code instituted civil marriage (by requiring the presence of a special state employee at the ceremony) and banned marriages not based on consent (Kandiyoti, 1991b, p. 36). In addition, it extended to the Hanafi school what had already been practiced under Maliki law: greater access to divorce for women. Women now had the right to divorce in the event of desertion, incarceration, disease, refusal to pay maintenance, insanity, threat of bodily harm, or continuous strife in the home (Esposito & DeLong-Bas, 2001, p. 51).

The Ottoman Code inspired reforms throughout the Muslim world. Egypt was a pioneer, first through registration requirements and later through bans on child marriage and provisions for women's protection. In 1897 and later in 1910, Egyptian laws instructed courts to require written documentation of marriage, divorce, and inheritance claims. Then, in 1923, the state forbade marriage officials from issuing certificates unless brides were sixteen and grooms eighteen (Esposito & DeLong-Bas,

2001, pp. 49–50). Algeria did not introduce a law requiring marriages to be registered until 1959, as French rule was waning. The same law established a minimum marriage age of fifteen for women and eighteen for men (Charrad, 2001, pp. 137–8).

In 1920 and 1929, Egypt introduced reforms stipulating grounds under which women could sue for divorce. These same laws extended the age of maternal custody to nine for boys and eleven for girls, and revised laws on divorce. *Talaq al-bidah* (irrevocable divorce by triple pronouncement) was rendered ineffective through rules declaring that all divorces were single and revocable. What is more, a valid divorce had to be intended as such: pronouncements made while intoxicated, in jest, or as threats were no longer valid, as they had been under Hanafi law (Esposito & DeLong-Bas, 2001, pp. 50–7).

British India-Pakistan adopted reforms in the 1939 Dissolution of Muslim Marriages Act, though stipulations about lack of maintenance and desertion were not as generous as in Egypt. On the other hand, the grounds for proving cruelty were expansive and included inequitable treatment by husbands who had taken on additional wives (Esposito & DeLong-Bas, 2001, pp. 76–8).

Pakistan introduced further reforms after partition. The Muslim Family Laws Ordinance of 1961, which still applies in Pakistan and Bangladesh, aimed to improve women's position in various ways. As in Egypt, it required the written registration of marriage and limited *talaq al-bidah* by ruling that all divorces were revocable. Divorces were to be processed through an Arbitration Council, required written notice, and were valid only after a ninety-day waiting period.[2] Finally, men wanting to marry additional wives were required to apply and obtain permission from the Council.

Egypt, by contrast, has been unable to restrict polygamy. To this day, court permission is not required for a man to marry again. In 1985, reforms introduced the requirement that a wife be notified if her husband marries again and granted her the right to divorce if she deemed herself harmed by the additional marriage. Husbands are also required to give legal notice of divorce to their wives. This seems incredible. How could a wife not know if she was divorced? But in fact, there were cases of husbands divorcing by *talaq* without the wife's knowledge and continuing

---

[2] Divorces not processed through the arbitration council, however, were still considered valid. Failure to observe legal procedures would incur a light fine or up to one year in prison.

to live with her, rendering her vulnerable to charges of *zina* and denying her the right to maintenance.

In addition, men's traditional right to restrict women to the home was modified in 1985: They were subsequently required to summon their wives to return home via official channels, after which time the wife had thirty days to appeal and recourse to divorce. In 2000, additional reforms granted wives the right to unilateral divorce historically held by men, but under the condition that they forfeit their right to the *mahr*, maintenance during *iddah*, and support for children in her custody.[3]

Iran introduced reforms to expand women's rights in 1967 and 1975. These were framed as "royal grants," not the result of women's lobbying (Najmabadi, 1991, pp. 60–2). Under the Family Protection Act and its revision, women had equal rights to divorce and equal guardianship rights over children. The law also increased women's freedoms by revoking a husband's right legally to prevent his wife from working. Instead, he had to seek such an order from a judge. What is more, a husband was entitled to maintenance from his wife. These reforms also raised the minimum marriage age to eighteen for girls and twenty for boys (Mirvahabi, 1975; Pakizegi, 1978). The timing of these changes reflected the Shah's whims and his perceived need to improve the country's image abroad, though feminists had long been agitating for the changes (Najmabadi, 1991, pp. 63–4).

In Malaysia, family law for many Muslims is governed by the Islamic Family Law (Federal Territories) Act of 1984. Under this law, which conforms fairly closely to classical Muslim law, fathers serve as legal guardians of children. In 1999, however, Malaysian civil law governing non-Muslims was modified to grant equal guardianship rights to mothers and fathers. Muslim feminists have lobbied for a similar reform of religious family law. In response, the government issued an administrative act granting mothers (as well as fathers) the right to sign a child's application for school, an identity card, and a passport. This decree softened the edges of the paternal authority upheld in the previous legislation.[4]

---

[3] See Howard Schneider, "Women in Egypt gain broader divorce rights; wide coalition pushed for legal equality," Washington Post, April 14, 2000, at A16. For a criticism of the reforms as not going nearly far enough, see Human Rights Watch, *Egypt: Ensure Women's Equal Right to Divorce: Despite Reforms, Women Suffer Discrimination under Legal System* (November 28, 2004).

[4] Sisters in Islam, "Islamic family law and justice for Muslim women," Conference report. June 2001, http://asiasociety.org/policy-politics/social-issues/women-and-gender/islamic-family-law-and-justice-muslim-women?order=ASC.

Overall, these twentieth-century codifications and reforms of Muslim family law led to greater public regulation and control of what had previously been seen as private family matters. Through marriage registration requirements and the participation of courts and Arbitration Councils in divorce, the state asserted its authority. Reforms raised the minimum marriage age to restrict child marriage and imposed conditions on polygamous marriages (while still permitting them). They expanded women's rights to divorce, most prominently in the event of a failure to provide maintenance, and offered them greater protection, including access to the dower and maintenance after divorce (Esposito & DeLong-Bas, 2001).

Reforms granting women greater rights were not uncontested, however. After the Islamic revolution of 1979, several of Iran's earlier advances were reversed. The minimum marriage age was lowered to nine for girls and fifteen for boys. Women's grounds for divorce were restricted and they lost their right to equal guardianship rights over children (Bernardi, 1986).

Later, however, Iran reversed these reversals, but stopped short of granting women equal rights with men. In the early 1990s, parallel to policy changes granting women greater opportunities in employment, equal pay, and family planning, women gained further rights to divorce in the event of hardship and also the right to alimony, signaling compensation for their contributions to marriage (provided they did not initiate divorce and were not at fault) (Women Living under Muslim Laws, 2006, p. 287). In 1997, a new law required that the amount of the dower (*mahr*) be indexed to inflation, creating an additional disincentive to husband's unilateral divorce of women (Women Living under Muslim Laws, 2006, p. 36). In 2002, women gained rights to initiate divorce proceedings without their husband's consent, but they still lacked the unilateral right to divorce enjoyed by men.[5] At around the same time, the minimum marriage age was raised to thirteen for women, though courts could offer permission for younger girls to get married. What's more, a woman's guardian could authorize a pre-pubescent marriage if he claimed it was in her best interest (Women Living under Muslim Laws, 2006, p. 127). In 1995, the law was amended to require husbands divorcing their wives to pay a salary compensating them for years of unpaid household labor (Women Living under Muslim Laws, 2006, p. 317).

---

[5] http://news.bbc.co.uk/2/hi/middle_east/2534375.stm. Also www.wluml.org/node/907.

Processes of Islamicization led to greater restrictions on women's rights in Indonesia. The Compilation of Islamic Laws, issued by presidential decree in 1991, was designed to unify policies on marriage and divorce for Muslims. It put Muslim women at a disadvantage in at least two respects over the 1974 Marriage law: Women no longer had equal inheritance rights with men and their consent was no longer required to make a marriage valid. Marriage was defined as a contract between the groom and the wife's father or *wali* (Musawah, 2009, p. 17).

Pakistan also saw backtracking with the Hudood Ordinances – adopted by General Zia-ul-Haq in 1979 following a military coup, and part of his Islamicization initiatives. The Ordinances classified *zina* – extramarital sex – as an offense against the state, as opposed to against individual men; noncompoundable, meaning the police may continue to prosecute even if the accuser withdraws their complaint; nonbailable; and punishable by death.[6] The law thus conflated two distinct practices – fornication (extramarital sex) and adultery (illicit sex outside marriage) – and also included rape under its rubric, defined as extramarital sex without consent. As a result, rape victims who were unable to offer "adequate" proof of coercion ended up being considered guilty of *zina*. In the two decades following adoption of the Ordinances, hundreds of thousands of cases of women were accused of *zina*, and many sentenced to public whippings (Khan, 2011). These injustices were amended only in 2006, under the Women Protection Act, which made *zina* impossible to prosecute, though it still remained a crime (Shaheed, 2010).

Table B.1 presents a summary of the main provisions of classical Muslim family law and contemporary, reformed versions. There are variations across countries, with women enjoying greater and lesser freedoms for divorce, guardianship rights, and rights to maintenance. As the table shows, most twentieth-century codifications vary little from classical Muslim family law, though the differences that do exist are important. Modern laws preserve the patriarchal structure of marriage – including men's responsibilities and women's obedience, and men's far greater rights to divorce and guardianship over children. However, women have gained greater rights to divorce, to custody of their children, and to maintenance and alimony in some countries.

---

[6] The death penalty and other aspects of the Ordinances were widely held to be contrary to Muslim principles and also in violation of Pakistan's constitution. In a 1981 ruling, the Federal Shariat Court revoked the death penalty as punishment for *zina*, as the Quran had stipulated that the maximum penalty would be 100 lashes (Khan, 2011).

TABLE B.I *Main features of classical Muslim family law*

Area	Classical version	Majority of twentieth-century codifications	Morocco's 2004 *Moudawana*
Conditions of marriage	* Eligibility for marriage at puberty (nine for girls; thirteen for boys) * Male guardian consents and contracts on behalf of woman * Women may not marry non-Muslims	* Minimum marriage age of sixteen for girls, eighteen for boys (some variation) * Male guardian consents and contracts on behalf of woman (some variation) * Women may not marry non-Muslims * Written registration of marriage	* Minimum marriage age of 18 for both spouses (Article 19) * Guardian's participation is optional; women may delegate right to contract marriage (Articles 13, 25) * Civil registration and authorization of marriage
Rights and duties in marriage	* Women must obey their husbands, care for home and children * Husbands must support wives and children * Husbands can prevent wives from working and going into public	* Women must obey their husbands, care for home and children * Husbands must support wives and children * Male power to prevent wives' work varies	* Rights and duties are the same for both spouses (Article 51) * Husbands are required to maintain their wives (Article 194)
Property	* Separation of property during marriage * Husband provides dower (*mahr*) * Husband retains marital home after divorce	* Separation of property during marriage * Husband provides dower (*mahr*) * Husband retains marital home after divorce	* Separation of property during marriage (Article 49) * Common marital property administrated by agreement (Article 49)[1] * Husband provides dower, but it should be modest (Article 28)

(continued)

Area	Classical version	Majority of twentieth-century codifications	Morocco's 2004 Moudawana
Divorce	* Husbands may divorce by order (*talaq*) and immediately (*talaq al-bidaī*) * Wives have access to divorce under extremely limited circumstances (Hanafi) or grounds including cruelty, desertion, failure to maintain (Maliki) * Husband must pay *mahr* to wife in full upon divorce * Husband pays maintenance during *iddah*	* Husbands may divorce by order (*talaq*) * Wives have access to divorce on grounds including cruelty, desertion, imprisonment, failure to maintain (some variations) * Divorce processed through courts and formal notification required * Wives may divorce unilaterally if they forfeit *mahr* and maintenance (Egypt) * Husband must pay *mahr* to wife in full upon divorce * Husband pays maintenance during *iddah*	* Divorce permitted by repudiation (a right seemingly granted to both spouses: Articles 78–9), mutual consent, or cause * All divorces processed judicially
Guardianship	* Fathers are legal guardians of minor children * Mothers may retain temporary custody after divorce until age 7 (boys) and 9 (girls)	* Fathers are legal guardians of minor children * Mothers may retain temporary custody after divorce for longer periods of time * Some countries allow courts to grant mothers greater custody and even guardianship rights	* Fathers are the first legal guardians of minor children; mothers serve as guardians when fathers are absent or incapacitated (Articles 231, 236) * At divorce, custody awarded first to the mother (Article 171)[2]

| Inheritance | * Female Quranic heirs receive around half of men's share
 * Freedom to bequest up to one-third of estate to nonheirs
 * Waqf (endowment) for religion, charity, or family | * Female Quranic heirs receive around half of men's share
 * Inheritance rights for orphaned grandchildren (Egypt 1946; Pakistan 1961)
 * Freedom to bequest up to one-third of estate, even to heirs (Egypt 1946)
 * Waqf (endowment) could no longer be used to circumvent other inheritance laws (Egypt 1946); family waqfs abolished altogether in Egypt 1952 but not in Pakistan | (Unable to find translation of book on inheritance) |

[1] In the absence of formal agreement, "recourse is made to general standards of evidence, while taking into consideration the work of each spouse, the efforts made as well as the responsibilities assumed in the development of the family assets." Unofficial translation prepared by Human Rights Education Associates, 2005, www.hrea.org/moudawana.html.

[2] A mother may lose custody of a child over seven years of age, however, if she has remarried and is not the child's legal representative.

Only one country with classical Muslim law – Morocco – has over-hauled its family code to eliminate most of the disadvantage suffered by women. Morocco's provisions are summarized in the final column of Table B.1. The law purports to remain faithful to Islamic values and traditions while giving women significantly more rights. The reformed *Moudawana* declares that spouses have equal rights and duties in marriage (Article 51), men and women have the same rights to initiate divorce, and the minimum marriage age is eighteen for both sexes. Though men and women administer their separate property during marriage, common property is managed by agreement and not by the husband (Article 49). Some inequalities remain: For example, the father is the presumed legal representative and tutor of his children, while the mother exercises these rights only if he is absent or incapable (Articles 231, 236). What is more, though the law imposes equality between spouses, it also requires men to pay maintenance for their wives after the marriage has been consummated (Article 194).[7]

Contemporary debates about reform are informed by different views of how to interpret classical doctrine. Perspectives of clerics, scholars, and other feminist activists vary on whether or not the Koran, the sunnahs, and so forth can be interpreted to endorse modern notions of gender equity (Mir-Hosseini, 1999). Reformers argue that the Quran reflects social conditions prevailing in the era of its revelation, that times have changed, and that the doctrine must evolve accordingly. These Muslim feminists search for textual support for women's rights.

Feminist reformers exercise the right of *itjihad* (judicial reasoning), arguing that gender equality promotes the Islamic principle of social justice and community well-being (Balchin, 2009, p. 200). Arguments made from within Islam have helped push reforms in Iran that instituted an equal division of property following divorce (provided the wife was not at fault) and also provisions for maintenance based on a wife's nonmonetary contributions to the household (Balchin, 2009).

Others, by contrast, claim that the search for theological justification ends up upholding the legitimacy of the Quranic reference point (as opposed to universal human rights standards), as well as the existence of religious states such as the Islamic Republic of Iran. Real emancipation requires secular arguments and institutions that defend rights regardless of religion (Moghadam, 2002).

---

[7] www.hrea.org/moudawana.html.

Since the 1980s, women's demands for family law reform have gained momentum in the Muslim world. Concepts such as gender equality and human rights have become normalized. Even Islamist parties feel compelled to explain how their positions will advance women's rights (Balchin, 2009, p. 213).

MULTIPLE LEGAL SYSTEMS

Several countries of our study have multiple legal systems. This means that parallel systems of law coexist, even though their rules vary and may even contradict one another. Almost all countries in this situation are former British colonies. Yet legal pluralism is more than a legacy of colonialism. It can also be the product of postconflict processes of reconstruction, including attempts to forge a new social contract between state and citizens (as in South Africa) (ICHRP, 2009). In addition, several advanced democracies with culturally diverse populations tolerate a degree of legal pluralism as a way to protect cultural group rights, often with deleterious consequences for the rights of individual women (Benhabib, 2002; Cohen, 2012; Okin, 1999; Shachar, 2001; Song, 2007).

Historically, multiple legal orders were tolerated – and even encouraged – by states seeking to hold onto power and avoid conflict. The Mughal and Ottoman empires permitted minority groups to retain their own laws and religion in exchange for paying tribute (ICHRP, 2009, p. 7). British colonial policies of indirect rule in Africa enhanced the power of traditional, local authorities to administer local laws (Lugard, 2013).

British policy on family law was developed in South Asia and later extended to colonies in Africa. As mentioned in Chapter 4, this approach rested on the principle of "noninterference" in the personal laws of the so-called Hindu and Muslim religious communities, at least when it came to marriage, divorce, guardianship, inheritance, and so forth. Even after Independence, the government of India – along with its counterparts in Kenya and Nigeria – chose to continue the "noninterference" policy and upheld the religious personal laws that had been codified under colonial rule. By codifying and applying religious personal laws, the British transformed – if not outright invented – not just the laws but also the communities (Williams, 2006).

British colonial authorities codified Muslim personal laws in the 1930s, including the Shariat Act of 1937 and the Dissolution of Muslim Marriages Act of 1939. These laws were designed to conform to classical texts that upheld male prerogatives in marriage and divorce, property, and guardianship, while enhancing women's dependence and vulnerability.[8] The Acts aimed to unify diverse practices and build a stronger sense of pan-Muslim identity. Abrogating local customs and practices that had denied inheritance rights to women, the Acts extended Maliki teachings on divorce to women previously governed by Hanafi law. The purpose, however, was less to expand women's divorce rights than to prevent Muslim women from converting to other religions in order to obtain a divorce (Williams, 2006, pp. 85–8).

Codification of Hindu law began under the British but, due to debate and opposition, was concluded only after Independence. A committee of experts appointed by the government formulated the original version, which represented a progressive change over most existing law. Hindu personal laws had varied across region and caste and over time, and parts of the country even upheld matriarchal systems. Women's rights to property, inheritance, and guardianship therefore varied from place to place, as did the possibilities for divorce and customs like dowry. Among upper-caste Hindus, the bride provided a dowry upon marriage; among lower classes, the groom supplied it (Ray, 1952, pp. 270–1). The government proposed to unify these diverse practices in a Code that granted women equal inheritance and property rights, abolished polygamy, and permitted divorce, even among upper-caste Hindus.

After Independence, the cause of the Hindu Code Bills was assumed by Dr. Babasaheb Ambedkar, the first Minister of Law, and strongly supported by Prime Minister Nehru. Yet proposals to grant women greater rights – especially equal inheritance rights – provoked considerable controversy. Ambedkar eventually resigned as minister out of frustration over what he perceived as the government's unwillingness to confront the opposition and force the bills through (Williams, 2006, pp. 104–5). Hindu conservatives opposed provisions on divorce, from changes in the joint family property system that would give daughters more inheritance rights to the granting of greater property rights to widows, among others. Eventually adopted in 1955 and 1956, the Hindu Code Bills represented significant progress over earlier law but was a watered down

---

[8] Codification occurred rather late in the colonial period, with initial attempts in the 1920s but and formal codes approved for Muslims and Hindus in the 1930s and 1940s, respectively. Criminal laws, civil laws, and laws on criminal and civil procedure had been codified during the nineteenth century, but the noninterference principle, combined with a lack of demand from Hindu leaders, delayed codification of personal laws until the twentieth century.

version of what had been proposed by Ambedkar.[9] Women still faced discrimination with respect to inheritance and agricultural land was excluded from the purview of the Code's terms on succession (Williams, 2006, chapter 4).

Adoption of the Hindu Code Bills – which departed in significant ways from prevailing laws and customs – demonstrated that Congress party governments were more willing to interfere in Hindu than in Muslim personal laws (Hasan, 2010). This trend continued, as the Hindu Succession Act was significantly modified in 2005. Academics, feminist activists, and civil society organizations worked with members of parliament to see that agricultural land was brought within the purview of inheritance regulations, daughters were made copartners in family property and gained rights to the family home, and widows gained greater inheritance rights (Agarwal, 2005).

Indian government policy toward Muslim personal laws has followed the opposite trajectory: resistance to reform. The courts had introduced piecemeal modifications in favor of women, principally by applying the colonial-era Code of Criminal Procedure to compel husbands to pay maintenance to destitute ex-wives. In its famous *Shah Bano* ruling in 1985, the Supreme Court upheld this practice. Conservative politicians objected, claiming that Muslim personal law required husbands to pay maintenance only during the *iddah* period; afterward, the obligation to support destitute women belonged to the women's children, fathers, siblings, and so forth (Williams, 2006, chapter 5). The Congress party government capitulated to these demands for adherence to the policy and instructed its deputies to support the Muslim Women's (Protection of Rights on Divorce) Bill, which rejected *Shah Bano* in favor of the more limited interpretation of the ex-husband's obligations. Subsequently, the Hindu nationalist Bharatiya Janata Party (BJP) was able to capitalize on what it called the government's capitulation to "minority" religious opinion (Hasan, 2010, pp. 943–4). India continues to uphold different personal laws, as a constitutional mandate to adopt a Uniform Civil Code governing all Indians has proven extraordinarily controversial. Secular feminists oppose a Uniform Civil Code due to its association with Hindu nationalism. They have opted to pursue reforms within each of the distinct family law traditions and realized some success with

---

[9] The Code included the Hindu Marriage and Divorce Act, the Hindu Succession Act, the Hindu Minority and Guardianship Act, and the Hindu Adoptions and Maintenance Act.

reforms to the Hindu Succession Act in 2005, described earlier in the chapter.

The experience of British colonialism produced similar effects in Southeast Asia, the Middle East, and sub-Saharan Africa. In Malaysia, colonial authorities granted Malay sultans relative autonomy over religious and cultural matters, including laws of personal status to gain their allegiance to the state. As in India, British policy tended to invent religious doctrine in the face of diverse and fluid customary practices.

Israel, another former British colony, upholds multiple legal systems. Following practices under the Ottoman empire, British rulers in Palestine recognized the rights of different cultural groups to apply their respective family laws. This legacy persists today. Rules on marriage, divorce, and support are determined by the religious affiliation of the parties involved. Orthodox Jewish law – hardly egalitarian – thus applies to the majority population. Though feminists have campaigned for reforms promoting gender equality, opposition from religious parties renders "change in the near future ... inconceivable. The maintenance of religious law in matters of marriage and divorce is still considered a basic tenet in the Israeli polity in general and in the delicate construction of Jewish identity in particular" (Halperin-Kaddari, 2003, p. 228).

With the exception of Tanzania, which applies a uniform family law incorporating principles of statutory, customary, and Muslim law, sub-Saharan African polities formerly under British rule maintain multiple legal systems. In Botswana, customary law is a parallel legal system to statutory law (modeled largely on South African law) and forms the "framework of norms within which the large majority of the people of Botswana think and act" (Garey & Townsend, 1996, p. 191).

Nigeria upholds a tripartite legal system, the complexity of which is exacerbated by its federal structure. First, Nigeria has a body of statutory law inherited from the British that applies to family issues. Marriage and divorce are governed by the 1914 Marriage Act and the 1970 Matrimonial Causes Act, which largely emulated the 1968 and 1969 divorce reforms adopted in Australia and the United Kingdom, respectively. Second, multiple and diverse sets of laws are respected by different ethnic groups, regions, and even villages. Largely uncodified, customary law is still upheld in court. Finally, Muslim law is widely applied in the north of the country. These three bodies of law differ, particularly when it comes to divorce. Conflicts occur since marriages under both customary and statutory law are common (Rahmatian, 1996).

Statutory law permits only monogamous marriages between men and women based on consent. Provisions for divorce, the rights and responsibilities of spouses, and rules on maintenance and custody are largely similar to those of Anglo-American common law. Customary law, by contrast, is more similar to Islamic law in several respects, though internally variable. As in classical Muslim family law, the marriage contract is usually concluded between two families and the bride's consent is often not necessary. The husband's family pays the wife's family a bride price, in contrast to Muslim family law, when the dower is paid to the woman herself. Upon divorce, the bride price must be repaid. Divorce is most commonly arbitrated by family members – with marital breakdown the most frequent reason – but can also be processed through the courts. Women have no right to maintenance under customary law and custody is usually held by the father (Rahmatian, 1996).

Nigeria has made few changes to family law. An exception is the Child Rights Act, adopted in 2003, which established a minimum marriage age of eighteen for both sexes and made it a criminal offense for a husband to consummate a marriage with a girl under eighteen, equating the act with rape. It also introduced equal inheritance rights for male and female children. These provisions challenge classical Muslim law's provisions on marital eligibility and inheritance. The President of the Supreme Council for Sharia in Nigeria claimed that the Act amounts to "a conspiracy against Islam ... and a direct attack on Islam ... no Muslim will obey this law. It doesn't matter who passes it" (quoted in Toyo, 2006, p. 1309).

But the country's political institutions make the Act extremely difficult to implement. Under the prevailing interpretation of the federal constitution, national laws in some areas, including areas of concern to women and children, may be passed but state legislatures must adopt similar legislation in order to take effect there. As of 2005, only four states had passed child rights laws, though twenty more were considering it and twelve had not responded at all (Toyo, 2006).

What is more, the extension of "shariah" law beyond family to criminal law in twelve northern states has led to further abuses of women's rights. The emphasis in these states has been on criminal punishment for alcohol use, theft, and *zina* (extramarital sex). As in Pakistan, victims who are unable to prove rape, which requires a confession from the rapist and two male witnesses, are considered to be guilty of *zina*. Under the Maliki law applied in Nigeria, pregnancy outside of marriage constitutes prima facie evidence of *zina*. While men have been able to practice "transgressive" sexuality with impunity, the brunt of criminal punishment has been borne by women (Pereira & Ibrahim, 2010). In 2001, for example, a teenage girl was sentenced to 100 strokes of a cane for giving birth to a baby outside of marriage.

Kenya historically had four different family law regimes: customary law, the Hindu Marriage and Divorce Act, the Mohammedan Marriage and Divorce Act, and the Marriage Act (governing people who choose to marry under statutory law, regardless of their religious background). After Independence, the government attempted to unify these multiple laws dating from British rule. It appointed a Commission on the Law of Marriage and Divorce in 1967, which presented its recommendation in 1968. However, the proposal was repeatedly defeated in parliament for being too Western and un-African and giving too many rights to women. Though it failed initially in Kenya, the proposal for legal unification was adopted virtually verbatim in Tanzania in 1971 (Baraza, 2009; Rahmatian, 1996, p. 297). Due to this legal paralysis, Kenya continued to apply antiquated laws until well into the twenty-first century. In the area of marital property, for example, courts used the Married Women's Property Act, an English statute from 1882 (Baraza, 2009 p. 11)!

The Tanzanian law permits marriage to be either monogamous or polygamous if both spouses agree. Marriage can be religious but has to be registered with civil authorities. Divorce has to be processed through the courts and requires a waiting period as well as attempts at reconciliation, except for divorce by *talaq*, which the law accepts as valid. Elsewhere, Tanzanian law conforms to common law principles by giving women equal custody rights and rights to maintenance, and prescribing that the division of property after divorce take into account the wife's nonmonetary contributions (Rahmatian, 1996).

After 2010, Kenya's adoption of a new constitution with a generally progressive bill of rights gave a push to family law reform. The constitution established the equality of men and women during and after marriage, but also called for the accommodation of religious law. Parliament adopted new Matrimonial Property and Marriage Acts in 2013 and 2014, respectively. These Acts recognized multiple forms of marriage, including Christian, civil, customary, Muslim, and Hindu. Like the constitution, the Acts upheld principles of equal rights, while also deferring to customary and religious laws. Like Tanzania, Kenyan law recognizes polygamous marriages. This means that in practice, many women who marry will not enjoy the same rights as men (Murungi, 2015). South Africa and Botswana uphold parallel legal systems of customary and statutory law but have introduced extensive reforms to the latter to promote gender equality. The South African Marital Property Act of 1984 largely abolished the institution of marital power and the male prerogatives it upheld. Botswana followed suit with the Abolition of Marital Power Act of 2004. The South African Constitution of 1996 endorses sex equality and a range of women's rights. It recognizes customary law (as did the Recognition of Customary Marriages Act of 1998), but renders its provisions subject to constitutional norms, including the clause on sex equality. Muslim marriages, however, are not recognized by law. In the 2000s, Parliament considered a Muslim marriage bill which codified classical rules on divorce, maintenance during *iddah*, and so forth, but was criticized by feminists and human rights advocates (Manjoo, 2007).

Other sub-Saharan African countries, including Ivory Coast and Senegal, (both former French colonies) have unified family laws modeled on the civil law tradition, to which we now turn.

CIVIL LAW

Based on Roman law, civil law is the most widely used system in the world. The Napoleonic Code, promulgated in 1804, was extremely influential for family law as it was copied and adopted in continental Europe and Latin America. The German Civil Code, adopted in 1900, was shaped by the Napoleonic Code but had a different structure and was far more detailed.[10] It, in turn, influenced the codes adopted in Japan, Korea, and China. Moves for reform in favor of gender equality began in the late nineteenth century, but many countries remained faithful to both Codes' patriarchal provisions until the mid- to late twentieth century. The first part of this discussion focuses on the Napoleonic Code, while noting significant differences with the German Code.

Like classical Muslim family law, the Napoleonic Code put women at a disadvantage relative to men. Article 213 states: "The husband owes protection to his wife, the wife obedience to her husband." This means that "The wife is obliged to live with her husband, and to follow him to every place where he may judge it convenient to reside: the husband is obliged to receive her, and to furnish her with every thing necessary for the wants of life, according to his means and station" (Article 214). Even

---

[10] The Code represented "twenty two years of careful study and research by the most eminent German jurists" and has been called "the most carefully considered statement of a nation's laws that the world has ever seen" (quoted in Wang, 1907).

if she is a "trader" or has separate property, a wife cannot plead in her own name or give, sell, or acquire any property (Articles 215 and 217). The German Code gave the husband similar prerogatives, though it did not contain an explicit clause about obedience, opting instead to compel both spouses to "live together in a matrimonial community of life" (quoted in Glendon, 1989, p. 91).

As Vogel describes, these articles reflect the concepts of male power (*puissance*) and female incompetence (*incapacité*) upheld by the Code. *Puissance* refers to the husband's control over the person, property, and activities of his wife. It enables him to monitor her friendships and correspondence, prevent her from working, deny her a passport, fix the marital home, and manage her property. As Napoleon himself declared: "The husband shall have the right to say to his wife: 'Madame, you will not go out today; Madame, you will not visit the theater; Madame, you will not visit this person; in short, Madame you are mine with body and soul'" (quoted in Vogel, 1998, p. 34).

The wife's *incapacité* implied that she was unable to engage in legally valid transactions without her husband's authorization on a case-by-case basis. What is more, all property she had upon entering marriage was lumped together as common property and managed by the husband, though wives were entitled to an equal share of marital assets upon dissolution of the marriage. However, most Catholic countries in Europe and Latin America did not permit divorce until the mid- to late twentieth century. Women could not sell, trade, or lease marital property without the husband's authorization.

As in classical Muslim family law, fathers had guardianship rights over minor children. Unlike in the Muslim tradition, however, mothers could become guardians in the event of a father's death. These rights were not absolute: A father could appoint a special council to share guardianship rights with the mother. What is more, if a woman remarried, the law required convocation of a family council to decide whether she could retain guardianship rights (Code Napoleon, Articles 389–96).

The Code sets the minimum ages of marriage at fifteen for women and eighteen for men. Unlike classical Muslim law, it requires the consent of both parties to the marriage and additionally requires parental consent if spouses are less than twenty-one and twenty-five years old (Code Napoleon, Articles 144–8). Marriages must be performed publicly, before a civil official (Article 165).

Divorce is permitted by mutual consent, bad conduct, imprisonment, or adultery. The notion of adultery, however, differs for women and men.

This discrepancy proved enduringly influential. A man may demand divorce if his wife commits adultery but a woman has grounds to terminate the marriage only if the man brings his concubine to live in the family home (Articles 229–33). As this suggests, French civil law was similar to classical Muslim law in permitting polygamy, as long as it was not formalized and places of residence were kept separate. Women have rights to alimony and guardianship of children after divorce unless they are the guilty party.

Family law in most civil law countries has undergone profound transformation since the original Code but the process has not been uniform. Some countries changed earlier, while others such as Chile held on to the famous clause on the husband's protection and wife's obedience until 1989. Some countries legalized divorce in the late nineteenth century; others waited until the middle to end of the twentieth (Italy, Spain, Portugal, Brazil, Argentina, Colombia) and even the first decade of the twenty-first (Chile). The rate and scope of change also varied, as Chapter Four showed. The rest of this section briefly summarizes the nature of these changes so that their import can be fully appreciated.

The first set of widespread changes concerned the property rights of married women. Married Women's Property Acts, passed in the late nineteenth century in Europe (and incorporated into the German Civil Code of 1900) and the early twentieth century in Latin America, kept the wife's earned income separate from the pool of common property managed by the husband and granted her full control over it. Reforms in the southern cone of South America also allowed couples to opt for separation of property regimes, common in classical Muslim family law (Htun, 2003, pp. 48–9). In 1887, Costa Rica became the first Latin American country to adopt separation of property as the default marital property regime (Deere and León, 2001, p. 51).

The next set of changes involved granting married women full civil capacity and revoking clauses obliging them to obey their husbands. In Mexico and some Central American countries, reforms around the turn of the twentieth century granted married women full civil capacity and changed rhetorical images of marriage, though some, such as El Salvador, opted to retain the obedience clause (Deere and León 2001, pp. 41–4). Elsewhere, these changes came about only in the mid-twentieth century. In France the obedience clause was deleted in 1938, but the wife had to seek her husband's permission to work until 1965 and the law called him the "head of the family" until 1970 (Glendon, 1989, p. 89). Brazilian law upheld the man as the head of the household until the civil code was reformed in 2001 following twenty-five years of feminist agitation for change (Htun, 2003, pp. 127–32). Similar reforms were adopted in Colombia in 1974 (Deere and León, 2001, p. 43). Germany reformed patriarchal provisions of its Code in 1957 but women did not gain equal rights to work outside the home until the Social Democratic Marriage Law of 1976, which declared that "the spouses will conduct the running of the household by mutual agreement" and "both spouses have the right to be employed" (Glendon, 1989, pp. 92–3).

Some countries made these changes as part of a big package that also included granting wives equal control over common marital property and reforms to the system of parental authority (equal guardianship rights for mothers and fathers): Spain in 1981, Peru and Switzerland in 1984, Korea in 1990 (Deere & León, 2001, 43; Valiente, 1996). Elsewhere, reforms were adopted on a piecemeal basis. Marital property reforms were intended to accommodate competing principles of individual rights, sharing between spouses, and compensation for unpaid household work. In Latin America, several countries, including Brazil, Mexico, and Colombia, adopted versions of the "deferred community" and "participation in earnings" regimes prevalent in Nordic countries and in Germany. Under these systems, husband and wife administer their separate property during marriage. If the marriage is terminated, however, common property – and sometimes just the increase in the monetary value of their estates during marriage – is pooled and split evenly (Glendon, 1989, pp. 132–4; Htun, 2003; Deere & León, 2001).[11] In addition, mothers were granted equal guardianship rights with fathers in Argentina in 1985 (after forty years of feminist activism on the issue)[12] and in Chile in 1998 (Htun, 2003).

Finally, divorce. As described earlier, classical Muslim law always permitted divorce but the terms of divorce discriminated against women, where not denying it to them altogether. In many civil law countries, especially Catholic ones, divorce was not legally available until the mid- to late twentieth century, with some exceptions. Though the Napoleonic Code permitted divorce in the wake of its legalization during the French Revolution, indissoluble marriage was reinstated in France in 1816. In 1884, the *Loi Naquet* relegalized divorce. In Latin America, Mexico

---

[11] Deferred community was introduced in Argentina in 1968 and Brazil in 1977; participation in earnings as an alternative property regime in Chile in 1994 (Htun, 2003).

[12] The Argentine Congress had approved a law for equal parental rights in 1975 but it was vetoed by President Isabel Perón.

legalized divorce in 1917, after the revolution, and Uruguay legalized it in 1907, during liberal rule. Other countries – including Costa Rica – permitted legal divorce at an early stage.

Elsewhere, the civil law upheld the Roman Catholic principle that marriage was indissoluble and precluded legal divorce. In Brazil, even the constitution contained a clause defining marriage as indissoluble. The principal challenge for liberal reformers was to challenge the political authority of Catholic bishops in order to render divorce legally available. Partisans of divorce struggled for decades, tending to succeed when conflicts erupted between Roman Catholic bishops and the state over authoritarian rule, control of education, human rights, and other issues (Htun, 2003, chapter 4). Once this occurred, the divorce laws adopted – in Italy in 1970, Brazil and Portugal in 1977, Spain in 1981, Argentina in 1987, Colombia and Paraguay in 1991 – were generally egalitarian in their provisions about grounds, property division, and child custody, though not all permitted divorce by mutual consent.[13]

Korea and Japan deserve special mention, since their laws were shaped by customary norms as well as European influences. Japan's Meiji-era civil code (modeled on the Napoleonic Code), adopted in 1898, was patriarchal and upheld the power and prerogatives of the male head of the house (*ie*). Departing from the French Code and conforming to customs during the Edo period (1600–1868), however, the Code permitted easy divorce. Couples could merely inform the civil registry official that they had divorced; processing through the court was not necessary (the courts would, however, process contested divorces) (Fuess, 2004). The Meiji Code lacked provisions on division of property and alimony after divorce and allowed parents to establish their own custody arrangements, while stipulating that the father's word would prevail in a disagreement. It preserved the control of families over marriage by requiring parental or ancestral consent for women and men marrying under the ages of twenty-five and thirty, respectively (Fuess, 2004, pp. 115–17).

---

[13] Divorce in several countries was legalized, banned, and then relegalized over the course of the twentieth century, following changes in political regimes more or less close to the Roman Catholic Church. Portugal, for example, legalized divorce in 1910, but then restricted the practice to non-Catholics in 1940 under a concordat with the Vatican. In 1966, mutual consent was removed as a ground for non-Catholic divorce. The overthrow of Salazar in 1974 led to a revision of the concordat and divorce was legalized for all citizens in 1977. In Spain, divorce was legal during the 1930s, banned under the Franco regime, and then made legal again after the transition to democracy. Argentina enjoyed legal divorce during a brief period of Peronist rule during the 1950s; it was banned following a military coup in 1956 (Phillips 1991, pp. 121–2; Htun, 2003, pp. 95–6).

After World War Two, U.S. occupation forces overhauled Japanese law. The Civil Code was reformed in light of the 1947 constitution, which upheld principles of sex equality in the family and society at large. It aimed to shift power from the *ie* and toward an equitable marital relationship. The "New Civil Code," adopted in 1948, thus promoted women's equal rights to property, parenting, and activities outside of the home. But it retained the customary and Meiji-era provisions on private, consensual divorce, requiring only that spouses inform the staff at the local government office, orally or in writing, that they were divorcing (Fuess, 2004, pp. 146–8; Schmidt, 2005). Unlike other advanced economies in Europe and North America, Japan never experienced a revolution in divorce law: Policies on divorce have remained remarkably stable over hundreds of years and rates have actually declined (Fuess, 2004).

One area of gender disadvantage that persisted into the twenty-first century in Japan concerned the marital name. The civil code requires that couples assume a common marital name. In 98 percent of cases this is the husband's (Schmidt, 2005). Women are required to use their marital name on all official documents, including driver's licenses, ID cards, health insurance cards, and so forth (Gelb, 2003). The rationale for this comes from the civil registration system (*koseki*) that lists all citizens (and residents) by household. Every household has a family head, which is usually the man (Mackie, 2003, p. 130). When Mala Htun lived in Japan in 2006 and 2007, her national ID card registered her husband's name as her "householder."

A comparable situation exists in Germany, where the law before 1976 required that couples assume the husband's name after marriage. After the Social Democratic Marriage Law of 1976, couples still had to have a common name, and unless they specified otherwise, it would default to the husband's (Glendon, 1989).

In Korea, gender-equitable changes came much later than in Japan. The Korean Code was influenced by the German Code but also by local, Confucian customs. Like the Napoleonic and German codes, as well as Muslim law, it designated the man as the head of the family and stipulated that other members owed him obedience. Fathers held guardianship rights over children, even if mothers held temporary custody after divorce, and only "innocent" wives could claim maintenance from former spouses. Unlike the European laws, and more in line with classical Muslim (and classical Hindu) practice, women had fewer inheritance rights than men. Married daughters received one-quarter the share of men of equivalent rank. What is more, the law prohibited people from marrying someone with the same last name (Cho, 1994). A major civil code reform in 1990 changed these provisions, but men continued to be considered the head of household. In 1997, the Constitutional Court ruled the marriage ban unconstitutional; a law to amend the Code – which banned marriage only between relatives – came into effect in 2005.[14]

Table B.2 summarizes the main differences between the Napoleonic Code of 1804 and the situation in most civil law countries after mid- to late-twentieth-century reforms. As the table makes clear, the changes have been dramatic. Most governments replaced patriarchal and discriminatory laws with measures endorsing gender equality.

SOCIALIST/COMMUNIST LAW

Socialist theory endorsed equality within the family and the termination of religious influence over family law and society in general, as Chapter Four described. The Soviet decrees on marriage and divorce of 1917 and the Family Code of 1918 were designed to produce a sharp break with the religious principles guiding prerevolutionary family law. The Soviet's primary aim was to reduce the influence of the Eastern Orthodox Church. Marriages had to be registered with the state: Religious marriages were no longer valid (Hazard, 1939, pp. 225–6). These early laws banned polygamy and the concept of illegitimacy, made divorce easy to obtain, and introduced equality between the spouses and between parents. The laws aimed "to deliver the woman from her traditional legal disabilities and to emancipate her from all subservience to her husband" (Berman, 1946, pp. 39, 48).

The Russian Family Code of 1926 further relegated marriage and divorce to the sphere of private agreement, with only a minimal role for the courts and the state (Berman, 1946, p. 40).[15] Private agreement, however, did not mean religious. Similar to the situation in Japan, divorce had merely to be recorded at the civil registry, whether by mutual consent or at the petition of one spouse. Only conflict over the division of property and child custody had to be processed through the courts (Hazard, 1939, pp. 238–9).

---

[14] www.state.gov/g/drl/rls/hrrpt/2009/eap/135996.htm.
[15] The constitution of the Soviet Union of 1924 had vested the right to formulate family law with each republic. Most followed the spirit of the Russian Code.

TABLE B.2 *Main features of civil law*

Area	Napoleonic Code, 1804	Situation after reforms in mid- to late twentieth century
Conditions of marriage	Minimum age of marriage sixteen for women, eighteen for men	Minimum age of marriage eighteen for both spouses
Rights and duties in marriage	* Husband must protect the wife; wife must obey the husband * Marital power → husband has rights over person, property, and activities of his wife * Female incapacity → women cannot work, appear in court, engage in financial transactions without husband's permission	Rights and duties are equal; some codes describe equitable marriage
Name	Law requires a common marital name, usually husband's (varies)	Couples can keep their own name or use a common name (some variation)
Property	* Men controlled common property during marriage, including wife's property * Property divided after divorce but guilty spouses lose rights	Wife and husband control separate property and/or common property administered by both spouses
Divorce	* Permitted for mutual consent; bad conduct; imprisonment; adultery (by woman) * Illegal in most Roman Catholic countries until twentieth century (timing of legalization varies)	Equal access for both spouses; grounds and waiting periods vary
Guardianship	Fathers hold rights of parental power over children; mothers assume conditional guardianship at father's death	Parental power exercised jointly or indiscriminately by mother and father
Inheritance	Equal rights in intestate succession (some variation, e.g., Korea)	Equal rights in intestate succession

Also notable was the recognition of (common law marriage) rights (Hazard, 1939, p. 229). And in a precursor to communist China's requirement of medical exams prior to marriage, the 1926 Family Code required each spouse to be properly informed of the other's health, especially venereal diseases, tuberculosis, and mental health (Ibid, 232). Note that U.S. states had similar provisions, including bans on marriage to people with diseases.

Some legal changes in the 1930s and 1940s – dramatically, including the ban on abortion in 1936 – amended these earlier liberal provisions, for example by imposing some restrictions on divorce, including the requirement of spousal summons (Hazard, 1939, p. 239; Berman, 1946, p. 41). These reforms were motivated by a plummeting birth rate and delinquency in payment of child support and included, in addition to the abortion ban, state allowances paid upon the birth of third (and subsequent) children and improvements to social services for women and children. Rhetorical emphasis was shifted away from women as equals to men and toward women as mothers. However, the key principles of the 1917 reforms, including monogamy, lifelong marriage, equality of husband and wife, and protection of illegitimate children, endured. Communist states of the global South also introduced egalitarian family laws, including North Korea in 1946, China in 1950, North Vietnam in 1959, South Yemen in 1974, and Cuba in 1975. See Table B.3 for a comparison of the early Soviet family codes with more recent laws in other countries.

The Chinese Marriage Law of 1950 was intended to produce a radical break with traditional, Confucian family traditions and the social order they upheld. The law's inspirations, however, had been brewing for decades. Intellectuals and nationalists of the May Fourth movement of the late 1910s and early 1920s had offered profound critiques of the traditional family system, especially the ways it oppressed and dehumanized women (Johnson, 2009, pp. 28–9). Meanwhile, the immense suffering of peasants in the first decades of the twentieth century – brought about by starvation, migration, warlordism, and civil war – broke families apart at the same time that it made traditional family forms seem more desirable. Resolving this contradiction proved a challenge to the Communist Party in the aftermath of the Marriage Law (Johnson, 2009).

The first article of the 1950 Marriage Law states that

the feudal marriage system based on arbitrary and compulsory arrangement and the supremacy of man over woman, and in disregard for the interests of the

TABLE B.3 *Socialist family law*

Area	Soviet Family Code 1918; Russian Code of 1926/7	Other countries
Conditions of marriage	Minimum marriage age of sixteen for women and eighteen for men; only civil marriages recognized	China (1950) and Vietnam (1959) banned child marriage, forced marriage, polygamy
Rights and duties in marriage	Equality between spouses	Equality between spouses (China, Vietnam, Cuba 1975)
Name	Common surname not required	Common surname not required (China, Vietnam, Cuba)
Property	1918 Code prescribed separation of property; 1926 Code established community property, with division after divorce to be determined by court according to spousal needs and interests of children	Equal enjoyment and use of property; household labor considered productive labor at divorce (Vietnam)
Divorce	Divorce had to be recorded with the civil registry at petition of both spouses or one spouse (other spouse served a summons)	Divorce processed by a notary public, not the courts (Cuba 1994)
Guardianship	Equality between parents	Equality between parents (China, Vietnam, Cuba)
Inheritance	Equality between males and females	Equality between males and females (China, Vietnam, Cuba)

children, is abolished. The new democratic marriage system, which is based on free choice of partners, on monogamy, on equal rights for both sexes, and of the protection of the lawful interests of women and children, is put into effect.

(Cited in Johnson, 2009, p. 235)

The law states that "husband and wife are companions living together and enjoy equal status in the home" (Article 7). Both have equal rights to work and to engage in social activities outside the home; to possession and management of family property; to use their own name; and to inherit (Articles 9–12). Divorce is granted "when husband and wife both desire it"; in the event of disagreement, the local people's government can grant the divorce after attempts at reconciliation have failed. Issues of custody and division of property are subject to agreement between the spouses or court decision, taking the wife and children's interests into account.

Vietnam's Marriage and Family Law of 1959 had similar features. It banned forced marriages, child marriages, and polygamy and introduced equality between men and women in rights, obligations, property, and parenting. The law also recognized household labor as productive labor relevant to the division of property in the event of divorce (Article 29).[16] In a precocious move for a socialist society, Article 3 also bans wife beating and abuse. China's marriage laws did not recognize the problem of domestic violence until 2001 (Woo, 2003; Htun, interviews in Shanghai in 2007).

Cuba's Family Code, adopted in 1975, conforms to communist trad-itions of equal rights. The Code offers detailed descriptions of the duties of spouses in marriage and parenting, stating that "both partners must care for the family they have created and must cooperate with each other in the education, upbringing and guidance of the children according to the principles of socialist morality. They must participate, to the extent of their capacity or possibilities, in the running of the home." As this suggests, even men who work outside the home are encouraged to con-tribute to housework. Parents jointly exercise parental power and spouses are equal executors of marital property. What is more, the Code avoids gendered language, opting instead to refer to spouses, parents, guardians, and providers (Htun, 2007).

Lest readers run out to champion socialist achievements for women's rights, it is important to recognize that sex equality was not a feature of all spheres of life. With the exception of the Vietnamese law mentioned earlier in this Appendix, male socialist leaders generally refused to acknowledge the reality of male dominance in the family and of problems of domestic and sexual violence. As Chapter 2 showed, communist and postcommunist countries on average performed more poorly than other countries. In the Latin American region, for example, Cuba lags far behind the rest of the region in the adoption of policies to prevent and punish violence against women (Htun & Piscopo, 2010).

---

[16] The text of the 1959 law (in Vietnamese) is available at the National Assembly's website: www.na.gov.vn/sach_qh/vkqhtoantap_1/nam1959/1959_18.html.

References

Abramovitz, Mimi. (1996). *Regulating the Lives of Women: Social Welfare Policy from Colonial Times to the Present*. Boston, MA: South End Press.

Abu-Odeh, Lama. (2004). Modernizing Muslim family law: the case of Egypt. *Vanderbilt Journal of Transnational Law*, 37(October), 1043–1146.

Adams, Julia. (2005). *The Familial State: Ruling Families and Merchant Capitalism in Early Modern Europe*. Ithaca, NY: Cornell University Press.

Addati, Laura, Cassirer, Naomi, & Gilchrist, Katherine. (2014). Maternity and paternity at work: law and practice across the world. International Labor Organization, May 13, 2014, www.ilo.org/wcmsp5/groups/public/—dgreports/—dcomm/—publ/documents/publication/wcms_242615.pdf.

Agarwal, B., & Panda, P. (2007). Toward freedom from violence: the neglected obvious. *Journal of Human Development*, 8(3), 359–88.

Agarwal, Bina. (1994). *A Field of One's Own: Gender and Land Rights in South Asia*. New York, NY: Cambridge University Press.

(1997). "Bargaining" and gender relations: within and beyond the household. *Feminist Economics*, 3(1), 1–51.

(2005). Landmark step to gender equality. *The Hindu*, www.hindu.com/mag/2005/09/25/stories/2005092500050100.htm.

Ahmed, Leila. (1992). *Women in Gender in Islam: Historical Roots of Modern Debate*. New Haven, CT: Yale University Press.

Alemika, E. E. O., Chukwuma, I., Lafratta, D., Messerli, D., & Souckova, J. (2005). *Rights of the Child in Nigeria: Report on the Implementation of the Convention on the Rights of the Child by Nigeria*. Geneva: Committee on the Rights of the Child, 38th Session.

Alexander, Amy C., & Welzel, Christian. (2009). *Islam's Patriarchal Effect: Spurious or Genuine?* August 19, 2009, https://ssrn.com/abstract=1458000 or http://dx.doi.org/10.2139/ssrn.1458000.

Alvarez, Sonia E. (1990). *Engendering Democracy in Brazil: Women's Movements in Transition Politics*. Princeton, NJ: Princeton University Press.

Amenta, Edwin, Bonastia, Chris, & Caren, Neal. (2001). US social policy in comparative and historical perspective: concepts, images, arguments, and research strategies. *Annual Review of Sociology*, 27, 213–34.

Amenta, Edwin, Caren, Neal, Chiarello, Elizabeth, & Su, Yang. (2010). The political consequences of social movements. *Annual Review of Sociology*, 36, 287–307.

Amirthalingam, Kumaralingam. (2005). Women's rights, international norms, and domestic violence: asian perspectives. *Human Rights Quarterly*, 27(2), 683–708.

Amnesty International. (n.d.). Sexual and reproductive rights health fact sheet, www.amnestyusa.org/pdfs/SexualReproductiveRightsFactSheet.pdf.

Annesley, Claire, Engeli, Isabelle, & Gains, Francesca. (2015). The profile of gender equality issue attention in Western Europe. *European Journal of Political Research*, 54(3), 525–42.

Anwar, Zainah, & Rumminger, Jana S. (2007). Justice and equity in Muslim family laws: challenges, possibilities, and strategies for reform. *Washington & Lee Law Review*, 64, 1529.

(1993). *In My Father's House: Africa in the Philosophy of Culture*. New York, NY: Oxford University Press.

Appiah, Kwame Anthony. (1997). Race, culture, identity: misunderstood connections. In Anthony Appiah & Amy Gutmann, eds., *Color Conscious: The Political Morality of Race*. Princeton, NJ: Princeton University Press, pp. 30–105.

Arabic Network for Human Rights Information. (2009). http://old.openarab.net/en/node/1400.

Armstrong, Elizabeth, & Bernstein, Mary. (2008). Culture, power, and institutions: a multi-institutional politics approach to social movements. *Sociological Theory*, 26(1), 74–99.

Aromaa, Kauko, & Heiskanen, Markku, eds. (2008). *Report Series 56. Victimisation Surveys in Comparative Perspective*. Helsinki: The European Institute for Crime Prevention and Control, affiliated with the United Nations (HEUNI), www.heuni.fi/en/index/publications/heunireports/reportseries56.victimisationsurveysincomparativeperspective_0.html.

(2008). *Victimization Surveys in a Comparative Perspective*. Stockholm Criminological Symposium 2007. Helsinki: UN European Institute for Crime Prevention and Control. www.heuni.fi/material/attachments/heuni/reports/6KmBUXHhv/PainoonHR56_1.pdf.

Avdeyeva, Olga. (2007). When do states comply with international treaties? Policies on violence against women in post-communist countries. *International Studies Quarterly*, 51(4), 877–900. doi:10.1111/j.1468-2478.2007.00481.x

(2009). Enlarging the club: when do states enforce gender equality laws? *Comparative European Politics*, 7(1), 158–77. doi:10.1057/cep.2008.34

(2010). States' compliance with international requirements: gender equality in EU enlargement countries. *Political Research Quarterly*, 63(1), 203–17.

Avelino, George, Brown, David S., & Hunter, Wendy. (2005). The effects of capital mobility, trade openness, and democracy on social spending in Latin America, 1980–1999. *American Journal of Political Science*, 49(3), 625–41.

Ayoub, Phillip. (2016). *When States Come Out: Europe's Sexual Minorities and the Politics of Visibility*. New York, NY: Cambridge University Press.

Bachrach, Peter, & Baratz, Morton. (1962). Two faces of power. *American Political Science Review*, 56(4), 947–52.

Badran, Margot. (2009). *Feminism in Islam: Secular and Religious Convergences.* Oxford: Oneworld.

Balchin, Cassandra. (2009). Family law in contemporary Muslim contexts: triggers and strategies for change. In Zainah Anwar, ed., *Wanted: Equality and Justice in the Muslim Family.* Kuala Lumpur: Musawah, pp. 209–36.

Baldez, Lisa. (2004). Elected bodies: the adoption of gender quotas in Mexico. *Legislative Studies Quarterly*, 29(2), 231–58.

(2014). *Defying Convention: US Resistance to the UN Treaty on Women's Rights.* New York, NY: Cambridge University Press.

Banaszak, Lee Ann. (1996). *Why Movements Succeed or Fail: Opportunity, Culture, and the Struggle for Woman Suffrage.* Princeton, NJ: Princeton University Press.

Banaszak, Lee Ann, Beckwith, Karen, & Rucht, Dieter. (2003). *Women's Movements Facing the Reconfigured State.* Cambridge: Cambridge University Press.

Baraza, Nancy. (2009). Family law reforms in Kenya: an overview. Paper presented at the Henrich Böll Foundation's Gender Forum in Nairobi, www.boell.or.ke/downloads/Nancy_Baraza_-_Family_Law_Reforms_in_Kenya.pdf.

Barrett, Jacqueline K. (1993). *Encyclopedia of Women's Associations Worldwide: A Guide to Over 3,400 National and Multination Nonprofit Women's and Women-Related Organizations.* London: Gale Research.

Barro, Robert J., & McCleary, Rachel M. (2005). Which countries have state religions? *The Quarterly Journal of Economics*, 120(4), 1331–70.

Bashevkin, Sylvia. (1998). *Women on the Defensive.* Chicago, IL: University of Chicago Press.

Basu, Amrita, & McGrory, C. Elizabeth. (1995). *The Challenge of Local Feminisms: Women's Movements in Global Perspective.* Boulder, CO: Westview Press.

Bauer, David, & Ameringer, Carl F. (2010). A framework for identifying similarities among countries to improve cross-national comparisons of health systems. *Health & Place*, 16 (6), 1129–35.

Baumgartner, Frank, & Mahoney, Christine. (2005). Social movements, the rise of new issues, and the public agenda. In Valerie Jenness & Helen Ingram, eds., *Routing the Opposition: Social Movements, Public Policy and Democracy.* Minneapolis, MN: University of Minnesota Press, pp. 65–86.

Bayat, Asef. (2007). *Making Islam Democratic: Social Movements and the Post-Islamist Turn.* Stanford, CA: Stanford University Press.

Becker, Gary Stanley, & Becker, Gary S. (2009). *A Treatise on the Family.* Cambridge, MA: Harvard University Press.

Beckwith, Karen. (2000). Beyond compare? Women's movements in comparative perspective. *European Journal of Political Research*, 37(4), 431–68. doi:10.1111/1475-6765.00521

Belsky, J., Bell, B., Bradley, R. H., Stallard, N., & Stewart-Brown, S. (2006). Socioeconomic risk, parenting during the preschool years, and child health age 6. *European Journal of Public Health*, 17(5), 508–13.

Benhabib, Seyla. (2002). *The Claims of Culture: Equality and Diversity in the Global Era*. Princeton, NJ: Princeton University Press.

(2009). Claiming rights across borders: international human rights and democratic sovereignty. *American Political Science Review*, 103(4), 691–704.

Bensusán, Graciela. (2007). *La efectividad de la legislación laboral en América Latina*. Geneva: Instituto Internacional de Estudios Laborales.

Berkman, Michael B., & O'Connor, Robert E. (1993). Do women legislators matter? Female legislators and state abortion policy. *American Politics Quarterly*, 21(1), 102–24.

Berman, Harold J. (1946). Soviet family law in the light of Russian history and Marxist theory. *Yale Law Journal*, 56(1), 26–57.

Bernardi, Albert. (1986). Iran: family law after the Islamic Revolution. *Journal of Family Law*, 25, 151.

Bernstein, Anya. (2001). *The Moderation Dilemma: Legislative Coalitions and the Politics of Family and Medical Leave*. Pittsburgh, PA: University of Pittsburgh Press.

Berry, Frances Stokes, & Berry, William D. (1999). Innovation and diffusion models in policy research. In P. A. Sabatier, ed., *Theories of the Policy Process*. Boulder, CO: Westview, pp. 169–200.

Bianchi, S., Cohen, P., Raley, S., & Nomaguchi, K. (2004). Inequality in Parental Investment in Child Rearing. In K. Neckerman, ed., *Social Inequality*. New York, NY: Russell Sage, pp. 189–219.

Bird, Robert C. (1997). More than a congressional joke: a fresh look at the legislative history of sex discrimination of the 1964 Civil Rights Act. *William & Mary Journal of Women and the Law*, 3, 137.

Bleijenbergh, Inge, & Roggeband, Conny. (2007). Equality machineries matter: the impact of women's political pressure on European social-care policies. *Social Politics: International Studies in Gender, State & Society*, 14(4), 437–59.

Blofield, Merike. (2012). *Care Work and Class: Domestic Workers for Equal Rights in Latin America*. University Park, PA: Pennsylvania State University Press.

(2013). *The Politics of Moral Sin: Abortion and Divorce in Spain, Chile and Argentina*. New York, NY: Routledge.

Blofield, Merike., & Haas, Liesl. (2005). Defining a democracy: reforming the laws on women's rights in Chile, 1990–2002. *Latin American Politics and Society*, 47(3), 35–68.

(2013). Policy outputs. In G. Waylen et al, eds., *Oxford Handbook of Gender and Politics*. Oxford: Oxford University Press, pp. 677–700.

Blofield, Merike, & Lambert, Priscilla. (2008). Parental leave and childcare policy and the fertility crisis in familial welfare states: a comparison of Italy, Spain, and Japan. *US–Japan Women's Journal*, 38, 43–67.

Blofield, Merike, & Martínez Franzoni, Juliana. (2014a). *Maternalism, corresponsibility, and social equity: a typology of work–family policies*. Social Politics 22(1), 38–59.

(2014b). *Work–Family Relations and Inequality in Latin America: The Case of Parental Leave and Care Services*. Background paper commissioned for the UN Report, The World's Women, 2015–2016.

(2015). *Are Governments Catching Up? Work–Family Policy and Inequality in Latin America.* UN Women Discussion Paper, No. 7.

Bohn, D. K., Tebben, J. G., & Campbell, J. C. (2004). Influence of income, education, age, and ethnicity of physical abuse before and during pregnancy. *Journal of Obstetrics and Gynaecology*, 33(5), 561–71.

Boling, Patricia. (2015). *The Politics of Work–Family Policies: Japan, France, Germany and the United States.* New York, NY: Cambridge University Press.

Borchorst, Anette. (2006). *Daddy Leave and Gender Equality – the Danish Case in a Scandinavian Perspective.* Aalborg University, Denmark/Aalborg: Institut for Historie, Internationale Studier og Samfundsforhold, Aalborg Universitet. FREIA's tekstserie, No. 60. doi:10.5278/freia.4691293/

Borchorst, Anette, & Siim, Birte. (2002). The women-friendly welfare states revisited. *NORA: Nordic Journal of Women's Studies*, 10(2), 90–8.

Boushey, Graeme. (2010). *Policy Diffusion Dynamics in America.* Cambridge: Cambridge University Press.

Bowen, Donna Lee. (1997). Abortion, Islam, and the 1994 Cairo Population Conference. *International Journal of Middle East Studies*, 29 (2), 161–84.

Boyd, Susan B., & Young, Claire. (2002). Who influences family law reform? Discourses on motherhood and fatherhood in legislative reform debates in Canada. *Studies in Law, Politics, and Society*, 26, 43–75.

Brady, David. (2003). The politics of poverty: left political institutions, the welfare state and poverty. *Social Forces*, 82, 557–88.

Brady, David, Beckfield, Jason, & Seeleib-Kaiser, Martin. (2005). Economic globalization and the welfare state in affluent democracies, 1975–2001. *American Sociological Review*, 70(6), 921–48. doi:10.1177/00031224050 7000603

Brambor, Thomas, Roberts Clark, William, & Golder, Matt. (2006). Understanding interaction models: improving empirical analyses. *Political Analysis*, 14(1), 63–82. doi:10.1093/pan/mpi014

Bratton, Kathleen A., & Ray, Leonard P. (2002). Descriptive representation, policy outcomes, and municipal day-care coverage in Norway. *American Journal of Political Science*, 46(2), 428–37.

Brauer, Carl M. (1983). Women activists, southern conservatives, and the prohibition of sex discrimination in Title VII of the 1964 Civil Rights Act. *Journal of Southern History*, 49(1), 37–56.

Braun, Robert. (2016). Religious minorities and resistance to genocide: the collective rescue of Jews in the Netherlands during the Holocaust. *American Political Science Review*, 110(1), 127–47.

Brinks, Daniel M. (2007). *The Judicial Response to Police Killings in Latin America: Inequality and the Rule of Law.* New York, NY: Cambridge University Press.

Brown, David S., & Hunter, Wendy. (1999). Democracy and social spending in Latin America, 1980–92. *American Political Science Review*, 93(4), 779–90.

Brown Thompson, Karen. (2002). Women's rights are human rights. In S. Khagram, J. V. Riker, & K. Sikkink, eds., *Restructuring World Politics: Transnational Social Movements, Networks, and Norms*. Minneapolis, MN: University of Minnesota Press, pp. 96–122.

Brownmiller, Susan. (1975). *Against Our Will: Men, Women and Rape*. New York, NY: Simon & Schuster.

Bruenig, Elizabeth. (2015, November 6). What Paul Ryan could learn from Pope Francis about maternity leave. *The New Republic*. Available at: https://new republic.com/article/123364/what-gop-could-learn-pope-francis-about-family-leave.

Brunell, Laura, & Johnson, Janet Elise. (2010). The New WAVE: how transnational feminist networks promote domestic violence reform in postcommunist Europe. In Katalin Fabian, ed., *The Politics of Domestic Violence in Postcommunist Europe and Eurasia: Local Activism, National Policies, and Global Forces*. Bloomington, IN: Indiana University Press, pp. 261–92.

Brush, Lisa D. (2003). *Gender and Governance*. Walnut Creek, CA: AltaMira Press.

(2011). *Poverty, Battered Women, and Work in U.S. Public Policy*. New York, NY: Oxford University Press.

Bunch, Charlotte. (2012). How women's rights became recognized as human rights. In Minky Worden, ed., *The Unfinished Revolution: Voices from the Global Fight for Women's Rights*. New York, NY: Seven Stories Press, pp. 29–39.

Butler, Judith. (1990). *Gender Trouble: Feminism and the Subversion of Identity*. New York, NY: Routledge.

(1994). Contingent foundations: feminism and the question of "postmodernism." In Steven Seidman, ed., *The Postmodern Turn: New Perspectives on Social Theory*. Cambridge: Cambridge University Press, pp. 153–70.

(2004). *Undoing Gender*. New York, NY: Routledge.

Bystydzienski, J. (1995). *Women in Electoral Politics: Lessons from Norway*. Santa Barbara, CA: Praeger.

Canada. Royal Commission on Equality in Employment; Abella, Rosalie S. (1984). *Report of the Commission on Equality in Employment*. Ottawa: Minister of Supply and Services Canada.

Careja, Romana, & Emmenneger, Patrick. (2009). The politics of public spending in post-communist countries. *East European Politics and Societies*, 23(2), pp. 165–84.

Carrillo, Roxanna, Connor, Melissa, Fried, Susana, Sandler, Joanne, & Waldorf, Lee. (2003). *Not a Minute More: Ending Violence against Women*. New York, NY: UNIFEM.

Casanova, Jose. (1994). *Public Religions in the Modern World*. Chicago, IL: University of Chicago Press.

Castles, Frances G. (1998). *Comparative Public Policy: Patterns of Post-War Transformation*. Northampton, MA: Edward Elgar Publishing.

Catholics for Choice. (2015). *You Are Not Alone: Catholic Women and the Abortion Decision*. Washington, DC: Catholics for Choice.

Celis, Karen, Childs, Sarah, Kantola, Johanna, & Krook, Mona Lena. (2008). Rethinking women's substantive representation. *Representation*, 44(2), 99–110.

Chalk, Rosemary, & King, Patricia. (1998). *Violence in Families*. Washington, DC: National Academy Press.

Chan-Tiberghien, Jennifer. (2004). Gender-skepticism or gender boom: poststructural feminisms, transnational feminisms, and the World Conference against Racism. *International Feminist Journal of Politics*, 6(3), 454–84.

Chant, Sylvia H. (2007). *Gender, Generation and Poverty: Exploring the Feminisation of Poverty in Africa, Asia and Latin America*. Northampton, MA: Edward Elgar Publishing.

Chappell, Louise. (2010). Comparative gender and institutions: directions for research. *Perspectives on Politics*, 8(1), 183–9.

Charrad, Mounira. (2001). *States and Women's Rights: The Making of Postcolonial Tunisia, Algeria, and Morocco*. Berkeley, CA: University of California Press.

Chasin, Alexandra. (2001). *Selling Out: The Gay and Lesbian Movement Goes to Market*. Basingstoke: Palgrave MacMillan.

Chaves, Mark, & Cann, David E. (1992). Regulation, pluralism, and religious market structure: explaining religions vitality. *Rationality and Society*, 4(3), 272–90.

Checkel, Jeffrey T. (1997). International norms and domestic politics: bridging the rationalist-constructivist divide. *European Journal of International Relations*, 3(4), 473–95.

Cheibub, J. A., Gandhi, J., & Vreeland, J. R. (2009). Democracy and dictatorship revisited. *Public Choice*, 143(1/2), 67–101.

Chen, Martha Alter. (2001). Women and informality: a global picture, the global movement. *Sais Review*, 21(1), 71–82.

  (2005). *Rethinking the Informal Economy: Linkages with the Formal Economy and the Formal Regulatory Environment*. Vol. 10. United Nations University, World Institute for Development Economics Research.

Cherif, Feryal M. (2010). Culture, rights, and norms: woman's rights reform in Muslim countries. *Journal of Politics*, 72(4), 1144–60.

Childs, S., & Krook, M. L. (2006). Should feminists give up on critical mass? A contingent yes. *Politics & Gender*, 2(4), 522–30.

Chitnis, Varsha, & Wright, Danaya. (2007). Legacy of colonialism: law and women's rights in India. *Washington & Lee Law Review*, 64, 1315.

Chivens, Thomas. (2010). The politics of awareness: making domestic violence visible in Poland. In Katalin Fabian, ed., *The Politics of Domestic Violence in Postcommunist Europe and Eurasia: Local Activism, National Policies, and Global Forces*. Bloomington, IN: Indiana University Press, pp. 171–94.

Cho, Mi-Kyung. (1994). Korea: the 1990 family law reform and the improvement of the status of women. *University of Louisville Journal of Family Law*, 33, 431.

Chronholm, Anders. (2009). Sweden: individualisation or free choice in parental leave? In Peter Moss & Sheila Kamerman, eds., *The Politics of Parental*

Leave Policies: Children, Parenting, Gender and the Labour Market. Bristol: Policy Press, pp. 227–41.

Clark, Catherine, Caetano, Raul, & Schafer, John. (1998). Rates of intimate partner violence in the United States. *American Journal of Public Health*, 88(11), 1702–4.

Clark, Martin, Hine, David, & Irving, R. E. M. (1974). Divorce – Italian style. *Parliamentary Affairs*, 27(June), 333–58.

Clark, Tom S., & Linzer, Drew A. (2015). Should I use fixed or random effects? *Political Science Research and Methods*, 3(2), 399–408.

Coates, Ta-Nehisi. (2015). *Between the World and Me*. New York, NY: Spiegel & Grau.

Cohen, Jean L. (2012). The politics and risks of the new legal pluralism in the domain of intimacy. *International Journal of Constitutional Law*, 10(2), 380–97.

Cohn, Jonathan. (2013). The hell of American day care: an investigation into the barely regulated, unsafe business of looking after our children. *New Republic*, 6, 15–29.

Collins, P. H., & Chepp, V. (2013). Intersectionality. In G. Waylen, K. Celis, J. Kantola, & S. L. Weldon, eds., *Oxford Handbook of Gender and Politics*. New York, NY: Oxford University Press, pp. 57–87.

Collins, Patricia Hill. (1990). *Black Feminist Thought: Knowledge, Consciousness, and the Politics of Empowerment*. Boston: UnwinHyman.

Committee on Women. (1978). What's Been Done? A Report on Progress towards Implementation of the Report by the Parliamentary Select Committee on Women's Rights, 1975, edited by the Committee on Women. New Zealand Parliament. Select Committee on Women's Rights. Wellington, NZ: Committee on Women.

Connell, R. W. (1987). *Gender and Power: Society, the Person, and Sexual Politics*. Stanford, CA.: Stanford University Press.

  (1990). The state, gender, and sexual politics. *Theory and Society*, 19(5), 507–44.

Cook, Alice Hanson, & Hayashi, Hiroko. (1980). *Working Women in Japan: Discrimination, Resistance, and Reform*. Ithaca, NY: New York State School of Industrial and Labor Relations.

Cook, Rebecca J. (1994). Feminism and the four principles. *Principles of Health Care Ethics*, 17, 193–206.

Cools, Sara, Fiva, Jon H., & Kirkebøen, Lars J. (2015). Causal effects of paternity leave on children and parents. *Scandinavian Journal of Economics*, 117(3), 801–28.

Coontz, Stephanie. (2016) *The Way We Never Were: American Families and the Nostalgia Trap*. New York, NY: Basic Books.

Corrales, Javier, & Pecheny, Mario. (2010). Introduction: the comparative politics of sexuality in Latin America. In Javier Corrales & Mario Pecheny, eds., *The Politics of Sexuality in Latin America*. Pittsburgh, PA: University of Pittsburgh Press, pp. 1–32.

Correa, Sonia, & Reichmann, Rebecca Lynn. (1994). *Population and Reproductive Rights: Feminist Perspectives from the South*. London: Zed Books.

Costain, Anne N. (1998). Women lobby Congress. In Anne N. Costain & Andrew S. McFarland, eds., *Social Movements and American Political Institutions*. Lanham, MD: Rowman and Littlefield, pp. 171–84.

(2005). Social movements as mechanisms for political inclusion. In Christina Wolbrecht & Rodney Hero, eds., *The Politics of Democratic Inclusion*. Philadelphia: Temple University Press, pp. 108–21.

Costain, Anne N., & Majstorovic, Steven. (1994). Congress, social movements and public opinion: multiple origins of women's rights legislation. *Political Research Quarterly*, 47(1), 111–35.

Cott, Nancy F. (1987). *The Grounding of Modern Feminism*. New Haven, CT: Yale University Press.

(2000). *Public Vows: A History of Marriage and the Nation*. Cambridge, MA: Harvard University Press.

Cotter, A. M. (2004). *Gender Injustice: An International Comparative Analysis of Equality in Employment*. Farnham: Ashgate.

Council of Europe. (2006). *Combating Violence against Women: Stocktaking Study on the Measures and Actions Taken in Council*. University of Osnabruck, Germany.

Coward, Harold G., Lipner, Julius, & Young, Katherine K. (1989). *Hindu Ethics: Purity, Abortion, and Euthanasia*. Albany, NY: SUNY Press.

Crenshaw, Kimberlé. (1993). Demarginalizing the intersection of race and sex. In D. Kelly Weisberg, ed., *Feminist Legal Theory: Foundations*. Philadelphia, PA: Temple University Press, pp. 383–98.

Creppell, Ingrid. (2010). Secularization: religion and the roots of innovation in the political sphere. In Ira Katznelson & Gareth Stedman Jones, eds., *Religion and the Political Imagination*. New York, NY: Cambridge University Press, pp. 23–45.

Crocker, Adriana M. (2005). *Gender Quota Laws in Latin America: Explaining Cross-National and Sub-National Diffusion*. Ph.D. Dissertation, Northern Illinois University.

Crowell, Nancy A., & Burgess, Ann W. (1996). *Understanding Violence against Women: Panel on Research on Violence against Women*. Commission on Behavioral and Social Sciences and Education, National Research Council. Washington, DC: The National Academies Press. http://doi.org/10.17226/5127.

Dahlerup, Drude. (2006). *Women in Politics: Electoral Quotas, Equality and Democracy*. London: Routledge.

Dahlerup, Drude, & Friedenvall, Lenita. (2005). Quotas as a fast track to equal representation for women. *International Feminist Journal of Politics*, 7(1), 26–48.

Daly, Mary, & Rake, Katherine. (2003). *Gender and the Welfare State: Care, Work and Welfare in Europe and the USA*. Cambridge: Polity Press.

Däubler, Thomas. (2008). Veto players and welfare state change: what delays social entitlement bills? *Journal of Social Policy*, 37(4), 683–706. doi: doi:10.1017/S0047279408002274

Davies, Miranda. (1994). *Women and Violence: Realities and Responses Worldwide*. London: Zed Books.

Dawson, Michael. (1994). *Behind the Mule: Race and Class in African-American Politics*. Princeton, NJ: Princeton University Press.

De Beauvoir, Simone. (1953). *Le deuxième sexe*. New York, NY: Random House LLC.

De la Fuente, Alejandro. (2001). *A Nation for All: Race, Inequality, and Politics in Twentieth-Century Cuba*. Chapel Hill, NC: University of North Carolina Press.

Deere, Carmen Diana, & León, Magdalena. (2001). *Empowering Women: Land and Property Rights in Latin America*. Pittsburgh, PA: University of Pittsburgh Press.

Devor, Aaron. (1989). *Gender Blending: Confronting the Limits of Duality*. Bloomington, IN: Indiana University Press.

Díez, Jordi. (2015). *The Politics of Gay Marriage in Latin America: Argentina, Chile, and Mexico*. New York, NY: Cambridge University Press.

Dobbin, Frank. (2009). *Inventing Equal Opportunity*. Princeton, NJ: Princeton University Press.

Domínguez, Jorge I. (1978). *Cuba: Order and Revolution*. Cambridge, MA: Belknap Press of Harvard University Press.

Donno, Daniela, & Russett, Bruce. (2004). Islam, authoritarianism, and female empowerment: what are the linkages? *World Politics*, 56(4), 582–607.

Dore, Elizabeth. (2000). One step forward, two steps back: gender and the state in the long nineteenth century. In Elizabeth Dore & Maxine Molyneux, eds., *Hidden Histories of Gender and the State in Latin America*. Durham, NC: Duke University Press, pp. 3–32.

Driessen, Michael D. (2010). Religion, state, and democracy: analyzing two dimensions of church–state arrangements. *Politics and Religion*, 3(1), 55–80.

Dryzek, John, Downes, David, Hunold, Christian, Sclosberg, David, & Hernes, Hans-Kristian. (2003). *Green States and Social Movements: Environmentalism in the United States, United Kingdom, Germany and Norway*. Oxford: Oxford University Press.

Dryzek, John S. (1990). *Discursive Democracy: Politics, Policy and Political Science*. Cambridge: Cambridge University Press.

Duerst-Lahti, Georgia. (1989). The government's role in building the women's movement. *Political Science Quarterly*, 104(2), 249–68.

Duncan, Simon. (1995). Theorizing European gender systems. *Journal of European Social Policy*, 5(4) 263–84.

   (1996). The diverse worlds of European patriarchy. In Maria Dolors Garcia-Ramon and Janice Monk, eds., *Women of the European Union: The Politics of Work and Daily Life*. New York, NY: Routledge, pp. 74–110.

Dunn, William N. (2011). *Public Policy Analysis*. Pearson Higher Ed.

Duverger, Maurice. (1954). *Political Parties: Their Organization and Activity in the Modern State*. New York, NY: John Wiley & Sons, Inc.

Ehrenreich, Barbara, & Hochschild, Arlie Russell. (2003). *Global Woman: Nannies, Maids, and Sex Workers in the New Economy*. Basingstoke: Palgrave Macmillan.

Ekberg, Gunilla. (2004). The Swedish law that prohibits the purchase of sexual services best practices for prevention of prostitution and trafficking in human beings. *Violence against Women*, 10(10), 1187–1218.

Ellingsæter, Anne Lise, & Leira, Arnlaug, eds. (2006). *Politicising Parenthood in Scandinavia: Gender Relations in Welfare States.* Bristol: Policy Press.

Elman, R. Amy. (1996). *Sexual Subordination and State Intervention: Comparing Sweden and the United States.* Oxford: Berghahn Books.

(2001). Unprotected by the Swedish welfare state revisited: assessing a decade of reforms for battered women. *Women's Studies International Forum,* 24(1), 39–52.

(2003). Refuge in reconstructed states: shelter movements in the United States, Britain, and Sweden. In Lee Ann Banaszak, Karen Beckwith, & Dieter Rucht, eds., *Women's Movements Facing the Reconfigured States.* New York, NY: Cambridge University Press, pp. 94–113.

(2007). *Sexual Equality in an Integrated Europe: Virtual Equality.* Basingstoke: Palgrave Macmillan.

Engels, Friedrich, & Morgan, Lewis Henry. (1978). *The Origin of the Family, Private Property and the State.* Moscow: Foreign Languages Publishing House.

Esping-Andersen, Gösta. (1990). *The Three Worlds of Welfare Capitalism.* Princeton, NJ: Princeton University Press.

(2009). *Incomplete Revolution: Adapting Welfare States to Women's New Roles.* Malden, MA: Polity Press.

Esposito, John L., & DeLong-Bas, Natana J. (2001). *Women in Muslim Family Law.* Syracuse, NY: Syracuse University Press.

Estevez-Abe, M., Iverson, T., & Soskice, D. (2001). Social protection and the formation of skills: a reinterpretation of the welfare state. In P. Hall & D. Soskice, eds., *Varieties of Capitalism: The Institutional Foundations of Comparative Advantage.* Oxford: Oxford University Press, pp. 145–83.

Estevez-Abe, Margarita. (2006). Gendering the varieties of capitalism. *World Politics,* 59(1), 142–75.

Estrich, Susan. (1987). *Real Rape.* Cambridge, MA: Harvard University Press.

Eurobarometer Survey. (2010, October). Retrieved from http://ec.europa.eu/ public_opinion/ archives/ebs/ebs_127_en.pdf.

Fabian, Katalin. (2010). *Domestic Violence in Postcommunist States.* Bloomington, IN: Indiana University Press.

Fausto-Sterling, A. (1993). The five sexes: why male and female are not enough. *The Sciences,* March/April, 20–4.

Ferree, Myra Marx. (2002). *Shaping Abortion Discourse: Democracy and the Public Sphere in Germany and the United States.* New York, NY: Cambridge University Press.

Finnemore, Martha, & Sikkink, Kathryn. (1998). International norm dynamics and political change. *International Organization,* 52(Autumn), 887–917.

Fish, M. Steven. (2002). Islam and authoritarianism. *World Politics,* 55(1), 4–37.

Fisher, Bonnie S., Cullen, Francis T., & Turner, Michael G. (2000). The sexual victimization of college women. *NIJ Research Report.* Retrieved from www/ ncjrs.gov/pdffiles1/nij/182369.pdf.

Forester, Summer. (2016). *The Social Policy Paradox: Securitization, Policy Agendas, and the Family Protection Act in Jordan.* Paper presented at the American Political Science Association Annual Meeting, Philadelphia, PA, USA.

Fox, Jonathan. (2008). *A World Survey of Religion and the State.* New York, NY: Cambridge University Press.

(2013). *An Introduction to Religion and Politics.* New York, NY: Routledge.

Franceschet, Susan. (2010). Explaining domestic violence policy outcomes in Chile and Argentina. *Latin American Politics and Society,* 52(3), 1–29.

Franzoni, Juliana Martínez. (2008). Welfare regimes in Latin America: capturing constellations of markets, families, and policies. *Latin American Politics and Society,* 50(2), 67–100.

Franzoni, Juliana Martínez, & Voorend, Koen. (2011). Who cares in Nicaragua? A care regime in an exclusionary social policy context. *Development and Change,* 42(4), 995–1022.

Fraser, Nancy. (1997). *Justice Interruptus: Critical Reflections on the "Postsocialist" Condition.* New York, NY: Routledge.

(2000). Rethinking recognition. *New Left Review,* 3, 107–20.

(2001). Recognition without ethics? *Theory, Culture, and Society,* 18(2–3), 321–42.

(2003). Social justice in the age of identity politics: redistribution, recognition, and particpation. In Nancy Fraser & Axel Honneth, eds., *Redistribution or Recognition? A Political-Philosophical Exchange.* New York, NY: Verso, pp. 7–109.

(2007). Feminist politics in the age of recognition: a two-dimensional approach to gender justice. *Studies in Social Justice,* 1(1), 23–35.

Freedom House. (2011). *Freedom in the World 2011.* New York, NY: Freedom House.

Freeman, Jo. (2008). *We Will Be Heard: Women's Struggles for Political Power in the United States.* Lanham, MD: Rowman & Littlefield Publishers.

Friedman, Elisabeth J. (1995). Women's human rights: the emergence of a movement perspective. In J. Peters & A. Wolper, eds., *Women's Rights, Human Rights: International Feminist Perspectives.* New York, NY: Routledge, pp. 18–35.

(2003). Gendering the agenda: the impact of the transnational women's rights movement at the UN Conferences of the 1990s. *Women's Studies International Forum,* 26(4), 313–331.

(2009). Re(gion)alizing Women's Human Rights in Latin America. *Politics & Gender,* 5, 349–75.

(2012). Constructing "the same rights with the same names": the impact of Spanish norm diffusion on marriage equality in Argentina. *Latin American Politics and Society,* 54(4), 29–59.

Fuchs, Victor R. (1990). *Women's Quest for Economic Equality.* Cambridge, MA: Harvard University Press.

Fuess, Harald. (2004). *Divorce in Japan: Family, Gender, and the State, 1600–2000.* Stanford, CA: Stanford University Press.

Garay, Candelaria. (2016). *Social Policy Expansion in Latin America.* New York, NY: Cambridge University Press.

Garey, Anita Ilta, & Townsend, Nicholas W. (1996). Kinship, courtship, and child maintenance law in Botswana. *Journal of Family and Economic Issues,* 17(2), 189–203.

References   315

Gelb, Joyce. (1989). *Feminism and Politics: A Comparative Perspective*. Berkeley, CA: University of California Press.
    (2003). *Gender Policies in Japan and the United States: Comparing Women's Movements, Rights and Politics*. New York, NY: Palgrave.
Gelb, Joyce, & Palley, Marian Lief. (1982). *Women and Public Policies*. Princeton, NJ: Princeton University Press.
    (1996). *Women and Public Policies: Reassessing Gender Politics*. Charlottesville, VA: University of Virgina Press.
Gerhard, Roberto, & Staab, Silke. (2010). *Childcare Service Expansion in Chile and Mexico: For Women or Children or Both?* Gender and Development Programme Paper No 10, May 2010. United Nations Research Institute for Socail Development (UNRISD). Geneva: UNRISD.
Gerntholtz, Liesl, Gibbs, Andrew, & Willan, Samantha. (2011). The African women's protocol: bringing attention to reproductive rights and the MDGs. *PLoS Med*, 8(4), e1000429.
Gill, Anthony. (1998). *Rendering unto Caesar: The Catholic Church and the State in Latin America*. Chicago, IL: University of Chicago Press.
    (2001). Religion and comparative politics. *Annual Review of Political Science*, 4, 17–138.
Githens, Marianne, & Stetson, Dorothy McBride. (2013). *Abortion Politics: Public Policy in Cross-Cultural Perspective*. New York, NY: Routledge.
Glendon, Mary Ann. (1987). *Abortion and Divorce in Western Law*. Cambridge, MA: Harvard Unversity Press.
    (1989). *The Transformation of Family Law*. Chicago, IL: University of Chicago Press.
Glendon, Mary Ann, Gordon, Michael, & Osakwe, Christopher. (1985). *Comparative Legal Systems*. St. Paul, MN: West Publishing.
Global Network. (2009). *Decent Work Conditions in Egypt 2009*. Solidar. www.solidar.all2all.org/IMG/pdf/e1_decent_work_conditions_in_egypt_2009.pdf.
Godoy, Lorena. (2004). *Understanding Poverty from a Gender Perspective*. Santiago: CEPAL.
Goetz, Anne Marie. (1998). Women in politics and gender equity in policy: South Africa & Uganda. *Review of African Political Economy*, 25(76), 241–62.
Goldin, Claudia. (2014). A grand gender convergence: its last chapter. *American Economic Review*, 104(4), 1091–1119.
Goldman, Alvin L. (1970). *Ancient Polynesian Society*. Englewood Cliffs, NJ: Prentice Hall.
Goodey, J. (2004). Sex trafficking in women from Central and East European countries: promoting a "victim-centered" and "women-centered" approach to criminal justice. *Feminist Review*, 76, 26–45.
Gornick, Janet C., & Meyers, Marcia K. (2003). *Families That Work: Policies for Reconciling Parenthood and Employment*. New York, NY: Russell Sage.
    (2008). Creating gender egalitarian societies: an agenda for reform. *Politics & Society*, 36, 313–49.
Gotell, Lise. (1998). Violence against women: some implications for feminist politics and women's citizenship. In Manon Tremblay and Caroline Andrew,

eds., *Women and Political Representation in Canada*. Ottawa: University of Ottawa Press, pp. 39–84.

Gough, Ian. (2004). Welfare regimes in development contexts: a global and regional analysis. In Ian Gough & Geof Wood, eds., *Insecurity and Welfare Regimes in Asia, Africa and Latin America: Social Policy in Development Contexts*. Cambridge, MA: Cambridge University Press, pp. 15–48.

Gouws, Amanda, & Galgut, Hayley. (2016). Twenty years of the Constitution: reflecting on citizenship and gender justice. *Agenda: Empowering Women for Gender Equity*, 30(1), 3–9.

Graham-Kevan, N., & Archer, J. (2003). Intimate terrorism and common couple violence: a test of Johnson's predictions in four British samples. *Journal of Interpersonal Violence*, 18(11), 1247–70.

Greenfeld, Lawrence. (1997). *Sex Offenses and Offenders: An Analysis of Data on Rape and Sexual Assault*. Washington, DC: US Department of Justice, Office of Justice Programs.

Grey, Sandra. (2002). Does size matter? Critical mass and New Zealand's women MPs. *Parliamentary Affairs*, 55(1), 19–29.

Grim, Brian J., & Finke, Roger. (2006). International religion indices: government regulation, government favoritism, and social regulation of religion. *Interdisciplinary Journal of Research on Religion*, 2(1), 1–40.

Grzymała-Busse, Anna. (2015). *Nations under God: How Churches Use Moral Authority to Influence Policy*. Princeton, NJ: Princeton University Press.

The Guardian. (2015). Chinese police release feminist activists. US edition, World section, April 13, 2015.

Haas, Liesl. (2006). The rules of the game: feminist policymaking in Chile. *Política. Revista de Ciencia Política*, 46, pp. 199–225.

(2010). *Feminist Policymaking in Chile*. University Park, PA: Pennsylvania State University Press.

Haas, Linda. (1992). *Equal Parenthood and Social Policy: A Study of Parental Leave in Sweden*. Albany, NY: SUNY Press.

Haas, Linda, & Hwang, C. Philip. (2008). The impact of taking parental leave on fathers' participation in childcare and relationships with children: lessons from Sweden. *Community, Work and Family*, 11(1), 85–104.

Habermas, Jürgen. (1996). *Between Facts and Norms: Contributions to a Discourse Theory of Law and Democracy*. Cambridge, MA: MIT Press.

Haggard, Stephan, & Kaufman, Robert R. (2008). *Development, Democracy, and Welfare States: Latin America, East Asia, and Eastern Europe*. Princeton, NJ: Princeton University Press.

Hagopian, Frances. (2008). Latin American Catholicism in an age of religious and political pluralism: a framework for analysis. *Comparative Politics*, 40(2), 149–68.

(2009). Social Justice, moral values, or institutional interests? Church responses to the democratic challenge in Latin America. In Frances Hagopian, ed., *Religious Pluralism, Democracy, and the Catholic Church in Latin America*. Notre Dame, IN: University of Notre Dame, pp. 257–332.

Hajjar, Lisa. (2004). Religion, state power, and domestic violence in Muslim societies: a framework for comparative analysis. *Law & Social Inquiry*, 29(1) (Winter), 1–38.

Hall, Peter. (1993). Policy paradigms, social learning, and the state: the case of economic policymaking in Britain. *Comparative Politics*, 25(3), 275–96.

Hall, P., & Soskice, D. (2001). *Varieties of Capitalism: The Institutional Foundations of Comparative Advantage*. New York, NY: Oxford University Press.

Halley, Janet, & Rittich, Kerry. (2010). Critical directions in comparative family law: Genealogies and contemporary studies of family law exceptionalism. *The American Journal of Comparative Law*, 58, 753–75.

Halperin-Kaddari, Ruth. (2003). *Women in Israel: A State of Their Own*. Philadelphia, PA: University of Pennsylvania Press.

Hamayotsu, Kikue. (2003). Politics of Syariah reform: the making of the state religio-legal apparatus. In Virginia Hooker and Norani Othman, eds., *Malaysia: Islam, Society and Politics*. Singapore: Institute of Southeast Asian Studies (ISEAS), pp. 55–79.

Hancock, Ange-Marie. (2007). When multiplication doesn't equal quick addition: examining intersectionality as a research paradigm. *Perspectives on Politics*, 1, 63–79.

(2016). *Intersectionality: An Intellectual History*. New York, NY: Oxford University Press.

Hansen, Susan B. (1993). Differences in public policies toward abortion: electoral and policy context. In Malcolm Goggin, ed., *Understanding the New Politics of Abortion*. Newbury Park, CA: Sage, pp. 222–48.

Harris, Angela P. (1990). Race and essentialism in feminist legal theory. *Stanford Law Review*, 42(3), pp. 581–616.

Hasan, Zoya. (2010). Gender, religion, and democratic politics in India. *Third World Quarterly*, 31(6), 939–54.

Hassim, Shireen. (2003). The gender pact and democratic consolidation: Institutionalizing gender equality in the South African state. *Feminist Studies*, 29(3), 505–28.

Hatem, M. F. (1992). Economic and political liberation in Egypt and the demise of state feminism. *International Journal of Middle East Studies*, 24(2), 231–51.

Hawkesworth, Mary. (2013). Sex, gender, and sexuality: From naturalized presumption to analytical categories. In Georgina Waylen et al., eds., *Oxford Handbook of Gender and Politics*. New York, NY: Oxford University Press, pp. 31–56.

Hayashi, H. (2005). *Labour Law, Work and Family*. New York, NY: Oxford University Press.

Hazard, John N. (1939). Law and the Soviet family. *Wisconsin Law Review* [1939], 224.

Hegel, G. W. F. (1999). *Elements of the Philosophy of Right* (Allen W. Wood, ed.). Cambridge: Cambridge University Press.

Heise, L., Ellsberg, M., & Gottemoeller, M. (1999). *Ending Violence against Women*, vol. 11. Baltimore, MD: John Hopkins Unviersity School of Public Health, Population Information Program.

Heise, Lori, & Germain, Adrienne. (1994). *Violence against Women: The Hidden Health Burden.* Washington, DC: World Bank.

Henderson, Ailsa, & White, Linda A. (2004). Shrinking welfare states? Comparing maternity leave benefits and child care programs in European Union and North American welfare states, 1985–2000. *Journal of European Public Policy,* 11(3), 497–519.

Hessini, Leila. (2007). Abortion and Islam: policies and practice in the Middle East and North Africa. *Reproductive Health Matters,* 15(29), 75–84.

Heston, Alan, Robert Summers, & Bettina Aten. (2006). Penn World Table Version 6.2, Center for International Comparisons of Production, Income and Prices at the University of Pennsylvania, September.

Hobcraft, John. (1993). Women's education, child welfare, and child survival: a review of the evidence. *Health Transition Review,* 3(1), 159–75.

Hochschild, Arlie Russell, & Machung, A. (1989). *The Second Shift.* New York, NY: Penguin Books.

Hoff, Joan. (1991). *Law Gender and Injustice: A Legal History of U.S. Women.* New York: New York University Press.

Holland, Alisha (2016). Forbearance. *American Political Science Review,* 110(2), 232–46.

(2017). *Forbearance as Redistribution: The Politics of Informal Welfare in Latin America.* New York, NY: Cambridge University Press.

Hook, J. (2006). Men's unpaid work in 20 countries, 1965–1998. *American Sociologcal Review,* 71, 639–660.

Hooker, Juliet. (2005). Indigenous inclusion/black exclusion: Race, ethnicity and multicultural citizenship in Latin America. *Journal of Latin American Studies,* 37(2), 285–310.

Howell, Jude. (2003). Women's organizations and civil society in China making a difference. *International Feminist Journal of Politics,* 5(2), 191–215.

Hrycak, Alexandra. (2010). Orange harvest? Women's activism and civil society in Ukraine, Belarus and Russia since 2004. *Canadian–American Slavic Studies,* 44(1–2), 151–77.

Htun, Mala. (1998). *Laws and Public Policies to Prevent and Punish Violence against Women in Latin America.* Unpublished paper. Weatherhead Center for International Affairs, Harvard University.

(2003). *Sex and the State: Abortion, Divorce, and the Family under Latin American Dictatorships and Democracies.* New York, NY: Cambridge University Press.

(2004). From "racial democracy" to affirmative action: changing state policy on race in Brazil. *Latin American Research Review,* 39(1), 60–89.

(2005). What it means to study gender and the state. *Politics & Gender,* 1(1), 157.

(2007). Gender equality in transition polities: comparative perspectives on Cuba. In Marifeli Pérez-Stable, ed., *Looking Forward: Comparative Perspectives on Cuba's Transition* Notre Dame, IN: University of Notre Dame Press, pp. 119–37.

(2009). Life, liberty, and family values: church and state in the struggle over Latin America's social agenda. In Frances Hagopian, ed. *Religious Pluralism,*

Democracy, and the Catholic Church in Latin America. Notre Dame, IN: University of Notre Dame Press, pp. 335–64.

(2016). *Inclusion without Representation in Latin America: Gender Quotas and Ethnic Reservations*. New York, NY: Cambridge University Press.

Htun, Mala, & Jensenius, Francesca Refsum. (2016a). *Institutionalizing Gender Equality: Anti-discrimination Laws and Social Norms in Mexico*. Paper presented at the Midwest Political Science Association Annual Meeting, April 7–10, Chicago, IL.

(2016b). *Violence against Women as a Violation of Human Rights? Legal Power and the Resilence of Social Norms in Mexico*. Paper presented at the American Political Science Association Annual Meeting, September 1–4, Philadelphia, PA.

Htun, Mala, O'Brien, Cheryl, & Weldon, S. Laurel. (2014). Movilización feminista y políticas sobre violencia contra las mujeres. *Foreign Affairs Latinoamérica*, 14(1), 2–13.

Htun, Mala, & Ossa, Juan Pablo. (2013). Political inclusion of marginalized groups: indigenous reservations and gender parity in Bolivia. *Politics, Groups, and Identities*, 1(1), 4–25.

Htun, Mala, & Piscopo, Jennifer. (2010). *Presence without empowerment? Women and politics in Latin America and the Caribbean*. Conflict Prevention and Peace Forum, Social Science Research Council, New York, NY.

Htun, Mala, & Power, Timothy J. (2006). Gender, parties, and support for equal rights in the Brazilian congress. *Latin American Politics and Society*, 48(4), 83–104.

Htun, Mala, Weldon, Laurel, & O'Brien, Cheryl (2010). *Women's rights in Nigeria*. Paper presented at the Midwest Political Association Annual Meeting, Chicago.

Htun, Mala, & Weldon, S. Laurel. (2010). When do governments promote women's rights? A framework for the comparative analysis of sex equality policy. *Perspectives on Politics*, 8(1), 207–16.

(2012). The civic origins of progressive policy change: combating violence against women in global perspective, 1975–2005. *American Political Science Review*, 106(3), 548–569.

(2015). Religious power, the state, women's rights, and family law. *Politics & Gender*, 11, 1–27.

Huber, Evelyne, & Stephens, John D. (2001). *Development and Crisis of the Welfare State: Parties and Policies in Global Markets*. Chicago, IL: University of Chicago Press.

(2012). *Democracy and the Left: Social Policy and Inequality in Latin America*. Chicago, IL: University of Chicago Press.

Hudson, Valerie M., & Den Boer, Andrea M. (2004). *Bare Branches: The Security Implications of Asia's Surplus Male Population*. Cambridge, MA: MIT Press.

Hug, Simon. (2003). Selection bias in comparative research: the case of incomplete data sets. *Political Analysis*, 11(3), 255–74.

Human Rights Watch. (2014). *World Report 2014: China*. Retrieved from www .hrw.org/world-report/2014/country-chapters/china-and-tibet.

Hussin, Iza. (2007). The pursuit of the Perak Regalia: Islam, law, and the politics of authority in the colonial state. *Law & Social Inquiry*, 32(3), 759–88.

Iannaccone, Laurence R. (1991). The consequences of religious market regulation: Adam Smith and the economics of religion. *Rationality and Society*, 3(2), 156–77.

Iannaccone, Laurence R., Finke, Roger, & Stark, Rodney. (1997). Deregulating religion: the economics of church and state. *Economic Inquiry*, 35(2), 350–64.

ICHRP. (2009). *When Legal Worlds Overlap: Human Rights, State, and Non-State Law*. Versoix, Switzerland: International Council on Human Rights Policy.

Ihsan, Fatimah, & Zaidi, Yasmin. (2006). The Interplay of CEDAW, National Laws and Customary Practices in Pakistan: A Literature Review. *Conceptualising Islamic Law, CEDAW and Women's Human Rights in Plural Legal Settings: A Comparative Analysis of Application of CEDAW in Bangladesh, India and Pakistan*. New Delhi: UNIFEM Regional Office, pp. 200–63.

Incite Women of Color against Violence. (2007). *The Revolution Will Not Be Funded: Beyond the Non-Profit Industrial Complex*. Cambridge, MA: South End Press.

Inglehart, Ronald, & Norris, Pippa. (2003). *Rising Tide: Gender Equality and Cultural Change around the World*. New York, NY: Cambridge University Press.

(2004). *Sacred and Secular: Religion and Poltics Worldwide*. New York, NY: Cambridge University Press.

International Labor Organization (ILO). (2010a). *Maternity at Work: A Review of National Legislation* (2nd edn.). Geneva: International Labour Organization.

(2010b). *Women in Labour Markets: Measuring Progress and Identifying Challenges*. Geneva: ILO.

Inter-Parliamentary Union. (2011). Women in national parliaments, www.ipu .org/wmn-e/world.htm.

Iversen, Torben, & Rosenbluth, Frances. (2006). The political economy of gender: explaining cross-national variation in the gender division of labor and the gender voting gap. *American Journal of Political Science*, 50(1), 1–19.

(2010). *Women, Work, and Politics: The Political Economy of Gender Inequality*. New Haven, CT: Yale University Press.

Jackman, Robert W. (1985). Cross-national statistical research and the study of comparative politics. *American Journal of Political Science* 29(1), 161–182.

Jacobs, Rachel. (2017). *Cooperative Reorganization in the Village: The Regulation of Marriage and Collective Living during Democratic Kampuchea*. Paper presented at the Southern Political Science Association, New Orleans, LA.

Jawad, Haifaa. (1998). *The Rights of Women in Islam: An Authentic Approach*. New York, NY: St. Martin's Press.

Jelen, Ted Gerard, & Wilcox, Clyde. (2002). Religion: the one, the few, and the many. In Ted Gerard Jelen & Clyde Wilcox, eds., *Religion and Politics in Comparative Perspective: The One, the Few, and the Many*. Cambridge: Cambridge University Press, pp. 1–26.

Jenson, Jane. (1995). Extending the boundaries of citizenship: women's movements of Western Europe. In Amrita Basu, ed., *The Challenge of Local Feminisms*. Boulder, CO: Westview, pp. 405–34.

Jhappan, Radha. (2002). *Women's Legal Strategies in Canada*. Toronto: University of Toronto Press.

Joachim, Jutta. (1999). Shaping the human rights agenda: the case of violence against women. In M. K. Meyer & E. Pru, eds., *Gender Politics in Global Governance*. Lanham, MD: Rowman & Littlefield, pp. 142–60.

(2003). Framing issues and seizing opportunities: the UN, NGOs, and women's rights. *International Studies Quarterly*, 47, 247–74.

Johnson, Holly. (1995). Seriousness, type and frequency of violence against wives part 3. In M. Valverde, L. MacLeod, & K. Johnson, eds., *Wife Assault and the Canadian Criminal Justice System: Issues and Policies*. Toronto: University of Toronto, pp. 125–47.

Johnson, Holly, & Sacco, Vincent. (1995). Researching violence against women: Statistics Canada's national survey. *Canadian Journal of Criminology*, 37, 281.

Johnson, Janet Elise. (2007). Domestic violence politics in post-Soviet states. *Social Politics: International Studies in Gender, State and Society*, 14(3), 380–405.

Johnson, Janet Elise, & Zaynullina, Gulnara. (2010). Global feminism, foreign funding, and Russian writing about domestic violence. In Katalin Fabian, ed., *Domestic Violence in Postcommunist States: Local Activism, National Policies, and Global Forces*. Bloomington, IN: Indiana University Press, pp. 78–110.

Johnson, Kay Ann. (2009). *Women, the Family, and Peasant Revolution in China*. Chicago, IL: University of Chicago Press.

Jones, Mark P. (2009). Gender quotas, electoral laws, and the election of women: Evidence from the Latin American vanguard. *Comparative Political Studies*, 42(1), 56–81.

Jordan-Zachery, Julia. (2007). Am I a black woman or a woman who is black? Some thoughts on the meaning of intersectionality. *Politics & Gender*, 3(2), 254–63.

Kabeer, Naila. (1994). *Reversed Realities: Gender Hierarchies in Development Thought*. London: Verso.

(2012). Women's economic empowerment and inclusive growth: labour markets and enterprise development. *International Development Research Centre*, 44(10), 1–70.

Kahl, Sigrun. (2005). The religious roots of modern poverty policy: Catholic, Lutheran and Reformed Protestant traditions compared. *European Journal of Sociology*, 46(1), 91–126.

Kalyvas, Stathis. (1996). *The Rise of Christian Democracy in Europe*. Ithaca, NY: Cornell University Press.

Kamerman, Sheila B., & Moss, Peter. (2009). *The Politics of Parental Leave Policies: Children, Parenting, Gender and the Labour Market*. Bristol: Policy Press.

Kandiyoti, Deniz. (1991a). Introduction. In Deniz Kandiyoti, ed., *Women, Islam and the State*. Philadelphia, PA: Temple University Press, pp. 1–22.

(1991b). End of empire: Islam, nationalism and women in Turkey. In Deniz Kandiyoti, ed. *Women, Islam and the State*. Philadelphia, PA: Temple University Press, pp. 22–47.

Kang, Alice J. (2015). *Bargaining for Women's Rights: Activism in an Aspiring Muslim Democracy*. Minneapolis, MN: University of Minnesota Press.

Kantola, Johanna. (2006). *Feminists Theorize the State*. Basingstoke: Palgrave MacMillan.

Karshenas, Massoud, & Moghadam, Valentine M. (2009). Bringing social policy back in: a look at the Middle East and North Africa. *International Journal of Social Welfare*, 18(s1), S52–S61.

Katzenstein, Mary Fainsod. (1989). Organizing against violence: strategies of the Indian women's movement. *Pacific Affairs*, 62(1), 53–71.

(1995). Discursive politics and feminist activism in the Catholic Church. In Myra Marx Ferree & Patricia Yancey Martin, eds., *Feminist Organizations: Harvest of the New Women's Movement*. Philadelphia, PA: Temple University Press, pp. 35–52.

(1998). *Faithful and Fearless*. Ithaca, NY: Cornell University Press.

Katznelson, Ira, & Stedman-Jones, Gareth. (2010). Introduction: multiple secularities. In Ira Katznelson and Gareth Stedman-Jones, eds., *Religion and the Political Imagination*. New York, NY: Cambridge University Press, pp. 1–22.

Kaufman, Robert R., & Segura-Ubiergo, Alex. (2001). Globalization, domestic politics, and social spending in Latin America: a time-series cross-section analysis, 1973–97. *World Politics*, 53(4), 553–87.

Kaufmann, Daniel, Kraay, Aart, & Mastruzzi, Massimo. (2011). The worldwide governance indicators: methodology and analytical issues. *Hague Journal on the Rule of Law*, 3(2), 220–46.

Keck, Margaret, & Sikkink, Kathryn. (1998). *Activists beyond Borders: Advocacy Networks in Transnational Politics*. Ithaca, NY: Cornell University Press.

Kenworthy, Lane, & Malami, Melissa. (1999). Gender inequality in political representation: a worldwide comparative analysis. *Social Forces*, 78(1), 235–68.

Kerber, Linda K. (1998). *No Constitutional Right to Be Ladies: Women and the Obligations of Citizenship*. New York, NY: Hill and Wang.

Kerbsbergen, Kees van, & Philip, Manow. (2009). *Religion, Class Coalitions, and Welfare States*. New York, NY: Cambridge University Press.

Khagram, Sanjeev, Riker, James V., & Sikkink, Kathryn. (2002). *Restructuring World Politics: Transnational Social Movements, Networks, and Norms*. Minneapolis, MN: University of Minnesota Press.

Kimani, Mary. (2016). Taking on violence against women in Africa: international norms and local activism start to alter laws attitudes. *Africa Renewal*, 21(2), 4.

Kingdon, John W. (1984). *Agendas, Alternatives, and Public Policies*. Boston, MA: Little, Brown.

Kingstone, Peter, Young, Joseph K, & Aubrey, Rebecca. (2013). Resistance to privatization: why protest movements succeed and fail in Latin America. *Latin American Politics and Society*, 55(3), 93–116.

Kitschelt, Herbert, Hawkins, Kirk A., Luna, Juan Pablo, Rosas, Guillermo, & Zechmeister, Elizabeth J. (2010). *Latin American Party Systems*. New York, NY: Cambridge University Press.

Kittilson, Miki Caul. (2008). Representing women: the adoption of maternity leave in comparative perspective. *Journal of Politics*, 70(2), 323–34.

Kittilson, Miki Caul, Sandholz, Wayne, & Gray, Mark. (2006). Women and globalization: a study of 180 countries, 1975–2000. *International Organization*, 60(2), 293–333.

Kittilson, Miki Caul, & Schwindt-Bayer, Leslie A. (2012). *The Gendered Effects of Electoral Institutions: Political Engagement and Participation*. New York, NY: Oxford University Press.

Klotz, Audie. (1995). Norms reconstituting interests: global racial equality and US sanctions against South Africa. *International Organization*, 49(3), 451–78.

Knapp, Kiyoko Kamio. (1995). Still office flowers: Japanese women betrayed by the Equal Employment Opportunity Law. *Harvard Women's Law Journal*, 18, 83.

Kohn, Melvin L., ed. (1989). *Cross-National Research in Sociology*. Newbury Park: Sage.

Kollontai, Alexandra. (1977). Communism and the family. In *Selected Writings of Alexandra Kollontai* (trans. Alix Holt), www.marxists.org/archive/kollonta/1920/communism-family.htm.

Korpi, Walter. (1983). *The Democratic Class Struggle*. London: Routledge.

(2006). Power resources and employer-centered approaches in explanations of welfare states and varieties of capitalism: protagonists, consenters, and antagonists. *World Politics*, 58(2), 167–206.

Kotsadam, Andreas, & Finseraas, Henning. (2011). The state intervenes in the battle of the sexes: causal effects of paternity leave. *Social Science Research*, 40(6), 1611–22.

Koven, Seth, & Sonya Michel, eds. (1993). *Mothers of a New World: Maternalist Politics and the Origins of Welfare States*. New York, NY: Routledge.

Krook, Mona Lena. (2009). *Quotas for Women in Politics: Gender and Candidate Selection Worldwide*. New York, NY: Oxford University Press.

Krook, Mona Lena, & O'Brien, Diana Z. (2010). The politics of group representation: quotas for women and minorities worldwide. *Comparative Politics*, 42(3), 253–72.

Krook, Mona Lena, & Schwindt-Bayer, Leslie A. (2013). Electoral institutions. In Georgina Waylen, Karen Celis, Johanna Kantola, & S. Laurel Weldon, eds., *Oxford Handbook of Gender and Politics*. New York: Oxford University Press, pp. 554–78.

Landes, Joan B. (1988). *Women and the Public Sphere in the Age of the French Revolution*. Ithaca, NY: Cornell University Press.

Laqueur, Thomas Walter. (1990). *Making Sex: Body and Gender from the Greeks to Freud*. Cambridge, MA: Harvard University Press.

Lavrin, Asunción. (1998). *Women, Feminism, and Social Change in Argentina, Chile, and Uruguay, 1890–1940*, vol. 3. Lincoln, NE: University of Nebraska Press.

Layton, Azza Salama. (2000). *International Politics and Civil Rights Policies in the United States, 1941–1960*. New York, NY: Cambridge University Press.

Leira, Arnaug. (1992). *Welfare States and Working Mothers: The Scandinavian Experience.* Cambridge: Cambridge University Press.
  (1993). The "women-friendly" welfare state? The case of Norway and Sweden. In J. Lewis, ed., *Women and Social Policies in Europe: Work, Family and the State.* Brookfield, VT: Edward Elgar, pp. 49–71.
  (2002). *Working Parents and the Welfare State: Family Change and Policy Reform in Scandinavia.* New York, NY: Cambridge University Press.
Levinson, David. (1989). *Family Violence in Cross-Cultural Perspective.* Newbury Park, CA: Sage.
Levitsky, Steven, & Murillo, María Victoria. (2009). Variation in institutional strength. *Annual Review of Political Science*, 12, 115–33.
Levitsky, Steven, & Roberts, Kenneth M. (2011). Introduction. Latin America's left turn: a framework for analysis. In Steven Levitsky & Kenneth M. Roberts, eds., *The Resurgence of the Latin American Left.* Baltimore, MD: Johns Hopkins University Press, pp. 1–30.
Lewis, Jane. (1992). Gender and the development of welfare regimes. *Journal of European Social Policy*, 2(3), 159–73.
  ed. (1993). *Women and Social Policies in Europe: Work, Family and the State.* Brookfield, VT.: Edward Elgar.
  ed. (1998). *Gender, Social Care and Welfare State Restructuring in Europe.* Brookfield, VT: Ashgate.
Liebowitz, Debra J. (2002). Gendering (trans) national advocacy. *International Feminist Journal of Politics*, 4(2), 173–96.
Lindvert, Jessica. (2007). The rules of the game: organizing gender policies in Australia and Sweden. *Social Politics: International Studies in Gender, State & Society*, 14(2), 238–57.
Livingstone, Sonia. (2003). On the challenges of cross-national comparative media research. *European Journal of Communication*, 18(4), 477–500.
Locke, John. (1988). *Two Treaties of Government* (Peter Laslett, ed.). Cambridge: Cambridge University Press.
Loveman, Mara. (2014). *National Colors: Racial Classification and the State in Latin America.* New York, NY: Oxford University Press.
Lovenduski, Joni, & Outshoorn, Joyce, eds. (1986). *The New Politics of Abortion.* Newbury Park, CA. Sage Publications.
Lowi, Theodore. (1964). American business, public policy, case-studies, and political theory. *World Politics*, 16(4), 677–715.
Lozano, Genaro. (2013). The battle for marriage equality in Mexico, 2001–2011. In Jason Pierceson, Adriana Piatti-Crocker, & Shawn Schulenberg, eds., *Same-Sex Marriage in Latin America: Promise and Resistance.* Lanham, MD: Lexington Books, pp. 151–66.
Lugard, Lord Frederick JD. (2013). *The Dual Mandate in British Tropical Africa.* London: Routledge.
Luker, Kristin. (1984). *Abortion and the Politics of Motherhood.* Durham, NC: Duke University Press.
Lynch, Julia. (2006). *Age in the Welfare State: The Origins of Social Spending on Pensioners, Workers, and Children.* New York, NY: Cambridge University Press.

MacKay, F. (2014) Nested newness, institutional innovation and the gendered limits of change. *Politics & Gender*, 10(4), 549–71.

Mackie, Vera C. (2003). *Feminism in Modern Japan: Citizenship, Embodiment and Sexuality*. New York: Cambridge University Press.

MacKinnon, Catharine. (1989). *Toward a Feminist Theory of the State*. Cambridge, MA: Harvard University Press.

Mainwaring, Scott. (1986). *The Catholic Church and Politics in Brazil, 1916–1985*. Stanford, CA: Stanford University Press.

(1999). *Rethinking Party Systems in the Third Wave of Democratization: The Case of Brazil*. Stanford, CA: Stanford University Press.

Mainwaring, Scott, & Pérez-Liñán, Aníbal S. (2013). *Democracies and Dictatorships in Latin America: Emergence, Survival, and Fall*. New York, NY: Cambridge University Press.

Mainwaring, Scott, & Scully, Timothy. (1995). *Building Democratic Institutions: Party Systems in Latin America*. Stanford, CA: Stanford University Press.

Mamdani, M. (1996). *Citizen and Subject: Contemporary Africa and the Legacy of Late Colonialism*. Princeton, NJ: Princeton University Press.

Manjoo, Rashida. (2007). *The Recognition of Muslim Personal Laws in South Africa: Implications of Women's Human Rights*. Islamic Law and Law of the Muslim World Paper, 08–21.

Mansbridge, Jane (1986). *Why We Lost the ERA*. Chicago, IL: University of Chicago Press.

(1995). What is the feminist movement? In Myra Marx Ferree & Patricia Yancey Martin, eds., *Feminist Organizations: Harvest of the New Women's Movement*. Philadelphia, PA: Temple University Press, pp. 27–34.

(1999). Should blacks represent blacks and women represent women? A contingent "yes." *The Journal of Politics*, 61(3), 628–57.

Mansbridge, Jane, & Morris, Aldous. (2001). *Oppositional Consciousness: The Subjective Roots of Social Protest*. Chicago, IL: University of Chicago Press.

Mares, Isabela, & Carnes, Matthew E. (2009). Social policy in developing countries. *Annual Review of Political Science*, 12, 93.

Martinez, Manuela, & Schrottle, Monika. (2006). State of European research on the prevalence of interpersonal violence and its impact on health and human rights. CAHRV-Report 2006. Co-ordination Action on Human Rights Violations funded through the European Commission, 6th Framework Programme, Project No. 506348.

Marx, Anthony W. (1998). *Making Race and Nation: A Comparison of South Africa, the United States, and Brazil*. New York, NY: Cambridge University Press.

Massell, Gregory J. (1968). Law as an instrument of revolutionary change in a traditional milieu: the case of Soviet Central Asia. *Law and Society Review*, 2(2), 179–228.

Mazur, Amy G. (2002). *Theorizing Feminist Policy*. Oxford: Oxford University Press.

Mazur, Amy G., & McBride, Dorothy E. (2007). State feminism since the 1980s: from loose notion to operationalized concept. *Politics & Gender*, 3(4), 501–13.

McAdam, Doug, & Su, Yang. (2002). The war at home: antiwar and congressional voting, 1965 to 1973. *American Sociologcal Review*, 67(October), 696–721.

McAdam, Doug, Tarrow, Sidney, & Tilly, Charles. (2001). *Dynamics of Contention.* New York, NY: Cambridge University Press.

McBride, Dorothy, & Mazur, Amy. (2010). *The Politics of State Feminism.* Philadelphia, PA: Temple University Press.

(2011). Gender machineries worldwide. *Background Paper, World Development Report 2012.* Washington, DC: The World Bank.

Melby, Kari, Ravn, Anna-Birte, & Wetterberg, Christina Carlsson. (2009). *Gender Equality and Welfare Politics in Scandinavia: The Limits of Political Ambition?* Chicago, IL: University of Chicago Press.

Mentzer, M. S. (2002). The Canadian experience with employment equity legislation. *International Journal of Value-Based Management,* 15(1), 35–50.

Merry, Sally Engle. (2006). *Human Rights and Gender Violence: Translating International Law into Local Justice.* Chicago, IL: University of Chicago Press.

Meyer, David. (2005). Introduction: social movements and public policy. In D. S. Meyer, V. Jenness, & H. Ingram, eds., *Routing the Opposition: Social Movements, Public Policy and Democracy.* Minneapolis, MN: University of Minnesota Press, pp. 1–26.

Meyer, Mary K. (1999). Negotiating international norms: the Inter-American Commission on Women and the Convention on Violence against Women. In M. K. Meyer & E. Pru, eds., *Gender Politics in Global Governance.* Lanham, MD: Rowman and Littlefield, pp. 59–70.

Milazzo, Annamaria, & van de Walle, Dominique P. (2015). Women left behind? Poverty and headship in Africa. *Demography,* 54(3), 1–27.

Mink, Gwendolyn. (1998). *Welfare's End.* Ithaca, NY: Cornell University Press.

Minkenberg, Michael. (2002). Religion and public policy. *Comparative Political Studies,* 35(2), 221–47.

(2003). The policy impact of church-state relations: family policy and abortion in Britain, France, and Germany. *West European Politics,* 26(1), 195–217.

Minow, Martha. (1987). We, the family: constitutional rights and American families. *Journal of American History,* 74(3), 959–83.

Mir-Hosseini, Ziba. (1999). *Islam and Gender: The Religious Debate in Contemporary Iran.* Princeton, NJ: Princeton University Press.

(2006). Muslim women's quest for equality: between Islamic law and feminism. *Critical Inquiry,* 32(4), 629–45.

Mirescu, Alexander. (2011). *Communism and Communion Religious Policy, Church-Based Opposition and Free Space Development: A Comparative Study of East Germany, Poland and Yugoslavia from 1945 to 1989.* Ph.D. Dissertation, New School for Social Research.

Mirvahabi, Farin. (1975). The status of women in Iran. *Journal of Family Law,* 14, 383.

Mlundak, Guy. (2009). The law of equal opportunities in employment: between equality and polarization. *Comparative Labor Law and Policy Journal,* 30(2), 213–41.

Moghadam, Valentine. (2003). *Modernizing Women: Gender and Social Change in the Middle East* (2nd edn.). Boulder, CO: Westview.

(2005). *Globalizing Women: Transnational Feminist Networks*. Baltimore, MD: John Hopkins University Press.

(2009). *Globalization and Social Movements: Islamism, Feminism, and the Global Justice Movement*. Lanham, MD: Rowman & Littlefield.

Moghadam, Valentine, & Gheytanchi, Elham. (2010). Political Opportunities and Strategic Choices: Comparing Feminist Campaigns in Morocco and Iran. *Mobilization: An International Journal*, 15(3), 267–88.

Mohamad, Maznah. (2009). Islam and Family Legal Contests in Malaysia. *Asia Research Institute Working Paper Series*, 109.

(2010). Making majority, undoing family: law, religion and the Islamization of the state in Malaysia. *Economy and Society*, 39(3), 360–84.

Moi, Toril. (2001). *What Is a Woman? And Other Essays*. Oxford: Oxford University Press.

Molyneux, Maxine. (1985a). Family reform in socialist states: the hidden agenda. *Feminist Review*, 21, 47–64.

(1985b). Mobilization without emancipation? Women's interests, the state, and revolution in Nicaragua. *Feminist Studies*, 11(2), 227–54.

(1998). Analysing women's movements. *Development and Change*, 29(2), 219–45.

(2007). *Change and Continuity in Social Protection in Latin America*. UNRISD Ginebra.

Montoya, Celeste. (2009). International initiative and domestic reforms: European union efforts to combat violence against women. *Politics & Gender*, 5(3), 325–48.

(2010). The European Union, transnational advocacy and violence against women in post communist states. In Katalin Fabian, ed. *The Politics of Domestic Violence in Postcommunist Europe and Eurasia: Local Activism, National Policies, and Global Forces*. Bloomington, IN: Indiana University Press, pp. 293–307.

Morgan, Kimberly J. (2006). *Working Mothers and the Welfare State: Religion and the Politics of Work–Family Policies in Western Europe and the United States*. Stanford, CA: Stanford University Press.

(2008). The political path to a dual earner/dual carer society: pitfalls and possibilities. *Politics & Society*, 36(3), 403–20.

Morgan, Kimberly, & Ann Shola Orloff. (2016). Introduction. In Kimberly Morgan & Ann Shola Orloff, eds., *The Many Hands of the State*. New York, NY: Cambridge University Press, pp. 1–34.

Mottier, Veronique. (2013). Reproductive rights. In Georgina Waylen, ed., *The Oxford Handbook of Gender and Politics*. New York: NY: Oxford University Press, pp. 213–45.

Moustafa, Tamir. (2013). Islamic law, women's rights, and popular legal consciousness in Malaysia. *Law & Social Inquiry*, 38(1), 168–88.

Murungi, Lucyline Nkatha. (2015). Consolidating family law in Kenya. *European Journal of Law Reform*, 17, 317.

Musallam, Basim F. (1983). *Sex and Society in Islam: Birth Control before the Nineteenth Century*. New York, NY: Cambridge University Press.

Musawah. (2009). *Home Truths: A Global Report on Equality in the Muslim Family*. Kuala Lumpur: Musawah.
Muzaffar, Chandra. (1987). *Islamic Resurgence in Malaysia*. Petaling Jaya: Fajar Bakti.
Najmabadi, Afsaneh. (1991). Hazards of modernity and morality: women, state and ideology in contemporary Iran. In Deniz Kandiyoti, ed. *Women, Islam and the State*. Philadelphia, PA: Temple University Press, pp. 48–76.
Nasr, Seyyed Vali Reza. (2001). *Islamic Leviathan: Islam and the Making of State Power*. New York, NY: Oxford University Press.
Nayak, M. B., Byrne, C. A., Martin, M. K., & Abraham, A. G. (2003). Attitudes toward violence against women: a cross-national study. *Sex Roles*, 49, 333–42.
Neier, Aryeh. (2005). *Taking Liberties: Four Decades in the Struggle for Rights*. New York, NY: Public Affairs.
  (2012). *The International Human Rights Movement: A History*. Princeton, NJ: Princeton University Press.
Nelson, Sara. (1996). Constructing and negotiating gender in women's police stations in Brazil. *Latin American Perspectives*, 23(1), 131–48.
Neo, Jaclyn Ling-Chien. (2003). Anti-God, anti-Islam, and anti-Quran: expanding the range of participants and parameters in discourse over women's rights and Islam in Malaysia. *Pacific Basin Law Journal*, 21(29), 29–74.
Nicholson, Linda J. (1986). *Gender and History: The Limits of Social Theory in the Age of the Family*. New York, NY: Columbia University Press.
Nie, Jing-Bao. (2011). Non-medical sex-selective abortion in China: ethical and public policy issues in the context of 40 million missing females. *British Medical Bulletin*, 98(1), 7–20.
Niedzwiecki, Sara. (2014). The effect of unions and organized civil society on social policy: pension and health reforms in Argentina and Brazil, 1988–2008. *Latin American Politics and Society*, 56(4), 22–48.
  (2015). Social policy commitment in South America: the effect of organized labor on social spending from 1980 to 2010. *Journal of Politics in Latin America*, 7(2), 3–42.
  (Forthcoming). *Uneven Social Policies: The Politics of Subnational Variation in Latin America*. New York, NY: Cambridge University Press.
Norgren, Tiana. (2001). *Abortion before Birth Control: The Politics of Reproduction in Postwar Japan*. Princeton, NJ: Princeton University Press.
Norris, Pippa. (1987). *Politics and Sexual Equality: The Comparative Position of Women in Western Democracies*. Boulder, CO: Lynne Rienner.
O'Brien, E. (2004). The double-edged sword of women's organizing: poverty and the emergence of racial and class differences in women's political priorities. *Women & Politics*, 26(3/4), 25–56.
O'Brien, R., Goetz, A. M., Scholtem, J. A., & Williams, M. (2000). *Contesting Global Governance: Multilateral Economic Institutions and Global Social Movements*. New York, NY: Cambridge University Press.
O'Connor, Julia S., Orloff, Ann Shola, & Shaver, Sheila. (1999). *States, Markets, Families: Gender, Liberalism, and Social Policy in Australia, Canada, Great Britain and the United States*. Cambridge: Cambridge University Press.
Oduro, Abena D. (2010). *Formal and informal social protection in Sub-Saharan Africa*. Paper prepared for the Workshop "Promoting Resilience through

Social Protection in Sub-Saharan Africa," organised by the European Report on Development in Dakar, June 28–30, 2010.

OECD. (2015). *Social Institutions and Gender Index. 2014 Synthesis Report.* OECD Development Center, www.oecd.org/dev/development-gender/Bro chureSIGI2015-web.pdf.

Okin, Susan Moller. (1989). *Justice, Gender and the Family.* New York, NY: Basic Books.

(1999). *Is Multiculturalism Bad for Women?* Princeton, NJ: Princeton University Press.

Olsen, Frances E. (1985). The myth of state intervention in the family. *University of Michigan Journal of Law Reform,* 18(4), 835–43.

Omelicheva, Maria Y. (2011). *Counterterrorism Policies in Central Asia.* London: Routledge.

Orloff, Ann Shola. (1993). Gender and the social rights of citizenship: the comparative analysis of gender relations and welfare states. *American Sociological Review,* 58(3), 303–28.

Organization of the Islamic Conference (2006). Statement at the 65th General Assembly of the United Nations. www.un.org/womenwatch/daw/documents/ga65/Org-of-Islamic-Conference.

Othman, Norani, Anwar, Zainah, & Kasim, Zaitun Mohamed. (2005). Malaysia: Islamization, Muslim politics, and state authoritarianism. In Norani Othman, ed., *Muslim Women and the Challenge of Islamic Extremism.* Petaling Jaya, Malaysia: Sisters in Islam, pp. 78–108.

Outshoorn, Joyce. (1996). The stability of compromise: abortion politics in Western Europe. In Marianne Githens and Dorothy McBride Stetson, eds., *Abortion Politics: Public Policy in Cross-Cultural Perspective.* New York, NY: Routledge, pp. 145–64.

Panda, Pradeep, & Agarwal, Bina. (2005). Marital violence, human development and women's property status in India. *World Development,* 33(5), 823–50.

Parkinson, Loraine. (1989). Japan's equal employment opportunity law: an alternative approach to social change. *Columbia Law Review,* 89(3), 604–61.

Parmley, Suzette. (2001, February 19). Hopes and fear greet NJ Paid-Leave Bill. The Philadelphia Inquirer, p. A01.

Paschel, Tianna S. (2010). The right to difference: explaining Colombia's shift from color-blindness to the law of black communities. *American Journal of Sociology,* 116(3), 729–69.

Paxton, Pamela, Hughes, Melanie, & Green, Jennifer. (2006). The international women's movement and women's political representation, 1893–2003. *American Sociological Review,* 71(6), 898–920.

Pearce, Diana (1978). The feminization of poverty: women, work, and welfare. *The Urban Social Change Review,* 11(1–2), 28–36.

(1990). The feminization of poverty. *Journal for Peace and Justice Studies,* 2(1), 1–20.

Pereira, Charmaine, & Ibrahim, Jibrin. (2010). On the bodies of women: The common ground between Islam and Christianity in Nigeria. *Third World Quarterly,* 31(6), 921–37.

Phillips, Anne. (2012). Representation and inclusion. *Politics & Gender,* 8(4), 512–18.

Phillips, Roderick. (1991). *Untying the Knot: A Short History of Divorce*. Cambridge: Cambridge University Press.

Pierson, Paul. (1994). *Dismantling the Welfare State? Reagan, Thatcher, and the Politics of Retrenchment*. Cambridge: Cambridge University Press.

(1996). The new politics of the welfare state. *World Politics*, 48(2), 143–79.

(2004). *Politics in Time: History, Institutions, and Social Analysis*. Princeton, NJ: Princeton University Press.

Pitanguy, Jacqueline. (1996). Movimento de mujeres y políticas públicas en Brasil. In N. Lycklama, V. Vargas, S. Wieringa, & J. Pitangui, eds., *Triángulo de poder*. Bogotá: TM Editores, pp. 55–80.

Piven, Frances, & Cloward, Richard. ([1971] 1993). *Regulating the Poor: The Functions of Public Welfare*. New York, NY: Vintage Books.

Pressman, Jeffrey L., & Aaron B. Wildavsky. (1979). *Implementation: How Great Expectations in Washington Are Dashed in Oakland : Or, Why It's Amazing that Federal Programs Work At All, This Being a Saga of the Economic Development Administration as Told By Two Sympathetic Observers Who Seek to Build Morals on a Foundation of Ruined Hopes*. Berkeley, CA: University of California Press.

Pribble, Jennifer. (2013). *Welfare and Party Politics in Latin America*. New York, NY: Cambridge University Press.

Putnam, Robert D. (2016). *Our Kids: The American Dream in Crisis*. New York, NY: Simon and Schuster.

Putnam, Robert D., Leonardi, Robert, & Nanetti, Raffaella Y. (1994). *Making Democracy Work: Civic Traditions in Modern Italy*. Princeton, NJ: Princeton University Press.

Quraishi, Asifa. (2008). Who says Shari'a demands the stoning of women? A description of Islamic law and constitutionalism. *Berkeley Journal of Middle Eastern & Islamic Law*, 1(1), 163–77.

(2012). The separation of powers in the tradition of Islamic statehood. In Rainer Grote & Tilmann Röder, eds., *Constitutionalism in Islamic Countries*. New York, NY: Oxford University Press, pp. 73–86.

Raaum, N. (2005). Gender equality and political representation: a Nordic comparison. *Western European Politics*, 28(4), 872–97.

Raday, Frances. (2009). Equality, religion and gender in Israel. In Jewish Womens Archive, ed., *Jewish Women: A Comprehensive Historical Encyclopedia*, https://jwa.org/encyclopedia/article/equality-religion-and-gender-in-israel.

Raghunathan, Abhi. (2001, February 4). A feud brewing over family leave. *New York Times*.

Rahmatian, Andreas. (1996). Termination of marriage in Nigerian family laws: the need for reform and the relevance of the Tanzanian experience. *International Journal of Law, Policy and the Family*, 10(3), 281–316.

Rai, Shirin. (2007). *Mainstreaming Gender, Democratizing the State: Institutional Mechanisms for the Advancement of Women*. New Brunswick, NJ: Transaction Publishers.

Randall, Vicki, & Waylen, Georgina. (1998). *Gender Politics and the State*. New York, NY: Routledge.

Ranger, Terence. (1983). The invention of tradition in colonial Africa. In Eric Hobsbawm & Terence Ranger, eds., *The Invention of Tradition*. New York, NY: Cambridge University Press, pp. 211–62.

Raphael, Jody. (1996). Domestic violence and welfare receipt. *Harvard Women's Law Journal*, 19, 201–27.

Rawls, John. (1971). *A Theory of Justice*. Cambridge, MA: Harvard University Press. (1993). *Political Liberalism*. New York, NY: Columbia University Press.

Ray, Renuka. (1952). The background of the Hindu Code Bill. *Pacific Affairs*, 29(3), 268–77.

Razavi, Shahra, & Jenichen, Anne. (2010). The unhappy marriage of religion and politics: problems and pitfalls for gender equality. *Third World Quarterly*, 31(6), 833–50.

Razavi, Shahra, & Staab, Silke. (2012). Introduction. Global variations in the political and social economy of care: worlds apart. In Shahra Razavi & Silke Staab, eds., *Global Variations in the Political and Social Economy of Care: Worlds Apart*. New York: Routledge, pp. 1–28.

Restrepo, Eduardo. (2004). Ethnicization of blackness in Colombia: toward de-racializing theoretical and political imagination. *Cultural Studies*, 18(5), 698–715.

Rhode, Deborah L. (1989). *Justice and Gender: Sex Discrimination and the Law*. Cambridge, MA: Harvard University Press.

Rich, Adrienne. (1980). Compulsory heterosexuality and lesbian existence. *Signs*, 5(4), 631–60.

Richie, Beth E., & Kanuha, Valli. (2000). Battered women of color. In Anne Minas, ed., *Gender Basics: Feminist Perspectives on Women and Men* (2nd edn.). Belmont, CA: Wadsworth Publishing, pp. 213–20.

Ridgeway, Cecilia L. (2001). Gender, status, and leadership. *Journal of Social Issues*, 57(4), 637–55.

Robnik, Sonja. (2010). Domestic violence against women: when practice creates legislation in Slovenia. In Katalin Fabian, ed., *Domestic Violence in Post-communist States: Local Activism, National Policies, and Global Forces*. Bloomington IN: Indiana University Press, pp. 195–220.

Rochon, Thomas R. (1998). *Culture Moves: Ideas, Activism, and Changing Values*. Princeton, NJ: Princeton University Press.

Rochon, Thomas R., & Mazmanian, Daniel A. (1993). Social movements and the Policy Press. *Annals of the American Academy of Political and Social Science*, 528(July), 75–87.

Rodrik, Dani, & Richard Zeckhauser. (1988). The dilemma of government responsiveness. *Journal of Policy Analysis and Management*, 7, 601–20.

Rosenbluth, F. M. (2007). *The Political Economy of Japan's Low Fertility*. Stanford, CA: Stanford University Press.

Ross, Michael L. (2008). Oil, Islam and women. *American Political Science Review*, 102(1), 107–123.

Rossin, Maya. (2011). The effects of maternity leave on children's birth and infant health outcomes in the United States. *Journal of Health Economics*, 30(2), 221–39.

Ruddick, Sara. (1995). *Maternal Thinking: Toward a Politics of Peace.* Boston, MA: Beacon Press.

Rudra, Nita. (2002). Globalization and the decline of the welfare state in less-developed countries. *International Organization,* 56(2), 411–45.

(2007). Welfare states in developing countries: unique or universal? *Journal of Politics,* 69(2), 378–96.

Ruhm, Christopher J. (1996). The economic consequences of parental leave mandates: lessons from Europe. *The Quarterly Journal of Economics,* 113(1), 285–317.

(1997). Policy watch: the family and medical leave act. *The Journal of Economic Perspectives,* 11(3), 175–86.

Rule, Wilma. (1987). Electoral systems, contextual factors and women's opportunity for election to parliament in twenty-three democracies. *Western Political Quarterly,* 477–98.

Rupp, Leila J., & Taylor, Verta. (1987). *Survival in the Doldrums.* New York, NY: Oxford University Press.

(1999). Forging feminist identity in an international movement: a collective identity approach to 20th century feminism. *Signs: Journal of Women in Culture and Society,* 24(2), 363–86.

Sainsbury, D. (2001). Gender and the making of welfare states: Norway and Sweden. *Social Politics,* 8(1), 113–43.

Sanbonmatsu, Kira. (2004). *Democrats, Republicans, and the Politics of Women's Place.* Ann Arbor, MI: University of Michigan Press.

Sanday, Peggy Reeves. (1981). *Female Power and Male Dominance: On the Origins of Sexual Inequality.* New York, NY: Cambridge University Press.

Sawer, Marian. (1996). Femocrats and Ecorats: Women's Policy Machinery in Australia, Canada and New Zealand. Occasional paper no. 6. Geneva: United Nations Research Institute for Social Development.

Sawyer, Mark Q. (2006). *Racial Politics in Post-Revolutionary Cuba.* New York, NY: Cambridge University Press.

Sayare, Scott, & Maïa de la Baume (2010, December 15). In France, civil unions gain favor over marriage, *New York Times,* www.nytimes.com/2010/12/16/world/europe/16france.html?_r=1&scp=1&sq=france%20marriage&st=cse.

Scheve, Kenneth, & Stasavege, David. (2006a). The political economy of religion and social insurance in the United States, 1910–1939. *Studies in American Political Development,* 20(Fall), 132–59.

(2006b). Religion and preferences for social insurance. *Quarterly Journal of Political Science,* 1(3), 255–86.

Schmidt, Petra. (2005). Family law. In Wilhelm Rohl, ed., *History of Law in Japan since 1868.* Leiden: Brill Academic Publishers, pp. 262–304.

Schoppa, Leonard J. (2008). *Race for the Exits: The Unraveling of Japan's System of Social Protection.* Ithaca, NY: Cornell University Press.

Schuler, S. R., Hashemi, S., Riley, A., & Akhter, S. (1996). Credit programs, patriarchy, and men's violence against women in rural Bangladesh. *Social Science and Medicine,* 42(12), 1729–42.

Schwedler, Jillian. (2011). Review article: can Islamists become moderates? Rethinking the inclusion-moderation hypothesis. *World Politics,* 63(2), 347–76.

Schwindt-Bayer, Leslie, & Mishler, William. (2005). An integrated model of women's representation. *Journal of Politics*, 67(2), 407–28.

Segura-Ubiergo, Alex. (2007). *The Political Economy of the Welfare State in Latin America: Globalization, Democracy, and Development*. New York, NY: Cambridge University Press.

Sen, Amartya. (1990). Millions of women are missing. *New York Review of Books*, 37(20), 61–6.

(2001). The many faces of gender inequality. *Frontline*, 18(22), 35–9.

Sezgin, Yuksel. (2009). Legal unification and nation building in the post-colonial world: a comparison of Israel and India. *Journal of Comparative Asian Development*, 8(2), 273–97.

(2011). Women's rights in the triangle of state, law, and religion: a comparison of Egypt and India. *Emory International Law Review*, 25, 1007–28.

Sezgin, Yüksel. (2013). *Human Rights under State-Enforced Religious Family Laws in Israel, Egypt and India*. New York, NY: Cambridge University Press.

Shachar, Ayelet. (2001). *Multicultural Jurisdictions: Cultural Differences and Women's Rights*. New York, NY: Cambridge University Press.

(2008). Privatizing diversity: a cautionary tale from religious arbitration in family law. *Theoretical Inquiries in Law*, 9(2), 573–607.

Shaheed, Farida. (2010). Contested identities: gendered politics, gendered religion in Pakistan. *Third World Quarterly*, 31(6), 851–67.

Sharfman, Daphna. (1994). Women and politics in Israel. In Barbara J. Nelson & Najma Chowdhury, eds., *Women and Politics Worldwide*. New Haven, CT: Yale University Press, pp. 380–95.

Sharma, Kumud, ed. (2012). *Changing the Terms of the Discourse: Gender, Equality and the Indian State*. Delhi: Center for Women Development Studies (CWDS).

Sheppard, Colleen. (2010). *Inclusive Equality: The Relational Dimensions of Systemic Discrimination in Canada*. McGill: Queen's University Press.

Shipan, C., & Volden, C. (2008). The mechanisms of policy diffusion. *American Journal of Political Science*, 52(4), 840–57.

Sibasish, Samyak. (2013, March 24). The issue of reproductive rights in India: how is it different from other societies? *Journal of Indian Law and Society*, https://jilsblognujs.wordpress.com/2013/03/24/the-issue-of-reproductive-rights-in-india-how-is-it-different-from-other-societies/.

Sigelman, Lee, & Zeng, Langche. (1999). Analyzing censored and sample-selected data with Tobit and Heckit models. *Political Analysis*, 8(2), 167–82.

Simmons, Beth A. (2009). *Mobilizing for Human Rights: International Law in Domestic Politics*. New York, NY: Cambridge University Press.

Singerman, Diane. (2005). Rewriting divorce in Egypt. In Robert Hefner, ed., *Remaking Muslim Politics: Pluralism, Contestation, Democratization*. Princeton, NJ: Princeton University Press, pp. 161–88.

Skocpol, Theda. (1992). *Protecting Soldiers and Mothers: The Political Origins of Social Policy in the United States*. Cambridge, MA: Harvard University Press.

(2003). Voice inequality: the transformation of American civic democracy. *American Political Science Association Presidential Address, 2012*.

Skorge, Øyvind Søraas. (2016). *The Century of the Gender Revolution: Empirical Essays.* Ph.D. Dissertation. The London School of Economics and Political Science (LSE).

Skrentny, John. (2002). *The Minority Rights Revolution.* Cambridge, MA: Harvard University Press.

Smooth, W. (2006). Intersectionality in electoral politics: a mess worth making. *Politics & Gender,* 3, 400–414.

    (2011). Standing for women? Which women? The substantive representation of women's interest and the research imperative of intersectionality. *Politics & Gender,* 7(3), 436–41.

Snajdr, Edward. (2010). Balancing acts: women's NGOs combating domestic violence in Kazakhstan. In Katalin Fabian, ed., *Domestic Violence in Postcommunist States.* Bloomington, IN: Indiana University Press, pp. 111–32.

Song, Sarah. (2007). *Justice, Gender, and the Politics of Multiculturalism.* New York, NY: Cambridge University Press.

Spelman, E. V. (1998). *Inessential Woman: Problems of Exclusion in Feminist Thought.* Boston, MA: Beacon Press.

Stadelmann-Steffan, Isabelle, & Traunmuller, Richard. (2011). Der religiose Faktor in der Familienpolitik: Ein empirischer Test klassischer und neurerer Ansatze im Vergleich von 27 OECD-Landern. *Zeitschrift fur Sozialreform,* 57(4), 383–408.

Stanton, Elizabeth Cady. (1848). The Seneca Falls Declaration. AMDOCS, Documents for the Study of American History, www.vlib.us/amdocs/texts/seneca .htm.

Stark, Rodney, & Iannaccone, Laurence R. (1994). A supply-side reinterpretation of the "secularization" of Europe. *Journal for the Scientific Study of Religion,* 33, 230–52.

Stepan, Alfred C. (2000). Religion, democracy, and the "Twin Tolerations." *Journal of Democracy,* 11(4), 37–57.

Sternbach, Nancy, Navarro-Aranguren, Marysa, Chuchryk, Patricia, & Alvarez, Sonia E. (1992). Feminisms in Latin America: from Bogota to San Bernardo. *Signs: A Journal of Women in Culture and Society,* 17(3), 393–434.

Stetson, Dorothy McBride. (1998). *Women's Rights in the USA* (2nd edn.). New York, NY: Garland.

Stetson, Dorothy McBride, & Mazur, Amy G. (1995). *Comparative State Feminism.* Thousand Oaks, CA: Sage.

    (2010). Introduction to comparative state feminism. *Women, Gender, and Politics. A Reader,* pp. 319–25.

Stokes, Susan C. (2001). *Mandates and Democracy: Neoliberalism by Surprise in Latin America.* New York, NY: Cambridge University Press.

Strach, Patricia. (2006). The politics of family. *Polity,* 38(2), 151–73.

Streeck, Wolfgang, & Thelen, Kathleen. (2005). Introduction: Institutional change in advanced political economies. In *Beyond Continuity: Institutional Change in Advanced Political Economies.* New York, NY: Oxford University Press, pp. 1–39.

Strolovitch, Dara Z. (2006). Do interest groups represent the disadvantaged? Advocacy at the intersections of race, class, and gender. *Journal of Politics*, 68(4), 893–908.

(2007). *Affirmative Advocacy: Race, Class, and Gender in Interest Group Politics*. Chicago, IL: University of Chicago Press.

Swank, Duane. (2001). Mobile capital, democratic institutions, and the public economy in advanced industrial societies. *Journal of Comparative Policy Analysis*, 3(2), 133–62.

Swers, Michele L. (2002). *The Difference Women Make: The Policy Impact of Women in Congress*: Chicago, IL: University of Chicago Press.

Tarrow, Sidney. (1998). *Power in Movement: Social Movements and Contentious Politics* (2nd edn.). Cambridge: Cambridge University Press.

Telles, Edward. (2004). *Race in Another America: The Significance of Skin Color in Brazil*. Princeton, NJ: Princeton University Press.

Teorell, Jan, Nicholas Charron, Marcus Samanni, Sören Holmberg, & Bo Rothstein. (2011). The Quality of Government Dataset, version 6Apr11. University of Gothenburg: The Quality of Government Institute, www.qog.pol.gu.se.

Thomas, Dorothy. (2012). The revolution continues. In Minky Worden, ed., *The Unfinished Revolution: Voices from the Global Fight for Women's Rights*. Bristol: Policy Press, pp. 325–32.

Thomas, Gwyn. (2011). *Contesting Legitimacy in Chile: Familial Ideals, Citizenship, and Political Struggle, 1970–1990*. University Park, PA: Pennsylvania State University Press.

Timpson, Annis May. (2002). *Driven Apart: Women's Employment Equality and Child Care in Canadian Public Policy*: Vancouver: UBC Press.

Tjaden, Patricia, & Thoennes, Nancy. (1998). *Stalking in America: Findings from the National Violence against Women Survey*. US Department of Justice, Office of Justice Programs, National Institute of Justice.

Tønnessen, Liv. (2014). When rape becomes politics: negotiating Islamic law reform in Sudan. *Women's Studies International Forum*, 44, 145–53.

Toyo, Nkoyo. (2006). Revisiting equality as a right: the minimum age of marriage clause in the Nigerian Child Rights Act, 2003. *Third World Quarterly*, 27(7), 1299–1312.

Traunmuller, Richard, & Freitag, Markus. (2011). State support of religion: making or breaking faith-based social capital? *Comparative Politics*, 43(3), 253–369.

Tribe, Laurence H. (1992). *Abortion: The Clash of Absolutes*. New York, NY: WW Norton & Company.

Tripp, Aili Mari, Casimiro, Isabel, Kwesiga, Joy, & Mungwa, Alice. (2009). *African Women's Movements: Changing Political Landscapes*. New York, NY: Cambridge University Press.

True, Jacqui. (2012). *The Political Economy of Violence against Women*. New York, NY: Oxford University Press.

True, J., & Mintrom, M. (2001). Transnational networks and policy diffusion: the case of gender mainstreaming. *International Studies Quarterly*, 45, 27–57.

Tucker, Judith E. (2008). *Women, Family and Gender in Islamic Law*. Cambridge: Cambridge University Press.

UNESCO International Bureau of Education (IBE). (2006). *Nigeria. Early Child-hood Care and Education (ECCE) programmes.* Country profile prepared for the Education for All Global Monitoring Report 2007 Strong Foundations: Early Childhood Care and Education. Geneva, Switzerland: UNESCO. IBE/ 2006/EFA/GMR/CP/62, http://unesdoc.unesco.org/images/0014/001472/147 201e.pdf.

United Nations. (1993). Directory of National Machinery for Advancement of Women. Vienna: Division for the Advancement of Women.

(1995). *Beijing Declaration and Platform for Action.* New York: Fourth World Conference on Women.

(1998). National Machineries for gender Equality. Expert Group Meeting. Santiago, Chile, August 31–September 4, 1998. Report. United Nations. Division for the Advancement of Women(DAW) Economic Commission for Latin America and the Caribbean (ECLAC). www.un.org/womenwatch/daw/ news/natlmach.htm.

United Nations Population Fund (UNFP). (2007). *Programming to Address Vio-lence: Ten Case Studies.* New York, NY: United Nations. United Nations document E/CN.4/2003/75.

United Nations Statistics Division. (2012). Statistics and Indicators on Women and Men, Table 5g. Maternity Leave Benefits, http://unstats.un.org/unsd/ demographic/products/indwm/default.htm https://unstats.un.org/unsd/demo graphic/products/indwm/.

UN Treaty Database. (2011). http://treaties.un.org/Home.aspx?lang=en.

UN Women (n.d.) Declarations, Reservations and Objections to CEDAW. Conven-tion on the Elimination of all Forms of Discrimination against Women. Avail-able at: www.un.org/womenwatch/daw/cedaw/reservations-country.htm.

U.S. Bureau of the Census. (2016). *America's Families and Living Arrangements* www.census.gov/data/tables/2016/demo/families/cps-2016.html.

U.S. Department of State. (2012). *2011 Human Rights Report: China (includes Tibet, Hong Kong, and Macau).* Retrieved from www.state.gov/j/drl/rls/ hrrpt/2011/eap/186268.htm.

Vail, Leroy, ed. (1989). *The Creation of Tribalism in Southern Africa.* Berkeley, CA: University of California Press.

Valiente, Celia. (2006). *El feminismo de estado en España: el Instituto de la Mujer (1983–2003).* Universitat de València. Institut Universitari d'Estudis de la Dona.

Van Cott, Donna Lee. (2005). *From Movements to Parties in Latin America : The Evolution of Ethnic Politics.* New York, NY: Cambridge University Press.

Van der Vleuten, Anna. (2013). *The Price of Gender Equality: Member States and Governance in the European Union.* Hampshire: Ashgate Publishing.

Vargas, Virginia, & Wieringa, Saskia. (1998). The triangle of empowerment: Processes and actors in the making of public policy for women. In Geertje Lycklama a Nijeholt, Virginia Vargas, and Saskia Wieringa, eds., *Women's Movements and Public Policy in Europe, Latin America, and the Caribbean.* New York: Garland, pp. 3–48.

Viterna, Jocelyn. (2012). The left and "life" in El Salvador. *Politics & Gender,* 8(2), 248–54.

Vogel, Ursula. (1998). The state and the making of gender: some historical legacies. In Vicky Randall & Georgina Waylen, eds., *Gender, Politics and the State*. New York: Routledge, pp. 29–44.

Wade, Peter. (2009). Defining blackness in Colombia. *Journal de la Société des Américanistes*, 95(1), 165–84.

   (2011). Multiculturalismo y racismo. *Revista Colombiana de Antropología*, 47(2), 15–35.

Wang, Chung Hui. (1907). *The German Civil Code*. London: Stevens.

Wängnerud, Lena. (2009). Women in parliaments: descriptive and substantive representation. *Annual Review of Political Science*, 12, 51–69.

Warner, Michael. (2002). Beyond gay marriage. In Wendy Brown & Janet Halley, eds., *Left Legalism/Left Critique*. Durham, NC: Duke University Press, pp. 259–89.

Warshaw, Robin. (1994). *I Never Called It Rape: The Ms. Report on Recognizing, Fighting, and Surviving Date and Acquaintance Rape*. New York, NY: Harper Paperbacks.

Weathers, Charles. (2005). In search of strategic partners: Japan's campaign for equal opportunity. *Social Science Japan Journal*, 8(1), 69–89.

Weber, Max. (1978). *Economy and Society* (Guenther Roth, ed.). Berkeley, CA: University of California Press.

Weldon, S. Laurel. (2002a). Beyond bodies: institutional sources of representation for women in democratic policymaking. *Journal of Politics*, 64(4), 1153–74.

   (2002b). *Protest, Policy, and the Problem of Violence against Women: A Cross-National Comparison*. Pittsburgh, PA: University of Pittsburgh Press.

   (2004). The dimensions and policy impact of feminist civil society: democratic policymaking on violence against women in the fifty U.S. states. *International Feminist Journal of Politics*, 6(1), 1–28.

   (2006a). Inclusion, solidarity, and social movements: the global movement against gender violence. *Perspectives on Politics*, 4(1), 55–74.

   (2006b). Women's movements, identity politics and policy impact: a study of policies on violence against women in the 50 United States. *Political Research Quarterly*, 59(1), 111–22.

   (2010). Perspectives against interests: sketch of a political theory of "women." *Politics & Gender*, 7(3), 441–6.

   (2011). *When Protest Makes Policy: How Social Movements Represent Disadvantaged Groups*. Ann Arbor, MI: University of Michigan Press.

Weyland, Kurt. (2005). Theories of policy diffusion: lessons from Latin American pension reform. *World Politics*, 57(2), 262–95.

Wickham, Carrie Rosefsky. (2004). The path to moderation: strategy and learning in the formation of Egypt's Wasat Party. *Comparative Politics*, 36(2), 205–28.

Wilensky, Harold. (1975). *The Welfare State and Equality*. Berkeley, CA: University of California Press.

Williams, Fiona. (1995). Race/ethnicity, gender, and class in welfare states: a framework for comparative analysis. *Social Politics: International Studies in Gender, State & Society*, 2(2), 127–59, https://doi.org/10.1093/sp/2.2.127.

Williams, Patricia J. (1988). On being the object of property. *Signs*, 14(1), 5–24.

Williams, Rina Verna. (2006). *Postcolonial Politics and Personal Laws: Colonial Legal Legacies and the Indian State*. New York, NY: Oxford University Press.

Williams, Sope. (2004). Nigeria, its women and international law: beyond rhetoric. *Human Rights Law Review*, 4, 229.

Wilson, William Julius. (2012). *The Truly Disadvantaged: The Inner City, the Underclass, and Public Policy*. Chicago, IL: University of Chicago Press.

Winkelmann, Rainer. (1997). *Econometric Analysis of Count Data* (2nd edn.) New York, NY: Springer.

Wolbrecht, C. (2000). *The Politics of Women's Rights: Parties, Positions, and Change*. Princeton, NJ: Princeton University Press.

Women Living under Muslim Laws. (2006). *Knowing Our Rights: Women, Family, Laws and Customs in the Muslim World* (3rd edn.). London: Women Living under Muslim Laws.

Woo, Margaret. (2003). Shaping citizenship: Chinese family law and women. Yale Journal of Law and Feminism, 15(1), 99–134.

World Bank. (n.d.) Gender Statistics. https://data.worldbank.org/data-catalog/gender-statistics.

(2012). *World Development Report 2012: Gender Equality and Development*. Washington, DC: The World Bank.

(2013). *Women, Business, and the Law 2014: Removing Restrictions to Enhance Gender Equality*. London: Bloomsbury.

World Conference on Human Rights. (1993). *Vienna Declaration and Programme of Action*. Vienna: United Nations. Retrieved from www.ohchr.org/EN/ProfessionalInterest/Pages/Vienna.aspx.

World Health Organization. (2010). *Preventing Intimate Partner and Sexual Violence against Women: Taking Action and Generating Evidence*. Geneva: World Health Organization, www.who.int/violence_injury_prevention/publications/violence/9789241564007_eng.pdf.

(2015). *Trends in Maternal Mortality, 1990 to 2015*. Geneva: World Health Organization, http://apps.who.int/iris/bitstream/10665/194254/1/9789241565141_eng.pdf.

(2016a). *Family Planning/Contraception Fact Sheet*, www.who.int/mediacentre/factsheets/fs351/en/.

(2016b). *Preventing Unsafe Abortion. Fact Sheet*, www.who.int/mediacentre/factsheets/fs388/en/.

World Values Survey Association. (2009). World Values Survey 1981–2008 Official Aggregate v.20090901, www.worldvaluessurvey.org.

Wright, Erik Olin. (1997). *Class Counts: Comparative Studies in Class Analysis*. New York, NY: Cambridge University Press.

Young, Iris Marion. (1990). *Justice and the Politics of Difference*. Princeton, NJ: Princeton University Press.

(2000). *Inclusion and Democracy*. New York, NY: Oxford University Press.

(2002). Lived body vs gender: reflections on social structure and subjectivity. *Ratio*, 15(4), 410–28.

(2005). *On Female Body Experience: "Throwing Like a Girl" and Other Essays*. Oxford: Oxford University Press.

Index

Abella Commission. *See* Royal Commission
on Equality in Employment
abortion, 136, 299
  Abortion Law Index, 212–22, 266
  abortion legality and reproductive rights
    indices, various regression techniques,
    1975 to 2005, 223
  access to, 11
  Catholicism restrictions on access to, 201,
    215
  church and state restriction of,
    224
  class inequality in access to, 208
  communism and, 216–17
  doctrinal politics and, 209
  feminist movements and, 218–20
  France funding of, 215
  Global North funding of,
    213–14
  Hinduism acceptance of, 203
  Islam on, 204
  in Latin America, 212–13
  left parties and, 217–18
  legal guarantees of, 1, 222
  legal status of, 207–8
  mean value of abortion index, by region,
    1975–2005, 213
  mean value of abortion law index, by
    year, 213
  physicians opposed to, 211
  public funding for, 21, 211–12
  religion and, 9, 215–16
  sex-selective, 207

  state funding for reproductive rights, by
    year, 213
  in U.S., 206–7
  variance in legality of, 210–11
  WHO estimates on, 202
abusive relationships, 32
Action Travail des Femmes (ATF), 102
administrative reforms, 34
Affordable Care Act (2010) (U.S.), 254
Africa, violence against women in, 43–4
African Charter on Human and People's
    Rights (2003), 64–5, 107
  protocol to, 67
African National Congress (ANC), 103–4
African-American experience, 250–1
Afrodescendants, 251–2
agenda-setting, 54
alcohol use, 31
ALI. *See* American Legal Institute
Ambedkar, Babasaheb, 286
American Legal Institute (ALI), 218–19
ANC. *See* African National Congress
Anglo Countries, index of violence against
    women, 39
Anwar, Zainah, 134–5
Apartheid, 253
Arab Spring, 67
Arabic Network for Human Rights
    Information, 92
Asia
  customary laws in south of, 138
  parental leave in, 170
  violence against women in, 48–50

ATF. *See* Action Travail des Femmes
Australia, 99–100
  Commonwealth Sex Discrimination Act
    (1993), 109
  feminist movements in, 106–7
  Women's Electoral Lobby, 108–9
authoritarian backlash, 45
autonomy, 2, 11
  determining, 57
  economic, 118
  non-autonomous feminist movements,
    57
  reforms for, 219
  reproductive, 21
Ayoub, Phillip, 250

Baldez, Lisa, 100, 238–9
Barro and McCleary, 270
Beijing Platform for Action (1995), 31–2,
  42, 50, 106
biomedical research, 253–4
birth control. *See also* population control
  access to, 219
birth defects, 218–19
birth rates, 299
black markets, 218
Braun, Robert, 157
Brazil, 252
  Brazilian Congress, 249
  divorce in, 134
  Married Women's Statute (1962),
    141–2
breastfeeding, 90, 172, 187–8
bureaucratic reprisals, 54
Bush, George W., 176

Cambodia, 126
Canada, 101–2
  Family Violence Initiative (1988), 38
  Federal Employment Equity Act (1986),
    102
Canadian Charter of Rights and Freedoms
  (1982), 92
Canadian Human Rights Commission,
  102
Canadian National Railway, 102
capitalism, 166
Cardoso, Fernando Henrique, 253
care work, 161
  public value of, 158, 169
cash transfers, 187

Catholicism, 157, 237. *See also* Roman
  Catholic Church
  abortion access restrictions from, 201,
    215
  divorce and, 137
  lack of government action from, 50
Catholics for a Free Choice (CFC), 206
CEDAW. *See* Convention on the
  Elimination of Discrimination against
  Women
CFC. *See* Catholics for a Free Choice
child care, 193, 267
  Child care Leave Law (1991) (Japan),
    161–73
  class politics of, 158–9
  cross-national trends in, 186
  dynamics driving, 168
  factors in strength of, 190
  feminist movements and, 194
  in France, 189
  government actions on, 162, 186–7
  left parties and, 190–3
  national wealth and, 190
  in Nigeria, 188
  policy by region, 193–200
  quality of, 189
  variations in policy on, 189–90
Child care Leave Law (1991) (Japan),
  161–73
Chile, 142
China, 48–50, 299
Chrétien, Jean, 102
church and state. *See also* state-religion
  relations
  abortion restriction from, 224
  challenges to, 122
  close, 18
  full separation of, 24
  fusion between, 152
citizenship, 210
civil law, 291–7
Civil Rights Act (1964) (U.S), 105
civil society, 243
  domestic, 68
  international norms and global, 61–8
  organizing in, 81–2
  state regulation and, 30–1
  weak countervailing forces in, 249
class inequality, 243–4
  in abortion access, 208
  social policy and, 164

class politics, 3, 16–17, 236–41, 247–8
  doctrinal, 239
  family leave and child care as, 158–9
  mobilization of, 19
  religion and, 21
  status politics and, 10–14
Clay, William, 174
Clinton, Bill, 175
coitus interruptus, 205
colonialism, 221, 242, 285
  family law under, 123, 138–9
  France cultural assimilation emphasis in,
    138–9
  laws of personal status under, 288
  statistical analysis on, 154
color of violence conferences, 56
Commission on the Status of Women (1969)
  (UN), 38, 105
Commonwealth Sex Discrimination Act
  (1993) (Australia), 109
communism, 116–17, 241
  abortion and, 216–17
  contraception and, 216–17
  countries after, 164
  family law under, 123, 126, 139–41,
    297–301
  family leave and, 180, 182
  important legacy of, 195, 241
  reproductive rights and, 216–17
  sex equality under, 140
  statistical analysis on, 154
comparative politics, 243, 246
consent, 205, 289
contraception
  availability of, 202
  communism and, 216–17
  feminist movements and, 218–20
  Islam on, 204
  left parties and, 217–18
  low-dose pill for, 209–10
  state funding for, 211–12
  U.S. funding for, 201–19
controls, 69–70, 79–80
Convention of Belém do Pará, 40–1
Convention on the Elimination of
  Discrimination against Women
  (CEDAW) (1979), 37–8, 47
  Committee, 63
  compliance with, 42
  different effects of, 66
  effectiveness of, 41

  importance of, 143
  ratification of, 66, 78, 114, 155
  reproductive rights affirmed by, 220
  violence against women not mentioned
    in, 52
Council of Europe, 64
criminal justice procedures, 13
cross-national studies, 30
Cuba, 252, 301

daddy leave, 20, 178
  in Denmark, 178
  normalizing effect of, 169
  sexual division of labor shifted by, 162
  Social Democratic parties championing,
    178
data, 25
  on formally existing organizations, 57
  multi-issue dataset, 247
  on violence against women, 34
  women's rights dataset, 4
Database of Political Institutions (DPI), 69
day care
  Day Care Act (1975) (Norway), 20
  fertility rates and, 193, 197–200
  for infants and toddlers, 188
Declaration on the Elimination of Violence
  against Women (1993) (UN), 28, 62
deliberative politics, 247
Democratic Party, U.S., 176
democratization, 45, 80–1, 243
  in Global South, 166
  social spending and, 181–2
Denmark, 178
dependent variables, 259–60
dignity, 10
Dissolution of Muslim Marriages Act
  (1939) (British India-Pakistan), 277
division of labor, sexual, 6
  class in, 99
  daddy leave shifting of, 162
  norms reinforcing, 12
  responsibility in, 11–12
divorce, 292–5
  in Brazil, 134
  Catholicism and, 137
  domestic violence as cause for, 48
  ease to obtain, 140
  Islam and, 274–5
  judicial, 275–6
  vulnerability from, 161

doctrinal politics, 3, 16–17, 236–7, 244, 247–8
  abortion legality shaped by, 209
  non-doctrinal policies and, 14–16
domestic violence
  divorce cause from, 48
  in Latin America, 41
  Law on the Prevention of Domestic Violence (2001) (Ukraine), 42
  in Morocco, 46
  shelters, 32–3
domestic workers, 172
DPI. *See* Database of Political Institutions

Eastern Europe
  double burden for women in, 160
  violence against women in, 42–3
ecclesiastical laws, 14–15
economic development, 167–8
economic equality, 18, 85
  disaggregating, 85–9
  feminist movements and, 101–6
  statistical analysis on, 110–18
  women in parliamentary seats and, 117
EEOL. *See* Equal Employment Opportunity Law
Egypt, 92, 277
  New Unified Labor Law (2003), 187
Elman, R. Amy, 39, 165
empowerment
  from social policies, 162–3
  triangle of, 100, 226
  from work, 85
Equal Employment Opportunity Law (EEOL) (1985) (Japan), 88, 106
Equal Status Act (1978) (Norway), 105–6
equality. *See also* economic equality; formal equality; substantive equality
  conditions of, 248–55
  guarantees of, 91
  indices on government actions on work, 93–6
  left parties and, 115
  legal, 94–6, 111
  racial, 18
  religion and, 127
  sex, 134
  uneven trends in, 245–6
  workplace, 264–5

equality, formal, 128, 264–5
  degrees of, 90
  legal, 140
EU. *See* European Union
eugenics, 14
Eurobarometer survey, 52
Europe, 28–9, 141
European Union (EU), 39
  fertility rates low in, 197
  parental leave in, 170
  violence against women in, 64
everyday politics, 56

families
  such transfers to, 187
  family law definition of, 124
  in Global South, 160–1
  normative arrangement of, 160
  political institutions growing from, 124
  traditional form of, 161
Family and Medical Leave Act (1993) (U.S.), 20, 174–6
Family Code (1926) (Russia), 297
family law
  in 19th century Europe, 141
  in Cambodia, 126
  under colonialism, 123, 138–9
  under communism, 123, 126, 139–41, 297–301
  control with, 125
  distributive function of, 125
  egalitarian, 126–7, 130
  exclusion from, 11
  families defined by, 124
  feminist movements and, 141–3
  guide to family law coding in countries with multiple legal systems, 263
  Islam and, 237, 273–85
  liberalized, 121
  in modern states, 125–6
  in North Africa, 15
  patriarchal interpretations of, 122
  reform of, 134, 137
  religion and, 122, 133–8
  social norms codified by, 120
  state regulation of, 14
  in Tanzania, 288
  women in parliamentary seats and, 156
Family Law Index, 129, 261–2
  coefficient plot, 150

GLS random effects models, 146
map of, 131
in Muslim-majority and non-Muslim-majority Countries, 145
religiosity scale and, 151
religious legislation index and, 150
family leave, 267
class politics of, 158–9
communism and, 180, 182
different forms of, 168
dynamics driving, 168
economic development and, 167–8
feminist movements and, 181
generosity, 183, 185
guaranteeing, 162
national wealth and generosity of, 182
in Norway, 176–7
treaties and, 181
in U.S., 244
family planning, 218–19
Family Planning Services and Population Research Act (1970) (U.S.), 201–19
Family Violence Initiative (1988) (Canada), 38
Federal Employment Equity Act (1986) (Canada), 102
feminism
analytic definition of, 57
second wave, 141–2
feminist movements, 52–8
abortion and, 218–20
in Australia, 106–7
change from, 17
child care and, 194
contraception and, 218–20
economic equality and, 101–6
effectiveness of, 41
family law and, 141–3
family leave and, 181
fertility rates and, 199
government control of, 48
high and low levels of, 24
international norms magnified by, 68–9
Israeli Feminist Movement, 102–3
lack of progress without, 51
in MENA, 45–6
non-autonomous, 57
policy agencies and, 59
relative importance of, 69
reproductive rights and, 225–6

second wave, 218
statistical analysis on, 154–5
strength in, 55
transnational and domestic, 2
in U.S., 8, 38, 195
violence against women combated by, 29–30
women in parliamentary seats and, 239–40
fertility rates, 172
day care and, 193, 197–200
declining, 161–73
EU low, 197
feminist movements and, 199
parental leave and, 194
Fonseca, Romy Medeiros da, 141–2
formal equality, 128, 264–5
degrees of, 90
legal, 140
Fourth World Conference on Women, 62–5, 220
Fox, Jonathan, 145–9
France, 293–4
abortion funding in, 215
child care in, 189
colonialism of, 138–9
marriage in, 133
Napoleonic Code (1804), 273–4
Fraser, Nancy, 241

Gelb, Joyce, 8
gender
dimensions of, 4–6
as institutional phenomenon, 5, 245
quotas, 11, 248–50
schemas, 31
German Civil Code, 293
Glendon, Mary Ann, 255
Global North, 197, 213–14
Global South
deaths in, 202
emerging democracies in, 166
employer mandates in, 187
familialism in, 161–2
family arrangements in, 160–1
social policies in, 159
government actions, 2, 25, 81–2, 245
Catholicism not producing, 50
on child care, 162, 186–7
on equality at work, 93–6
feminist movements weakened by, 48

government actions (cont.)
    indices on equality at work from, 93–6
    to investigate status of women, 142
    Islam not producing, 50
    on reproductive rights, 209
    for substantive equality, 89
    violence against women and, 31–7, 51
Griswold v. *Connecticut*, 209–10
Grzymała-Busse, Anna, 135

Hadenius and Teorell database, 68
Hall, Peter, 8
Halley, Janet, 125
Hastings, Warren, 138
health care, 03
health policy, 253–4
Henderson, Ailsa, 165
heterosexuality, 6
Hindu Code Bills (1955) (India), 286–7
Hindu Succession Act (2005) (India), 287
Hinduism
    abortion acceptance by, 203
    Hindu Code Bills (1955) (India), 286–7
    Hindu Succession Act (2005) (India), 287
    personhood of fetal life in, 207
historical changes, 96–101
HIV/AIDS, 226
Holocaust, rescue networks during, 157
Htun, Mala, 9, 25, 296
human rights. *See also* Arabic Network for
        Human Rights Information; Universal
        Declaration of Human Rights; Vienna
        Declaration at the World Conference
        on Human Rights; World Conference
        on Human Rights
    treaties, 46–7
    universalist claims of, 82
    violations of, 29
Human Rights Watch, 62
Hussin, Iza, 138, 288

I Never Called It Rape (Warshaw), 53
ICESCR. *See* International Covenant on
        Economic, Social, and Cultural Rights
illegitimacy, 140
ILO. *See* International Labour Organization
implementation, 254–5
independent variables, 267–9
Index of Government Response to Violence
        against Women, 70
India, 48

Dissolution of Muslim Marriages Act
        (1939) (British India-Pakistan), 277
    Hindu Code Bills (1955), 286–7
    Hindu Succession Act (2005), 287
    after Independence, 285
    Muslim personal laws in, 287–8
indigenous movements, 251–2
indirect rule, 285
infants and toddlers, 188
Inglehart, Ronald, 135, 215–16
institutions
    approaches with, 241
    challenges to, 3
    gender phenomenon of, 5
    importance of, 4
    political institutionalization, 134
    privileges of, 156
    of state-religion relations, 135
Inter-American Consultation on Women
        and Violence (1990), 40–1
Inter-American Convention on the
        Prevention, Punishment and
        Eradication of Violence against Women
        (1994), 40–1, 64
international agreements, 37–8, 226–7
International Conference on Population and
        Development, 220
International Covenant on Economic,
        Social, and Cultural Rights (ICESCR),
        84, 193
International Labour Organization (ILO),
        101–2
international law, 66
international norms, 106–8, 220, 242
    diffusion of, 77
    feminist movements magnification of,
        68–9
    global civil society and, 61–8
    progressive policies and, 115
    on women's rights, 2
International Women's Year (1975), 37
intersectionality, 10
Iran, 278–9
Islam. *See also* Sisters in Islam
    on abortion, 204
    on contraception, 204
    divorce and, 274–5
    family law and, 237, 273–85
    Islamicization, 280
    lack of government action from, 50
    law of, 19

Ottoman Law of Family Rights (1917), 276
 personal laws, 285–8
 pregnancy and, 205
Islamic Family Law Act of 1984 (Malaysia),
  278
Israel, 136, 288
 Ottoman millet system in, 126
 unions in, 102–3
Israeli Feminist Movement, 102–3
Israeli Women's Network, 103

Jacobs, Rachel, 126
Japan, 89, 295–6
 Child care Leave Law (1991), 161–73
 Constitution (1947), 87–8
 Equal Employment Opportunity Law
   (EEOL) (1985), 88, 106
 Labor Standards Law (1947), 87
Jordan, 46–7

Kabyle customary law, 274
Kamerman, Sheila B, 166
Kazakhstan, 43
Keck, Margaret, 100
Kenya, 142, 285, 290
Khmer Rouge, 126
kinship, 247
 governance of, 3
 networks, 12
 reproductive labor via, networks, 161–2
 state regulation of, 14
Kittilson, Miki Caul, 165
Kollontai, Alexandra, 13, 139, 297
Korea, 296–7

labor mobilization, 19
 strength of, 21, 164
 in U.S., 165
Labor Standards Law (1947) (Japan), 87
Latin America
 abortion in, 212–13
 domestic violence in, 41
 informal sector in, 91–2
 left parties in, 164–5
 maternity leave in, 171
 violence against women in, 40–2, 244
Latin American and Caribbean Feminist
   Network against Domestic and Sexual
   Violence, 40
Law on the Prevention of Domestic Violence
   (2001) (Ukraine), 42

lawfulness, 24–5
Leadership Conference on Women
   Religious, 206
left parties, 69–70
 abortion and, 217–18
 child care and, 190–3
 contexts of, 166
 contraception and, 217–18
 egalitarian values of, 164
 equality and, 115
 failures of, 109–10
 in Latin America, 164–5
 literature on, 165–6
 parental leave and, 163–4
 policy expansion from, 194–5
 power of, 182, 270–1
 reproductive rights funding and, 224–5
 social justice and, 179
 strength of, 166, 238
 in U.S., 195
 women's rights and, 165
Legal Center for Women's Rights, 103
legal reform, 33
legislative elections, 1–2
lesbian, gay, bisexual, transgender,
   questioning (LGBTQ)
 law developments on, 7
 rights, 249–50
A Letter from Japanese Women (Women's
   Circle), 88
LGBTQ. *See* lesbian, gay, bisexual,
   transgender, questioning
Lindvert, Jessica, 99–100
lipstick lobby, 108
lobbying, 56
Lowi, Theodore, 8, 240–1

Malaysia, 19, 278
marginalized social groups, 251
Marital Property Act (1984) (South Africa),
   290–1
market regulation, 13
marriage
 consent basis of, 289
 in France, 133
 marital rape, 16
 minimum age for, 279
 same-sex, 248–50
 as site of rights, 249
Married Women's Statute (1962) (Brazil),
   141–2

maternity leave
  employer mandates for, 171
  importance of, 169
  as labor issue, 168
  in Latin America, 171
  paid, 12–13, 27, 170–6
Mazur, Amy G., 99–100
media presence, 58
mental illness, 31
Middle East and North Africa (MENA)
  attitudes in, 136
  feminist movements in, 45–6
  religious courts in, 14
  reproductive rights funding in, 213–14
  social policies in, 187
  violence against women in, 44–7
migrant women, 12
military service, 160
minimum wage, 91
Minkenberg, Michael, 216
monarchical authority, 124
Montoya, Celeste, 39
Morocco, 284
  domestic violence in, 46
  National Action Plan, 45–6
Moss, Peter, 166
motherhood, 19
  limited public support for, 202
Mozambique, 44
Mulroney, Brian, 102
multiple legal systems, 285–91
Muslim Family Laws Ordinance (1961)
  (Pakistan), 277

Nairobi conference, 43, 60
Napoleonic Code (1804) (France), 273–4,
  276, 291–3
National Institutes of Health, 253–4
National Organization for Women (NOW),
  105, 219
national wealth, 80, 166–8, 243
  child care and, 190
  family leave generosity and, 182
Neier, Aryeh, 62
Netherlands, 173
New Unified Labor Law (2003) (Egypt), 187
NGOs. See non-government organizations
Niger, 139
Nigeria
  child care in, 188
  legal system of, 288

minimum wage in, 91
Nomura Securities, 89
non-feminist groups, 83
non-government organizations (NGOs),
  60–1
non-interference, 138
norms
  international, 2, 61–9, 77, 106–8, 115,
    220, 242
  regional, 64, 77–8, 107
Norris, Pippa, 135, 215–16
North Africa, 15
Norway
  Day Care Act (1975), 20
  Equal Status Act (1978), 105–6
  family leave in, 176–7
  women's coup in, 177
NOW. See National Organization for
  Women

OAS. See Organization of American States
Obama, Barack, 251
occupational segregation, 10
OECD. See Organisation for Economic
  Co-operation and Development
Open Society Institute, 42–3
ordered logit models, 222
Organisation for Economic Co-operation
  and Development (OECD), 26
Organization of African Unity, 107
Organization of American States (OAS), 64
  women's commission, 40
Ottoman Law of Family Rights (1917)
  (Islamic law), 276
Ottoman millet system, 14–15, 126

Pakistan, 142
  Dissolution of Muslim Marriages Act
    (1939) (British India-Pakistan), 277
  Hudood Ordinances, 280
  Muslim Family Laws Ordinance (1961),
    277
Palley, Marian Lief, 8
parental leave, 20, 169
  in Asia, 170
  in EU, 170
  fertility rates and, 194
  generosity by region, 180
  left parties and, 163–4
patriarchal norms, 6
  authority of, 124

defenders of, 18–19
religious doctrine historically enforcing, 134
PDA. *See* Pregnancy Discrimination Act
Persian Gulf, 167
police, 49–50
  brutality, 11, 46
policy, 3. *See also* social policy; women's
    policy machineries
  actors and institutions for, 17
  child care, by region, 193–200
  domestic, 78–9
  dynamics, 9
  feminist movements and, 59
  international norms and progressive,
    115
  left parties expansion of, 194–5
  of non-interference, 285
  salient actors and institutions for each
    policy type, 230–1
  scope, 34
  social movements changing, 82, 221
  state-religion relations shaping of, 216
  transnational, 12
  typology of, 4, 9, 230–1
  underlying paradigm setting the
    parameters of, 8
  variations in child care, 189–90
  on violence against women, 29
  on women legal status at work, 86
POLITY score, 69
polygamy, 274, 277–8
population control, 218
Power Resources Theory, 179
pregnancy, 210
  complications around, 202
  Islam and, 205
  protections for, 100
Pregnancy Discrimination Act (PDA) (1978)
    (U.S.), 174–6
prevention programs, 33
Project Haven, 38
protest, 56
  mass, 58
  of sexual harassment, 49
public funding, 1–2
public health initiatives, 219
public opinion, 56

racial inequality, 250–3
rape, 280
  attitudes toward, 53

crisis centers for, 33
marital, 16
rape-prevention, 53
recognition, 10
regional conventions, 114
regional norms, 64, 77–8, 107
religion, 80, 96, 133, 269–70. *See also*
    church and state; state-religion
    relations
  abortion and, 9, 215–16
  challenging authority of, 27
  class politics and, 21
  effects of, 69, 116
  equality and, 127
  establishment of official, 222–4
  family law and, 122, 133–8
  as field of contestation, 157
  health care support from, 83
  multivocal understanding of, 122, 206
  official, 145–9, 151, 270
  patriarchal norms historically enforced
    by, 134
  politics of, 18
  religious nationalism, 250
  statistical analysis of, 144–5
  U.S. and, 216
  violence against women and, 16
religion and the state database, 145–9
religiosity scale, 151–3
religious legislation, 145–9
religious party, 153–4
reproductive and sexual health, 201–3
reproductive labor, 11
  private transactions of, 13
  purchasing of, 12
  socializing, 13
  via kinship networks, 161–2
reproductive rights, 247–8
  abortion legality and reproductive rights
    indices, various regression techniques,
    1975 to 2005, 223
  CEDAW affirmation of, 220
  communism and, 216–17
  feminist movements and, 225–6
  funding for, 222, 266
  government actions on, 209
  left parties funding for, 224–5
  MENA funding of, 213–14
  state funding for reproductive rights, by
    year, 213
  as status politics, 228

Ridgeway, Cecilia, 5
Rittich, Kerry, 125
Roe v. *Wade*, 219
role equity, 8
Roman Catholic Church, 14
  bishops of, 15
  theology, 204
Roman law, 291
Royal Commission on Equality in
    Employment (Abella Commission),
    101–2
rubella epidemic, 218–19
Rudra, Nita, 164
Russia, Family Code (1926), 297

sacralization, 133
Sanbonmatsu, Kira, 241
Schroeder, Patricia, 174
secularization, 133–4
segregation, 84, 252
Seneca Falls Convention, 141
sex
  binary distinction of, 7
  sexual freedom, 8
  sexual pleasure, 205
  trafficking, 28–9, 42
  in Western world, 5
sexual division of labor, 6
  class in, 99
  daddy leave shifting of, 162
  norms reinforcing, 12
  responsibility in, 11–12
sexual harassment
  protest of, 49
  workplace, 88–9
Sexual Offenses Act (1998) (Tanzania), 44
Sezgin, Yuksel, 126
Shachar, Ayelet, 125
shadow reports, 23
shariah law, 289–90
SIGI. *See* Social Institutions and Gender
    Index
Sikkink, Kathryn, 100
Sisters in Islam, 134–5
Social Democratic parties, 178
Social Institutions and Gender Index (SIGI),
    26
social knowledge, 54
social movements, 30
  conservative, 82
  policy change from, 82, 221

social norms, 3, 86–7, 120
social policy
  class inequality and, 164
  contemporary systems of, 160
  empowerment from, 162–3
  in Global South, 159
  in MENA, 167
social workers, 32
socially desirable outcomes, 85
South Africa, 44, 253
  Constitution of, 103
  Marital Property Act (1984), 290–1
  Women's National Coalition, 103
spousal abuse, 49–50
spousal benefits in Hungary, 161
state feminism, 59
State Funding Index, 212–22
state regulation
  civil society and, 30–1
  of compliance with equality guarantees, 91
  of family law, 14
  of kinship relations, 14
state-market relations, 167–94
state-religion relations
  institutionalized, 135
  policy shaped by, 216
state-sponsored discrimination, 85, 95–6
  assessing, 90
  laws upholding, 94–5
statistical analysis, 70–1
  approach to, 258–9
  case selection for, 257
  on colonialism, 154
  on communism, 154
  on economic equality, 110–18
  on feminist movements, 154–5
  of religious factors, 144–5
status hierarchy, 6, 240
  changes in, 246–7
status politics, 3, 16–17, 247
  actors in, 17
  class politics and, 10–14
  non-doctrinal, 235
  reproductive rights as, 228
sterilization, 219
Stetson, Dorothy McBride, 100
Strolovitch, Dara, 52–3
Sub-Saharan Africa, 14
substantive equality, 87, 95, 114, 265
  attention to, 91
  government actions for, 89

problems addressed by, 92–3
in Turkey, 92
Summit of the Americas, 40–1
Sweden, 20, 99–100
Violence against Women Act (1998), 39

Tanzania, 290
family law in, 288
Sexual Offenses Act (1998), 44
tax credits, 187
terrorism, 28–9
TFNs. *See* transnational feminist networks
thalidomide epidemic, 218–19
Third World Conference on Women, 64–5
Thomas, Dorothy, 62
tipping points, 65–7
Title VII, Civil Rights Act (1964) (U.S), 105
training professionals, 33
transgender people, 7
transnational feminist networks (TFNs),
    60–1, 143
treaties, 65
family leave and, 181
human rights, 46–7
normative leverage from, 68–9
specific regional, 65
vernacularized, 155
Turkey, 45, 92

Uganda, 15
Ukraine, Law on the Prevention of Domestic
    Violence (2001), 42
UN. *See* United Nations
UN Women. *See* United Nations Fund for
    Women
United Arab Emirates, 172
United Nations (UN), 23
Commission on the Status of Women
    (1969), 38, 105
Decade for Women, 108
Declaration on the Elimination of
    Violence against Women (1993), 62
United Nations Fund for Women
    (UN Women), 42
United States (U.S.)
abortion in, 206–7
biomedical research in, 253–4
Civil Rights Act (1964), 87, 104
contraception funding in, 201–19
Democratic Party power in, 176
Family and Medical Leave Act (1993), 20

family leave in, 244
Family Planning Services and Population
    Research Act (1970), 201–19
federal government in, 1–2
feminist movements in, 8, 38, 195
labor mobilization in, 165
left parties in, 195
National Organization for Women, 105
Pregnancy Discrimination Act (PDA)
    (1978), 174
racial politics, 104–5
rape attitudes in, 53
religion and, 216
Violence against Women Act (1994), 38
Universal Declaration of Human Rights, 52
unpaid leave, 8
U.S. *See* United States

Vienna Declaration at the World Conference
    on Human Rights (1993), 31–2
demands before, 50
effectiveness of, 41
Vietnam, 301
violence against women, 11, 54, 240
in Africa, 43–4
Anglo Countries index of, 39
in Asia, 48–50
CEDAW not mentioning, 52
data on, 34
in Eastern Europe, 42–3
in EU, 64
Eurobarometer survey on, 52
Europe index of, 40
feminist movements combating, 29–30
first recognition of, 62
global problem of, 28–9
government responsiveness to, 31–7, 51
index of, 35–6, 260–1
international agreements on, 37–8
international law on, 66
in Latin America, 40–2, 244
in MENA, 44–7
parliamentary seats held by women and,
    50–1
policy on, 29
professionalization of services, 33
religious authorities and, 16
Violence against Women Act (1994)
    (U.S.), 38
Vogel, Ursula, 292
vulnerable populations, 32–3

Warshaw, Robin, 53
WBL. *See* Women, Business, and the Law
WEAL. *See* Women's Education and Action
    League
Weldon, S. Laurel, 32, 34, 53
welfare states
    contemporary, 167
    difference among, 162
    expansion of, 19
    gender and, 159–60
    spending contestation in, 163
    trajectory of, 21
    work-life integration shaped by, 162
White, Linda A., 165
whiteness, aesthetic valuation of, 56
Women, Business, and the Law (WBL), 23,
    26, 128
women in Parliament
    economic equality and, 117
    family law and, 156
    feminist movements and, 239–40
    violence against women and, 50–1
women of color, 56
Women's Circle, 88
Women's Education and Action League
    (WEAL), 105
women's policy machineries, 59, 77, 108–9,
    115, 242
women's rights, 7

cross-national variation in, 22
dataset on, 4
international norms on, 2
left parties and, 165
multiple areas of women's rights, linear
    regression with panel-corrected
    standard error, 70 countries,
    1985 – 2005, 234–5
work, 264–5
    breastfeeding at, 90
    circumstances of, 86
    discrimination in, 11
    empowerment from, 85
    indices on government actions on equality
        88, 89 t
    legal equality at, 94–6
    policy on women legal status at,
        86
    seasonal employment, 91–2
    sexual harassment at, 88–9
    work-life balance, 100, 162
World Bank, 23, 26. *See also* Women,
    Business, and the Law (WBL)
World Conference on Human Rights, 62
World Health Organization (WHO),
    202
World Values Survey, 151–2, 215–16

Young, Iris Marion, 5